MW00654268

# ONE IS THE LONELIEST NUMBER

ON THE ROAD AND BEHIND THE SCENES WITH THE LEGENDARY ROCK BAND THREE DOG NIGHT

**JIMMY GREENSPOON**

WITH MARK BEGO

PHAROS BOOKS
A SCRIPPS HOWARD COMPANY
NEW YORK

For my mother and father



First published in 1991.

Library of Congress Cataloging-in-Publication Data
Greenspoon, Jimmy.
One is the loneliest number: on the road and behind the scenes
with the legendary rock band, Three Dog Night / Jimmy Greenspoon with Mark Bego.
p. cm.
Discography : p.
ISBN 0-88687-647-8 : $18.95
1. Three Dog Night (Musical group) 2. Rock musicians—United States—Biography.
I. Bego, Mark. II. Title.
ML421.T55G7 1991
782.42166'092'2—dc20
[B] 91-22691 CIP MN

Pharos Books are available at special discounts on bulk purchases
for sales promotions, premiums, fundraising or educational use.
For details, contact the Special Sales Department, Pharos Books, New York, NY 10166.

Printed in the United States

Pharos Books
A Scripps Howard Company
200 Park Avenue
New York, New York

10 9 8 7 6 5 4 3 2 1

# Contents

# Preface

I have been a Three Dog Night fan since 1969, the year they began their recording career. Their *Suitable For Framing* album was in "heavy rotation" on my own personal soundtrack that year, and as their career grew and evolved, I eventually bought every album they recorded.

Three Dog Night's phenomenally successful recording career included a five-year reign on the international music charts and encompassed a varied repertoire of classics including "Mama Told Me (Not To Come)," "One," "Easy To Be Hard," "Old Fashioned Love Song," "Black and White," and "Joy To The World." As a group they were unique for several reasons: they had three talented and totally different lead vocalists, their hits were culled from the creme de la creme of rock and pop songwriters, and their music was crafted by four top-notch musicians whose scope seemed boundless.

The keyboard player, Jimmy Greenspoon, was classically trained — and born to rock and roll. He still is one of the most highly respected keyboard players in the business. In addition to his million-selling musicianship with Three Dog Night, his reputation as a "party animal extraordinaire" is equally legendary. A seasoned pro when it came to having a good time, there was nothing that he wouldn't do for a thrill: pot, pills, coke, booze, sex, heroin, orgies. You name it: he did it.

At first Jimmy's drug use was strictly for "fun" — like dropping liquid acid and going to the Monterey Pop Festival, or for a particular gig where a psychedelic vantage point would come in handy. After Three Dog Night was formed and they hit the top of the charts, the drugs soon became a survival tactic: "uppers" to stay awake at all-night recording sessions, coke to maintain a "buzz," and then "downers" to unwind with. As the money rolled in at an astonishing rate, it seemed the party would never end. But as with all good things, it did. Group polititcs and individual drug problems began to sabotage its once-brilliant career, and Jimmy watched his life spiral downward into ten years of hard-core heroin addiction.

With all of the substances that he has filtered through his body, it's a wonder he's alive today to tell his story. On one hand, Jimmy's teenage drug use is humorous and as indicative of the era as Woodstock and Arlo Guthrie's "Alice's Restaurant." However, at the lowest depths of his heroin-induced hell, his life became every junkie's nightmare. His ultimate detoxification and recovery is truly an inspirational saga of courage.

In September of 1987, when I received a call from my agent and was asked, "How would you like to do a book with one of the guys from Three Dog Night?" I jumped at the opportunity to meet Jimmy and discuss it. When it was explained to me that Jimmy was a ten-year heroin addict and alcoholic who had been on the wagon for two years, I was apprehensive. My original fear was that with all of the drugs he had taken, he wouldn't be able to remember a thing that he had done, or would have the brainpower of broccoli.

With fascination I read some of the excerpts from his detox journal and was instantly hooked. We talked on the phone and discussed his life and the direction he wanted the book to take. A couple of weeks later, I drove to Philadelphia to catch a Three Dog Night concert and to meet him. Sitting in a Chinese restaurant in Philly, Jimmy began to tell me of his outrageous adventures with Three Dog Night. I was amazed to discover that he not only remembered everything he had ever done, but what he was wearing while he was doing it! We were both laughing so uncontrollably that I thought we were going to get thrown out of the restaurant.

Following our visit, I found that I was charmed by his energetic personality and his crazy sense of humor. I knew then and there that I had met a "best friend for life," and I had hit upon a story that truly needed to be told.

The following month I flew to Tucson, Arizona, to visit Jimmy and his lovely wife, Karen, and it was there that we began working on the initial pieces that ultimately became this book. In the meantime I interviewed him on the phone, traveled to see him on the road with Three Dog Night, and he visited me in New York City on two occasions. Finally, I returned to Tucson in November 1989, and we completed the manuscript.

Jimmy Greenspoon has the kind of boundless energy that is kinetic, and he has a wildly dramatic way of describing everything. It was my intention to preserve this outrageousness on these pages.

In addition to his musical creativity, Jimmy is also the kind of person who must be doing something at all times. Cleaning up the house, the yard, and/or the car are among his favorites. Whenever he and I get together, we act like a rock and roll version of "The

Odd Couple." He is the neat-freak, and I am the slob. I would go to the bathroom to brush my teeth, and return to the guest bedroom to find that Jimmy had made my bed, alphabetized my CDs, and neatly stacked all of my belongings according to size, color, and subject. Karen and I couldn't put down a coffee cup without Jimmy picking it up, washing it, and putting it away — whether we had finished the coffee or not!

Knowing the post-detox Jimmy, I was as amazed as anyone to have him relate to me the unscrupulous lengths to which he would go to maintain his "high," at the height of his drug use. It was as if there were two Jimmy Greenspoons: the current big-hearted sober one, and the single-minded one he was while on drugs.

I'm glad that he made it back from the dark side of his self-imposed drug horrors. I'm also thrilled that I was able to help him tell his colorful tales of sex, drugs, and rock and roll. Life backstage in the upper stratosphere of the rock world *is* every bit as raw and raucous as one would guess. One of the reasons for this is Jimmy Greenspoon.

— Mark Bego

# Acknowledgments

I would like to acknowledge and thank: God for giving me strength and wisdom, my mother for all her love, my father for trying the only way he knew how, my sister Lyla for understanding, my daughter Heather for forgiving me, my daughters Cheri and Kim for accepting me, and most of all my wife Karen for her inspiration, patience and never-ending love.

I would also like to thank the following people who touched my life in some way: Timmy Alvarado, Steve Barnett, Steve Bristow, Doug Burch, Rusty Carlson for being there, Shaun Cassidy, Richard Cole for his friendship, Durrie, George Englund, Lenny Fagan, Henry and Becky Freeman, Mike "Tiny" Gossen, Tom Hulett, Gerry Landry, Mark and Carla Leap, Michael Lloyd for helping me to get started in the business, Hugh Lynch, Mario for putting up with my attitude, Roger McGuinn for inspiration, Bill and Debbie McKenzie for sorting out the money, Larry McNiney, John Meglen for his valued friendship and good times, Julia Negron for saving my life on more than one occasion, Ronnie Portilla for getting me there in one piece, Ken Schwarz, Barbara Shore for being there when things were tough, Bernie Stewart, Wendie for being a good friend, Elmer Valentine for a place to start, Ron Berry for his words of wisdom and my wardrobe, Mary Margaret for introducing me to my first real love, and my new friend Mike Nachtigal for a bright future.

Also everyone connected with Three Dog Night: Danny Hutton, Chuck Negron, Cory Wells, Michael Allsup, Floyd Sneed, Joe Schermie, Jack Ryland, Skip Knote, Jay Gruska, Al Ciner, Dennis Belfield, Mickey McMeel, Richard Grossman, Paul Kingery, Scotty Manzo, Steve Ezzo, Mike Keeley, T. J. Parker, Gary Moon, Mike Cuneo, Richard Campbell, Bob Tomasso, Anthony Ragonese, Joel Cohen, Larry Fitzgerald, Burt Jacobs, Bill Utley, Reb Foster, Bill Cooper, Richard Podolor, Jimmy Ienner, Bobby Ward, and anyone else I may have forgotten.

A special thanks to the bands I manage: Bad Habit and About Face.

Also, thanks to Joe Stunkard for solving our computer problems, and to Geary Chansley and Lauri Scalise of MCA for help with the photos.

And last, but by far not the least, thanks to Mark Bego for his hard work, friendship, and patience; and to Tony Seidl for believing in us.

—Jimmy Greenspoon

# Introduction

I had it all, and I lost it.

For twenty three years I had flirted with death. I made it through hundreds of acid trips, pounds of cocaine, pills, codeine cough syrup, grass, and more alcohol than I thought humanly possible to consume. All of this culminated in a $500-a-day heroin habit. After everything that I have done to myself, it is a miracle that I'm alive to tell my story.

I grew up in the fairy-tale world of Beverly Hills and spent my summers at our house in Palm Springs, where I rubbed elbows with movie stars and presidents. All the while I was trying to make my father, Maury Greenspoon, proud of me.

I had a loving, if not overly protective, mother who happened to be a silent film star: Mary O'Brien. Like my father, she too gave me a standard to live by, and I tried to adhere to it.

Our family vacations were spent in Hawaii. I attended the best schools. When I expressed an interest in music, my mother made sure I had the best equipment, musical training, and a suitable atmosphere that was conducive to learning my craft. When I was old enough, she bought me my first car, my second, and so on. In a nutshell, I had everything a young boy could ask for — and more.

By the time I was sixteen, I was carving out a name for myself in local Hollywood rock bands. We had record contracts, nightclubs, girls, parties, and all the trappings of potential success.

When I was nineteen, I was in on the ground floor of what was to become my meal ticket for life. I didn't know at the time that the fledgling Three Dog Night would become one of the best-selling groups in rock and roll history, and that we would continue to make music together in four different decades.

As the keyboard player for this group, how could I have known that our first hit single, "One," would catapult us to immediate international stardom? I never suspected that we would have twelve consecutive Gold albums, seven Gold singles, two Grammy nominations, three Number One songs, twenty-two Top Forty hit singles, and that we would become one of the top ten largest grossing groups in rock and roll history.

By the time I was twenty, I had earned over a million dollars, and I had a wife and a child on the way. I owned a three-story house high in the Hollywood Hills complete with a swimming pool and an indoor elevator. I had two Mercedes Benz, for which I paid cash, and enough money to keep this idealistic lifestyle going forever . . . or so I thought.

However, there was one thing I hadn't counted on amid my nonstop life in the fast lane: I was an addict. I had an insatiable appetite for sex, drugs, and rock and roll. It eventually led me into my own private hell, where my worst nightmares were to become painful reality. Every demon that could be summoned from the depths of despair would ride with me on my roller-coaster life — from the heights of rock and roll stardom all the way down to the absolute bottom.

In the end, I would become just another burned-out junkie looking for my next fix, and a restless womanizer looking for another short skirt with a cute ass. My fairy-tale existence would give way to hedonistic excesses. The very things that I dreamed of as a child — success, wealth, and power — would be my undoing as an adult.

Too many people I knew and respected had consumed lesser amounts of abusive substances than I — and died. Jimi Hendrix, Janis Joplin, Jim Morrison, Cass Elliot, John Bonham, Keith Moon, and countless others saw an early grave.

Before my charade was over, a part of me would die, only to give way to someone I never thought I would become.

It is next to impossible in one book to chronicle all of the events that almost led to my demise, simply because for twenty-three years they existed every single day. I can only relate some of the self-inflicted anguish I went through along with the temporary joy that I experienced in my life.

I don't claim to have a magical cure for the illness known as "addiction," because there is none. One can only keep the disease dormant through clean living, support from fellow addicts, and most importantly — love. Love of yourself, love of God, and love of another human being. I have found that love for the first time in my life.

Because of my wife, Karen, my family, and my newfound self-respect, I have learned that even the worst day sober is better than the best day stoned. This wasn't a revelation that came to me easily. I had to nearly kill myself through my own excesses to realize that my own will to live outweighed my self-destructive tendencies.

If just one person reads these pages and decides to turn their life around by seeking help, no matter where they seek it, I'll know that the part of my life that I threw away was not spent in vain. It is with this new insight that I dedicate this book: to everyone who has ruined their life because of substance abuse. It is my hope that they too will find the courage to turn their lives around.

— Jimmy Greenspoon
Tucson, Arizona
1991

# 1 / Shot Down

The bloodstained walls of the bathroom looked like a Jackson Pollock painting. On the bathroom sink lay the tools of my trade: a broken, dirty needle; a used piece of cotton; a blackened spoon; and an almost empty "bindle" that only hours ago contained over two grams of heroin.

I was still feeling the effects of the shot that I took just thirty minutes before. But this time something was wrong. I couldn't seem to get high enough. I wanted more.

Every time you stick the needle in, there's that remote feeling in the back of your mind that this is *the one*. Once your finger pushes down on the plunger, there's no turning back. Death is an ever-present character in a junkie's life. Most of the time it's lingering in the background. It would rather claim your life slowly, over a long period of time, than quickly, in a moment of stupidity. This time, however, as soon as I felt the warm rush of pleasure in my veins, I thought that this was *the fatal one*. I somehow knew that I had just taken that last step over the boundary of life.

It was too late to undo the damage that was inevitable, and I suddenly found myself praying. Throughout my life, I had never been a spiritual person. I believed in God, but in my sick addicted mind, I thought that He had turned His back on me. My prayer at that moment was one of complete selfishness: *Why hadn't I spread this fantastic but deadly poison over a period of time, say . . . a few hours?* I thought in my prayer: *Why did I have to do it all in one shot? By tomorrow, I could have still had enough for my morning wake-up fix. After all, why make something so sinful and so deadly, so easy to do?*

If I wasn't going to die this time, I was going to have to work real hard to bring myself around, I decided. *Maybe this fear of death is a blessing in disguise. This might be what I've needed all along to make me wake up and stop this insanity.* After about a minute of sheer terror, I realized that this wasn't *the one,* and death wasn't touching its icy finger to my soul. I breathed a sigh of relief. The last thing I wanted to do was to give up my life of drugs, booze, and nonstop partying.

That bitch had won again. She was a sly one. Of all the girls I've known or had affairs with, this one just wouldn't take "no" for an answer. She was no different from the rest. She took all of my money, my time, my very creative inner self. In return, I was given a feeling of warmth and security. This woman had me by the balls, on my knees on the bathroom floor in front of my toilet, praying to her. She occupied all of my time. Where to find her? When? How much would she cost me this time? I thought I never loved anyone as much as I loved her. Her name was "Heroin." This scenario had been repeated over and over and over again, until that night when, for a few short moments, death did indeed come to claim my soul.

May 23, 1985, started out just like any other night. I called my connection to place an order for the evening. Even as I placed my order, somewhere in the back of my mind I knew something was wrong. To this day, I can't quite put my finger on it. Somehow I knew that I was at the end of this deadly lifestyle I had chosen for the past twenty-three years. When my dealer asked me how much I wanted, I replied, "More than I need."

This new batch was even more powerful than the last. He warned me that anything over half of a gram would be stupid, and possibly fatal. But then again, he was a dealer, and a large sale only meant that he could increase his supply even faster. I bought a gram for $600. He gave me a break on the price of this poison — and I felt lucky.

That night, somewhere around La Cienega and Fountain avenues in Los Angeles, my luck ran out. Before I shot up the gram, I had already taken three quaaludes and downed half a bottle of vodka. Some might think this was a death wish, but to me it was just my last cry for help. It was a cry not so much made to others, but to myself. Because, in the end, it's your own ass on the line. When you stand alone in the presence of God, and ask His forgiveness for the fucked-up mess you've made of your pitiful life, it's a one-on-one confrontation. There's no one there who's going to help you but yourself. If and when you finally realize this, that's when the first faint light of victory over your demons becomes clear.

When I left the dealer's house that night, I drove my white sports car down Sunset Boulevard, slightly faster than usual. I wanted to get home before everything I had taken kicked my ass. The last thing I remember before I "came to," lying in the street, was turning left onto La Cienega from Sunset. By the time I made the turn, my body was on auto pilot. The heroin and the 'Ludes had worked together, and the vodka acted as a catalyst.

I don't think there are words that can describe the feeling of lying in the street, with four or five paramedics and policemen around you, and knowing that something is very wrong. There was a throbbing pain in my head, but it was ever so slight. The drugs had done their job to numb my mind and body. My shirt was covered with warm blood. At the time, I didn't know that it was blood from a head wound I received after I hit the windshield. Had I not had my seatbelt on when I left my dealer's house, I might have been thrown out of the car. I thought to myself, *I must have hit something, or even worse . . . someone.* My first words were: "Oh my God, did I kill someone?" A policeman assured me that no one was hurt in the accident but me. I had, however, hit the police car broadside.

The way the policeman said, "No one but you," started a chain reaction in my still numb brain. *This is it,* I thought to myself. *This time, Jimmy, you fucked up real bad.* They instructed me to lie still and informed me that the ambulance would be right there. It was only a few minutes before I heard the wail of the sirens. However, to me the wait seemed to take forever. Everyone appeared to be moving in slow motion. Then the sickness of my addiction crept in.

Was I supposed to reflect on my life, my family, and everything that I had ever done wrong, so that I could meet my Maker with a clean conscience? That would have taken me hours — possibly days — and I thought I only had minutes. My warped mind conjured up all types of bizarre images: *Will I be on the cover of* Rolling Stone *again? . . . How many people will be at my funeral?* Not one of my thoughts was of my family, or the emotional and financial mess that my premature exit from life would cause.

The images of my funeral soon subsided, and I now seemed to be in a state of suspended animation. Nothing moved. No sounds were made. If this was death, why were all of these people still around? Then, out of nowhere, a wall of confusion surrounded me. Bright lights . . . voices talking loudly over the police radio . . . people rushing everywhere. It was this flurry of activity that stuck out in my mind. To the passerby, it might have looked like the aftermath of a terrorist bombing. I shouldn't flatter myself in the face of death, but I'm sure that anyone who was "rubber necking" to catch a view of this scene probably thought it was just some poor guy who was hurt. Little did they know that on the ground lay a member of one of the best-selling rock groups of all time, dying from a drug overdose.

The turning point came swiftly. As soon as the ambulance doors were closed, I knew that this ride was more than routine. I had been through such an ambulance ride twice before, so I knew that this time around there was something horribly different. I distinctly remember hearing three words: "We're losing him!" The first time the paramedics said that, I didn't hear them clearly. The second time they said it, it was clear as a bell. It rang true and hit the very center of my being. "We're losing him!" I repeated the three words to myself over and over again.

Just before we pulled into the emergency entrance of Cedars Sinai Hospital, they said the words again. Only this time the words were followed by someone pounding their fists on my chest, presumably to stop the cardiac arrest that I was going into. I found out later that I had no pulse or heartbeat for about a minute. It was a short span of time compared to the thirty-seven years that I had lived, but it was long enough to let me know that I was not ready to die.

For twenty-three years I had flirted with death. I had snorted several mountains of cocaine, taken enough pills to open a pharmacy, shot up so much heroin my arm looked like a dart board, and had drunk enough alcohol and cough syrup to embalm all of the inhabitants of Cincinnati, and somehow I had survived. And now I was going to be another rock and roll casualty? Bullshit!

I'm not quite sure of what happened next. I do know that I mustered up every bit of energy left in my limp body and called out one last time to God to please save me. Then it all went black.

When I woke up, I was in a brightly lit white room. No one was in sight. No sounds could be heard. *Ah ha, this is heaven,* I thought to myself. *Death wasn't that painful, thanks to the incredible mixture of drugs I had taken.* I was alone on a cold steel table — the kind they had in hospitals back on earth. Maybe this was some sort of way station where the angels cleaned you up before you got to see God. After all, you couldn't meet Him covered in blood. Funny, they even dressed me in the same stupid white gown. I laughed out loud. *It's on backwards just like on earth,* I thought to myself. *Maybe I get to make one last phone call to tell everyone what happened. In my best Chevy Chase impersonation I'll say: "Hello, I'm dead and you're not."* But I quickly ruled that out since I hadn't paid my phone bill for over two months, and they probably took away all privileges in heaven.

Then I saw it. That little label on the gown. As I mouthed the words, I began to laugh and cry at the same time. "Made in Japan. . . . Made in fucking Japan!" Unless God was Japanese, which I doubted, this could only mean one thing: *"I'm alive!"* In my motion picture-oriented mind, I immediately thought of the movie *Frankenstein.* I could see Dr. Frankenstein shouting, "It's alive!" as he stood over the monster he had just created.

"I'm alive!" I shouted.

"Yes, you're alive," another voice said with a slight chuckle. This took me by surprise. I turned my head to see a young doctor with a rather sardonic grin on his face, standing over me. "This time," he continued. "But don't press your luck, Mr. Greenspoon. You were legally dead for over a minute. Your body can't take another round like that." He then tried to piece together the events that led up to my temporary demise.

To fully understand all that had happened, he had to know everything that I took that evening. With rapid-fire accuracy I began reeling off the various quantities of drugs that I had consumed earlier that night. My words were obviously those of a well-seasoned drug pro, and as he listened, the doctor just shook his head every so often. He put his clipboard down and prepared an injection of Narcon, a drug used to reverse the effects of other drugs.

As soon as the Narcon was administered, I began to feel something that I hadn't felt before. The shot completely eradicated the high that I had worked so hard to achieve. I was straight for the first time in years, and I didn't like it. After all the time and money I had spent that night getting stoned, it was all reversed in one second. *How dare someone take this all away from me!* I thought to myself. I was too wrapped up in my own private hell at the time to realize that this doctor and the paramedics had just saved my life. Did I seriously think that I could have pulled this off myself?

There were, and still are to this day, many unanswered questions about that night. Considering all that I had done to myself that night, I should have been dead. I know now that God stepped in and took me from the jaws of death and deposited me on a higher plane of consciousness. It was to be another year before I would fully understand where I was or why I had been spared that night.

I can now, with total clarity, begin to understand my other near brushes with death and come to grips, honestly, with the fact that I am an addict and an alcoholic. The amazing thing is that I never thought I had a problem. Denial is at the very core of an addict's life. There were many times in the past when I was near death, but still I had managed to come out of it unscathed. However, instead of being thankful and learning from my mistakes, I always willingly jumped right back into my own personal drug-induced nightmare.

How did I get on this path of self-destruction? Why was it that everything I did and enjoyed became an addictive obsession? I began to look into my past to find the answers . . .

# 2 / A Change Is Gonna Come

My life began on February 7, 1948, at 5:00 A.M. This wondrous event took place at the Cedars of Lebenon Hospital in Los Angeles. I don't remember much about the birth. But judging from later baby pictures, I was completely irresistible — and totally vain.

One of my earliest memories was being pushed around in my stroller in front of our house in Beverly Hills. I was probably only a year old at the time. My red hair was so long and curly then that everyone mistook me for a girl. This was a constant source of irritation for my mother.

I was the second of two children. My sister, Lyla, was nineteen years older than me. I always thought it odd that there was such an age difference between us, and that my mother waited so long to have a second child. However, if there was a logical explanation for this, it was never presented to me.

Due to our age difference, Lyla and I were never as close as other brothers and sisters. In that way, I almost felt like an only child. The one love that we did share was that which we had for our gray Angora cat named Amber.

My mother was born Mary Thompson in Cleburn, Texas, just after the turn of the century. Having ultimately become a Hollywood actress, she lied about her age so many times that to this day I'm not sure in which year she was born. She was the youngest of three sisters. I don't recall my maternal grandfather, because he had already died by the time I was born, but I distinctly remember spending summers in Kansas City, Missouri, with my mother, grandmother, and two aunts. Mother and the family had moved to Kansas City from Texas while she was still a young girl.

My mother was one-quarter Cherokee, and the whole Thompson family seemed to be quite independent and feisty. It was in the middle of the 1920s that my mother, grandmother, and aunts decided to move west to California. They headed for Hollywood.

Mother realized that she would have to become the breadwinner of the family, so she decided to try her hand at acting. She was incredibly good-looking, so due to her own moxie, she began making the rounds of the movie studios, looking for work. It wasn't long before she landed work at such famous 1920s studios as R.K.O., the Max Sennett Studio, and Hal Roach.

She never talked a lot to me about her movie career, but the one film that she mentioned to me time and time again was having appeared in *The Butler,* with Charlie Chaplin. She also spoke very highly of her work with Buster Keaton. Her career in films just began as silent films were on the wane. When Hollywood converted to "talkies" in the late 1920s, Mother found that she was able to easily make the transition into films with sound.

While earning her own spending money, and making enough money to support the family, Mother decided to declare her own independence. She moved out of the house and out on her own. Young girls back then didn't actually live alone; she roomed with someone who was also in the movie business. One of her first roommates was another hopeful actress named Lucille LeSueur. Lucille had made a name for herself in movies as a Charleston dancer, and later changed her name when her career picked up. She became known as Joan Crawford.

Although Mother was aggressive about her career, her personality was more proper and reserved. Joan, however, was known as quite a party girl. I'm certain that a lot of the adventures that they became involved in were instigated by Joan.

One story that Mother recalled to me with fondness concerned a certain actor who persistently telephoned her, asking her out for dates. Mother was the serious type, and she was more concerned with learning her lines for the next day's shoot at the studio than hopping into bed with one of those smooth-talking Hollywood types. This particular suitor finally became so persistent that he would even call her while she was visiting my grandmother's house. Finally, after putting him off numerous times, she told him flat-out that she wasn't interested in going out with him. However, she was certain that her roommate, Joan, would love to go out with him.

The persistent caller turned out to be none other than Douglas Fairbanks, Jr. How could Mother have known what she started? Fairbanks, the heir to a vast Hollywood fortune, fell madly in love with Joan and became her first husband. This caused quite a Hollywood scandal at the time, as Douglas' father, the famous swashbuckling silent film star, and his stepmother, Mary Pickford, were appalled at the prospect of Joan as a daughter-in-law. Douglas Fairbanks, Jr., disavowed his parents' wishes and married the social-climbing Crawford, and really set the wheels of her career in motion.

Meanwhile, my mother's acting career continued at a steady pace. Although she never attained the type of stardom that Joan Crawford had, she continued to work well into the 1930s. Through the years, her intimate circle of friends included several members of the movie community. George Burns and Gracie Allen were close friends, as were Mary and Jack Benny. For a long period of time she had told me that Jack Benny was my godfather, when, much to my later disappointment, I was to find out that he was my sister's godfather — not mine.

Mother's first marriage was to a vaudeville star named Benny Rubin. He was a comedian she had met in Hollywood. They spent a lot of time on the road together, while he was still working on the stage. Later he would land several bit parts in movies, which was preferable for my mother, because she wanted to stay in Hollywood. The most important thing that came out of that marriage was the birth of my older sister. They divorced after a number of years, but they remained close friends until his death in the mid-1980s. I remember Benny attending family holiday dinners. He was always encouraging me to pursue my piano playing, and to do whatever it was that made me happy in life.

I never knew the reason that my mother divorced Benny. To me, he was always part of the family. Rather than being an ex-husband of my mother, he was more like an uncle to me. In fact, my mother always encouraged me to call him "Uncle Benny."

My father was born Adolph Maurice Greenspoon in Arvada, Colorado, in the early part of the century. He came from a family of strict Russian Jews. My paternal grandmother was, however, Protestant, so I remember getting Chanukah *and* Christmas presents from that side of the family. I didn't know much about religion, but I loved the double presents, and all the strange food (especially the wine!) at the formal Jewish holiday dinners.

Father attended the University of Colorado at Boulder, majoring in accounting and business management. After he graduated, he moved west to California. Once in California, he and a cousin started a manufacturing business called the Art Pillow Company. I remember that they had a huge factory/warehouse on Wall Street in downtown Los Angeles. The company manufactured pillows, draperies, and custom-made bedspreads for retail stores such as Barker Brothers, Robinsons, and Sears. When he met my mother, he was exactly the type of man she was looking for. After her marriage to Benny Rubin, she had had enough of unstable Hollywood actors. They were married in the mid-'40s in Los Angeles, and together they bought the beautiful corner duplex at 174 North Swall Drive in Beverly Hills.

My dad was a total workaholic. I have so many memories about my mother, because she was always at home, but my father was always down at the factory. He was never much of a dad to me, in the sense that he never took me on fishing or camping trips, or to baseball games. I think that's one of the reasons that my mother encouraged me to take piano lessons — to fill that void that was missing from my life.

When my father and I did do things together, it took the form of his offering me small oddjobs and tasks at his factory. Although we were supposedly doing something together, in actuality he would set me up with a task on the assembly line floor with his workers.

My first job at the pillow factory was operating an airhose to blow off the excess stuffing off of the pillows. Another time I operated the manual device that stamped the various covering material onto the cloth-covered buttons. After gaining the respect of the factory workers, and of my dad, I graduated to my first incentive-based task at the shop, at the age of seven. This was known as "turning pillows," for which I would be paid the whopping sum of one cent per pillow.

My dad probably figured that this task would keep me busy — and out of his hair — for hours on end. What he didn't realize was how hyper I was. I was not only temporarily entertained by this task, but it wasn't long before I figured out how to finish the job hours ahead of schedule, only to show up at the closed door of his private office to ask him "What's next?" and to inform him how much money he owed me.

When lunch time came, Dad would never invite me to join him. I always had lunch with the workers. That gave me a sense, early on, of what it was like to be an employee. And I knew, at an early age, that I would never be interested in being one.

The funny thing was that during my excursions to my father's factory, my mother thought that he and I were spending time together like other fathers and sons did, when in reality he was forcing me to become that much more independent. Although I respected him greatly for his accomplishments, that bond of love was never there between us. The feeling of estrangement continued up until the time he died in 1985.

At my father's insistence, my parents built a house in Palm Springs, located at 286 Camino Alturas, near the end of Palm Canyon Drive. The idea was to have a family home away from Los Angeles. We started out going down there on weekends, because my father was a member of the prestigious Tamarisk Country Club. In theory, this sounded like a great opportunity for the family to have a place to go, so that we could be together as a family. Unfortunately, it ended up driving us further apart, as my father would spend all of his time on the golf course or at the clubhouse with all of his buddies. My mother and I both hated golf, so we would do things together to pass the time while Dad golfed.

My dad was having such a great time in Palm Springs that he decided in the mid-'50s to move the family down there for an entire year. That caused us to grow even further apart, because he would drive into Los Angeles during the week to the factory, and on the weekends he would be out golfing. Instead of seeing more of him, we saw even less of him.

One would think my family had an idyllic existence in Palm Springs. But in reality, it was becoming increasingly trauma-filled. My father's quest for independence on the golf course was finally getting to my mother, and I would often be witness to horrendous fights between my parents. My mother, with her Cherokee heritage, was not to be tangled with when she got angry. She often wound up picking up and throwing anything that was handy — usually dishes or a lamp. For my dad, this led to severe bouts of manic depression.

Depression was a word that wasn't even in my vocabulary at that time, but it was something that I was to become quite familiar with in later years. The most extreme example of this was when my father took an emotional turn for the worse and became suicidal. I received a harsh dose of reality when I came home from school one day and found him floating facedown in the swimming pool. Something had compelled me to go to the backyard. I wasn't a great swimmer, so I was paralyzed with fear. I immediately thought he was dead. Fortunately, my mother and my uncle had just pulled into the driveway and heard me screaming. My uncle dived into the pool and dragged Dad out of the water, while my mother called the paramedics. I don't remember much else about that day, but thank God they got to him in time. After a few days at the hospital, he was released. That was the beginning of his long association with psychiatrists and antidepressant drugs.

After my father's attempted suicide, my mother decided that she would find things that they could do together. Getting out and meeting people at parties seemed like a reasonable way to get him into the mainstream of social life. I was all of eight years old at the time — but too old for babysitters, I thought — so I convinced my mother that I could stay home alone. She would leave me with the phone number of the place where they would be and tell me to phone if anything at all went wrong in their absence. Being a horror film fanatic, as soon as they left the house I would turn on my favorite TV show: "Thriller," hosted by Boris Karloff. After one particularly scary episode, I went to the kitchen got several butcher knives to protect myself. If anything jumped out at me, I was armed and ready! It was a good thing that my parents were rather vocal when they returned from these parties, because if they had snuck in silently that night, they would have been made into paté by their knife-wielding son!

A lot of celebrities owned houses in Palm Springs. Since my dad played golf with several of them, it wasn't long before he was invited to the "A list" parties. These usually lasted until the wee hours of the morning. Often the local school would have a nighttime babysitting service for the children of these social climbers. However, on one occasion, my mom and dad took me along to a party at Frank Sinatra's house. After being introduced to him, I was ushered into a large, toy-filled room where the children of the other guests were imprisoned with such torture devices as Lincoln Logs and Erector Sets.

Being so young, I wasn't that impressed by movie stars and their accomplishments, unless they were someone I really admired or whose movies I had seen. Right across the street lived Esther Williams and Fernando Lamas. I remember walking by daily and seeing their kids playing in their front yard. We exchanged the usual, "Hello, how are you," but we had never become friends. One day, though, while I was playing alone in front of my house, the kids across the street called out to me to come over and play with them. I stopped what I was doing and jumped at the opportunity to meet some new people, because I was bored. I went over there and walked back by their pool. Moments later, their mother came out and introduced herself. I told her that I lived across the street, and she asked me my name. I told her, "Jimmy Greenspoon." At that point her whole demeanor changed. Suddenly, out of left field, she said, "I'm sorry but you're Jewish, and we're Catholic, so you can't play with the boys."

Devastated, I ran home crying, not understanding what any of this had to do with friendship. My mother, upon finding out what happened, stopped making dinner and stormed across the street. I'm not sure what words were exchanged, but I do know that the next day I was invited back to the house to play with the boys.

My father, in an attempt to do more things together, would often take me to the golf course with him. Sometimes I would play caddy, and he would even let me drive the golf cart and hand him his clubs. On one particular occasion, he was bubbling over with excitement because some special guests were playing cards in the clubhouse. I waited for him in the locker room while he showered and changed, and then followed him into a room to meet these "mystery guests." In this room a group of men were playing cards. At the far end of the table sat a rather distinguished-looking, balding man, surrounded by people who looked like they didn't belong there at all. My father proudly introduced me to the balding man: "Son, I'd like you to meet the president of the United States, Dwight Eisenhower." With a rather polite but curt "It's nice to meet you, Mr. President," I turned and saw someone I recognized sitting at the opposite end of the table. With a big smile on my face, I walked that way and proceeded to introduce myself to Danny Thomas. Extending my hand, I said, "My name is Jimmy Greenspoon, and if Rusty Hamer ever gets sick and can't appear on your T.V. show, I'll be your son!" With that, Danny Thomas cracked up, and even the president and my father laughed. Taking a cue from the president, even those men who looked out of place (who turned out to be Secret Service agents) joined in on the laughter.

After spending a year in the desert, battling tarantulas and scorpions and other insidious desert vermin, we packed our bags and headed back to Swall Drive. My dad didn't seem as depressed as he had when we we were living in Palm Springs. He was, however, taking more and more trips to Japan to purchase fabric, and when he returned he seemed to be in an even better mood than when he left. I thought it was great — but my mother knew instinctively that something was up.

At this point in their lives, my parents were sleeping in separate rooms. While my mother's bedroom was filled with antiques, and her king-sized bed was covered with a big quilt, my father's room was becoming a virtual Japanese shrine, complete with kimonos and Japanese pictures on the wall. Finally, one day my mother's curiosity got the best of her, and she began going through his drawers. It was there that she discovered several pictures of Dad with a beautiful Japanese woman.

My mother wasn't too fond of the Japanese anyway, having lived through the threats of air raids during the Second World War and Pearl Harbor. After this she was as mad as a samurai. She went into the living room, grabbed a bottle of vodka, and quietly sat waiting for my father to return from work. When he returned, I took my cue and went out to play. Later my mother told me that she had confronted him about the affair. He admitted that it was going on.

The next day when I came home from school, my mother said to me, "Come on, and get into the car, we're going for a little ride." We got into the car, and she drove me over to the Park LaBrea Towers, on the other side of the Tar Pits. When we got there, she informed me, "This is our new home — without your father."

I wasn't too pleased with her decision, mainly because it meant that I had to change schools in the middle of the year and attend the notoriously tough John Burrows Junior High School. For me, life without my father wasn't all that different, and as mother informed me, it was a trial separation while they worked things out. My biggest concern then was for my mother's well-being during the separation.

I distinctly remember my first day at John Burrows Junior High School. Beginning at the new school was sheer terror for me. It's one thing starting out at a new school during the first of the school year, but when you are led into a classroom midsemester, and introduced in front of the class, your palms start to sweat.

The kids were decidedly different from the ones I was used to having as classmates in lily white Beverly Hills. It was sort of like a scene from the famous juvenile delinquency movie *The Blackboard Jungle*. The school was half black and Latino, and I had visions of being knifed and stuffed into my locker. Also, it didn't help having a name like "Greenspoon." It was times like these that I wished my name was "Smith" or "Jones" — or better yet, "Leroy" or "Bubba" or "Gomez."

I complained to my mother that attending this school was a living hell, so she did what she could to get me transferred to another junior high in the same school district. This didn't bother me, because I hadn't made any friends there anyway. Unfortunately, the other junior high school in the district, LeConte, was the basement of hell. Located on Bronson Avenue in Hollywood, it was predominantly Mexican/Latino with a few blacks, a few Asians, and one Greenspoon.

My first day there, I was thrown against my locker and told that I had to "buy insurance."

"Insurance for what?" I asked.

"Your life," said the friendly Neanderthal insurance salesman who was threatening to squash me like a bug. At that point, I couldn't thank my mother enough for transferring me.

I promptly told the thug that I didn't have any money.

"Did you bring lunch?" he asked me.

"No," I stupidly replied, "my mother gave me money for lunch."

"Well, you're in luck," I was informed, "because that is exactly the price of insurance."

Like a well-oiled machine, every day the Neanderthal would approach me, and I would surrender my lunch money. I was afraid to complain to my mother, because I might be sent to Siberia to go to school. Or worse yet, Mother might fly off the handle and show them what "kicking ass" was all about.

After six or seven months of taking that abuse, I came home one day and found out to my surprise and relief that we were moving back to Swall Drive. My mother said there had been a change of plans. My father was moving down to Palm Springs so that we could occupy the house on Swall Drive. He knew how miserable we both were.

Returning to Horace Mann Junior High School was a wonderful feeling. Not only did I not have to pay insurance anymore, but I could return to eating lunch on a daily basis.

In summer of 1961, my mother and I, as well as my best friend, Michael Lloyd, and his mother (also an actress), started what turned out to be an annual event: spending our entire vacation in Hawaii together. I was twelve years old, and Michael and I had already formed our first band together. We were not only close friends, but also constant writing partners.

In Hawaii, Michael and I surfed every day; at night, we'd sit on the beach and Michael would play his guitar. We attracted a circle of locals, who would join in on our singalongs. I felt somewhat left out, because it was a little difficult to wheel a nine-foot grand Steinway piano out onto the beach so that I could play too. It was times like those that I wished my mother had given me guitar lessons instead of piano lessons.

In Honolulu, between the main drag and the beach, there were dozens of little surf shacks. One in particular fascinated me every day when I passed by. Two totally radical dudes lived there and seemed to be having the time of their lives. To me, it looked like they had the ideal existence. There were surfboards on the front porch, and a Zigzag mat over the front door. However, the most amazing sight was a gigantic floor-to-ceiling wall of beer cans stacked on top of each other. I remember thinking to myself how totally cool it was that they had emptied all of those beer cans.

While I thought this was the absolute coolest, Michael thought it completely stupid. At thirteen, peer pressure was beginning to get to me, but he was like the Rock of Gibralter. I later thought that his idol must have been Pat Boone, because he was so squeaky clean and afraid to take chances. In retrospect, I wish I had followed his lead all of those years ago.

One night, after we had returned to the bungalow and went to bed, I set the alarm clock and snuck out in the middle of the night to go to a party. It was there that I embraced my future lifestyle — with open arms and an open mouth. I drank beer after beer after beer until I couldn't see straight. After getting totally smashed, someone pointed me in the direction of the bungalow, and I staggered back to my room, trying to quietly sneak back in unnoticed. This is not an easy task when you have no sense of balance whatsoever.

I tried to sneak in through the window, quietly, but I ended up waking up my mother in the process. I thought she was going to kill me. She knew immediately what I had been up to. Instead of punishing me, she told me that sufficient punishment would come to me in the morning. When I woke up the next day, I found that she was right. I spent the better part of the day "praying to the porcelain god." There seemed to be pneumatic drills and jackhammers going off in my head. My teeth were asleep, my tongue itched, and it tasted like a herd of water buffalo wearing sweaty gym socks had run through my mouth.

As bad as I felt then, I knew that I wanted to do it all over again the next night.

My first taste of rock and roll fame came that summer when Michael and I were spotted by a photographer on the beach at Waikiki. He informed us that he was shooting an album cover for the popular surf group, the Sentinels. He already had two gorgeous surf bunnies lined up for the shoot, and all he needed were two bitchin' dudes and one surfboard. When I look at that album cover shot now, and the way I looked then, I'm appalled.

Although I loved surfing and drinking beer, and an occasional nod from the opposite sex, my first true addiction was playing music. That habit dates back to my first taking piano lessons when I was seven years old.

Maybe growing up in Beverly Hills had something to do with my future addiction. I know that financially and socially, it certainly didn't hurt. I felt as if I always had to be "on" — not to please my parents, even though my mother demanded a lot more out of me than my father did. Instead, it was for myself. I always felt that I wanted to be better than most kids, at whatever I did. I was just competitive.

When I was seven and Mother decided that I should learn to play the piano, I resented it. Later in my life I thanked her for it many times over. Of course, I had to have the best lessons from the best teachers. Her ultimate goal was for me to become an accomplished classical pianist. I, however, had something completely different in mind. I practiced four hours a day to become someone my mother could be proud of. I'm sure she never dreamed that someday I would gain worldwide fame doing something that she was, basically, against.

From the moment I first heard a rock and roll record on the radio, I knew that's what I wanted to do. As far back as I can remember, I would save up my weekly allowance (fifty cents a week) and on the weekend ride my bicycle two miles to the May Company store on Wilshire and Fairfax and head for the record department. There I would purchase the latest records that I had been hearing on the radio.

Since I became a record connoisseur at the early age of seven, I tried to buy virtually every record that I could. Even at sixty-nine cents a single, this soon exceeded my allowance. I often found myself borrowing extra money from my mother to supplement my growing habit. Soon I had amassed dozens of records for my collection.

The Top Ten records that influenced me the most during the first eleven years of my life are permanently etched in my mind. They are (including highest chart position and year of release):

1. "Maybellene" by Chuck Berry (#5/1955)
2. "Diana" by Paul Anka (#1/1957)
3. "Venus" by Frankie Avalon (#1/1959)
4. "Day-O (The Banana Boat Song)" by Harry Belefonte (#5/1957)
5. "Loveletters in the Sand" by Pat Boone (#1/1957)
6. "You Send Me" by Sam Cooke (#1/1957)
7. "Catch a Falling Star" by Perry Como (#1/1958)

8. "Lollipop" by the Chordettes (#2/1958)
9. "What'd I Say" by Ray Charles (#6/1959)
10. "There Goes My Baby" by the Drifters (#2/1959)

Obviously, my musical tastes were eclectic. I listened to the radio every day and practiced the piano religiously. When I heard Danny and the Juniors' statement of musical longevity, "Rock and Roll Is Here To Stay," I knew that I would become a famous rock star, no matter how long I had to work at it or how many dues I would have to pay.

As far as I knew, there were no other rockers from Beverly Hills. I stuck with my classical training, studying at the L.A. Conservatory of Music. There was an ironic twist to that particular building because it later became the world-famous Whiskey-A-Go-Go on Sunset Boulevard. I would later play there in various groups, and also do a lot of my most abusive drinking and drug taking there.

After five years of classical piano, I decided it was time to move on. My interest in modern and jazz music was growing daily. My mother could sense my need to satisfy my new musical tastes, so she found a great modern teacher named Harry Fields. His studio was just down Sunset Boulevard from the conservatory in West Hollywood. This was only a five-minute drive from our house in Beverly Hills. However, my mother would have driven any distance and spent any amount of money to make me happy. My father didn't care what I did as long as it made my mother happy. If I needed musical supplies or a better piano, he would hem and haw until I threw a tantrum and secretly went behind his back to my mother. Within a few days, I would get my way.

The things that I learned from Mr. Fields were invaluable later in my life. However, by the time I was twelve, I had gone as far with him as I could. He even suggested to my mother not to throw any more money away on my lessons. According to him, he couldn't teach me anything more. He said that I had natural talent and that I should direct it toward something I believed in. I knew just what the something was: rock and roll music.

I bought every record I could get my hands on and listened to the radio nonstop. One station in particular, KRLA in Pasadena, played all of the current hits as well as oldies. (I didn't know at the time that the program director and disc jockey, Reb Foster, would later become one of the managers of the group that would make all of my wildest dreams — and my worst nightmares — come true. I began to memorize the music and lyrics to all of the records. Then I took it a step further and could name the record label, songwriter, and the "B" sides. All the while, rock music filled the air at 174 North Swall Drive in Beverly Hills.

I had my first taste of success at the age of twelve. My childhood friend, Michael Lloyd, and I had the same musical background and awakening. Together, we formed a band in seventh grade and entered a talent contest at our school. He played the guitar, I banged on the piano, and another friend pounded away on the drums. Placing musical instruments in front of a group of chimpanzees would have met with better results. Nevertheless, we won the contest. That was all of the encouragement I needed. I had a taste of acceptance from a crowd. Granted, there were only fifty people in the audience, and they were between nine and thirteen years old, but I'll never forget the feeling that I got on stage that day in the spotlight.

We needed to "fatten up" the sound of our little band, so we added a bass/rhythm guitar player. Michael and I were at the core of the band. Over the next few years, a succession of drummers and rhythm guitarists came and went. Originally, we called ourselves the Alleykats. Later we became the New Dimensions. The line-up of musicians included Michael Lembeck on guitar, whose father was Harvey Lembeck of *Beach Party* movie fame. (In later years, Michael went on to become a regular on the hit TV series "One Day at a Time," playing the part of Mackenzie Phillips' husband.)

Michael Lloyd and I were writing songs every day. We hooked up with a manager who had us working all of the time. We were making about $50 apiece per night. We did dances, weddings, bar mitzvas, all of the surf fairs, the teenage fair at the Hollywood Palladium, private parties for movie stars, and just about everything else.

When it came time to record our "cute" little songs, we enlisted the help of a publisher by the name of Mike Curb, who was a friend of Michael Lloyd's. He published our songs for us, which was our first step toward landing a recording contract. Mike Curb later founded Warner/Curb Records and went on to become lieutenant governor of California.

Through the help of Curb and some family contacts, we were now ready to go into the studio to record our orignial compositions. Our recording sessions took place in a little studio on Melrose Avenue in Hollywood, across the street from what is now Paramount Studios. The owners of the studio were a husband and wife team, Hite and Dorinda Morgan. They had a song called "Barbie" that they wanted one of their groups, Kenny and the Cadets, to record, but the group wasn't too sure about the song. Although the song "Barbie" never turned into anything big, the group did. In a few short months, Kenny and the Cadets would break onto the music scene with a new record about the latest craze, "Surfin'," and they would change their name to the Beach Boys.

The Morgans still had the song "Barbie," written to capitalize on the Barbie doll craze that was sweeping the country, and my group, the Alleykats, ended up recording it. The song was recorded, pressed, distributed, and went promptly into the toilet. So much for our first single.

Kenny and the Cadets leaving the Morgans proved to be very much in our advantage, because it provided us with the opportunity to have more recording time. Under the direction of Hite and Dorinda, we figured that maybe we could break wide open like the Beach Boys. However, fame on a grand scale was not in the cards for us just yet. We kept on recording and landed record contracts with various independent labels, but with little or no response. Not to be discouraged, we kept on playing gigs every chance we could. For a bunch of kids just about to start high school, we became quite popular on the dance circuit.

The one thing I noticed about being in a rock band was that the girls suddenly took notice. Up to this point, I could only speculate what it was like to win the admiration of the opposite sex. The more popular we became, the more the girls hung out. I guess you could call it the early stages of "groupies." As did every virile young boy at the time, I too dreamed of being seduced by any one of the tender little things who waited for us after the show. The one big drawback was that we weren't quite initiated into the "school of cool." Since none of us had a driver's license, one of our mothers' would have to pick us up after we played. Definitely *not cool.* Another not so cool thing was that no one in the band drank or did the unspeakable — drugs! That is, no one but me. At that point, I had been introduced to only alcohol, but I greeted it with open arms.

I had my first taste of liquor when I was seven. The family was at my grandmother's house for one of the Jewish holidays, and I spied a bottle of dark, thick liquid. Nobody there tried to stop me when I became curious and decided to take a sip. I'll never forget that first taste of Mogen David 20/20 — or "Mad Dog 20/20," as hardcore alcoholics call it. I thought it would taste better on pancakes, but since there weren't any around, I poured myself a large glass and sat in the corner sipping away at it until I finished the whole thing. When I stood up, I felt dizzy and quickly sat down again. Then that wave of warmth and strength hit me. I was off and running. After that first time, whenever we went out to dinner, I'd ask my mom for a sip of whatever she was drinking. Soon, she would order some mixed drink, pretending it was for her. When the waiter walked away, she passed it over to me.

I found the more I drank, the easier it was to fall asleep. I also discovered that it gave me a certain sense of strength. I could do and say things that I couldn't do or say before. I drank more and more. By the time I was thirteen, I was well on my way to becoming a closet alcoholic. At the dances I attended at the time, I would sneak out of the room and have a belt with one of the hip girls or older guys who were there. I was on my way to being cool. The other band members had no idea I was drinking; it was my secret. I tried to hide it from my parents too. However, at home, when the vodka started to disappear, my mother questioned my sudden plunge into social drinking. I assured her it was harmless and that nothing would come of it.

That was my first mistake. Denial at thirteen is a hard thing to imagine. Of course, I didn't realize it was denial until I was thirty-seven years old and I had spent over twenty-three years simultaneously kidding myself and killing myself. It was already too late to turn back now.

The seed had been planted, and my addictive personality soon wasn't satisfied with mere alcohol. A certain part of me wanted to try other forbidden things, even though my own common sense told me that it was wrong. Sex and drugs would be the next frontiers for me to explore.

We kept on recording under the name the New Dimensions and continued to play all over Southern California. But there was something different. I was meeting new friends and running outside of my circle of school chums. The rest of the band saw a noticeable change in my behavior. Michael Lloyd was getting restless too and wanted to record and play with different people, keeping him and me as the core of the group.

During one of my late Friday night trips up to the Sunset Strip, I stumbled into one of the many rock clubs and was intrigued by a group whose name I've long since forgotten. What caught my eyes and ears were the guitar and bass players. They were introduced on stage as David and Mike Doud. There was a certain rawness in both their sound and their look. Dave was probably in his mid to late teens, while Mike was well over twenty. I thought to myself, *He must know all about cool. I'll bet he even smokes grass.* There was a James Dean quality to Mike, while David looked like he had just gotten up and couldn't find a hairbrush.

After their set, I sought them out, introduced myself, and told them that I liked their music. There was a plan already formulating in the back of my mind: "If we could get them together with Michael Lloyd and myself, and find a suitable drummer, we would really 'kick ass' — and get all the girls we wanted!" Besides, I could tell they were real party animals — in other words, my kind of people. I asked them when they would be playing again and found out it was not for six more weeks. That would work out perfectly, because I could pump Michael up and generate some interest in this new brainstorm of mine.

I set up a meeting with Michael Lloyd, the Douds, and myself. Since the older Doud had a car, they drove to meet us at Michael's house in Beverly Hills, which was just a few miles from me. We talked about music, the Beatles, recording (which was something the brothers didn't have access to), and our many contacts in the business. We all hit it off immediately and agreed to join forces. I could sense, however, a slight bit of apprehension in Michael Lloyd's complete trust of Dave and Mike. This was probably due to the fact that Michael was a clean-cut kid who had no desire whatsoever to discover "the high life." I have to give him credit. He never once questioned the brothers as to their lifestyle, even though he could clearly see it was radically different from his. However, I was drawn closer to them for that very reason.

By then the Beatles had three singles on the charts and had paved the way for the British Invasion. This provided an interesting dichotomy in our repertoire. We would write Beatle-influenced songs and still be able to cover all of the current British Top 40 hits in our live shows. This would be the best of both worlds, as far as I was concerned. The girls would flock to hear us. Since the majority of the public would never be able to see the Beatles "live" in-concert, we would be a popular substitute.

Within a few weeks, Michael and I had enough material — both new and old, plus most of the Beatle songs that were popular — to fill three or four sets. It was now time to put our merry band of boys together. But one major problem surfaced almost immediately. Mike Doud had a better offer from a group that was his own age. We understood his position and wished him well. We still had David, Michael Lloyd, and a friend from Beverly Hills, along with myself. Art Guy was a pro in every sense of the word. He played drums and played the shit out of them. David made an excellent suggestion to add a sax player who had been working with him on and off for a while. A phone call was made, and Danny Belsky was inducted into the group.

We started rehearsals, alternating between Michael's house and mine. Both of our mothers were very supportive of our new attempt at stardom. Michael and Dave traded off playing bass and lead guitar, although Dave was a better rock and roll player. He didn't have the formal training that Michael or I had, but he played from the heart, and that is something that can't be taught.

As I mentioned, we were first known as the Alleykats. This was certainly a laughable name for three kids from Beverly Hills and two from across town. We played all over Southern California and even got into the studio. Somewhere along the way, we decided to change the name back to the New Dimensions. Later we dropped the "New" and simply became the Dimensions.

We were suddenly being flooded with great job offers. Playing at the Surf Fair at the Santa Monica Civic Auditorium was a plus on our side. The Beach Boys, who were the biggest American group at the time, would headline, and we would go on before them. Also on the bill were various other popular surf groups of the time like the Crossfires, who later became the Turtles. There was excitement everywhere, even though the surfing craze had taken a backseat to the Beatles and their invasion.

I wanted something more out of the group and myself but couldn't pinpoint it. I knew in my heart it was time to move on. I wanted to play more aggressive rock.

David Doud had become a close friend. We shared the same lust for life and the same curiosity for things that we knew were wrong to do. This casual attitude I had developed was attributed to the fact that we were spending a lot of time in the Sunset Strip bars getting drunk. David was a few months away from getting his driver's license and would borrow his brother's car. On many occasions, Mike would join us on our hedonistic trips. He wasn't happy with the group either and really wanted to play with his brother again. They had a certain chemistry between them that came out when they played.

While making the rounds one night, we all came to the unanimous decision to stop screwing around and get a serious rock and roll band together. The music scene on the Sunset Strip was night and day from the mellow surf sounds of the lowlands. Something was happening up there that was going to explode at any moment.

We could all feel it. There were no less than a dozen clubs in a two-mile stretch that soon would spawn some of the best groups to come out of America — or anywhere, for that matter. The kids did what they wanted and seemed to have a general disregard for anything establishment. That suited me just fine, but I knew that Michael Lloyd, with his wholesome and conservative down-home values, would never be caught dead on Sunset. For me, this was going to be my ticket out.

The split was an amicable one, with Danny Belsky jumping ship to come with me. He too wanted to taste forbidden fruit. Mike Doud brought a drummer with whom he was working. He was also an excellent singer and had fantastic stage presence. We decided to make this Latin powerhouse, Joe Madrid, our front man and put Danny on drums. Since Danny was a multi-instrumentalist, he had no problem adjusting to the switch. He and Joe would trade off playing drums, leaving me the front of the stage for certain numbers to shake my ass and play "rock star."

We had to find a name that people would remember and that sounded ultra-hip at the same time. Since Mike was into jazz and R&B music as well, he suggested the title from a Mose Allison record: the Seventh Son. I liked it immediately for purely personal reasons, seeing as how I was born on the seventh day of February. We all agreed and started rehearsals at Dave and Mike's large house in the Hollywood Hills. Their parents had been killed in a plane crash a number of years before, and they were living off of the inheritance. Their grandmother occupied one of the rooms in the house, but she was hard of hearing and couldn't get around that well. The boys usually brought her food and she would inch her way down the steps to the kitchen. This would take so long sometimes that we could, literally, have a party in full swing, have everyone cleared out and the place cleaned up before she reached the bottom of the stairs. It became the perfect atmosphere for our drunken debauchery.

We met our goals sooner than anyone had anticipated. I was spending more and more time away from home with my new mentors. My mother gave me carte blanche to come and go as I pleased. In a way, I wished that she would exercise a little more control over me instead of the total independence she let me have. Still, I probably would have done what I wanted anyway.

The one thing that was suffering was my schoolwork. My grades were poor, and I didn't seem to fit in at Beverly Hills High School anymore. They looked at me as sort of a rebel. I started to grow my hair long, and my thoughts were always of rock music, girls, and partying.

The groundwork had been laid, and so with the '60s in full swing, I raced forward and never looked back. The real turning point was just around the corner, and I eagerly anticipated every challenge that lay in my path. I wanted to learn more about life. I had good teachers in the "party animal brothers" — David and Mike Doud — and I was willing to become the best possible student. Class was about to begin.

# 3 / Mama Told Me Not To Come

February 7, 1964. Aside from the fact that this was my sixteenth birthday, the single most important event so far in my life was about to take place on this day. I would get my driver's license and my mother would buy me my first car: a lime green SS Chevy Nomad station wagon. The first thing I did to the car was put a mattress in the back, in anticipation of the many girls I knew I would surely pick up. At Beverly High, it was a status symbol to have your own car.

I began to spend more time away from home, but my trusting mother never questioned where I was going or with whom I was spending all my time.

I was on the verge of flunking out of school at the time — not because I didn't have the brains, but simply because I didn't give a damn. The final straw was when I failed physical education for not "suiting up" for an entire semester. I didn't care for sports. The only form of exercise I wanted would be directed toward the opposite sex.

The Beatles had started a fashion revolution, but it seemed that most of the kids weren't that quick to pick up on it. Being aspiring rockers, Michael Lloyd and I went full speed ahead to turn the code of dress at Beverly upside down. We grew our hair longer and started wearing jeans and other clothes that were socially unacceptable. Even though we weren't working together, we remained close friends. His mother was in the process of setting up a recording studio for him in the back of their house. He had a keen ear for arranging and was leaning more toward the production and technical end of the business. He knew his place wasn't up there under the spotlights. That he left to me.

We were being pressured by the gym coaches and the boys' vice-principal to cut our hair and "straighten out our act," as they put it. The alternative was to pack up our books and get our walking papers. This chastisement lasted for about another two months, which was just before summer vacation of our junior year. Then they pushed us one time too many. I'm sure they thought that we could conform to their upper-class way of thinking. However, when we walked into the gym and the coach said, "Greenspoon! Lloyd! Either cut your hair, or you're out of here!" we took our cue and walked up the hill to our lockers for the last time.

Michael's mother knew of a school in Hollywood that catered to people in the entertainment industry. The next morning, we checked out of Beverly High and into Hollywood Professional School. It was housed in a slightly run-down, two-story white building on Hollywood Boulevard just past Western Avenue in a section of town light years away from Beverly Hills.

Just about the same time, not far away at Hollywood High School, David Doud was undergoing a similar metamorphosis. He was expelled from school for smoking and drinking on campus. I suggested he join the merry band of misfits at HPS. So, before summer vacation of 1964, David, Michael, and I were once again drawn together.

The great thing about HPS was that you got to pick your classes and there was no P.E. The best was yet to come. I found out, through continued efforts, that you could leave the school at any time, for any reason, as long as you had a note from anyone. I pushed this rather lax rule to the limit. This was about the same time that Michael and I met Kim Fowley.

Kim was somewhat of a legend around Hollywood for his sheer persistence when trying to secure a record deal. His track record already included two big hits: "Alley-Oop" by the Hollywood Argyles and "Popsicles Icicles" by the Mermaids. He was involved in the writing and/or production of both. If he had a group and walked into a record company, he wouldn't leave until he had secured a deal. His imagination was vivid and his disposition caused people to never question anything that he said or did. He tested it many times by showing up at HPS early in the morning, walking right into the classrooom, and loudly announcing to the teacher and the whole class something like, "Would you please excuse Mr. Greenspoon and Mr. Lloyd? They have to accompany me to Guam to do an Armed Forces radio show." The first time that he said that, I couldn't believe my ears. Fucking Guam! Couldn't he have picked someplace like London? The best part was that the teacher always bought it. There was only one small hitch. She would usually ask for a full report of where we were going, to be delivered in front of the whole class when we returned. No problem! I was great at the fine art of bullshitting. I'd just look up in the encyclopedia whatever I needed to know about a given place, memorize it, and deliver the speech to the class. They always fell for it hook, line, and sinker.

Summer was just around the corner, and I eagerly anticipated cutting my teeth with the grown-up rockers on Sunset Boulevard.

Aside from my sixteenth birthday and the change in learning institutions, there was one event that happened that would change my life forever. It was at this time in my life that I was introduced to and fully embraced the use of drugs.

We rehearsed new material with the Seventh Son at Mike and Dave's house at least four hours a day. Word spread quickly about this tough-sounding new band. When we played a dance in the valley, two men who owned one of the "in" Sunset Strip clubs came to check us out. It didn't take long for Ed Fontaine and Jerry Lambert to decide that they wanted us as the house band at their establishment.

This was our big break. The club that would become our home was Stratford on Sunset. It sat in a gulley on the southeast corner of Sunset Boulevard and Olive Drive in Hollywood. Across the street was Ciro's, already spawning some of the better bands around — bands with names that reflected the changing times: the Seeds, the Leaves, the Bees. There was obviously a nature theme running rampant.

The '60s was a turbulent and ever-changing time period for rock and roll. I remember one particular night at Ciro's during the summer of 1964. Mike Doud saw on the marquee that some friends of his were playing there. They had been known as the Southern California Gas Company, but had to change their name for obvious reasons. They now called themselves the Grassroots, but that too would have to be changed soon: for another group playing down the street at the Crescendo was already called the Grassroots and had a song out called "Where Were You When I Needed You?" that started to break locally.

The leader of the group at Ciro's was the first black man to front a racially mixed rock group, long before anyone ever heard of Jimi Hendrix. His name was Arthur Lee. He cut quite an imposing figure: dark glasses, a scarf around his neck, Edwardian shirts and, what was to become his trademark, an old pair of army boots with one unlaced. He had a mesmerizing presence. His music had a rawness and sound that was sure to be a hit, and his onstage persona was that of a stoned-out troubadour in King Arthur's court. That's just what the audience became: followers of King Arthur Lee. He was a Pied Piper who would lead them down the road to a different form of consciousness. I, for one, quickly fell under his spell.

Arthur was rumored to be growing a killer marijuana plant. I was fascinated by this aspect of the man. I knew that Mike and Dave had smoked grass, and I'm sure that our drummer Joe Madrid had also. Danny Belsky, our sax player, I wasn't sure about.

Mike had worked with Arthur and his guitarist at a few local dances a couple of years earlier, so we were invited over to Ciro's by Arthur, and then next door to the large apartment building where he and his killer weed lived. When we got there he instructed everyone to follow him into the bedroom. There I watched with wonder as he rolled the biggest joint I had ever seen. Actually, it was the first joint I had seen in person. Up to this point, my sole knowledge of marijuana came from the highly "educational" film, *Reefer Madness*. Like the people in the movie, I feared that if you smoked grass your brain would turn into silly putty, you would develop instant genetic damage, and you'd wake up the next morning with two heads. However, there was a part of me that wanted to experience a grass high. Since I had been drinking for quite some time now, in my mind I justified that taking one little toke off a joint wouldn't hurt.

Arthur and the boys could sense my apprehension at taking this step to become a full-fledged rocker. They suggested that I follow them into the huge walk-in closet and just breathe the smoke from the joint they would pass around. *No harm in that,* I thought. So, in I went.

Arthur lit the joint and passed it to Mike, who passed it to Dave. All the while they would blow the smoke in my direction. Within a few minutes, they were laughing at nothing in particular. They would pass the joint, look at me, and blow the smoke in my face. I thought this was pretty stupid until I made a comment about the lack of weight I was experiencing. Suddenly, everyone in the closet was quiet. They just looked at each other for a minute and started laughing even harder. "He's on his way," Arthur said.

My God, was this it? Was this what it was like to be stoned? If so, then I wanted more. Surely this couldn't be bad for you. I think I surprised them when I asked to be included in the next round of passing the joint. I'll never forget that shit-eating grin on Mike's face. He slapped me on the back. "OK, Greenspoon!" was all he said over and over again. In a while, we laughed at that too.

When we stumbled out of the closet, Arthur played us some of his new songs on the guitar and told us of an idea he had for his new group. They were being courted by Elektra Records, and he had everything planned out as to how he would take Hollywood by storm. First there would be the name change. He drew the proposed group logo in psychedelic lettering on a piece of paper. I remember the simplicity of that one word: "Love." *What a great name for a group,* I thought to myself. And so, Love came to be. They went on to record some of the better songs of the time, including "Alone Again Or," "7 + 7 Is" and the classic "My Little Red Book," which was Arthur's tour de force on stage.

Everything happened quickly in the '60s, so when Love vacated Ciro's to move over to the trendier Hollywood clubs, the Brave New World and Bido Lido's, the void was filled quickly by a group who, in a few short months, would leave a lasting impression on the music industry. They played electric folk music: songs by Pete Seeger along with brilliant originals and a stunning new version of Bob Dylan's "Mr. Tambourine Man." They too adopted a name with nature in mind, the Byrds, changing the spelling obviously just to be different.

I remember it vividly. I was walking out of Stratford's one night during a set break and was watching this endless parade of freaks across the street going into Ciro's to see the Byrds. By then I was well on my way to being a pot head. The only drawback was that the combination of pot and alcohol left me feeling like I was mired in the La Brea Tar Pits. One of the club regulars saw that I was leaning against the wall as if to hold it up, and he offered me an "upper." I had never taken one, but I was eager to find out what this high would be like. I didn't know that Danny Belsky would always take one before he went on stage. He would also always be talking a hundred miles an hour, and he'd chew countless toothpicks to shreds every night. I chased the tiny white pill down with a beer and continued to stare in awe at the scene that was unfolding across the street.

The Byrds seemed to attract people who had little regard for clothes, or any other conventional bourgeois trappings. A new era in rock was unfolding before our eyes, and I wanted to make sure that I ingested all I could. I continued to stare with amazement, all the while not even noticing that I was biting a hole in my lower lip. I was grinding my jaw at a rapid rate now. What the hell was this strange new sensation? My whole body was moving faster, even though I was standing in place. That quickly changed as I began to pace up and down in front of the club.

Break time was over, and I couldn't wait to get back on stage. Seeing the crowd across the street, coupled with the fact that the upper had kicked in, gave me renewed strength.

As I ran into the dressing room, I could hardly contain myself. I was rambling on about the side show over at Ciro's and that we should go over on the next break and check them out. Everyone agreed that something new, something wonderful, was about to take place in the music scene. We agreed that we should study it carefully.

The effect of the upper was now in full swing, and I bounded out of the dressing room, stopping only for a second. I turned and addressed my somewhat perplexed-looking band mates: "Come on! Let's play! There's people to entertain, girls to impress, music to be made!"

Mike and Dave eyed each other cautiously. Joe and Danny just rolled their eyes and laughed. Then everyone followed me onto the stage. Ten minutes later, when I launched into the intro of one of our ballads at freight train acceleration, Mike walked over to me with that damned shit-eating grin of his. He put his hand on my shoulder and whispered into my ear with knowing approval, "OK, Greenspoon!" The rest of the band gave me nods of approval. I was "in" now.

Every night after that, before going on stage, we would go through this little ritual of taking an upper, smoking a joint, all chased by some cheap wine — usually something of a fine vintage like Ripple or Thunderbird. That way, everyone in the band was on the same wavelength — or lack of one, I should say.

Time passed so quickly. Maybe that was because of the newness of the drug era, and the fact that everybody was so stoned — myself included. At any rate, it was sometime early in 1965 when we all made the short trip across the street and over to Ciro's to witness the first flight of the Byrds.

Ed Fontaine and Jerry Lambert, the owners of Stratford's, who had now become our personal managers as well, were also very curious and tagged along.

Aside from the obvious circus of people in front of the stage, the first thing that caught our eyes and ears was the ringing electric twelve-string guitar of Roger McGuinn (then known as Jim Mc-

Guinn). He wore a shaggy haircut and Ben Franklin glasses. McGuinn had a very distinctive vocal style that, even today, is copied with best results by Tom Petty. The cocky stage presence of David Crosby was also an obvious plus, as were their beautiful, soaring harmonies. The drummer, Michael Clarke, also caught my eye, not especially for his drumming, which was competent, but for his projected innocence. He reminded me a lot of myself. In the years to follow, Michael and I would become drinking buddies and fellow hell-raisers.

Chris Hillman, the Byrds' bass player, and I also became friends later when he and Michael and Gram Parsons formed the Flying Burrito Brothers. David Crosby and I never struck up a relationship. He always seemed to have his mind tuned into something else, and he tried to stay just one step ahead of everyone else. We talked on occasion or ran into each other at one of the '60s hangouts, like Ben Frank's on the strip, but we never seemed to hit it off. Their front man, Gene Clark, was also somewhat of a loner. They all ran within a tight circle of friends and were probably a little leery of any competition, especially from younger players like myself.

One thing I do know is that the Byrds not only made a lasting impression on me but on a whole generation as well. I will never forget the feeling I got that first night I saw them.

The Seventh Son was becoming a very popular group in L.A. Holding the house band position at Stratford's gave us the opportunity to do something that few bands could do. Whenever the club would change its format and bring in popular groups or single artists, it was the house band's job to always back them up. When the club went on a soul kick, we got to work with some people in the industry that we really respected. Among the performers we backed up were Mary Wells, Major Lance, the Coasters, the Olympics, Martha and the Vandellas, and more top acts than I can remember. Also at the time we were backing up a rather "mod" looking duo wearing wide bell-bottoms and fur vests. They were a young husband and wife team who called themselves Caesar and Cleo. Eventually, they began using their own first names, Sonny and Cher.

Also, on any given night, a crazy maniac with curly dirty black hair, torn clothes, who obviously hadn't bathed in months, would jump up on stage and launch into one of his bizarre tunes. The most famous of these tunes was a nonsensical piece of shit called "Merry-Go-Round (Boop, Boop, Boop)." This idiot, who called himself Wild Man Fischer, was actually signed to a record deal by Frank

Zappa, who had a knack for acquiring strange and unusual talent. Fischer recorded one totally forgettable waste of vinyl, but still persisted on ramming the songs down the unsuspecting throats of the public.

We still held the house band position at Stratford's, but two weeks out of the month we would be booked into all the other hip clubs in Hollywood and along the Strip, clubs like the super chic Red Velvet and the Purple Onion. The caliber of bands that played these clubs seemed to turn off the mainstream rockers, but we welcomed the challenge.

A little north of the Red Velvet, just off Hollywood Boulevard, was the Brave New World that played host to the always bizarre Frank Zappa and the Mothers of Invention. East of that was Bido Lido's, where Arthur Lee and his group Love reigned supreme. As you headed west on Sunset, on the corner of Crescent Heights Boulevard was Pandora's Box, a small pink monument to local talent. West of that was Stratford's and Ciro's, followed by a shoebox of a club, the Sea Witch. Two blocks west was the old Crescendo, which had been bought out by some very smart businessmen who turned it into the number-one showplace on Sunset Boulevard. They renamed it the Trip, which was an appropriate title for a club that hosted some of the most spaced-out people to come out of the '60s. Next came the Whiskey-A-Go-Go, which saw a radical policy change when the Trip came into existence. Up to that point, the Whiskey booked people like Trini Lopez and Johnny Rivers, both of whom had huge followings consisting of fairly straight, middle-class people. When the longhairs took over "the Strip" and turned it into a Southern California version of Haight Ashbury, these performers and their fans were threatened with possible extinction.

Next door to the Whiskey was a little hole in the wall called the London Fog. The house band there at the time was a struggling new group, the Doors, whose lead singer, Jim Morrison, was rumored to be the Marlon Brando of rock. His claim would have to bear close attention by the other local rockers. Two doors down from the Fog was the Galaxy. There, what was to become L.A.'s premier psychedelic band, the Iron Butterfly, was busy initiating hordes of people into the new realm of music. The last club on the Strip was Gazzari's. Any young, up-and-coming band could get a break there. To this day, it and the Whiskey are the only clubs still in business on a regular basis. Many groups, including the Knack, Ratt, and Mötley Crüe got their start there.

The scene was changing so rapidly with the emergence of new groups, new drugs, and a totally new lifestyle that the whole rock world from New York to San Francisco was focused on this last frontier of music and style. I embraced the changing times and welcomed any new philosophy based on sex, drugs, and rock and roll. This edict became a way of life, not only for myself, but for countless other young people growing up in this era.

The year 1965 was when everything would culminate in my search for knowledge about life, liberty, and the ubiquitous party. I grew up way too fast for my own good, but in retrospect, I'm thankful for being allowed to go through so much shit in my life and still be able to come out on top.

My mind and body were stimulated in two significant ways during this time period. I was introduced to complete "all-the-way" sex and LSD at about the same time. They were both incredible learning experiences to which I quickly became addicted. However, I didn't realize at the time that they could easily kill you.

My sexual awakening was supplied by an older woman at one of the previously mentioned clubs, the Sea Witch. Up until that point, I had gone on various dates with the usual necking and heavy petting in the back seat of the car. I would "cop a feel" or get my hands down the girl's pants and into her underwear. If I was real lucky, I'd even get a hand job. But now I was on stage, and there were girls who wanted to get into *my* pants!

We had just finished a real "smokin' " set at the Witch. I had noticed that all during our show a certain well-endowed older woman was throwing the "fuck darts" in my direction. I immediately responded by dancing, singing, and shaking my ass all over the stage in an attempt to turn her on. Lo and behold, it worked.

When I got off the stage, she made her way through the crowd. After the appropriate introductions, she led me by the hand into our own dressing room like she had done this countless times before. Mike and Joe were in there putting the moves on two other prime-looking candidates, so I quickly turned to make my exit, only to be blocked by my newfound friend. She then whispered into my ear, "Follow me. I know where we can go."

As we left the dressing room, I looked back at Mike with that stupid grin on his face, and before he could blurt it out, I said, "Don't even think of saying it." The grin got wider, and we made our exit.

She took me by the hand through the tiny, packed club to the front, where there was a small enclosed room that housed the pay phone. There were always people in line waiting to use the phone, or hanging out inside smoking a joint. We staked out a spot in front of the door, and she instructed me to wait right there. Then she dashed off to the bar to get a couple of drinks. She returned a few minutes later with two tumblers filled to the rim with Chivas Regal.

When the phone booth was vacated, she pulled me inside and locked the door. Then, without even missing a beat, she began to blow in my ear and kiss the back of my neck, alternately taking sips from her scotch. I'd polished off mine and was in the process of reaching for her tumbler when she dropped to her knees and proceeded to demonstrate the joys of oral sex for the first time.

The room began to spin, and I'm not quite sure how I reacted, but I could tell by her enthusiasm that she was enjoying herself. When she started to take off the rest of my clothes, I suddenly became a little apprehensive that someone would come in to use the phone and discover what we were doing. Being a red-blooded American teenage boy, I knew what the next logical progression was, although I didn't want it to happen in a crowded phone booth in a night club on Sunset Boulevard. I told her that my parents were on vacation in Europe, and we could go over there. That very moment I was simultaneously saved and embarrassed by the sound of Mike's voice over the club PA shouting "Showtime, Greenspoon! Get the hell out of the phone booth!"

When we both emerged from that tiny cubicle, I knew that my face was as red as my hair. My new friend just smiled at me and said, "I'll wait for you after the show."

We had two more sets to complete, and I ripped through them like a runaway freight train — playing every song ten times faster than it was meant to be played. Everyone in the band, except for Mike, thought I was overamping on speed. He, however, knew that the sudden burst of enthusiasm was directly attributed to the fact that I had just met a real L.A. woman, and not one of the virginal high school cuties who frequented the clubs. In between songs, Mike would bolt over to me, put his hand on my shoulder, and smile that Cheshire Cat grin, saying, "All right, Greenspoon!" We both broke out laughing.

At 2:00 A.M., as the band struck the last chord, I practically set the place ablaze beating a path to the front door. True to her word, she was waiting for me in front of the club.

I grabbed her by the hand and started to pull her down the street to the parking lot. "Slow down," she said. "What's your hurry? We have all night." *I've waited this long,* I thought to myself, *I might as well wait a little bit longer.*

A week prior to getting the engagement at the Sea Witch, I had traded in my old set of wheels for something that was more practical and conducive to the lifestyle I was now living. The new "Spoon-mobile" was a fire engine red MGB convertible. No matter what the weather, with the exception of a raging rain storm, I would always leave the top down. I began wearing brightly colored wool scarves and had let my hair grow well past my shoulders. It didn't take long to acquire a nickname: "The Red Baron."

I got my first taste of materialistic acceptance when we arrived at the parking lot and, having seen my car, she said, "Great! Let's take yours. Mine is a piece of shit."

It felt great driving down Sunset with the wind blowing in our faces and the music cranked up well beyond distortion. She suggested that we make a brief stop at Gil Turner's Liquor Store at the corner of Sunset and Doheny. Soon she emerged carrying two bottles of Dom Pérignon champagne. I was not only going to be initiated into the club of manhood, but also would acquire a taste for some of the finer things in life.

As we walked into the house, she asked me where the kitchen was, then proceeded to put both bottles of champagne in the freezer to chill them faster. She then took me by the hand and led me into my own living room, where we sat down on my parents' couch and engaged in some trivial small talk. After a few minutes she produced a Baggie full of some killer-looking weed and some rolling papers. Not missing a cue, I jumped right in and helped her roll about a half dozen "bombers." I picked one of the joints, and from the second I lit it, I knew that the stuff was mean. I took one long toke off of it and began choking violently. "Jesus Christ!" I said to her, coughing smoke out of my lungs. "What the hell is this shit?"

"It's a combination of some home-grown and Middle Eastern hash," she said.

"Great, now if I can just get past the choking, maybe it will work," I told her.

"Oh, it's working, all right," she smiled, "just sit back and give it a chance."

I took her advice and stretched out on the couch for a minute or two. *Well, nothing is happening so far,* I thought to myself, *I guess the stuff isn't that good after all.* About that time, I remembered the champagne chilling in the freezer. As I stood up, my knees buckled and I fell to the floor.

"Holy shit! I guess it *is* working!" I said. She stood over me with a smile on her face that soon gave way to uncontrollable laughter. In a second, I was caught up in it and laughing hysterically as well.

I picked myself up off the floor and started walking to the kitchen, all the while mumbling, "Good shit!" I soon returned with two glasses and two nearly frozen bottles of champagne. I popped the cork on one of them and then began to pour. We raised our glasses to toast the evening, and then she suddenly turned to me and said, "I bet you don't even remember my name."

"To tell you the truth, you're right — I don't," I replied. I really didn't care, but I pretended to be embarrassed and asked her anyway.

"It's Diane," she said.

"Hi, Diane. I'm Jimmy."

"Hi, Jimmy. It's a pleasure to meet you," she said as she shook my hand.

"Now that we have been formally introduced, what comes next?" I teased.

"How about some more champagne and another joint?" Diane answered.

*Ah, ha,* I thought to myself, *now, this is my kind of woman!*

Sometime in 1965 I discovered paradise on Hollywood Boulevard. It took the unlikely form of a quaint little record shop on the north side of the street about two blocks west of Vine. Even its name seemed to roll off the tongue like a whisper: Lewin's Record Paradise. Mr. Lewin's claim to fame was that he possessed the ability to secure the British import versions of albums, singles, and EPs long before their greatly inferior American copies hit the conventional record shops. The English records usually contained tracks not found on the American ones, as well as better sound quality and wonderful slick album covers. Mr. Lewin would go down to LAX customs and pick up a new crop of releases while a small contingent of would-be rockers, myself included, would wait patiently at the store for his return.

Although most European imports are today regarded as collector's items, the sole purpose then was to get a jump on the American version and learn a song by your favorite group long before it was even played on the local radio stations. Upon doing this, and by promptly including the selection in your set list, you almost instantly guaranteed yourself carte blanche with the best-looking groupies around. Another plus was that if you couldn't make out the words to a certain song, no one cared, because they didn't know the song either. You could actually make up your own words, and everyone would think that's the way the song was supposed to sound.

Case in point: when I tried to learn the Rolling Stones' "Get Off of My Cloud." Depending on what drugs I was on at the time, I only got as far as, "I live on the . . ." from the first verse. By the time I got to the chorus, which we encouraged the audience to sing along with, I had created a series of totally unintelligible sounds that vaguely resembled words. People would come up to me after our set and be completely flabbergasted that I knew the words. With a smug look, I would sarcastically retort, "Doesn't everybody?" By the time the song was a hit on the charts, most clubs' patrons were singing my lyrics, not those by Jagger and Richards. This ploy worked extremely well until the sheet music was published and people learned the right words, at which time we promptly dropped the song from our set.

I would order the records from a list that Mr. Lewin made up of the new releases and would wait outside the store for him to return from the airport with next month's crowd pleasers by the Hollies, the Rolling Stones, the Yardbirds, the Kinks, and a host of then unknown British bands. If he wasn't back by opening time, his wife would be there to let in the anxious stars of tomorrow. We would pass the time with tea and idle chatter until the moment when Mr. Lewin would walk through the door carrying a big box of records that still had the customs seal on it.

After parting with $4.95 for an album, $2.98 for an EP (extended play disc — usually four songs), or $1.10 for an import single (with the 45 rpm spindle already in the center), I would jump in the Spoonmobile and drive to the band house in Brensen Canyon with my foreign treasures. Once armed with a hit of speed, a bottle of cheap wine, and a good joint, the band would plunge "head first" into next weekend's show. After four hours of intense rehearsals, we would take a break, usually to go out and score some more drugs, and make a run to Victor's Liquor Store down the hill on Franklin Avenue. By midnight the set would be well-rehearsed, complete with the new lyrics that we made up to compensate for the lack of intelligible ones on the records.

As Friday night approached, we fine-tuned the set that included not only some R&B staples — like Mose Allison's "Parchman's Farm," "Walkin' the Dog" by Rufus Thomas, and the ten-minute version of "Smokestack Lightning" — but now we could dish up the Hollies' "Here I Go Again," "For Your Love" by the Yardbirds, Donovan's "Sunshine Superman," the Kinks' "Well Respected Man," the Searchers' "Someday We're Gonna Love Again," "Whenever You're Ready" by the Zombies, and countless other crowd-pleasers.

The songs, when played in the confines of a smaller club like Gazzari's or the Sea Witch, would almost always take on a tougher attitude. We had been performing these tunes for so long before they were bonafide hits that they took on an air of being our own.

When we were the opening act for a major headliner like the Byrds, Love, Buffalo Springfield, or the Lovin' Spoonful, we would magically transform the songs from mere cover tunes into a concert event. This worked especially well at the 2,500-seat Hullabaloo (which was later called the Kaleidoscope, the Aquarius Theater, and is now the home of TV's "Star Search"). The latter incarnation was apropos, since it was the home of the stars thirty years earlier when it was the Moulon Rouge. Having a large following in L.A., playing current and future rock staples, and having a downright "O.K. Motherfucker: Try to follow this set!" attitude, we more often than not took the wind out of the sails of the headliner.

Knowing a good thing when he saw one, Gary Bucasta, owner of the Hullabaloo (and manager of one of L.A.'s fave's, the Yellow Pages), promptly put us in the opening slot on a regular basis and even let us headline on the "off" nights, where we could build an even bigger following. This was acceptance on a large scale, and that suited my ego just fine. It didn't take too long to build on our rising local fame. I could walk into the most prestigious hangouts (usually Canter's Deli on Fairlax or Ben Frank's on the Strip) and not only be guaranteed a table (an almost impossible feat in those days) but have L.A.'s rock denizens call me by name. You knew you really had made it when at the table occupied by the various clubs' waitresses and regulars your name would be dropped like ice in a glass. As far as I was concerned, that was "paradise."

It was on one of the Hullabaloo's "off" nights, when we weren't playing but had gone down to check out the competition, that I had one of my more amusing solo acid trips.

Wallowing in my newfound notoriety, I had gone down early to prowl the cavernous club and catch a set by a much-hyped new band from Toronto called the Mandella (years later, their drummer, Penti "Whitey" Glan, would become a frequent drug partner). I demonstrated my final act of rock and roll acceptance when the bouncers and doormen let me in past the long lines of people twisting their necks and bodies into all sorts of grotesque positions just to see who the hell this VIP was. Once inside, I paused for some flirtatious chatter with whoever was at the ticket window that particular evening, then proceeded up the stairs and into the lion's den.

I usually made my way from table to table reticently, pausing only for a handshake or a quick "Hello," until I found one that contained suitable prey. Poised and ready to strike, I made my move quickly, to avoid a rush by the regular vermin that inhabited the place. Once my libido was unleashed, it was almost impossible to stop. However, on this night, quite suddenly, I had an uncharacteristic change of heart. On my way to the hunting ground, I stopped by a table to talk to Jim Pons of the Leaves, who were shaking up the charts with their version of the ubiquitous "Hey Joe." Seated with Jim was Jerry Penrod, the bass player for Iron Butterfly, and several members of the Sons of Adam, another local favorite.

Although I wanted to get laid, music was my first love, and once we started talking, all thoughts of my quest for flesh suddenly vanished. About ten minutes into a heated discussion on record companies, I noticed some out-of-place movement across the room. A girl I knew only by her first name, Kathy, was circulating something from a large shopping bag around the various tables. I got up from my seat at the table to get a better look, and upon closer inspection, I saw that she was freely giving out little glass vials that were about one-third full of a bright blue liquid. As I approached her, she reached into the bag and handed me one of the glass vials and simply said, "Enjoy," and continued on her way through the club.

I knew immediately that the blue liquid was some kind of wonderful new drug, but which one I wasn't quite sure. I turned around to catch up to her.

"Kathy!" I shouted over the roar coming from the opening act on stage. "What the hell is this?"

"It's Blue Liquid Owsley," she yelled back, "very powerful shit." And, with that, she was on her way again.

I knew that Owsley Stanley was a chemist who manufactured pharmaceutical LSD of rare quality and potency. He was especially famous for his dealings with the Grateful Dead. Without a doubt, this night was going to be special. I wasted no time. Unscrewing the cap, I tilted my head back, pressed the vial to my lips, and let the tasteless liquid roll down my throat. I was about to embark on a trip that didn't require any luggage. The only necessary tools were a strong imagination, which I possessed, and my car keys. Not knowing how strong this stuff was, I didn't want to come on to it in this hedonistic playground.

Within a few minutes, I was in the parking lot fumbling for my keys. I was starting to get that queasy feeling in my stomach, accompanied by a wonderfully warm rush all over my body. I opened the car door, got in, and started the engine. Then I cranked up the radio and, because it was a warm summer night, I put the top down. I turned right out of the parking lot, heading east toward Gower Street. There I turned left to Franklin Avenue and suddenly realized I was coming on to this faster than I had anticipated.

I laughed out loud and thought to myself, *Where the fuck am I going?* Then, without warning, I saw it. Horror of horrors: fog was slowly rolling in, blanketing most of the Hollywood Hills. I took Franklin to Beachwood Canyon Drive, where some unknown force compelled me to turn into the misty mire. Normal visibility was almost zero; "acid" visibility was on a completely different planet!

By now the effect of the drug was in full swing, and a frightening thought engulfed me. I was totally lost on a road that I usually knew like the back of my hand. To compound matters, they had sandblasted the center line off the road and painted a new one. This wouldn't be such a big deal, except that with my greatly altered perception, I clearly saw both lines going in different directions.

The only logical thing to do was throw the car into first gear and, driving at a snail's pace, open the door, lean out, and try to follow the darker of the two white lines (the current one). This worked well until a car came up behind me with its brights on. Trying to disguise my total panic, I motioned him to pass me — a rather ludicrous gesture, considering the fact that nobody could see more than a foot in either direction. Suddenly, my mounting paranoia got the best of me, and I made a sharp left turn up a steep hill. It was a bold, evasive maneuver, and I promptly lost the car on my tail. However, I could have achieved the same results by driving off a cliff, because now I was so hopelessly lost that I didn't even know what side of the hill I was on. This was quickly becoming drug hell.

I remember saying over and over out loud, "I'm not having fun now." I was practically at a standstill when somehow I saw a smooth stretch of pavement. *Salvation,* I thought to myself, and pointed the car in that general direction. The forward movement of the car was abruptly cut short by something solid. The fog momentarily dissipated long enough for me to make out a wall with a window right in the middle of it. I hadn't a clue as to what the fuck that was or how it got in the middle of the street. To make matters worse, there appeared to be a solid wall on either side of me, where arranged neatly and seemingly hanging in midair were . . . garden tools?

Then came the evening's piece de resistance. From overhead a light suddenly turned on. By now my skin had crawled about two inches off my bones, and my heart was somehow on the floor of the car. Ripping through the dead silence like a knife through flesh, a sound appeared. As it got closer I could make out someone shouting — a loud male voice, shouting at me — and by the tone I could tell he wasn't a happy camper.

"What the hell are you doing in my garage?"

Then, like the apocalypse, it hit me: I'm in a garage. This took a few minutes to figure out because of my temporarily displaced brain cells. However, my reflexes were in perfect working order, and without even thinking, I threw the car into reverse and floored it, only to meet another object blocking my hasty exit. This one, however, gave way to the force of the car hitting it, and with a loud crash I killed the gentleman's mailbox.

Knowing that the band house was only a few blocks away up Bronson Canyon, I pointed my car in a familiar direction. As I cruised cautiously down Beachwood, I turned the radio back up and searched for a station. The last thing I remember was hearing Gene Pitney singing "24 Hours From Tulsa," and thinking to myself, *My God, I really did go far. Maybe I'd better get a hotel room for the night.*

As the fog upon L.A. — and in my brain — slowly lifted, I glanced at my watch and noticed that this whole ordeal had taken roughly five hours out of my life. But in my altered state, it had seemed like an eternity!

Because of episodes like that one, when we first started dropping acid, no one wanted to leave the house. Usually Danny was our designated straight man. We were all a little afraid to go out in public. When someone made the suggestion, "Let's go out someplace," it was like: "You mean around people? No!" finally, we decided to attempt to venture out.

Getting into the car and trying to drive was a terrifying new adventure. Just finding your way for any more than a block was scary. Then, once we mastered that feat, someone suggested, "Let's go to a restaurant." That was another unique trip unto itself. You'd sit there tripping your brains out, and imagine that there were 4,500 people talking at once, because that's what the noise in the restaurant would sound like on acid. We'd be sitting there totally paranoid, imagining that they were all talking about us.

After we mastered restaurants, we progressed to doing really dumb things while tripping. There was a small amusement park called Pacific Ocean Park at the time, out on the pier, in Santa Monica. We'd drop acid and go there. I remember we got through all the rides: the octopus arms, and the roller coaster. One night we all went into the House of Mirrors while blitzed on acid. All of us got down on all fours, trying to find where the edges were, because we were bumping into the mirrors. We were obviously stoned when we started out. There we were on all fours, and in walks a family from Iowa, with a kid tugging at his mother's skirts going, "Mom, why is he doing that?" It took us hours to find our way out of there. It would take me years to find my way out of the drug adventure I had begun.

# 4 / Lean Back, Hold Steady

At 9:00 A.M. on December 3, 1965, I found myself once again standing outside Lewin's Record Paradise, waiting for Mr. Lewin's return from the airport. Only this time, the anticipation was of an extraordinary nature, for this was the day the Beatles released their landmark *Rubber Soul* album. I had stockpiled some Blue Owsley for just such an occasion.

Back at the Bronson Canyon house, Joe Madrid, our lead singer, and Dave and Mike Doud waited patiently for my return so we could "drop" and then dissect the creative artistry and the message contained on this fine piece of vinyl. Only Danny Belsky, our drummer, chose not to venture beyond the realm of consciousness. He didn't do half the amount of drugs that the rest of us did, and on this particular occasion he chose to remain the designated "straight man." His job would be to monitor Dave, Mike, Joe and myself, to make sure that we didn't have a bad trip. He really didn't care too much for acid, which naturally meant more for those of us who sought out the true meaning of life, and other complex thoughts.

Mr. Lewin was later than usual getting back from LAX, but due to the overwhelming feeling that this was going to change my whole outlook on conventional music as I knew it, I didn't mind the wait. I positioned myself at the front of the small line that was forming in front of the store, to insure that I was the first one on my block to own the British import copy of *Rubber Soul*. I felt like a kid at Christmas, although I don't think I ever received a present as rewarding as the one that was about to unfold over the next few hours. I was practically jumping out of my pants by the time Mr. Lewin finally pulled up in back of the store. The electricity in the air that was created by the kids in front of his shop must have been contagious, for I could see him grinning from ear to ear as he walked through, set the box of records down, and came to unlock the front door. My hand was firmly grasping the door knob, and my feet were already set in motion as I heard the click of the lock. I almost knocked him down to get to the box first.

"Hey, slow down mate!" were the words that Mr. Lewin said firmly for my sole benefit. But my ears didn't hear a thing. My senses had all but shut down, and my primal instinct was to nail the first copy. Throwing down a handful of bills on the counter, and not even waiting for my change, I ran to my car, jumped in, and drove as fast as I could back up Bronson Canyon. There the ritual would begin.

As I drove up, Mike and David were in the driveway waiting for me. I held the album above my head like a victory cup at a race, to show all of my waiting cohorts that I had indeed claimed the prize. At that moment, Joe stuck his head out of the living room window and informed us that the doctor was ready to see us. Sometimes when we dropped acid, Joe would feel like he was in charge of our trip, by administering the dose along with a joint and some wine.

As we went inside the house, Danny Belsky was sitting in the kitchen, chewing on his ubiquitous toothpick and looking rather put off at his impending babysitting job. Joe came in from the living room with a handful of goodies. He passed out the double-dose vials of Blue Liquid Owsley to Mike, Dave, and myself. He held the last one in his hand. There was a moment of exhilarating silence as we all looked at each other. Then, as if amid some strange ritual, we tilted our heads back at exactly the same time and consumed the blue liquid. Another moment of silence followed. Mike, always the philosophical one, broke the silence by saying, "Too late to turn back now."

"No shit!" was my quick reply.

Danny came out of the kitchen, taking a hit on a joint that he had rolled. He had a disgusted look on his face and was mumbling something that sounded like, "You're all a bunch of fucking assholes." True. And soon we were about to be some very stoned fucking assholes. Joe went into the kitchen to roll us some home-grown bombers and break the seal on the cap of the vintage Thunderbird wine.

About fifteen minutes had passed since we dropped, and the nausea and wonderful queasy, disoriented feeling that immediately precedes the initial rush was coming on strong. With the record in place on the turntable, and everyone positioned around the room, I let the needle drop on side one. From the moment of the opening guitar riff on "Drive My Car," so many things charged inside my head that it would be impossible to convey them honestly or accurately. What I will do, however, is give my evaluation of what I first heard on acid that night as near as I can remember.

Although car songs were nothing new to me growing up in California, somehow, in the hands of the Fab Four, this ultimate status symbol took on a new meaning. The sheer rawness and simplicity of "Drive My Car" was rock and roll at one of its finer moments. At the end of each verse, when they went into the ad-libbed "beep beep, mmm, beep beep, yeah" (although utterly stupid — even compared to some of today's airwave garbage), I thought that God had sent forth another commandment. We played this one about four times in a row before moving on to the second track.

"Norwegian Wood" is simply a delicate English folk waltz. *Beautiful acoustic guitars,* I remember thinking to myself. The interplay between John and Paul's voices on the bridge was as beautiful and smooth as a lake on a December morning. I remember we didn't even bother going back to the beginning of the song. We just kept playing the bridge over and over. The acid had come on so strong that I eased myself off the couch and climbed on top of a paint ladder left behind by some workmen who were doing some minor remodeling.

Joe, Dave, and Mike had positioned themselves in front of the speakers with their heads slightly cocked like the RCA Victor dog. Danny was on the love seat directly behind the ladder. The drugs and music were making it possible for me to completely detach myself from the room. I was now floating somewhere in time. (In reality I was still on top of the ladder.) I couldn't see or hear anything but the music. As far as I was concerned, there was nobody else in the room — or anywhere for that matter. It all happened so quickly. In the space of time it takes one song to fade out and another to start, I lost it somewhere. I remember thinking to myself that I should try to call the other guys. I was so stoned that I didn't even realize that they were only a few feet away from me, and in their own world. Somehow, I either couldn't find a phone wherever I was or I couldn't get through.

Then the third song came blasting out of what was now a pulsating mass of wood and wires. When the opening lines of "You

Won't See Me" hit my brain and simultaneously bounced off the walls, I knew that I had gone just a bit too far. Remember, I thought that I was alone, floating somewhere and trying to phone the others to tell them the wonderful message that this album was conveying not only to me but to the entire world. I only needed to hear the first eight words to know that the Beatles must be some all-powerful mystics who could read people's minds. As Paul started singing about calling up and finding "your line's engaged," I let out a scream and began to feel myself falling for what seemed like the longest time. As I looked down, the ladder was melting away with me on it!

It was like the wood had virtually melted from underneath me, like the clocks in a Dali painting. I could feel myself sinking into the floor, going downward in slow motion, and the next thing I knew, I was sprawled out on the floor. Obviously, I had fallen off the ladder, but in my stoned state the whole thing happened in my mind in slow motion.

I was quickly jolted back to reality when I hit the floor. At the same time, the music stopped, as Dave had turned it off when he saw me fall off the ladder onto the living room floor. Suddenly, everybody came back into view, including Danny, who was standing above me muttering, "You stupid asshole! Are you all right?" I slowly got up, shook the cobwebs loose, and turned to Dave to announce that I had been on a different level of consciousness and that everybody disappeared. I told him that I tried to call him but couldn't get through. They looked at each other, started laughing, and said, "Sit down on the couch you dumb shit. We're at the beginning of the third song on the album." Dumbfounded, I did as I was told, closed my eyes, and started to drift away again. The last thing I remember in that song was Paul singing about losing the time and then losing his mind "If You Won't See Me." After that, I phased out.

I must have had a temporary cranial shutdown, because the next song, George Harrison's "Think For Yourself," I don't remember at all. Next up was "The Word." Although a good song at the time, with its "so fine, it's sunshine" analogy, the world love theme didn't have nearly the same effect as some of the others, and merely served as a segue to the next song. In "Michelle" was a strange dichotomy for me. The song, while being hauntingly beautiful, was also very mundane at the same time. McCartney tried to do what he already had done on "Yesterday" but somehow missed the mark. Nevertheless, it sparked some beautiful images in my already acid-soaked brain. As the next song came on, Ringo's "What Goes On," I remember getting up off the couch and going upstairs to go to the bathroom. This acid was so intense that the record seemed to be playing all over the house. Sound literally seemed to come out of the walls. Although somewhat distant, I could make out the strains of a pleasant country song that was to become a Ringo staple. As quickly as that song came on, it faded out.

As I came out of the bathroom and started to descend the stairs, I realized that I was having trouble walking. I held on to the banister, while doing the elementary "left foot, right foot" routine. At the same time, I heard John Lennon's voice uttering the opening line to "Girl." When John asked in the lyrics of the song if anybody was going to listen to his story, I shouted out loud, "I'm listening John, I just can't fuckin' walk!"

"Come on, Greenspoon! You're missing the song," someone yelled from downstairs.

"What I'm missing are these goddamned steps," I shouted back as I tripped and tumbled into view at the bottom of the stairs. Everyone was so engrossed with the song that they neglected to notice my rather dramatic entrance.

"Don't get up. I'm fine, really. I'm not hurt," I was saying to nobody in particular, which was good, because nobody was listening to me at all.

I walked back into the living room and at that moment thought I heard the rather deafening sound of someone taking a hit off a joint. In actuality, it was in the song. Those Beatles were slick! They knew how to push all the right buttons. Right after John elongates the line "A girl," he takes a deep breath before repeating it. The microphone picked it up so clearly that it sounded like the sucking noise usually associated with pot smoking. Dave had gotten up to put that part on again and again. Reflecting on it today, it is amazing that something so natural as a person breathing into the microphone could have such a profound effect on us. Of course, one must realize that acid intensifies everything, so God only knows what we were hearing individually up to that point. I thought "Girl" was one of the better songs on the album. Was I ever wrong.

Side one and side two just melted into each other. The four of us were now so stoned that nobody could get up and turn the record over. That's why it was great to have a DSM (designated straight man) like Danny Belsky there for just such a task. Every word or musical note seemed to send me off on a different adventure now, so when I heard the country swing opening to "I'm Looking Through You," I had no idea what was in store for me in the next few seconds. I turned and faced David to say something about the Beatles' uncanny understanding of country music, when Paul's voice started singing the title line of "I'm Looking Through You," and then asked, "Where did you go?" At that very instant, Dave became transparent, and I thought I could put my hand through him like Casper the Ghost. It must have been a testament to the power of the drug, because although my hand met with resistance when I struck his chest, I could clearly see the wall through his body. I think he was getting a little pissed off at me for repeatedly hitting him, so I had to channel my energy somewhere else. Back to the sofa to assume the position: head back, eyes closed, mind on "stun."

The song "Wait" was next up, and although it's a little hazy as to how the song affected me — if at all — the urgency of John shouting "Wait" showed his incredible change of expressiveness in taking a simple song and turning it into a vehicle of emotion. With its twelve-string Rickenbacher intro, and a definite nod to the Byrds, "If I Needed Someone" was a prime example of simple elements blended together to form a perfect union. The playing, singing, execution, and production were flawless. I personally loved this tune. From the moment we heard the intro, the boys and I decided to cover it for our set. Actually, I'm quite surprised that the plethora of L.A. folk/rock bands around in the mid-'60s didn't cover this song and make a huge hit out of it. Instead, everyone chose the overused "Hey Joe."

"In My Life" was one of the finest love songs I had ever heard. While Paul's "Yesterday" and "Michelle" gave a positive and cheerful outlook on love from days gone by, Lennon chose the darker side of the coin. The chord structure and harmonies alone evoked the feeling of a man reflecting on his life in such a way that you couldn't help but empathize with him and feel that way too. This was where Lennon and McCartney could show their true colors. They could take the same subject and come up with two totally different ways of presenting it. Ultimately, it would stir different emotions about a single subject. Love in the hands of a realist and a cynic was something to behold when they put pen to paper.

For their last song, they slipped back into that country-tinged swing mode with "Run For Your Life." Everything about the song was pure country/pop. The acoustic guitar opening, the tightness of the harmonies, and most of all the lyrics — with lines about rather seeing his girlfriend dead than to catch her with another man (a line borrowed from an early Elvis Presley song) — was a field day for most country artists' way of thinking. "Live fast, drink hard, die young, and don't fuck with my woman" was their credo.

By the time we were through playing track after track over and over again, we were physically and emotionally drained. The acid was wearing off, and as I saw the sky becoming lighter through the window, I knew that we had been going almost twenty-four hours solid! The road was long and the trip took many unexpected turns, but I for one was so enlightened by it that every time I hear one of those songs from *Rubber Soul,* I will remember with fondness the innocence, wisdom, and new understanding for life that I gained on that vividly acid-soaked December day.

In early 1966, all hell broke loose on Sunset Strip. The western perimeter of the Strip began at Doheney Drive and ran eastward to Olive, where Ciro's and Stratford on Sunset were located. For everyone under the age of twenty, the Strip was *the* place to be. With about a dozen nightclubs and twice as much entertainment, it was a veritable cornucopia of sex, drugs, and rock and roll. What didn't take place nightly on the Strip would spill over every weekend to the now-infamous "love-ins" held at the carousel in Griffith Park. There, thousands of teenagers would converge in various stages of undress to drop acid, listen to music, engage in sex, and generally demonstrate their lack of respect for the establishment.

At night on Sunset, after the clubs closed, you could usually find hundreds of kids converging upon the only twenty-four-hour coffee shop, Ben Frank's, which was located directly across the street from the Trip. Anybody who was anyone, and people who were absolutely no one, would get together there for early morning breakfast and idle chatter. Various assorted characters with names like Beetle Bob, Vito, and Johnny Fuck-Fuck would be seen table-hopping at Ben Frank's, alternately passing out hits of acid and blueberry muffins. No one ever wanted to go home after the clubs closed and, consequently, would hang out until all hours of the morning, in spite of efforts by the police to disperse them. The longhairs who loitered on the Strip outnumbered the police by ten to one.

By the fall of 1966, the police were beside themselves with frustration. They couldn't seem to effectively control the crowds that the Strip attracted nightly. In October 1966 the L.A.P.D. had imposed a full curfew, forbidding anyone from loitering after 2:00 A.M. To add to the confusion, sheriffs would be bused in by the dozens to enforce the curfew. If someone didn't have a legitimate ID, or a purpose for being there, the hippie was handcuffed and herded into the buses with others, like cattle going to slaughter.

Beyond the mile-long Strip, numerous people thought that they could avoid the trouble by hanging out far away from the eye of the storm. They would congregate at Pandora's Box, Bido Lido's, or the

Brave New World, which were a couple of miles east of the main powderkeg of impending disaster.

It was only a matter of time before something had to give. The police were becoming less tolerant, and the crowds were becoming more unruly. Finally, by December, things came to a head with what is now known as the infamous riot on Sunset Strip. On December 11, 1966, when the police attempted to enforce the curfew, the crowds became an aggressive mob of rock-throwing, bottle-breaking, stoned and uncontrollable teenagers. The authorities, not well-versed in the tactics of crowd control, became overzealous and began to swing their nightsticks and bust heads.

Marching down Sunset was a wall of kids interspersed with members of every famous group appearing in the clubs on the Strip at that time. Sonny and Cher made headlines when the Associated Press snapped their pictures along with the other rioters that night, and newspapers across the country ran the story. The Buffalo Springfield best summed up everyone's feelings that evening when group member Stephen Stills wrote the now classic song "For What It's Worth." This marked the beginning of the end of the idyllic life-style of the "flower children." The rest of the '60s would be personified by protest marches, campus riots, and everyone's declaration of personal freedom. The war between the hippies and the establishment was officially under way, and would spill over into the early '70s.

After the riots, I was becoming increasingly more dissatisfied with the club scene, and with my band at the time, the East Side Kids. I made the decision to move on to other projects to develop my own career. I remember vividly, and with a certain fondness, the evening that I quit the band. It was a Friday night and we were playing at a little dive on Cahuenga Boulevard at Yucca, which used to be a coffee house called the Omnibus.

For our efforts that night, we were to receive half of the money that was collected at the door, in lieu of a set fee. This usually worked out well when the place was jam-packed, as we could walk away with $300 to $400 in our pockets.

On this particular night, I arrived early and set up my red Farfisa organ on the tiny stage. It was 8:15 P.M., and we were due to start our first of three sets at 9:00. As I was plugging in my organ, I looked up and noticed that there were only two people in the whole place — and I was one of them. What made it even more depressing was that the drunk who was at the bar turned out to be a friend of the owner, and had been let in for free. I remember saying to myself, "Fuck this!" I proceeded to unplug and then pack up my organ. I then walked quietly toward the front door and my freedom. As I was about halfway out of the club, the other band members arrived in time to catch my exit.

"Hey, what's going on?" Mike Doud asked.

"Look around, what do you see?" I replied.

He looked at the lone drunk at the bar, and answered "Nothing."

"Exactly — I quit!"

With that I turned to walk out the door, only to hear Mike say, "You're making a big mistake." I didn't answer him, but thought to myself, *I don't think so.*

After a relatively short period of time — which I refer to as a "creative sabbatical," where I did nothing but take drugs, frequent clubs, and find chicks — I began to make some phone calls to try to find another vehicle suitable for my talents. Once again I called my old childhood friend, Michael Lloyd, to see what he was up to. He informed me that he was working with an interesting group by the name of the West Coast Pop Art Experimental Band. They were basically playing the exclusive "in crowd" spots, such as the "members only" discotheque in Beverly Hills called the Daisy. They had just recorded an album for Warner Brothers records and had a number of other club dates and a few concerts lined up.

After learning of my availability, Michael asked me to join him in this already happening band. I jumped at the prospect of branching out into a different area of music. The songs that the band had recorded were very commercial-sounding pop songs, interspersed with radical psychedelic overtones.

One great thing about the band was the fact that they carried their own impressive light show. This was at a time when light shows were not expected fare. The light show, which was run by a brilliant man by the name of Buddy Walters, consisted of rear projection screen, mirror ball, colored pinwheel, strobe lights, and fog machines. Buddy also had what was later to become a staple of San Francisco rock: a clear-glass dish of colored water and cooking oil that was positioned on an overhead projector. When another glass dish was placed on top of the projector and moved around, the resulting projected image resembled that of a swirling, colored amoeba.

The group was led by Bob Markley, an eccentric gentleman who lived in the fashionable Trousdale Estates area of Beverly Hills. This was strictly a hobby to Bob, as his main source of income was a healthy trust fund set up by his oil-rich parents, somewhere in the Midwest. When I agreed to come on board, Michael set up a meeting between myself and Markley at his house. When I arrived there, three things became immediately apparent to me: (1) he preferred dating very young women (he was in his thirties at the time); (2) he was completely straight — he didn't drink or take drugs; (3) he was a complete asshole. If he didn't have the money to fund this project, he would have been completely useless.

Even though Michael was still straight as an arrow, and would never change, that was all right. He tolerated what I did and didn't try to impose his will on me. On the other hand, I wasn't ready for a complete stranger like Markley to start preaching to me about my lifestyle. The other band members consisted of two brothers — Sean and Dan Harris, who played bass and guitar, respectively — and drummer John Ware.

After we rehearsed and played a few dates together, it became readily apparent that as a musician Markley was less than useless. While he proclaimed to be a percussionist, playing tambourine and congas on stage, he had no sense of time or rhythm whatsoever.

One of the most significant aspects of the West Coast Pop Art Experimental Band was the fact that the personnel changed during the year that I was with them. An acquaintance of mine and Michael's, Stacey London, suggested a guitar player she knew named Ron Morgan. Ron had been part of the Electric Prunes, who had just recorded their only major hit song, "I Had Too Much To Dream Last Night," which made it to Number 11 on the national pop charts in early 1967. He left the Electric Prunes shortly after the record was released and filled in the lead guitar spot with us that was vacated by Dan Harris. Shortly after that, Sean left, and Michael moved over to playing bass. This posed a slight problem, in that we needed another guitar player. Ron had a friend from Colorado who was bumming around L.A. and looking for work. His name was Rob Yeazel, and he turned out to be not only a good guitar player but a good singer and songwriter as well.

Our first major gig with the new line-up was at the Teenage Fair in Portland, Oregon. We got a cheap motel for the band near the coliseum, and of course Markley booked himself a posh suite in a fancy hotel.

Ron, Rob, and I had an immediate common bond in that we all loved to smoke pot, drop acid, and generally get as fucked up as humanly possible. Michael Lloyd and Markley remained straight, while John vacillated somewhere in between.

The schedule for the Teenage Fair was such that it required a vast quantity of "uppers" for us to accomplish what we were expected to do. Over an eight-hour period, we would play ten-minute sets, with ten minute breaks. That came to three sets an hour, or twenty-four sets a day for four of the five days of the fair. On our off day, Ron and I would go to the local record store and catch up on all of the latest releases by the new bands.

One band in particular that influenced me greatly at the time was Moby Grape from San Francisco. They had a different line-up in that they used three guitars playing harmony with each other, as well as bass and drums. They also used incredibly intricate three- and four-part harmonies. They were light years ahead of their peers, since this formula was virtually unheard of by their peers. The unique thing about Moby Grape's recording career was that some dimwitted A&R man at their label, Columbia Records, decided to release every song on their debut album as a single, and to release them all simultaneously. This decision completely backfired, resulting in virtually no hit single off the album. (Years later, the *Moby Grape* album would become a cult classic and a collector's item.)

When we returned to L.A., Markley lined up a similar gig at the L.A. Teenage Fair, held at the Hollywood palladium. John Ware had left the band at this point, and we had hired a new drummer, Francesco Lupica, whom I had known since my Sea Witch days. The hectic schedule there afforded me the opportunity to branch out and experiment with new drugs. A friend of Buddy's came up to me before the show, carrying a large Mason jar filled with a clear liquid. He asked me if I'd ever tried amyl nitrate. I informed him that I hadn't, at which point he unscrewed the lid, dipped a piece of cotton inside, and then shoved it under my nose. For anyone who hasn't experienced an amyl nitrate rush, it's quite unique. Upon inhaling its fumes, an immediate head rush makes your cranium feel like it's just been overinflated by a tire pump. This all lasts about thirty seconds. You can feel the blood rushing through your veins like a runaway freight train. At the same time, your heart is beating so fast that you think it's going to explode. To top it off, you temporarily lose touch with reality and the outside world.

Meanwhile, back on stage, I'd be in the middle of a song, and with the combined blinding effect from the strobe light and the fog machine, I could barely see what I was doing to begin with. In the middle of all this, suddenly out of nowhere, Buddy's friend would toss amyl nitrate-soaked wads of cotton onto my keyboard. Playing with one hand, I would inconspicuously grab the wad of cotton with my other hand, hold it up to my nose, and snort the "popper" fumes. For a short while I would be transported to another planet, and while the other band members thought we were playing one song, I'd be off on my own composition. When the rush wore off, I would look back at Ron and Rob to inform them that I had indeed just returned from the cosmos.

One of the most memorable shows we did as the West Coast Pop Art Experimental Band was a concert at the Santa Monica Civic Auditorium, on the same bill with my current idols, Moby Grape. Also on the bill were two of the current crop of psychedelic bands, the Strawberry Alarm Clock ("Incense and Peppermints") and the Yellow Balloon (which was led by Don Grady of the TV show "My Three Sons," who had one hit song called "Yellow Balloon"). I also remember that Markley was at his nadir of horrendous. He was wearing a pair of white leather hot pants, knee-high white leather boots, and some other equally fashion-conscious creation as a top. This only drew more attention to him. Coupled with the fact that he was so horribly out of time with us, and insisted on playing a tambourine solo, this turned out to be one of the most embarrassing nights of my early career. I knew then that my days with this band were numbered.

On various occasions, Rob and Ron had also voiced their mutual disgust with Markley's asshole antics and the general direction of the band. Rob began formulating a new plan. He asked me if I was interested in leaving L.A. and starting a band with him and Ron in Denver. He said that until we could get things off the ground, we could stay with his parents, and avoid any immediate outlay of cash. The idea was sounding better to me all the time.

One morning, while sitting on top of a rock somewhere in Malibu Canyon, coming down off of a beautiful acid trip, I made the decision that my future was in Denver. We began making plans for the great exodus — immediately.

We formulated all of our plans to move to Colorado, and a couple of nights before we left L.A. for Denver I informed my mother I was going to go. As usual, she took the news well. Once that was taken care of, Ron and I decided that we were going to celebrate, so we scored a couple of tabs of acid. Before we took them, we agreed that we should drive to somewhere really spiritual and take it — Lake Hollywood or someplace like that — to go watch the sun come up or go down. So, we hopped into my car. We were driving along, and wouldn't you know: we were stopped by the cops.

Totally freaked out, I kept saying, "Ron! Ron! I know they are going to bust me. I just know it!"

Trying to be level-headed, and sensing that I was worried about the tabs of acid that we had yet to take, he said, "Now just take the stuff and hide it."

"It's not that, man. I've got warrants out for my arrest for parking tickets."

"Oh, my God. They're going to arrest you."

I said, "Yeah."

Ron bolted. He just took off and ran down the street. Well, I didn't want them to find the two tabs of acid, so I just took them both. I didn't think that I would have any real problem. I thought, "They will just question me and stuff, and later on I'll just be good and fucked up." I didn't think, "Wait a minute, they're gonna arrest me!"

They came over to my car and looked at the registration, and went back to their car to make the call. I was watching the police officer, and he didn't seem to have an amused look on his face. Suddenly, a sinking feeling came over me and I thought to myself, *OK, they're gonna nail me.*

He came back to my car and said, "Will you please step out of the car? We're going to have to take you in."

I said, "What for?"

"Well, you have a number of outstanding warrants for traffic tickets. Just lock your car up and leave it here. It will be all right."

As they were taking me in, we talked about this and that, and the music scene, and the various groups. All of the time they were being cordial and pleasant — really nice as far as the L.A.P.D. was in those days. Then the two hits of acid I had just taken started to come on. I was sitting there trying to act cool, while thinking, *Oh, my God! This is really going to be a drag!*

They took me down to the old Hollywood station on Wilcox. It was about 2:00 A.M. and nobody was there, besides the booking sergeant, and I could tell it was the end of his shift. He was like some old redneck guy from Alabama. The last thing that he wanted to see was some kid with hair down to his waist, wearing bells and beads, with a big peace sign on his shirt, saying, "Hi guy."

The next thing that I knew I was in the holding tank, which was unoccupied. Then they finally called my name.

"Greenspoon?"

"Yes?"

"You ever been arrested before?"

"No, no, no. This is all new to me."

There I was, just trying to compose myself, and the acid was really kicking in by this point.

So we went through the whole routine with the thumbprints and all of the paperwork.

"Do you understand what you are here for?" they asked me. "We're gonna hold you here. You can call your mother or whoever you want. Do you have a lawyer?"

I said, "Yeah, but I don't know his number. I'll call my mom."

By then I was really flying on the acid, so they put me in the last cell at the end. I proceeded to jump up on one of the bunks, and I sat there swinging my legs and checking things out. *It's not so bad,* I thought, *It's a little grungy in here. There's a little toilet over there, but absolutely no privacy. This* is *a jail, not a country club.* Sitting there counting the squares of tile on the floor and trying to entertain myself, all of a sudden I heard this screaming. I looked up, and there was this girl in one of the cells. *What is going on here?* I thought to myself. And I heard a cop shouting, "Shut up. Get over there."

"You can't make me!" the girl shouted back.

And the guard said, "Look — shut up!"

I was sitting there taking this all in, and thinking, *God, they're really pushing this girl around.* All of a sudden the guard grabs at the girl and rips her wig off! I'm stoned out of my mind, and thinking, *Wow! They just ripped this girl's hair off! This is too bizarre!*

Obviously, the cops knew this person, because the next thing she said was, "Do I have to again?"

"Yeah," they said roughly. So the girl takes off her shoes and her dress. I'm sitting there going, *Wait a second, what is going on here? First they're harassing this girl, now they're having her strip. What gives?* I didn't realize that it was a drag queen! I couldn't figure out what the hell was happening.

Then the guard said to the drag queen, "OK, get into the last cell with him." I'm looking around thinking, *Who? Me?* By this time the guy was crying, and mascara was running down his face. He gathered up his wig and dress and he shuffled into my cell, and they slammed the door shut. The cops turned and walked away, laughing.

After the guy who was now in my cell composed himself, he looked at me and said, "What are you in here for?"

Always the comedian, I said, "I killed a drag queen."

He started screaming, "Get me out of here!" I don't even know why I said that. Just for effect, I guess.

Eventually my mom came to my rescue and bailed me out. After that whole episode with the L.A.P.D. and the drag queen, I knew that leaving Los Angeles was a great idea. Colorado — here I come!

I had every intention of packing as many possessions as was humanly possible into my MG Midget and making my escape from L.A. by six in the evening. The plan was simple. Everything I needed for the journey and to set up temporary residence in Colorado would be crammed into the tiny sports car, saving only passenger space for Rob. We made arrangements to stay with his parents in Arvada temporarily, so most of his belongings were already there. But, as on so many other occasions, drugs innocently intervened and fucked up our well-made plans. God only knows why I chose our travel day to try out a new and powerful psychedelic called STP. It was basically the same as regular acid, except for one minor difference — it lasted over forty-eight hours. A two-day acid trip in the confines of one's familiar surroundings would be hard enough to take, but for the first journey away from my parents and home, and my sudden declaration of independence, this turned out to be a little extreme.

Somebody, I don't recall who, had given me the drug the night before at a going-away party. Being young and full of curiosity didn't seem to pose any serious problems for me, or anyone else in the '60s for that matter. This was my first chance to stretch my wings, and like a human sponge, I wanted to soak up every bit of knowledge and experience — good or bad — that I could. The person who gave me the STP at the party said that it would just make the long drive more enjoyable. What he neglected to tell me (which I found out later) was that no one he knew had ever tried the drug, so they weren't quite sure how potent it was or how long it really did last. Curious, yet just a little hesitant, I decided to split my dose with Rob.

I thought my plan was foolproof: have everything packed and ready to load into the car, then with tears and goodbyes exchanged between myself and my mother, drive the short distance to Trousdale Estates and Bob Markley's house, where Rob was staying. There we would pack the last few remaining possessions, take the STP, and head out on Interstate 10 toward the unknown. Nice plan — bad execution.

I guess leaving home was harder than I thought it would be, because beneath my hard exterior, my insides turned to mush. As I drove away and saw my mother standing on the corner crying, tears started to well up in my eyes too. I got about two blocks from the house and pulled over to Robert Burns Liquors on the corner of Burton Way and Doheney (where Beverly Hills Four Seasons Hotel stands today), and bought a bottle of juice to wash down my portion of the STP. I didn't want to wait until we left town. Had I known the pain my mother was going through to let me go — realizing that I was finally growing up — I would have turned the car around and abandoned this hare-brained scheme.

As I drove north on Doheney toward Sunset Boulevard, I

quickly became wrapped up in mixed emotions about my sudden freedom. I was also experiencing something unexpected and surprising. It seemed that the drug was coming on a lot faster than regular acid. By the time I turned onto Sunset, heading to Markley's Beverly Hills estate to retrieve Rob, I felt like I had been tripping for hours, when in reality it had been only about ten minutes.

Through my eyes, the trees were bending and swaying with the strong late summer breeze, which wouldn't have been bad, except that it was a calm day. As I was watching the parade of movement all around me, something flashed in front of the car. I slammed on the brakes, skidding to the curb, and sat motionless for a few seconds, trying to regain my displaced composure. Then reality crept back in. *Oh, my God!* I thought to myself. *I've run over a dog or a cat!* I slowly opened the door and got out to face the grisly outcome of my drug-induced carelessness. As I looked at the ground in front of the car, I let out a sigh of relief, followed by uncontrollable laughter. It seems that my only crime so far that day was that I had killed a leaf.

I got back into the car and proceeded to drive cautiously to Markley's house. I was quite anxious to get on the road, and equally as enthused to give Rob his hit, so he too could share in the destruction of innocent foliage. As I turned the corner and started up the driveway to the house, I saw what could only be described as a pitifully funny sight. There, at the top of the driveway, stood Rob and Ron, looking dazed and confused. Rob had the garden hose in his hand and was watering Markley's smoldering and expensive living room couch, which also doubled as Rob's bed. It was immediately apparent to me that Rob had fallen asleep on the couch while smoking a cigarette or a joint (more likely the latter) and had accidentally set it on fire. I literally fell out of the car onto the ground, I was laughing so hard! Of course the STP that I had taken was in full swing now.

After I regained my composure, I tried to speak through the tears of laughter. "What the fuck did you do? No, don't tell me, I don't even want to know." Not only was there a huge hole burned in the couch, but it now contained numerous gallons of Trousdale Estates water. "Let it go, it's dead," I said to Rob. "Here take this." I held out my hand and offered him the hit of STP. "I couldn't wait," I exclaimed. "I took mine two days ago — or was it only a half hour ago? It doesn't matter — it's great!"

Rob, without even breaking character, continued to extinguish the smoldering couch. With the hose in one hand, and a beer in the other, he threw down the hit I gave him and took a long swig of the beer. Then he dropped the hose and ran inside the house. I turned to Ron and said that we should get out of there before Markley came home and discovered the carnage.

"You guys get going, I'll drive out in a few days," Ron said.

"What about the couch?" I asked.

"Don't worry, I'll cover for you," he replied.

*What a pal!* I thought to myself, but how would he explain to Markley what happened? It didn't matter. If Ron said he'd take care of it, then he would.

Just then, Rob came running back out of the house with two suitcases, a shoulder bag, and numerous articles of clothing in tow. "Find a space and tie them down with a bungie cord," I instructed him. Like an obedient servant, he silently nodded and obliged. With most of our worldly possessions on board, we exchanged brief farewells with Ron, and hopped into the car. The real adventure was about to begin.

I had taken the I-10 freeway entrance off Sunset numerous times in the past, driving to Palm Springs, but this time we just zoomed right past it. Before long the high-rise buildings of downtown L.A. came into view.

"I think we missed our turn," I nonchalantly said to Rob.

"What turn?" was his rather dim reply. "I thought we could take this road all the way there."

"All the way there?" I asked.

"To Denver," he said.

I pulled the car over to the curb and just stared at him in a nonbelieving fashion, then we both started to laugh hysterically. We were both way too stoned to try to find Colorado, since we couldn't even get on the freeway to get out of L.A. If this was any indication of things to come, we were in deep trouble!

I stopped laughing long enough to look up and see a sign that said, "Interstate 10 East — straight ahead." *Salvation,* I thought. At this point I made the single most fatal error of the trip: I made Rob the navigator. Given the options, though, I really didn't have much of a choice. We headed east toward San Bernardino to pick up I-15 to Barstow and then Las Vegas. At one point we pulled over and carefully surveyed the map to make sure we didn't screw up.

There we were, two modern-day Lewis and Clarks, on an extraordinary journey — so stoned we couldn't even read a roadmap. As we drove toward that desert oasis known as Las Vegas, I felt for the first time on our trip a complete sense of independence. It was time to test my new wings. We found a truck stop about halfway to Vegas and stopped for a bite to eat. I could tell as we walked into the Choke and Puke (as some years later I would refer to truck stop restaurants) that the patrons of this first-class establishment weren't ready for two longhaired, hippie, weirdo, stoned-to-the-gills freaks like Rob and myself. We made our way to an empty booth and sat down. Then we began to wait and wait . . . and wait. I could detect some of the subtle comments from the people seated around us, and was getting a little pissed off at the lack of service. A glass of water and a menu would have been a nice start. Then came the inexpiable. Some redneck ya-hoo walked up to the table and matter of factly said, "I didn't know they let the animals out of the zoo."

Rob, surprisingly quick-witted, considering his present state of mind, shot back a great retort of his own: "I didn't know so much shit could be piled into one pair of boots."

I thought the guy was going to come unglued on the spot. Just then, two of his friends stepped up to restrain him.

I turned to Rob and said we weren't going to get any service anyway and we should make a hasty exit. Still hungry, but glad to be in one piece, we walked rather briskly to the car and drove on. I knew that I was too stoned to eat anyway, and wasn't really ready for that kind of challenge. Las Vegas would offer a more suitable cover for our current states of mind.

I had seen the lights of Vegas before, rising up from the desert floor like the mythical Phoenix out of its own ashes, but in my altered consciousness it became an entirely different scene. The night heat coming off the desert, along with the nonstop shimmering neon parade, produced a dreamlike scene. Rob and I pulled over at the top of the hill that overlooks Vegas and sat for what seemed like the longest time, just staring at this incredibly beautiful sight. After being completely mesmerized, I slipped the car back into first gear, and we drove off toward the neon jungle.

As we first drove onto the strip, things started to jump out of the lights almost immediately. We only got two blocks before we pulled over to explore. Besides the magnitude of the strip's southern-end hotels like the Dunes, the Tropicana, and the Rivera, we were completely blown away by this fantastic western-looking village across the street from the Desert Inn. It comprised the numerous curio shops at the Frontier, which were outrageous.

I didn't recall the lights being so intense. Of course, when I came through before, I wasn't stoned on STP. We had to find fuel fast, but I kept getting sidetracked by the marvelous liquid neon jungle. Finally, we broke through the maze and onto the other side of town. There I spotted a 7-11 that sold gas, so we could fuel up and buy some munchies at the same time.

Our planned route would take us through St. George, Utah. I

didn't know at the time that this town and the surrounding area was a cancerous breeding ground, due to the atomic bomb detonations in the desert nearby. This was where John Wayne and Susan Hayward made the motion picture *The Conqueror*. It was also the place where a good percentage of the cast and crew of that movie were exposed to cancerous agents due to the fallout, and suspiciously died of cancer. As we passed through the town in the predawn hours, it looked so peaceful and quiet, and not at all like a place that later in life would breed so much pain and suffering.

The STP was wearing off now but still possessed enough of a kick that, when coupled with the beautiful landscape of Utah, created an almost dreamlike scene. Somehow we timed it so that we arrived in Provo just as everything was opening up that morning. Hunger was rapidly overtaking us, so the first sign of life we encountered was the local McDonalds.

We ordered some cheeseburgers and fries, and then returned to the car to eat our gourmet breakfast in silence as we watched the town wake up and its fine citizens go about their everyday routines. Of course, after I scarfed mine down, I was ready to go.

We got on Route 70 heading east toward Green River. The sheer beauty of the mountains and surrounding area is now permanently etched in my brain. We must have pulled over two dozen times between Green River and Grand Junction. Good time we weren't making, but I didn't care. It seemed that just when I thought the drug had worn off, something would trigger it, and I'd be off and tripping again.

Once we reached Loveland Pass, there was already lots of snow on the ground — not enough to warrant chains on the tires, but still a significant amount. I was quickly becoming addicted to the clean air and fantastic natural surroundings. At one point, I turned to Rob and said that I wanted to move to this little town that we were passing through. It happened to be Georgetown. The Rockies offered so much beauty and inspiration: from the starkness of Grand Junction, to the awesome splendor of Glenwood Canyon (which a month later inspired a song), to the soaring peaks of Loveland Pass, to the quaintness of Georgetown, and finally the suburban hum of Denver itself. Although our trip was winding down, as we got on I-25 and headed north to Rob's parents' house in Arvada, I could sense an almost certain feeling of closeness with my new surroundings. It didn't matter at the time, and I don't know if it's a valid point even today, but since Arvada was where my father was born, it seemed only fitting that my first solo trip away from the complacency and safety of my parents, would end in that Colorado town.

As I drove up to Rob's parents' house, some three days after we left Los Angeles, and watched the sun set behind the Rockies, I could feel a sense of adventure and electricity in the air.

When we pulled into the driveway, Rob's mom and dad came out to greet us. Their excitement gave way to surprise and then a totally disbelieving look. What I wanted most was a hot shower, a good meal, and two days of uninterrupted sleep. What I got was immediate scrutiny from a Baptist minister and his wife. When I got in the house and went to the bathroom, I caught a quick glimpse of myself and didn't blame them at all. I looked like shit, and Rob looked even worse. It didn't matter what they thought of me at the time, because I would turn on the charm at the dinner table later. All they cared about was that their son was home and safe. Well, he was home anyway. Around me, nobody was safe for very long.

I quickly unloaded the car and set up temporary housekeeping in the Yeazels' basement. Rob, of course, got his old room, which was exactly as he had left it. The next day we would find new and wonderful ways of getting stoned and would start to write songs. We would also start making calls to find the best players in town to complement Rob, Ron, and myself. I wanted to start a group that would make Denver sit up and take notice.

I got far more than I bargained for: In a few weeks the ego-fueled "Superband" would be born, and with it some of the most carefree and crazy adventures of my life.

# 5 / Out In The Country

Rob suggested a bass player that he had worked with named Roger Bryant, who not only was a great player but a great singer as well. Never being one to procrastinate, the next day I told Rob to call Roger up and invite him over for a little impromptu jam session in Rob's basement. Roger was great and he fit right in, so we started writing some songs immediately. Among our early endeavors were such memorable titles as "Jill and the Muskrat," "I Ain't Got No Body," "Glenwood Canyons of Your Mind," and "Nottingham Daily" — our ode to Sherwood Forest. This was the first time I had been out of California, what did I know about Sherwood Forest?

The nuclei of the songs were written around riffs that I came up with on my Honer electric piano that I schlepped out from L.A. It turned out to be a real group effort. Roger and Rob would add their parts, leaving enough room for Ron's input and solos. We were trying to write and stockpile as many tunes as possible before the end of the week, when Ron would arrive from L.A.

Usually after a long rehearsal, we would hook up with some of Rob's college-age buddies who could order for us at bars, since we would usually get "carded." One of our favorite hangouts was the local bowling alley lounge. It was just dark enough in there so that no one could see how young we really were, so we usually got away with it.

Generally, we'd start off the evening by smoking a joint to get high and adding a Black Beauty (speed) for endurance. However, since we weren't a working band yet, and didn't have any money, this particular form of recreation was getting expensive.

On one particular night, one of our friends came in "amped to the max." That was Rob's term for someone who was so high that his eyes were bulging out of his head, sweat oozing from his pores, teeth ground down to stumps. To be in the same room with this person would be comparable to shock treatment. In other words, our main concern was "What is he on?" . . . "Where do we get it?" . . . "How much does it cost?"

We cornered this Tasmanian Devil long enough to find out that he was high on nasal inhalers. Upon close interrogation, we discovered a cheap new over-the-counter high. It was a very simple procedure: (1) enter the local drug store and steal as many inhalers (preferably Vick's) as you could stuff into your pocket; (2) unscrew the bottom; (3) remove the cotton inside; (4) cut into equal pieces; (5) swallow the drug-soaked cotton, and chase with your favorite alcoholic beverage (beer or Southern Comfort were two of my favorites); (6) clear the runway and prepare for "blast-off."

The high that this little procedure produced usually lasted about twenty-four hours. However, the down side of it was the fact that you kept belching up the camphor that was in the cotton. That generally nailed the coffin shut on meeting girls.

Ron arrived by the end of the week, and the next order of business was to find a drummer. Ron already had somebody in mind, so, as we did with Roger, we told him to contact his friend. The next day, one Myron Pollock showed up at Rob's parents' house. Although we took Ron's word for Myron's drumming expertise, we first wanted to take a look at him, to see if he fit in visually with our band. Ron, Rob, Roger, and I were the epitome of '60s psychedelic fashion. We wore beads, fringed jackets, sandals, and shoulder-length hair. When we opened the door and saw him standing there, my first thought was, "No fucking way!" There, standing before us, was a tall, skinny, frizzy-haired, bespectacled, large-nosed Jewish kid who looked like he was on his way from chemistry class to temple. This was definitely not the type of person we could offer a piece of inhaler cotton and a joint!

Nevertheless, we all agreed to give him a chance. Ron knew a club owner who ran one of Denver's hottest nightspots, the Exodus. The owner offered us his club to rehearse in during the day, the ultimate goal being, once we got a tight enough set put together, that he would start us playing on an off night (usually Tuesdays). At our first rehearsal we all headed for the club, still a little apprehensive about Myron. When we got there, his drums were already set up. We all walked in, took one look at the drums, and said to each other, "Looks impressive!"

We set up our equipment, then gathered around the bandstand with just the guitars to work on a tune. Right away, Myron started interjecting suggestions about where his parts would fit. That impressed us greatly. After running through the tune a couple of times, we were ready for full instrumentation. The moment of truth was near. From the first downbeat of Myron's rock-solid drumming, we knew that he was our man — even though he never did drugs. That was also the day we modestly chose our name: Superband!.

Our rehearsals progressed from there, and we were off and running. All the time we were rehearsing, the club owner would drop in. He was so impressed with us that he started us out in front of an audience that Friday night. And even though we were playing original tunes that no one had ever heard before, the response was so favorable that the owner immediately wanted to sign us to a management contract.

We got together after closing time, did a few inhalers, slammed down a few brews, and signed on the dotted line. The owner then informed us that he was going to buy us band transportation, in the form of an old Ford panel truck, and a PA system. He also agreed to pay us a weekly salary and a percentage of the "door." We were sitting on top of the world!

We kept writing more tunes, and rehearsing, and due to our success, the attendance at the club had doubled within a month. Our next coup was opening for Denver's top band at the time, Lothar and the Hand People. Our main objective was to blow them off the stage. That would have been considered kind.

That night we got together before the gig for a pep talk and agreed: "Tonight there would be no nasal inhalers." For something of this magnitude, we decided that we needed to graduate to a more up-scale drug: hash. It wasn't that we hadn't smoked hash before, but after being broke for so long, we needed to feel that this was a special occasion and it was going to be our night.

We took to the stage like five men possessed, and in a matter of minutes, we whipped the crowd into a seething den of sweating sexual excitement. We had our work cut out for us, because a lot of people in the crowd had come to see Lothar, and had little — or no — idea who we were. Slowly but surely, we broke through the barrier of skepticism and won them over. When we were done, we made sure that everyone knew who Superband was.

When Lothar took the stage, they knew that they had their work cut out for *them*. They were the headliners, but we had proven that we were more than just some bar band. We wanted the top spot in Denver, and we wanted it *now*.

The more popular we got, the more money we made. Since our manager was taking out money for the van and the PA, what was left over was ours to split. Living at Rob's house afforded me the opportunity to build up a little nest egg of money, since my only responsibility was my $125-a-month car payments. My mother had informed me when I had left home that this was my sole responsibility. Since we weren't making that much money when the band first began, I had to call Mom to help with the car payments. As always, she came to my rescue.

Although Rob's parents were cool about me living in their basement, I was careful not to abuse the privilege. I couldn't exactly bring girls back to the house at all hours of the night. My solution was to find a house.

As our fame started to grow, we attracted legions of worshiping girls who wanted to sleep with the band. I was more than happy to oblige on any given night. I told the rest of the band, "You'd better make your move fast, or I'll fuck her!"

After about two months, I figured that it was finally time to move out of Rob's parents' house. A friend of ours told us that he knew about a cabin for rent, about thirty-five miles southwest of Denver in Deer Creek Canyon. Everything sounded perfect: the rent was only $50 a month, and it was so remote that we could carry on, make noise, rehearse, and do anything that we wanted.

We got the key, and everyone except Myron (who was married and had a child) went to check it out. As we turned off of Deer Creek Canyon onto Star Route Road, I could tell by the remoteness of the location that this was perfect for our hedonistic exercises.

The house wasn't much. It was just a little cabin with a well in front of it, a small living room, kitchen, bathroom, and one tiny storeroom that could be used as a back bedroom. We loved it. We went down to the real estate office, signed the papers, and headed for Pier One Imports to furnish our band house.

Since there would be four of us living there, we'd have to divide the living room up into three little living quarters, and give someone the back room. That was the most desirable room, because it had a door that locked, which meant you didn't have to watch and/or listen to everyone else's sexual antics.

We ended up buying bamboo mats, which we strung up on clothesline to divide the room. Then it was up to each individual to furnish and decorate their own cubicle as he saw fit. It's amazing what a couple of bricks, a two-by-four, a beanbag chair, and a sleeping bag can do to make a place look like home. Everyone had their own supply of incense, joints and hash, and made sure that the fridge was always stocked with beer (and little else). Come to think of it, I can't remember ever having food in that place, except for an occasional piece of leftover pizza or some french fries that after a couple of months looked like something from another planet.

We all decided to set aside a certain day, usually on the weekend if we weren't working, to "raise the group consciousness." This would entail somebody scoring some acid, and basically having all of us dropping together. The theory was that if something threatening happened to any one of us — like wandering off and being attacked by a bull moose — the others could come to his aid.

This was the ideal lifestyle: playing at the club four nights a week, and dropping acid the other three. The only thing missing at the cabin was an animal, although at times we acted more like animals than the wildlife which inhabited the woods around us. One day, one of our friends brought over a German Shepherd puppy. They were moving into an apartment where animals weren't allowed, so we agreed to give her a home. She was very hyper, so I immediately named her Crystal (as in crystal methedrine — which is a form of speed). It didn't take Crystal long to start to develop human traits, and soon she was just one of the guys.

One night I decided to initiate her into our little fraternity, and I dropped a tab of acid into her drinking water. The other guys didn't know that I had done this. After about half an hour, she started to chase her tail. This became an obsession. I thought that she was going to run up her own asshole, she was chasing that thing so fast! She finally collapsed in the driveway from sheer exhaustion.

I wondered at the time what dogs saw when they dropped acid. Not that they regularly did it to have a good time. This was just the kind of thing that you'd think of when you were on acid. Crystal got totally into the scene. At one point we had her dressed in a bandana and love beads.

Later on that afternoon, Rob returned from the city, took one look at Crystal, and couldn't figure out what was wrong with her.

"She's on acid," I explained.

"Right," Rob said in disbelief, "give me my hit."

Half an hour later, when he was tripping as well, he finally believed me. He was so fried himself that he sat down in the driveway with Crystal and attempted to carry on a conversation: "So what do you see? Fire hydrants? What were your parents like? Are you having a good time?" I couldn't believe some of the shit he was saying to her. I could tell that she was thoroughly disgusted with him. Every now and then she would pick her head up and sigh.

Later that evening, Roger came back to the cabin and saw Rob sitting in the driveway talking to the dog. Under Roger's arm was a bag.

"What's with those two?" he asked.

"You don't even want to know," I replied. My main concern was what insidious torture device this asshole had purchased now. He was always plaguing us with practical joke paraphernalia. The last time he walked down the driveway, it was with a bag full of suction cup darts. "What's in the bag?" I cautiously asked him. With that he pulled out the latest pair of mind-altering audio devices: the Jimi Hendrix Experience's first album, *Are You Experienced?*, and the debut album from the group Vanilla Fudge. Everyone had arrived back at the cabin by then, and we were well on the way to neutralizing what was left of our precious brain cells.

Roger played DJ and previewed the Hendrix album first. We positioned ourselves around the massive eighteen-inch stereo speakers, salivating with anticipation. As the needle dropped onto the first cut and we heard the opening strains of "Foxy Lady" burst forth, we all snapped at the same time. We must have played the intro over and over again for about fifteen minutes before we even got into the first verse. I couldn't believe how new and fresh sounding this music was. It must have taken us hours to listen to the whole album, because we kept playing parts of it. It inspired us so much that we immediately decided to write a song with the same hard-edged feel that the Hendrix album had to it.

Hours passed, and the initial dose of drugs started to wear off. We still had the Vanilla Fudge album to listen to. What were we going to do? There was only one solution: drop more acid! And so we did. The Vanilla Fudge album totally baffled us. The main cut on the album was a version of the Supremes' song "You Keep Me Hangin' On," which had been slowed down extremely. We kept arguing about the accuracy of our turntable. Every time we tried to speed up the turntable to what we thought was the proper speed, the vocals sounded like the Chipmunks. When someone would turn it back down to the proper setting, and the music sounded like molasses. After listening to the whole album, we came to the brilliant conclusion that every song sounded slow. We thought it was a different concept, in that the album contained no originals — they had recorded nothing but cover versions of other people's songs. I remember thinking to myself, "Why would anyone want to do an album of songs by outside writers, and rearrange them so that they sounded new and fresh?" (Little did I know at the time, but that would later become Three Dog Night's claim to fame.)

On the following weekend, the guys decided when we dropped that we'd go on a nature hike. We had been inside the cabin tripping for so long, we were getting real cabin fever. Although I didn't mind a little fresh air, and some beautiful scenery, talking to squirrels and eating acorns wasn't my idea of spending a peaceful Sunday afternoon. My thoughts were focused skyward. Being an avid reader of science fiction novels, and an outer space junkie, I chose to pursue my alternate love — flying saucer hunting.

Sometime midday on the appointed Sunday afternoon of our nature excursion, we did what was becoming like a ritual: We'd gather in the living room and drop a tab of acid, down a couple of beers, and smoke a joint. This particular day, I was totally consumed with being whisked away in a flying saucer by some intelligent form of life, other than the assholes I was dropping with. Therefore, I just pocketed my dose of acid and informed them that I was going off on my own adventure. I wanted to have a clear head in case I did get captured, so that I could communicate with them on their own superior level and not sound like a blithering idiot. I got in my car and drove to the top of Star Route Road. Almost at the top of the mountain, the road ended near a little pasture. I stopped the car, got out, and sat down in the clearing. Then I patiently waited, thinking, "OK, I'm here, come take me away." Before I knew it, it was nighttime, and the sky was aglow with billions of stars. Somewhere in that shimmering void there must have been some form of intelligent form of life doing the exact same thing.

Time seemed to stand still. Then, all of a sudden, something caught my eye. I could distinctly detect movement in the sky. At first I thought it was a shooting star or a meteor. The thing that seemed strange to me was the fact that it was traveling along on a perfectly horizontal line, then it came to a sudden stop. I was totally mesmerized at this point. As I watched in amazement, it came hurtling down to the earth below and seemed to land in the pasture not far from where I sat. Part of me wanted to run in the opposite direction, and part of me wanted to embrace the unknown with open arms.

Just then, I heard what sounded like a hydraulic door being opened, followed by what seemed to be the noise of a metal hatch slamming shut. The sound reverberated throughout the canyon and sent a chill through my entire body. I stared in the direction of the sound, simultaneously praying that something would — and wouldn't — happen.

Venturing toward what I imagined to be a landing site, I stopped short of a clump of bushes. As I looked up I distinctly saw a sight that would stay with me for the rest of my life. There before me, in the darkness, were three intensely burning red eyes. I couldn't tell if there was a body attached to this vision — and frankly, I didn't give a shit! Just then, the thing let out the most blood-curdling, inhuman scream I had ever heard. I screamed, and it screamed even louder. Everything happened so fast that I didn't have time to think of what to do next. I simply took that as my cue to get the hell out of there.

I ran for the convertible and dived into it without even opening the door. Then I spun the car around, floored it, kicking up dirt and rocks, and beat a path toward the cabin, not once looking backward.

When I got back at the cabin everyone was still into their nature shit. While I had been making contact with beings from another planet, they were discussing the origin of tree bark and talking to leaves. I came to a screeching halt, leaped from the car, and began to share the details of my adventure — in a matter of seconds. My heart was pounding so fast, and I was talking at such an incredible speed, that there was no way they could comprehend what I was trying to tell them. They looked at me completely dumbfounded, as if I were the alien!

*Wait a minute,* I thought to myself, *I'm dealing with people who talk to dogs hoping they'll answer, shoot people with rubber darts for recreation, and I expect them to be rational?* Their explanation of the whole thing was that I was having a bad trip.

"Ah ha," I exclaimed, pulling the uneaten hit of acid out of my pocket. "I never took it, you hypocritical bastards!" With that, I went off into the house quite disgusted, took my hit, and sat quietly listening to the stereo with my headphones on.

To this day I can recall the encounter vividly. And I can honestly say that I was straight — that is, as straight as I could ever be in those wild years.

Two major irritations entered everyone's lives around that time. The first one was red-neck, shit-kicking, gun-toting, hippie-hating cowboys. The second one was pig-headed, fun-loathing, music-hating narcotics officers. Any way you sliced it, the party was about to end.

One particular thorn in our side was Sergeant Gray, the majordomo of the narcs. Every chance he got, he tried to bust one of us or one of our friends. He was always pulling us over, in hopes that he'd find some major quantities of illegal drugs. We were always one step ahead of him. We made sure that we had taken everything before we left the house, but weren't fucked up so badly that we couldn't pass the "Sergeant Gray Sobriety Test."

He used to come into the Exodus all of the time just to intimidate everybody. However, this usually backfired, since he was totally out of his element. The minute that he and his partner would walk into the club, we would stop whatever song we were playing, shine the spotlight on him, and announce to everyone in the place, "Ladies and gentlemen, would you welcome our special guest for the evening: Sergeant Gray of the Denver Police Department, and his personal pet." This would be the audience's cue to dispose of every illegal substance on them. "Boy, Sarge, I'll just bet you can hear the sound of toilets flushing all over this club." People would be swallowing joints, taking pills, hiding things in their girlfriends' hair and, in extreme cases, shoving a capsule up their ass.

He would be thoroughly disgusted with this little spotlight antic that I would pull. But he wouldn't leave before delivering one of his famous fear tactic speeches: "You guys had better be looking over your shoulders every minute. Because if you even spit wrong, I'll be right behind you, and you'll be mine." With that, one of us from the stage — usually Rob — would say something intelligent like, "Oh, we're really afraid!" And with a disgusted look on his face, Sergeant Gray and his assistant would leave. Once out of sight, they were but a memory.

Because of Sergeant Gray's surprise "raids," we were overly paranoid and always on our toes. On one afternoon I had just purchased some amazing Lebanese hash. We smoked a couple of bowls and decided to go down to the club to rehearse. Just in case the buzz wore off midafternoon, we took a large supply of the hash with us. When we got to the club, we fired up the instruments, downed a couple of beers (except for Myron, who had a Coca-Cola), and started to work out our latest tune. About an hour into the rehearsal I looked up to see three uniformed men walking through the front door of the club. We all completely lost it. Thinking that Sergeant Gray was making good on his threat, we ate every last bit of hash that we brought with us.

With that, one of the uniformed men asked, "Excuse me, are any of you the owner of the club?" "No," I dumbfoundedly replied.

"Well, when you see him, tell him that the fire marshal

dropped by for a routine inspection. We'll just stop in next week. Have a good afternoon."

After they disappeared, we sat there in total silence, just staring at each other. We had just eaten a chunk of hashish the size of a golf ball — for nothing. We immediately called off the rehearsal and told drug-free Myron that in a very short time we were going to be way too high to play music, let alone make sense. We jumped into the van and hauled ass back to the cabin before the hash hit and we were reduced to babbling, rubber-legged, mush-brained idiots.

One day we arrived at the club to be informed by our manager that he had set up a recording session for Superband. The plan was that we would record two of our best tunes, and then Denny, our manager, would front us the money to press a single that would be sold at all of our shows. The initial revenue would pay for the pressing costs and would complete our payments on the band gear and van. It seemed that he had a friend who owned a recording studio. The friend turned out to be a dentist, and the facility was located in the back of his office. We figured that if we didn't produce a hit record, we would at least get a discount on a root canal job!

We worked up two of our best received numbers, and off to the dentist's office we went. Both songs dealt with the joy and pain that came from doing drugs. My song, "I Ain't Got No Body," was a wonderfully melodic ode to an acid trip. Rob's song, "Acid Indigestion," was about as blatant as they come — no hidden meanings here.

After several hours we finished the recording session, turned the masters over to Denny, and placed our future in his hands. This was meant to be our big break in show business. After that the singles were pressed and began to sell like hotcakes at the club. We even received some local radio airplay, which proved to be icing on the cake. Although the records never saw the light of day beyond Denver, it still gave everyone the sense of hope that anything was possible in the world of rock and roll if you just took enough drugs and believed in it.

Before I left Los Angeles, I had begun a relationship that I wasn't interested in continuing, at least not on a serious basis. This was with my old friend Tracy. Like me, she was a fanatic rock and roll junkie. We had been friends since grammar school, and she had always taken an interest in me, but I had never reciprocated. She wasn't a beauty queen, but then again, I wasn't Robert Redford. I knew that sleeping with her, would jeopardize our friendship. Like me, Tracy had a passion for music, and I would call her on the phone and say, "have you heard this one?" Then I'd play the latest English import that I had gotten at Lewin's that day. Finally, after several years of going over to her house for dinner, numerous phone calls, and seeing her at all my shows (through the numerous bands I played in), I finally broke down. One night, I don't remember where or when, because I was really stoned, we did the dirty deed. From that point on, even though she knew she could never have a serious relationship with me, she carried the torch.

Meanwhile, back at the cabin, where I was bedding one of the waitresses from the Exodus, there was a knock on the mat that partitioned off my third of the living room. There was a message for me down at the club, to call Tracy in L.A. I said, "Thank you," and went back to discussing the meaning of life with the bimbo I was fucking at the time.

The next day, I drove down to the bottom of the canyon to the Country Store, where the nearest pay phone was, and returned Tracy's call. She said she wanted to come and visit. Being the selfish bastard I was, I thought to myself, *Great! It wouldn't hurt to have someone around to clean up the place. Maybe she'll get lucky with one of the other guys.*

No specific date was set for her proposed visit, and by that afternoon, I had forgotten about the phone call. Then one day, out of the clear blue sky, she came driving up the driveway in her car. I should have been happy to see her, but I wasn't. However, I wouldn't let that stop me from having fun. Basically, I was quite rude to her and ignored her as much as possible. (I wish now that I could apologize to her for acting like a complete asshole. Chalk it up to youth and the drugs I was doing.) She ended up sticking around for quite a while.

Tracy's presence at the cabin was cramping my style a bit, but I didn't let it stop me from picking up other girls during her visit. One night at the club, in between sets, I had been noticing a certain waitress. At the end of the evening, I asked her if she wanted to come back to the cabin and get high, and she agreed. Her name was Lee Smith. Although she had worked at the Exodus for a while, I had never paid much attention to her.

We went back to the cabin, got wasted, and little else happened, except we watched the sun come up together. The atmosphere at the cabin was starting to get to me. Here I was with a girl I really liked, and there were a bunch of stoned assholes running around talking to stoned dogs, playing with dart guns, and generally carrying on like a bunch of kids. The next night we decided to go back to her place after the club closed.

When we got to her place, she decided to take a bath. I sat down in her bedroom and started watching one of my favorite carnivorous plant movies: *The Day of the Triffids*. The bathroom door was closed, but there was a large piece of frosted glass in it. I kept sticking my face up to the glass, in hopes that I could watch her inside. Realizing that I couldn't, I got disgusted and went back to watching the movie.

When she came out of the bathroom, I rolled another joint, watched TV for a little while, turned out the lights, and then we made love. When I think back on it now, it all seems so simple and basic.

This turned out to be the first time that I thought that I wanted an actual relationship with someone, as opposed to a series of one-night stands. I can't say that I was in love with her from the very beginning, because I was too immature. But we enjoyed each other and I wanted to spend more time with her. Being only nineteen years old at the time, I was trying to act more grown up and sophisticated than I really was. At least, I wanted to give that impression to the other guys in the band. I figured, "What better way to do that than to have a serious relationship with someone?"

At this point, I had completely forgotten about Tracy and didn't care about her feelings. After a few times of taking Lee back to the cabin, Tracy saw the hopelessness of hanging around. She went home disillusioned and hurt.

Before Tracy left Denver, Rob took me aside and tried to give me a little talk about the way I was treating her. My basic reaction was, "If you're so concerned about her, why don't you fuck her?" After she left, I didn't give her another thought for a long time.

Lee, Rob, and I were on our way back to the cabin one day when we had one of our worst encounters with our other dreaded foe — the cowboys.

Up to that point, our only encounter with them would be to see them as we drove past their house, down the canyon from us. They would usually be setting fence posts, punching cows, branding steer, or some other task that suited their personalities — like shoveling shit. Generally, they would say something unoriginal to us, like, "Is that a boy or a girl under all that hair?"

We would wait until we drove past them, out of earshot, and shout one of our own original phrases, like, "Fuck you, Wyatt Earp." This particular day, however, two of the bigger, meaner-looking ones were standing in the middle of the road, blocking our path. Since there was a deep ravine on either side of us, we had to either stop for them or run them over (my first choice). No sooner had we stopped than Rob rolled down his window, and one of the inbreeds hauled off and punched him in the face. Since I was driving, and was in no mood to deal with this shit, I immediately floored the car and got the hell out of there.

Rob, who was holding his nose while blood trickled out from between his fingers, mumbled something to the effect of, "I had a nice buzz going up until now."

When we pulled into the driveway, we told Roger and Ron what had happened. They immediately ran for the cabin, and began to search through their possessions for something to defend themselves with. We locked all of the doors and stood guard by the windows all night, until the hash we had done earlier wore off. Once again it was a total waste of good drugs.

The next day, Roger and a friend of his pulled up in the driveway. When they got out of the friend's car, I could see that they were both carrying rifles. When they got out of the car, I said, "I guess this means that 'dropping' today is out of the question?"

Roger dispelled my worst fears by reaching into his pocket and producing a Baggie containing numerous hits of a brand new batch of acid. *Thank God,* I said to myself. *If we're going to play the Hatfields and the McCoys, I want to make sure that I am good and stoned!*

We dropped acid that evening, and basically it was pretty uneventful. I surmised that Roger was bluffing and that the rifles were unloaded. However, the next morning I was awakened by the sound of several members of "The Wild Bunch" shooting beer cans off a log. I looked out the door and saw Roger's friend walking down the driveway, saying, "Where's the chicken?"

*Where's the chicken?* I wondered, suddenly remembering that the cowboys had a chicken coop on the outskirts of their property. *Great,* I thought, *I'm going to be blown away over a couple of extra crispy drumsticks!*

Fortunately, he was too stoned to find the end of the driveway, let alone the moronic cowboys. After about an hour, he came wandering back into the cabin, rolled another joint, and sat down in front of the stereo.

Years later, when Jackson Browne released the song "Red Neck Friend," I thought of our encounter with the cowboys that day. After that incident, we tried to avoid them at all costs. If they were in our path when we pulled out into the road, we would just turn around and go back to the cabin until they disappeared. Sooner or later we were bound to have another confrontation with them, and our luck would have run out.

Since Superband was becoming so popular in the metropolitan Denver area, our manager, Denny Sheneman, decided to book us in other cities. We hit the club circuit, everywhere from Grand Junction, Colorado, to Laramie, Wyoming.

At this point, we were getting quite clever with our tunes. We had one tune that was patterned after Moby Grape's song "Omaha." Our song was called "Hey Skinhead." This went over particularly well at a club in Colorado Springs, whose sole clientele were the cadets from the Air Force Academy! Playing that song literally kept us on our toes, because we were constantly dodging the beer bottles thrown at the stage by the irate "fly boys." We just added fuel to the fire by playing our new break song called "Fuck You." We all made a conscious decision in the future to scope out the audience before we would play a song that we knew would piss them off.

Lee and I had been dating for a while by the winter of '67, and she thought that it was finally time for me to go over and meet her family. They lived in a modest home in Bear Valley, a suburb of Denver. It was convenient in that it was situated halfway between the club and the cabin. It was also only two miles from the local hangout, the Pancake House on Wadsworth Boulevard. This was the only place in the area that was open twenty-four hours a day, where everybody could congregate after the clubs closed.

Lee had warned me ahead of time that her parents were strict Seventh Day Adventists, and they might not approve of my lifestyle. *No problem,* I thought. As I was to do at many other times in my life, I simply turned on "the Greenspoon charm." I really didn't know how to act in front of them because I never had to be "approved of," except for an occasional date when I was younger, which was usually chaperoned anyway.

We arrived at her parents' house, and after exchanging introductions, I sat down on the living room sofa and we began the uncomfortable ritual of staring at each other, with nothing much to say. When we got the small talk out of the way, I found out that her father owned a security patrol service, and her mother, Ruth, worked at a blueprint shop. Lee also had two brothers: Donny, who had just gotten out of the service and loved to race cars, and Marvin, who helped his dad out with the business and was finishing up college. Also at their house lived three large but friendly German Shepherds, presumably retired from the patrol business.

After finding out a little bit about their family background, it was my turn to reciprocate. I told them about my parents and my upbringing in Beverly Hills, hoping that that would impress them. I also ran down a list of my musical accomplishments. It seemed that Marvin was the most interested in that particular aspect of my life. After a while, Lee, sensing that it was getting a little uncomfortable, made motions toward our exit. After making plans to attend a family dinner the following Sunday, we split.

I told her that I wanted to stop by and introduce her to one of my friends, who just happened to live only a few blocks from her parents. My friend was a lady named Carol Sturkel. She was a lot older — and I thought a lot wiser — than myself and the rest of the guys in the band. We had met through mutual friends. Carol would come down to the club to see us play, and then we would go back to her place to get stoned. She owned a 1967 silver Corvette that she let me drive on occasion.

I remember that we would be at her house getting stoned, and then she would excuse herself and head for the bathroom. When she returned to the living room, she acted like a totally different person. I had no idea at the time that she was going into the bathroom to shoot up heroin. This accounted for her drastic personality transformation. She was basically a kind person who was fun to be around, except when she went "mental" on us. And then it became increasingly uncomfortable to be around her.

When Lee and I eventually found out that Carol was a junkie, we were appalled. To us, that was only one step ahead of a child molester. We quickly dropped her out of our circle of friends after that.

One of the premier concert venues soon opened in Denver. It was called the Family Dog, and was located in a big warehouse on Evans Avenue. The Family Dog was run by Chet Helms, who had worked for Bill Graham at the Fillmore West in San Francisco. Helms had formed Family Dog Productions and was responsible for bringing into Denver some of the more interesting concert bookings at the time. He would usually have two major groups and one local opening act on the bill at the same time.

We had gotten a booking there, opening for Big Brother and the Holding Company, Quicksilver Messenger Service, and Blue Cheer. This was a dream come true for all of us. We wanted to blow the other major bands off the stage, so we consumed mass quantities of drugs and rehearsed for two solid weeks in preparation for the big night.

Not only did we want to sound good, but we also wanted to look the part. I immediately went on a scavenger hunt to all of the second-hand clothing stores in the area, and I came up with what I like to call my "Julius Caesar look." This consisted of a rather elaborate and heavy red velvet toga that was encrusted with several pounds of metal studs. To add to the excess weight, I also wore a half dozen strings of colored beads and a cow bell around my neck. To complete this pseudo-Roman ensemble, I bought a pair of leather sandals that laced up to the navel. I was an awesome sight, to say the least. It wouldn't have been so bad that I looked like an extra from *Ben Hur,* but it was December and ten degrees below zero outside. Anything for rock and roll . . .

On the night of the show, everybody — except, of course Myron — decided that to be in tune with the cosmos and the people in attendance, we all had to drop acid. We took our hits at the cabin, jumped into our respective vehicles, and headed for the Family Dog. Lee rode with me in my car. Once inside the club, we were greeted by one of the most incredible light shows that I had seen in quite some time. The acid was coming on slowly, but even though it was cold outside, my body temperature was rapidly rising. We all got together in the dressing room for a little pep talk and inspiration. At that point, Myron knew something was up, but he wasn't quite sure what.

We got our cue to go on stage, and by that time we were feeling the full effect of the drug. Our excitement was at a fever pitch. When we hit the stage, I noticed that everyone was looking up at the large screen behind us. The entire audience was mesmerized by the colored wall of swirling corn oil that was being projected in back of us. We all knew we had our work cut out for us, seeing how the entire audience's attention span, which was probably limited to begin with, was focused on a pulsating sea of Mazola.

We launched into the opening bars of "Hey Skinhead," and I immediately panicked. I had no idea where I was in the song, and was solely relying on the other guys to sense my dilemma and cover for me. This wasn't going to happen, because they were more lost than I was. At one point, I thought I had already finished the song and proceeded to play the next one. In reality, we were only one verse into our opening number. Thinking that they had fucked up royally, the Three "R's" — Ron, Roger, and Rob — followed my lead and started playing the tune that I was playing. To add to the confusion, poor Myron was totally lost.

After a series of missed cues, forgotten solos, and ad-libbed words, we finally got on track. By the third or fourth tune, we were a tight musical unit with one unified train of thought. When we got to the song "Nottingham Daily," it was time to stretch out and show this crowd just what we were made of. This meant that everyone got to take extended solos. It would have been fine, except that as the opening act, we only had twenty minutes on stage. Already we had eaten up most of our time trying to figure out what song we were doing.

By now we were flying, and every little movement seemed like a divinely inspired gesture. As the time approached for us to make our exit from the stage, we were still in the middle of Ron's guitar solo. I remember looking off to my right, only to see a large Nubian slave with his arms wildly flailing, giving us the traditional "Hey asshole! Get the fuck off the stage!" cue. All I could see in my altered state was a trail of arms, which I misinterpreted for his total enthrallment with the music. I thought that he wanted us to keep playing, so I turned to Ron and gave him the sign to extend his solo.

When I looked back to see how the Nubian bouncer was responding, I was greeted with two of them giving me simultaneous signs to "Cut it!" and "Vacate the stage!" Once again, I mistook their gestures as those of friendship. With this I immediately launched into a long solo.

The stage hands descended upon us like flies on shit and began to unplug our equipment and carry us off the stage. Bewildered by their gestures, and totally dazed by the light show, the next thing we knew we were off the stage and wondering what had just happened.

I remember turning to Rob and asking, "What do you think? Did they like it?"

"They seemed to," was his reply, not having a clue as to what had just transpired. I was feeling pretty good about the evening so far, and I wanted to stick around to hear the other groups. I went up to the bar and got a large Coke, which I immediately spilled down the inside sleeve of my toga and all down the front of myself. It didn't feel too bad and, being as stoned as I was, I simply went back to the bar and got myself another Coke.

After a short set change, Blue Cheer came on with an almost deafening wall of noise. I remember standing there in a trance, listening to them while trying to unglue my toga from my Coca-Cola soaked body. Quicksilver Messenger Service was next on the bill and did a fairly uninspiring set by my standards. To be quite fair, however, at that point I had become just another one of the children of the corn oil and was totally entranced.

Big Brother and the Holding Company came on after about a half hour set change. Two things immediately stood out to me about the band. One: they were incredibly out of tune. Two: I was fascinated by Janis Joplin's stage presence. Although her voice was like salt on an open wound, somehow, in my clouded state of mind, she sounded like an angel. I was also very curious about the fact that she and her bottle of Southern Comfort were inseparable. Whenever she took a swig off of it, the next note that came out of her was as irritating as the sound of chalk on a blackboard. She'd be unnervingly tense and unbearable to listen to one moment, and the next, she could sound like a whisper.

As her set came to a close, I wanted to beat the rush out of the parking lot and get back to the cabin. I rounded up Lee, and we beat a hasty retreat to the car.

I found my car buried under a snowdrift. After digging the car out of the snow, we got in and headed for the mountains. We got about two blocks from the Family Dog when, all of a sudden, I heard a loud noise, followed by the sound of engine parts falling into the road. Just then the car came to an abrupt stop and died a violent death. Not knowing what to make of this automotive carnage, we pushed the car to the side of the road and walked back to the parking lot, where we bummed a ride back to the cabin with the other band members.

The next day I called Carol Sturkel, since the car was only a couple of miles from her house. She called the people from AAA, and about fifteen minutes later, they arrived with a tow truck.

The driver immediately put his head under the hood and almost as quickly removed it, saying something to the effect of, "This baby's going nowhere in a big hurry." He then asked me when I last put oil and water into the car.

"Oil? Water?" I said with surprise. I thought to myself, *Maybe sometime last summer in L.A.?*

He then informed me that my freeze plugs had blown out, and that I had cracked the block. *Hmmmm? Sounds serious to me,* I thought.

We decided to tow the car to Carol's, while I thought of what to do. A couple of days later, Lee told me that an old boyfriend of hers was an excellent mechanic, and that she'd call and get a price quote on installing a new engine. She found out that he could put in a complete short block for $350, including labor. *A great price,* I thought. *All I have to do is save up the money.* In the meantime, transportation wouldn't be a problem, because there was always the band van, and Carol told me that I could borrow her Corvette.

I had been getting tired of living in the cabin, the commute up there, the cowboys, and all of the nonsense. Lee and I made the decision to get a place of our own, in town close to the club. We found a great old house on Sherman Street, about half a block from the Pizza Hut, where we hung out.

We didn't have much furniture to begin with. Our first bed was a dilapidated instrument of torture that threatened to swallow us like a Venus Fly Trap every time we'd lie down on it.

We finally made the wise decision to get rid of the frame and put the mattress on the floor. We also had the assorted furnishings of the era: bean bag chairs, assorted "black light" posters, and various incense burners. In the bathroom we hung various zig-zag mats, and from the ceiling we suspended the usual assortment of Indian paisley printed cloth. The kitchen was fairly basic, considering that we mainly lived on rice curry and tea. There was a small, enclosed area on the back porch that was perfect for Crystal, whom we had rescued from the depths of doggie drug despair and constant partying.

Around this time, Sergeant Gray had escalated his war on drugs to constant harassment of anyone with hair below their earlobes. I knew then that my days were numbered, and if I was going to get out of town, I had to scrape together enough money to repair the Spoonmobile.

I had already called my mother and warned her that I would be moving back to L.A. sooner than she thought. Not only could she expect my arrival, but that of my girlfriend and our dog Crystal. I could sense the fact that she was not too pleased with this particular decision, but seeing as how she never told me how to live my life, she declined comment. At that point in the conversation, I realized that it was the wrong time to ask for a loan to fix the car. So I did the next best thing: I called up Carol, explained my situation, and was immediately granted a $150 loan, which I promised to pay back. Lee called her mechanic boyfriend, we had the car towed to his garage, and the resurrection began.

When we arrived at the Exodus that night, we witnessed police officers leading a pair of drug offenders into the squad car. It seems that they had been busted for possession of a couple joints. Sergeant Gray really meant business — and it could only get worse. From that night on, I became increasingly more paranoid, and it now seemed that my every waking moment was spent looking over my shoulder. When I'd come out of the house in the morning and spot an unmarked car with two men sitting in it, I would immediately go back into the house and flush all of my drugs. Living under these conditions wasn't fun anymore. Consequently, a change had to come — and fast.

The day that the car was ready, I informed Lee to go over to the club, get her paycheck, quit her job, and pack. I would go over to the garage, pick up the car, and tell the mechanic that I would return the next morning with the balance of the bill. As a friend of Lee's, he didn't question my honesty. The whole time I knew that I had no intention of ever paying this guy for the wonderful job he did on my car.

I had already prepared Rob, Ron, Roger, and Myron for my inevitable escape, and instructed them to hang on to whatever possessions I left behind. Lee and I loaded up the car with as many things as we could take and allotted a small space for Crystal. We then drove to Lee's parents' house, said our "goodbyes," and left town without ever looking back.

Sergeant Gray and the cowboys had achieved their goal. They ran this fun-loving, drug-taking, girl-chasing, flying saucer-hunting, curry-eating, camphor-breathing, peace-loving hippie out of town.

I had left Los Angeles a teenager with a hit of acid and a dream, and now I was returning to town with two hits of acid, a dog, and a girlfriend. In my mind, I was well on my way to being what I considered a responsible adult. This wasn't to be the last time I deluded myself.

# 6 / It's A Jungle Out There

We arrived at my parents' house in Beverly Hills after only about thirty-two hours on the road — a considerably shorter time than it had taken Rob and me to get to Denver in an STP-fueled haze. When we pulled up, my mother came out to the street to greet us. I could sense right away that any misgivings she had about meeting Lee were immediately dispelled. After the obligatory introductions were made, and Crystal relieved herself on the front lawn, we all went inside for some food and sleep after our long drive.

Whereas most parents of teenagers would make certain that their sons and their girlfriends slept in separate beds, my mother was totally cool about us sleeping together. She had already made my bed up for the both of us.

In the time since my absence, virtually nothing had changed in my room. Everything was exactly where I left it. That suited me just fine, because that meant that she didn't discover my secret stash places. Since I was too tired to go score drugs up on the Strip, I immediately went to one of my favorite hiding spots, behind my television set, and discovered a cornucopia of grass, hash, and pills — aged to their fullest potential.

We rolled a joint, lit a stick of incense, and then I took a long, hot bath. As I sat completely submerged in Calgon, I contemplated the most crucial step to becoming "a responsible adult" — marriage!

Lee and I had already discussed such future plans on our drive from Colorado. I decided that the next day I would sit down with my mother and have a serious talk to reveal my intentions. After an hour in the tub, and nearly falling asleep and drowning myself, I dragged my shriveled, prunelike body out of the water and back into my bedroom. Within minutes I was sound asleep and dreaming of wedding plans.

The next morning I woke up quite early, as usual, and went into my mother's bedroom to wake her up.

"I'm really excited, and I have something important that I want to tell you . . ." I said.

Before I could even finish my sentence, she interjected, "I know, you want to get married."

This took me totally by surprise, but then again, a lot of things that my mother did took me by surprise.

My father, who had long since resumed living with my mother, was as much of an absentee member of the family as before. When he wasn't at work, he was on the golf course. And when he came home, he was so wrapped up with facts and figures pertaining to his business that he had little else to contribute to the household, or to my upbringing. With this in mind, my mom found herself with the seemingly impossible task of being both mother and father to me. I didn't understand how hard that was at the time, but years later I was able to appreciate her efforts.

Throughout her life, all that she wanted was for me to be happy. If I wanted to do something, she would never say no to me. Even if she realized that my actions could result in a total disaster, she allowed me to learn from my own mistakes.

To demonstrate her faith in me, she immediately began making plans for the wedding. We set a date and made plans to be married at the Beverly Hills Presbyterian Church. With only the immediate family and a small number of friends in attendance, we held the reception at my parents' house, where we would live for several months, until we could afford to get our own place.

My mother was so gracious that she even set up a charge account in our name at the ritzy Burton Way Market. We also had carte blanche at the Robert Burns drug and liquor store. It was just a matter of time before we would begin to abuse these privileges.

Ron, having broken up Superband and moved back to Los Angeles, was available for the role of "best man" at my wedding. The day before the wedding, my mother took me to Sy Ambers on Hollywood Boulevard to purchase my wedding suit. Always being fashion-conscious, I chose a tasteful green and white wool houndstooth ensemble.

As I did with so many major events in my life, on the day of my wedding I took as many drugs as possible to heighten the experience — and to compensate for the fact that I was scared shitless. Right after the ceremony, Ron and I both took a hit of acid. By the time the reception started, I was peaking. The events of the evening, needless to say, were a little hazy, but I do remember continually walking past the cake, looking at it, and breaking out with wild laughter. At one point during the reception, I wandered off into one of the back bedrooms and started to come on to some girl who was there. I can't remember if she was one of the bridesmaids or just one of the guests. For all I know, I probably came on to one of each.

Although things became a big blur, I distinctly remember waking up the next morning, picking up my left hand, and seeing a wedding ring on my finger. I emitted a silent scream of terror. *What the fuck have I just done!?!* I thought to myself. Not exactly the most reassuring note to begin a marriage on. But I was committed, and determined to make the best of it.

Sometime in late 1967, I crossed paths with Michael Lloyd once again and became involved in still another creative project. In my absence, Michael had purchased a small recording studio on San Vicente Boulevard in Los Angeles. He invited me to come down and record a couple of new tunes that he had written, and at the same time offered to record any tunes that I had or wanted to have recorded — free of charge. It was a great business arrangement, because I could go down there late at night when I knew he wasn't there and bring along an assortment of music-producing, drug-taking, sex-minded moral degenerates and other low-life scum. Another close friend of ours, the brilliant Sunset Strip con man, Kim Fowley, was also in possession of a key to the studio. He would come in during the early hours of the morning, dragging along with him the wretched refuse from the slowly disintegrating Sunset Strip scene.

I would try to coordinate it so that whenever I wanted to record any of my tunes, it wouldn't conflict with anyone else's recording schedule, especially Michael's. Although Michael was incredibly tolerant of my escalating drug use, he still voiced a concern over keeping the clientele at his recording studio somewhere within the boundaries of the human species.

About this time I met a young man who was hanging out at the studio. His name was Timmy Alvarado. He was a friend of Danny Hutton, a singer who had three solo hits in the mid-60's. Danny used to come into all of the Sunset Strip nightclubs and, although we were never formally introduced, we shared a mutual love for music. Due to this same understanding, he was soon to be instrumental in changing my life forever.

One night Timmy and I somehow started talking about lodging. I told him that I was living with my wife at my parents' house, and that the quarters were becoming a bit tight. He told me that he had a guest house for rent in back of his place, and I could have it cheap. The next day I packed up whatever possessions Lee and I had accumulated, and with Crystal in tow, we moved into Timmy's guest house on Morse Avenue in the upper middle-class neighborhood of Sherman Oaks.

What the guest house really amounted to was an enclosed patio. The floors were nothing more than loose bricks set on top of dirt, some of the windows were covered with sheets of thick plastic, and for warmth we bought a little electric heater. Luxuries were at a premium; however, there was a small kitchen and a bathroom. The main problem with the place was soon to surface as summer approached. There was virtually no way to keep the marauding bands of ravenous ants away from our cupboards (and my stash!). It seemed that no matter how much Raid I sprayed on them, they would just come back for more. Whenever we would leave for the evening, there would be thousands of them converging on a leftover piece of pie.

I got the brilliant idea to place all of my drugs in a Baggie and bury it in the backyard. I didn't give a thought to my plan until I got the sudden urge to roll a joint and I couldn't for the life of me remember where I buried the shit! I must have dug up half of the backyard in my search, and turned up nothing.

At the age of twenty, another of my pressing problems was my reoccurring draft status. The Vietnam War was raging, and there was no way I was going to go over there to risk my life for that senseless shit. However, my problem was even greater than I thought, since I was classified "1-Y." This meant that I was only temporarily deferred, for medical reasons, and could be called down to the induction center to take another physical examination, and be reclassified, at any time. In anticipation of this, my mother spent a vast quantity of money (in the $10,000 range) on various doctors and lawyers who could write me bogus notes, questioning my sanity.

I remember one "shrink" I went to, just for this purpose, was constantly prescribing the strangest assortment of pills for me. Probably he was hoping they would induce insanity and schizophrenia so that he could keep me as a patient long after the war was over. Among the pills I was instructed to take was Thorazine, which is an extremely strong sedative used for mental patients (it is also prescribed to bring people down from bad acid trips). The other pill that was prescribed was the most bizarre pill that I had ever taken in my life. It turned out to be nothing more than one-half sleeping pill, and one-half pharmaceutically produced LSD!

On one occasion I took one of the half-acid tranquilizers, and gave one to Timmy, then went back to my place to battle the killer ants. After about an hour, when I was peaking, I hacked my way through the jungle of trees and vines that separated the guest house from the main house. When I knocked on the door, and Timmy answered, I could tell he was just as fucked up as I was and was having equally as hard a time communicating. The stuff became so intense that all we wanted to do was to go to our respective beds to try and sleep it off.

The dreams that resulted were nothing less than spectacular visions in vivid Technicolor, ear-splitting stereophonic sound, and audience-participating cinerama. After about six or seven hours in the Land of Oz, I awoke only to discover that the acid had not worn off as it normally would have, but instead had become even more intense. Once again I tried to make my way through the jungle of killer vines and carnivorous carp that inhabited Timmy's fish pond. When I finally arrived at his front door, I knocked sharply, only to find it ajar. I pushed it open and walked inside, quietly calling out his name, careful not to scare the shit out of him. Just then I saw him lying on the living room sofa. He looked up at me and said, "It gets better." Then I turned around, stumbled back to my place, and proceeded to get another eight hours of cinematic dreams.

During this whole trip, Lee had declined to partake with us, and probably wound up smoking an entire lid of grass to entertain herself.

With regard to my draft status, I continued to take all of the pills prescribed to me, thinking that my "1-Y" status would keep me away from those war-mongering, pencil-pushing, Napalm-dropping bureaucrats at the induction center in downtown L.A. However, one day, when I went to get the mail, I had a rude awakening. There before me was my new draft card, and stamped on it — as plain as day — was my new classification: "1-A." Accompanying this horrifying piece of paper was a brief letter informing me when to appear for another physical. It also stated that if I passed the physical examination, I should bring along my toothbrush — because I wasn't going home. Drastic action had to be taken immediately, and I knew just what to do.

I had five days to prepare for my physical. The first thing that I would do was to score enough Black Beauties to keep me awake the entire five days. If I got a wee bit too edgy, I also made sure that there was a sufficient quantity of "reds" to mellow me out. I also scored a couple of lids of some killer weed too, and a large chunk of Nepalese hash. And if that didn't do the trick, just as a back-up, I had two tabs of acid. The next step would be for me to not take a shower or shave for the five days before the physical. By the end of this time, I should be sufficiently ripe enough to even turn the stomach of a wine-soaked bum on Skid Row.

I told Lee of my plan, apologizing in advance for my festering state of decomposure that week. She wasn't happy with my plan, but neither she nor my mother were ready to see me sent off to die in some fucking rice paddy in Southeast Asia.

When the fateful day arrived, I was already hallucinating from the lack of sleep. I was also quite on edge and cranky. I made the long torturous drive from the Valley to downtown L.A., went into the induction center, and gave the officer at the desk my papers. He then instructed me to pry my clothes off, put them in a locker, and to follow the yellow line down the hallway. *Where the hell was I going — Oz?* I thought to myself.

No sooner had I turned the corner than I began to be poked, pricked, and prodded by various pseudo-military doctors in long, white robes. Something strange was happening here. Every time I'd reach another point in this medical "receiving line" of examiners, they barely touched me, yet at every step of the way, I would be declared "positive" and suitable for induction. When it came time for a urine test, I couldn't pee. They simply said, "No problem, it's probably positive anyway." When they checked my heartbeat, the stethoscope had barely touched my chest, when my paper was stamped "positive." When one of the doctors drew my blood, he could barely find my vein. But when he finally did, he just stuck the unmarked sample in a rack with about 200 other unmarked samples and stamped my paper "positive."

I was getting pissed off. Obviously, they were going to declare me "positive," no matter what condition I was in. I turned to the officer who was standing there, pointed to my vial of blood, and asked, "Don't you want to put my name on this sample, in case you make a mistake?" He just turned to me and sarcastically shouted, as if I was already one of his grunts: "Boy, this is the military . . . we don't make mistakes." He then instructed me to follow the green line down the hall. *Great,* I thought to myself, *I could use a little color change right about now.*

As I walked down the green line, I knew that this wasn't working out in my favor. Drastic measures were called for immediately. A plan was formulating in my sleep-deprived brain. I stopped long enough to put my underwear on backwards. Did I think that was grounds for a discharge? Then I spied a blue line, and I decided to disobey orders and take that. I found that it led in the opposite direction from the yellow and green lines. A little ways further, I discovered that the blue line was intersected by a red line. I stopped for a second to gather my thoughts. Using my intuitive logic, I deduced that the red signified "Stop . . . Desist . . . Hold everything." Deciding that the forbidden path was the one to take, I followed the red line to a closed door. On the door was written someone's name, followed by the title "Commanding Officer." *Authority,* I thought to myself and swung the door open.

Just then the CO looked up in amazement, and shouted, "What the fuck do you want, son?"

"For one thing," I said with a wild look in my eyes, "I'm not your son, and for the other: I just want to *kill!!!* . . . I want to . . ."

Before I could say anything else, he cut me off in midsentence and shot back with his best army rhetoric, "Great! You're just what we're looking for! There's a definite place for you in 'Nam, son."

"No, Pops," I shot back, "you don't seem to understand. I just want to kill *you* and everyone in this fucking place!" With that, I ran wildly toward his desk, and in one graceful leap, reminiscent of Jim Thorpe, I jumped up on it and began to kick all of his files onto the floor. Then I picked up a handful of pencils that were in a coffee cup, broke them in half, and threw them at him. At that point, he told me to take my papers, follow the blue line, and go into Room 24 and take a seat.

I knew that I had made the desired impression. I calmly took my papers, hopped off of his desk, and said, "Thank you," as if nothing had even happened. Upon reaching Room 24, I found to my relief that it was the army psychiatrist. I handed my papers to a rather nondescript gentleman and sat down next to some other pond scum, who were obviously trying the same tact of forced mental derangement. I sat there for a while, clinging to my pile of letters from the various doctors and lawyers which stated that I was indeed unfit for any kind of military action.

After about half an hour, the doctor called me into his office and asked me to have a seat. He then proceeded to examine my assortment of files and papers. Just then, another uniformed officer stuck his head in the door, handed him a piece of paper, and said, "This one goes with the crazy redhead."

*Great,* I thought to myself, *he said the "C" word — they bought it!* I knew that my mother would be so pleased to find out that the $10,000 she had spent was well worth it.

From here on in, the rest of the formalities were pretty much painless. Mainly, I just sat there while they processed a bunch of paperwork. After a while, the doctor told me to get my clothes and go home. They would notify me in two weeks of my new draft status.

Relieved and extremely tired, I left the draft board and headed for the nearest pizza parlor. I drove home, ate a piece of the pizza, and slept for the next twenty-four hours. Not even the sound of the killer ants carrying away the leftovers could awaken me.

Two weeks later, I hacked my way from Timmy's guest house to the mailbox, as I had every day since I lived there. In anticipation of the formal letter from the government, I would usually stand on the curb a good half hour before the mailman arrived. At times I would even intercept him a few blocks before he approached the house. Finally, on that fateful day, among the usual bills, junk mail, and letters from Lee's parents, I saw the envelope bearing the words "Selective Service System." I hesitated for a moment, not knowing what the outcome might be, even though I was quite certain that my brainless antics at the draft board had assured me a "4-F."

I carefully opened the envelope in much the same way I had done as a kid to intercept my less-than-perfect report cards. I peered inside with my eyes half-closed. My fingers fumbled for the paper inside. As I pulled it out, I held my breath and gazed upon the final outcome of my most brilliant charade to date. There it was, staring back at me: "4-F." I let out a scream and ran back to the house. Lee was at the door to greet me, and by the look on my face she could tell that I had been spared the horrors of war.

In early 1968 Lee and I decided that we no longer wanted to be part of the Valley scene. It was time to make a geographic move, and since a lot of my friends and fellow party animals lived in the canyons of the Hollywood Hills, that seemed like a likely choice to relocate.

I went to Mann Realty, which was located under the Canyon Country Store on Laurel Canyon Boulevard. The woman everyone told me to contact was Elenore Marion. It seemed that she either owned or rented half the houses in the canyon. She was a wonderful woman who had a large family of her own, and she really liked rock music and all of the musicians and other people who lived up there.

I told her that I was looking for a rustic, two-bedroom home with a small backyard for Crystal. I had saved up a little money from doing various sessions and had also borrowed some from my mother. Mrs. Marion showed me various pictures of the homes available until one of them really caught my eye. It was exactly what I was looking for: a two-bedroom, one-bathroom house with a large kitchen, a two-car garage, and a large backyard that sloped up a huge, tree-lined lot. It was the second house on the left on Lookout Mountain Avenue, across the street from the Wonderland Avenue School.

Elenore told me that the neighbors on my immediate left were musicians also. It turned out that a friend of mine, Jim Pons, was living in the upstairs duplex. He was at that time the bass player with the Turtles (I had met him years earlier, when he was with the Leaves). Below him were Ian and Ruth Underwood, both very excellent avant-garde musicians who were currently members of the Mothers of Invention. Living next to them was a strange but likable fellow by the name of Millard Deutch. I had no idea what he did for a living, and never asked. Next to him was musician and solo artist Danny Hutton.

The house was perfect, and Lee and I both fell in love with it instantly. Not only was it just what we were looking for in a house, but the neighborhood seemed conducive to my rapidly escalating musical tastes. I especially liked the fact that several of my new neighbors would be musicians whom I knew and respected. Lee and I told Elenore that we'd take it. Two weeks later, we moved in.

Elenore was such a wonderful landlord and friend to everyone that late that summer the Turtles immortalized her with a composition. The song "Elenore" went on to become one of their biggest hits.

I had indirectly met Danny Hutton on and off years earlier when he had come into the various clubs that I was playing in on Sunset Strip with the East Side Kids. He had already recorded several solo singles at that point. His biggest hit was a song he had written, called "Roses and Rainbows," which was released in 1965 and made it to Number 73 on the *Billboard* chart. The follow-up single, "Big Bright Eyes," was another one of his compositions, and in 1966 he covered the song "Funny How Love Can Be," which had been a hit for an English group called Ivy League. Although his singles didn't reach the upper region of the national charts, they were all Top Ten hits in L.A. — thus assuring him star status and respectability among Hollywood's rock crowd.

I continued to record with Michael Lloyd on various projects that came up, and before long I was getting quite a reputation among L.A.'s rock community as a good session player. It was this newfound notoriety that one afternoon brought Danny Hutton to my door with an offer that would change my life forever.

I invited him in, and over a couple of killer joints, we discussed a project in which he was currently involved. It seems that he was doing a session that was being produced by legendary Hollywood eccentric Van Dyke Parks. He was vague as to who else was involved in it, but he mentioned that it was strong on vocals and vocal harmonies. He especially needed my expertise on one particular song they were recording. It was an obscure Lennon and McCartney song entitled "It's For You," which was originally recorded as a waltz by British singer Cilla Black. I quickly agreed to do the session with him and these other "mystery" people he was working with. I was especially interested in working with Van Dyke Parks, and we made plans for me to accompany him to the recording studio later that week.

On the appointed day, I arrived at Sunset Sound Studios in Hollywood and was introduced to Parks, who turned out to be just as eccentric and off-the-wall as everyone said he was. I found him to be a highly intelligent person who always seemed to be interspersing into his conversation large words that no one seemed to be able to define. He seemed to speak in riddles, and probably only he knew for sure what he was talking about.

Van Dyke put on a rough track of the song that I was to play on that had been recorded with some other Hollywood session musicians. They had taken the original 3/4 time of the song and made it a straight-ahead 4/4 rock tune. I could immediately picture the keyboard parts that I would play. To give it a slight baroque flavor, I suggested that I try the part on a harpsichord, and then maybe do some overdubs on other keyboards later, if necessary. Van Dyke was quite impressed with my fresh new ideas and quickly agreed. I went into the studio, put on the headphones, and played along with the track to get the chord structure. Everybody in the control room seemed to be jazzed by what I was playing, and we decided to go for one. After a few takes, it sounded great, and everybody thanked me. Then everybody promptly disappeared into the night. I returned to my new Canyon home to get stoned with my wife.

Originally, the song was one which Danny wanted to record as a solo, but Van Dyke suggested that he try using some additional singers to create something bigger. The song was to be part of a demo to shop around for a record deal.

For the next couple of weeks, I continued to do various recording sessions, and I sat in with friends at several of the local Sunset

Strip nightclubs. Unknown to me, at the same time Danny was working on yet another project with Van Dyke. In order to get a better record deal, Van Dyke wanted to try other creative collaborations. Since he was a writing partner with Brian Wilson of the Beach Boys, it seemed only logical that he bring Brian in to co-produce and help out. Brian brought with him the tracks for two completed new Beach Boys tunes. They were "Time To Get Alone" and "Darlin'." Danny and Van Dyke were completely knocked out by what they heard and mentioned that the songs sounded like material from the infamous *Pet Sounds* album. Everybody agreed that was the direction to go, and Danny immediately got on the phone to call some background singers that he knew.

One of the singers was Cory Wells, the leader of a band called the Enemies, who had played at the Whiskey-A-Go-Go and other Sunset Strip nightclubs the same time I was with the East Side Kids. I had met Cory indirectly years earlier when he came into the Trip, where I was working. Once, on our off night, he had borrowed my Farfisa organ. The other singer, Chuck Negron, was suggested by somebody else. He had a solo deal at the time with Columbia Records, under the name of Chuck Rondell. Columbia hoped to make him into a pop Johnny Mathis, since beautiful ballads were his forte.

Danny and the two background singers quickly learned the two songs and put their vocals down. The finished product was a great Beach Boys sounding track with an entirely unique vocal delivery. Each voice was so distinct and different, but blended so well, that it almost sounded like a group. Brian was so excited that he started talking about management and producing other things with Danny.

Later, Danny recounted the events of one particular night when Brian came in and told him, "I've got the perfect name to call you guys: you are now going to be known as 'Redwood!' " That was environmentally safe, and sure to catch the attention of some A&R man at a record label. However, there was just one fly in the ointment. When the other Beach Boys heard the finished songs, they got quite jealous and insisted that Brian keep the songs for them. Through some early group politics and bullshit, Danny and the other singers' voices were erased, and the Beach Boys' vocals were put on. Capitol Records wasted no time releasing "Darlin'," and soon it became a big hit. Not to be discouraged by this slight setback, Van Dyke and Danny continued to look for other songs that would be instant deal-getters.

Meanwhile, Danny was thinking more and more that he had

stumbled upon something new and wonderful with the vocal blend that was achieved with Cory and Chuck on the demos. He had decided to talk them into forming a group with the emphasis on three-part harmony. Each member would bring in a song reflecting his musical taste. Danny's was straight-ahead, pop-oriented; Cory's was heavily influenced by blues and R&B singers such as John Lee Hooker, Otis Redding, and Sam Cooke; and Chuck was the master of the ballad, and possessed an incredible falsetto.

Danny set up meetings with the other two singers at his house and they sat around singing songs and trying out various new approaches to harmony. Their voices seemed to blend so well that it sounded as if they had been singing together for years. Cory and Chuck decided to go along with Danny's idea to form a group, realizing there was strength in numbers, and it would be easy to snag a record deal as a trio. The only foreseeable stumbling block was Chuck's recording contract with Columbia Records. Since his contract was almost up, and there really hadn't been any chart success at this point, he didn't think there would be any problem dissolving the contract.

One thing that the three of them agreed upon almost immediately was the fact that if they had a hit record, they would have to have some sort of band backing them so they could reproduce on the road what would be on their records. All of a sudden, they had the task of assembling musicians to fill this slot. Wanting to work with something that was melodic to rehearse their tunes, they decided the first position to fill was that of keyboards. Danny told the other two that there just happened to be, living two doors down, an excellent keyboard player who had worked in various bands on the Sunset Strip. When Danny mentioned my name, Cory even said he knew of me and thought it was a good idea to give me a call.

One afternoon I was sitting on my living room sofa, smoking a joint and listening to an English import album of the Zombies, when there came a tapping at my front door. I opened the door and found Danny, looking rather excited. I invited him in and asked him, "What's up Dan?" He sat down and told me about his idea for a new vocal group. He also explained that there had been some contact with a manager, and in the not too distant future there would probably be a showcase performance at a local club to obtain a record deal. He asked me if I'd be interested in being the keyboard player. The idea appealed to me, but there was some hesitation on my part as I was comfortable doing sessions and other pick-up dates. If I committed to this project, there was no certainty that there would be any immediate money, or that it would be a hit at all.

Armed with that knowledge, I had a decision to make, considering I had a wife and new house to take care of. Danny told me to think about it and let him know my decision. I rolled another joint and discussed the infinite possibilities of this new venture with Lee.

Lee's theory was that it was all speculation, and that there were no guarantees. That was a valid point, but still a little voice in me said, *What the fuck? Go for it!* The change would be good, and I believed very strongly in the already assembled talent. Besides, if things didn't pan out, I could always do sessions or form another group.

So, after a mere twenty minutes of intense vacillating, I got off the couch and walked over to Danny's house. His door was already open, so I just walked in and found him on the phone in his music room.

"Count me in!" I exclaimed, then asked "What's the next move?"

He was already on the phone to Cory and set up a meeting for the three of them and me to go over some song ideas the following night. Danny also asked me to tap into my vast repertoire of songs to see if there was anything suitable for this new group. I ran back down the stairs and headed toward my house, where I spent the remainder of that day sifting through numerous albums — both domestic and imported — in hopes of finding the perfect song.

The next night I met with Danny, Chuck, and Cory, and we began listening to various tunes that everybody had brought. If we came across one that we especially liked, I would position myself at Danny's electric piano and pound out a rough arrangement while they harmonized. Besides working on the already recorded "It's For You," one of the earliest songs we worked up was a tune by the Rascals called "If You Knew." This musical marriage was already far exceeding anyone's expectations. We set out to find some other compatible musicians to round out the group. Cory said that he knew a bass player named Joe Schermie, who had worked with him in the short-lived Cory Wells Blues Band in Phoenix. He called up Joe, proposed the idea to him, and said that if he accepted, Joe could stay at his house until he found a place of his own. Joe agreed almost without hesitation and said he would be out the next day.

I suggested Ron Morgan, the excellent guitar player who had worked with me in Superband and the West Coast Pop Art Experimental Band. I found out by calling my old friend, Stacey London (she had since forgiven me for being so rude to her in Colorado), that Ron was living in Hollywood and was looking for something to get into. I called him up and let him talk to Danny, who set up a meeting with him.

The next night was my first meeting with Joe Schermie. Right off the bat, I could tell he had a loud and boisterous personality that bordered on the obnoxious. One thing he did possess, however, was an amazing sense of rhythm, deeply rooted in Latin music. This was a holdover from the days that he worked in various bars in the Phoenix area with the all-Mexican Jordan Brothers Band. He brought in his bass guitar from the car, along with his suitcase. Those seemed to be his only possessions, and he was ready to take Cory up on his offer of a temporary place to crash. He plugged his bass into Danny's small practice amp and began running through a plethora of various riffs and rhythms. It was an infectious beat that he was laying down. I quickly joined in, and we immediately began to improvise on a tune right on the spot. Danny looked at me, and then at the other singers, and nodded his approval. With that, I quickly taught Joe the rough chord structure to a song that we were considering.

After a few minutes, Danny, Chuck, and Cory joined in, and I distinctly remember stopping the song midway through it, totally blown away by what was developing. Everyone else was equally impressed with the chemistry of the five of us. We played around for a few more hours, then decided to call it a night. Our plan was to get together the following night, with the addition of Ron.

When Ron arrived the next evening, we set up our equipment in Danny's music room, and he and Joe and I launched into an extended jam. The things that were coming out of just the three musicians were raw and powerful, yet subtle and tasty. Ron picked up on the chords to one of the songs, as Joe had done the previous night, and once again, with the three singers joining in, the product was almost staggering. It sent shivers up my spine. Ron and Joe both agreed to sign on and give this yet-unnamed band a shot. (Although tentatively named "Redwood," when the songs recorded with Brian Wilson left, so did the name.) The only thing missing now was the drummer.

Danny suggested the drummer who had played on the demo of "It's For You" that Van Dyke Parks had produced. I don't recall his name, but I remember that he was a session player from Florida. He was technically a good drummer, but he had a tendency to overplay. He thought he had to put in some incredibly fast "fill" every other bar. After deliberating for a while, we decided that he wouldn't be right for us. Cory had kept a list of musicians that he had either worked with or that had been referred to him. He mentioned a drummer named Barry that a friend of his had said was excellent. He called him up and asked him about auditioning for the group. Barry had a family and a real job: he drove a 7-Up delivery truck.

He played drums as a second source of income and had done various rock sessions, although his roots were firmly planted in jazz.

Since Danny's music room was way too small for a full band to set up, we decided to rent a small rehearsal space in Hollywood. We found a place that suited our needs: Rainbow Studios, which in actuality was a dance studio by day. It was located upstairs in a building on the corner of Vine and Yucca streets in Hollywood.

Danny, Cory, and Chuck sat back while Ron, Joe, Barry, and I jammed for a while. We then went through the procedure of teaching Barry a few tunes, and shortly thereafter, the singers joined in. As a drummer, Barry seemed to be competent enough, but he lacked musical aggressiveness. For my taste, he just didn't play hard enough. That was probably due to his heavy jazz background. Nevertheless, he signed on, and we were now a complete seven-piece unit.

The next week Danny called me up and told me that there was a meeting at our newly acquired manager's office. I got in my car and drove to 211 South Beverly Drive, in Beverly Hills. That was the location of the management offices of Reb Foster and Associates. Their other clients at the time made up an impressive list of hit-makers, including the Turtles and Steppenwolf.

I had indirectly met Reb Foster many times in the past. He was the program director for the top-rated radio station in Los Angeles, KRLA. Prior to that, he was the owner of a nightclub in Redondo Beach, called the Revelaire, where I had worked with Michael Lloyd in our various surf bands. Also at that same time, the house band at Reb's club was the Crossfires, whom Michael and I shared the bill with at a "Battle of the Bands" at the Santa Monica Civic Auditorium. Ironically, my next-door neighbor, Jim Pons, was the bass player for the Crossfires, who had long since changed their names to the Turtles.

When I arrived at the office, I was led into a spacious conference room. I took a seat and waited for everyone else to arrive. When the meeting was about to begin, two older gentlemen entered the room and sat down. They were both very distinctive looking. One of them was neatly dressed in a three-piece, pin-striped suit. His hair was short but well-groomed, and he had a goatee that was an obvious holdover from the beatnik era. His name was Bill Utley, and I soon came to find out that he was the mastermind and brains behind the company. The other gentleman was slightly overweight, wore glasses, and had a very abrasive attitude. He almost reminded me of a Mafia hit-man. His name was Burt Jacobs. He was the "muscle" of the organization, and possessed a volatile temper. Later on, his ability to negotiate a hard bargain would help secure deals for the group. He had a take it or leave it attitude: "If you want Steppenwolf, you have to take Three Dog Night."

Even though the company was named after Reb Foster, we soon found out that it was in name only, as his expertise was his rapport with various disc jockeys and programmers. This would come in handy when it came time to get our records played. Bill did most of the talking at that initial meeting, plotting out his strategy for turning us into a hit group. He knew that until things got off the ground, he would have to bankroll us for a while, and he informed us that he wasn't adverse to doing so. The first thing that he had to do was to get us in front of an audience. As a group, we had to concentrate on our various functions and learn enough material for a set.

While Burt and Bill searched for the appropriate venue, the rest of us got antsy. We decided at first to take matters into our own hands, to put some immediate money in our pockets by auditioning at a couple of local clubs. Quickly we threw together a rough set of about four or five tunes. The first place at which we auditioned was a bowling alley called the Carolina Lanes, near the L.A. Airport. I got a good laugh when I found out that we were trying out there, because I had played there years earlier with Dave and Mike Dowd, and knew that it was a topless bar. We went in, set up our instruments, and without any introduction, began playing some of our songs. The owner quickly came up to Cory and complained that the girls were having trouble dancing — or should I say bouncing their tits — to the unfamiliar tunes that we were playing. Taking a cue from Cory, we began playing Cream's "Sunshine of Your Love." This fared a little better, but actually the whole thing was quite depressing, because no one was paying attention to our music. Everyone involved mutually agreed that we wouldn't be the right kind of band to play at such a prestigious place as that.

A few nights later, we had an audition at a long-forgotten club in Long Beach. We got there and found out that we had to drag our instruments up a long flight of stairs. We set up and began to play, and almost immediately I could tell by the expression on the owner's face that he wasn't impressed. He cut us off after a few tunes and said that we sounded good, but we didn't play any Top 40 songs. Until we did so, he said, we probably wouldn't have any success. Discouraged, we broke down our equipment, schlepped it back down the stairs, and went home.

Burt called with some good news a few days later. He had a show for us at a real club. We were to open for the Standells at the Ice House in Pasadena. In the past, this had primarily been known as a folk club, but the owners were desperately trying to breathe new life into it by changing formats.

A wave of excitement ran through the entire band, and we rehearsed diligently for our debut. Now we had the serious problem of coming up with a name. Everyone sat around Danny's living room with pieces of paper, writing things down and throwing names out for the others' approval or disapproval. However, we couldn't seem to agree on anything, and as the date was approaching fast, Bill took the bull by the horns and said, "For the sake of this show, to get some advertisement, just call yourself 'Tricycle.' " It was almost a forgone conclusion that the management wanted us to have a name that would reflect the use of three lead vocalists, which would be our main selling point, so for one night only, we were "Tricycle."

The show at the Ice House was basically uneventful, as the audience consisted of only a handful of friends of both bands. Not even the Standells' fame from their 1966 hit "Dirty Water" could draw a sizable crowd. The rockers apparently didn't know that the club had changed musical formats from folk to rock. And besides, Pasadena was a long way from Hollywood.

Until another club date came in, we began to "sit in" at various afterhours clubs in Hollywood. One of the best ones was the Red Velvet, a club Cory and I had frequented in our Sunset Strip band days. The lack of anything tangible happening with the group was quickly discouraging Barry. Deep down we knew that he longed for the comfort and financial security of his old job, which was understandable since he had a large family to support. He called Danny one day and said that he didn't think that things were working out, and that nothing would probably come of our project anyway. He informed Danny that he was quitting Tricycle and going back to delivering 7-Up.

This turned out to be a beneficial move for us, since by now everyone shared my opinion that his playing wasn't strong enough for the direction in which we were heading. We immediately started hanging out at the various nightspots in hopes that we'd hear a great drummer and be able to snag him. Once again, Cory heard through the musical grapevine some rumblings about an incredible black drummer who worked with a group called Heatwave, from Canada. We found out that they played a lot at the Red Velvet but weren't due to return there for another couple of weeks. However, after investigating a little more thoroughly, Cory discovered that Heatwave was playing at a club called the Carousel in Ventura, California, which was about forty-five miles north of Los Angeles.

We all agreed to meet at the club and check out this so-called "incredible" drummer. When we walked in, Heatwave was just finishing their first set of the evening. In the last few seconds of the song they were playing, I zeroed-in on the drummer and thought to myself, *This guy is incredible!* In that short time, I could tell that he had a very unorthodox way of playing, and although I knew it couldn't be possible, he seemed to be somehow hitting his high hat and snare drum at the same time with the same drumstick.

Everybody ordered a drink and waited for the next set. About halfway into the first song, Danny turned to me and whispered, "This guy's a bitch!" Joe was especially knocked out by the drummer's unique rhythms. They were almost African sounding, and with his unusual style, it sounded like two drummers were playing at the same time.

We all agreed that we had to have him in the group. After they took a break, Cory went over to the drummer, introduced himself, and brought him back to our table. He introduced the drummer to us as Floyd Sneed, and he sat down. "I hear you have a proposition for me," he addressed to no one in particular. Danny, being the early spokesman for the group, ran down all of the ideas to Floyd and highlighted the prospect of possibly being signed by a major record label. Although we were sure that Floyd wouldn't want to give up his comfortable club gig for something that right now was still very uncertain, we still pressed the issue. Floyd thanked us for our interest in him and said that he would have to think about it and get back to us. We all left the club hoping that a miracle would take place: that he would accept our offer.

A few days later, Danny called to inform me that a miracle had indeed happened. Floyd had just called him to say that he had quit Heatwave and was ready to forge ahead with us into the unknown.

With the addition of a hot new drummer, we had assembled the ultimate septet: Cory Wells, Danny Hutton, Chuck Negron, Ron Morgan, Joe Schermie, Floyd Sneed, and myself. Our personal and musical chemistry all seemed to click instantly, and we were ready to rock and roll!

Things began to happen quite rapidly then. We had to seriously come up with a name that the whole world would remember. We set up rehearsals at Rainbow Studios once again and began to work out our growing repertoire.

Throughout this whole time, everyone kept coming up with what they thought was the perfect name, only to find out after close inspection that their ideas were basically lame. I had discovered that Danny shared the same passion for science fiction and fantasy that I did, and we began to search through our libraries of books in hopes of finding the perfect moniker. But alas, once we put our ideas on paper, they seemed inappropriate and too far out in left field. After all, who would buy a rock record from a band calling themselves "The Martian Chronicles"?

Then one night, when we were all over at Danny's house, sitting around the fireplace, his girlfriend, June Fairchild, stumbled across an article in *Mankind* magazine about the Australian Aborigines. While we were wrapped up in our own little world of trying to find the perfect name, June began reading aloud from the article. Suddenly, everyone stopped what they were doing and looked up and said to her, "Read that part again!" She recounted the paragraph she had been reading about the various tribes who lived in the Outback and dug holes in the ground and slept with dogs for warmth, since they did not possess personal items like blankets or clothing. We listened intently when she came to the part about the slang term used for this particular survival procedure. According to the article, the phrase "three dog night" signified the coldest weather conditions and the number of canine sleeping partners required for warmth.

We kept repeating those words over and over to ourselves, each of us imagining the name on an album cover or a club marquee. That was it — our search was over! Right then and there, we christened ourselves "Three Dog Night."

# 7 / Celebrate!

Shortly after finding our group name, Burt Jacobs called Danny and told him that we had our first official gig at the Whiskey as Three Dog Night. Everyone was beside themselves with anxiety and anticipation. It was a homecoming of sorts for Cory and me, since we had played there dozens of times with other groups. We also had a good rapport with the owner, Elmer Valentine; his partner, Mario; the various bouncers, including our friend Don Stroud; and, of course, all the waitresses.

We rehearsed intensely to come up with the best possible rock and roll set that would kick L.A. in the butt. Our song line-up included "It's For You," "If You Knew," two Johnny "Guitar" Watson songs that Cory had found — "Nobody" and "Find Someone To Love" — and his tribute to Otis Redding, our cover version of "Try a Little Tenderness," which was destined to be the showstopper.

A few nights prior to the show, we all drove down Sunset Strip to stare at our name on the marquee and to take pictures of it. Although we had the opening slot for a local favorite band — Group Therapy, which included singer/songwriter Ray Kennedy (who later cowrote the Beach Boys' song "Sail On Sailor") — and our name was in small letters on the marque, it nevertheless impressed the hell out of us.

When the night of the show came, the band arrived at the club extra early. There was already a line forming outside. Since nobody knew who we were, we assumed that they were all Group Therapy fans.

As we all paced around in the dressing room with first-night jitters, Cory and I were experiencing a unique sense of déjà vu. For the two of us it was just like coming back home again. We were all bound and determined to go on stage and totally blow away everyone. To calm myself down a bit I ordered a double Black Russian from one of the waitresses and slammed it down in a matter of seconds. By the time we hit the stage, I had a nice little buzz going.

We opened the show with the extremely up-tempo and frantic "Find Someone To Love." From that moment on, everybody's eyes in the audience were totally riveted on the stage. Even the waitresses, who were quite blasé about seeing groups on stage, stopped dead in their tracks to listen to this incredible new band. We knew we had them in the palm of our hands.

The one unfortunate thing we discovered that night was that Ron had incredible stage fright. This was something that had never surfaced when he had played with me in other bands. When it came time for his guitar solos, he would either not play what he had in rehearsal or would completely hide behind his amplifier. This took everyone by surprise, and was actually quite disturbing. I thought to myself that maybe it was just opening-night jitters. But if it wasn't, we had a potential problem on our hands. Still, by the time Cory started "Try a Little Tenderness," everybody in the audience was on their feet cheering.

We finished off the set and received our first real standing ovation. We had to do an encore. The only problem was, we didn't know any other songs! So, being the professionals we were, we made one up on the spot. What we came up with that night was the basis for the song "Jam," which later appeared on our 1971 album, *Harmony*.

When we came off the stage, drenched in sweat, everybody was incredibly psyched up, and the amount of adrenaline pumping through our bodies was immeasurable. The various members of Group Therapy were standing backstage with rather shocked looks on their faces. When I walked by one of them, he said to me, "Great show man!" I thanked him, and thought to myself, *OK, motherfucker —your turn. Try and follow that!* On the way back to the dressing room, Danny pulled me aside and asked me what was wrong with Ron. I told him I didn't know, but that he'd probably be all right at the next night's show.

We once again arrived early the following night and saw a

larger line in front of the Whiskey. News traveled fast in Hollywood, and the word was already on the street that there was a hot new band playing there. We took the stage and did a carbon copy of the previous night's show. About halfway through the set, as I looked out to the audience, I could see that there were many famous musicians in attendance checking us out. At one table I noticed Eric Clapton sitting with a group of people. Between songs I did something that, in retrospect, I realize I shouldn't have done. I went over and told Ron to play like he had never played before, because Clapton was in the audience. When the spotlight hit him for his solo, Ron's spot on the stage was bare! Not only had he run behind his amp, as he had done the night before, but he was crouching down so low that you could hardly see him at all! I could tell that he was genuinely frightened. Once again Cory brought the house down with "Try a Little Tenderness," and we finished the set to yet another standing ovation.

The first night of the engagement, Group Therapy had come off like a poor man's Vanilla Fudge. Every song was played at a snail's pace and sounded like a funeral dirge. Their showstopper was supposed to be a pop version of the song "Exodus." But, compared to our up-tempo bombardment, they almost succeeded in putting the audience to sleep. The second night, we found that they had drastically changed their set. They tried to inject some enthusiasm into their playing, but fell just short of boredom.

When we went back into the dressing room, Bill and Burt were there, bubbling over with excitement. It seems that we had, in forty-eight hours, accomplished the unaccomplishable. We had taken L.A. by storm and were suddenly a hot property. This would virtually guarantee us a record deal. Also, they informed us that Elmer was so knocked out, and had such a positive response from the audience, that he was going to put us on a co-headlining bill later in the month with a San Francisco band called It's a Beautiful Day. After that, Elmer told Burt and Bill that we could headline. We were on Cloud Nine, but we had one major immediate problem: Ron.

The next day, Danny called Cory and Chuck, and then me, to discuss what to do about the situation. We all agreed that it wasn't working out with Ron. Although he was an excellent player in rehearsals, when he got in front of an audience he went from Dr. Jekyll to Mr. Hyde. As his friend, I felt obligated to talk to him to find out what the problem was. I never did fully understand the reason. When it came right down to it, I guess he was just afraid of the pressure of success on a large scale. The next day, everybody mutually agreed that it wasn't working out, and that Ron had to go. We were temporarily left without a guitar player. We had to act fast to find somebody new, as we had only three weeks until our next show at the Whiskey.

Joe had already moved out of Cory's place and had found a little efficiency unit at the Vine Street Motel at the corner of Yucca and Vine, across from Rainbow Studios. When we got together the next day to go over a few songs, Joe mentioned that a band from Northern California was living and rehearsing at the motel. He said the band was only 0K, but the guitar player was great. Maybe we should give him a listen, Joe suggested, and perhaps lure him over to our camp. Danny and I went over to Joe's and then walked next door to a vacant building where this band was rehearsing. Joe was correct in his evaluation. The guitar player was right on the money. When they took a break, Danny went over and introduced himself. Then Joe and I went over and were introduced to Michael Allsup.

Michael and the band, called Family Scandal, were from Modesto, California. Once again, I had proof of what a small world it really is. He informed me that we indirectly knew each other. His band was in town to record, and somehow they had hooked up with my old friend Kim Fowley. The song that Kim gave them to learn was a tune that I had written years earlier, called "October Country." It had already been a local hit by a band of the same name.

Danny ran down the whole story about Ron and all of the things that were going on, and Michael seemed very interested. He said he would have to think about it and get back to us the next day, as he felt obligated to his friends. The next day Mike called Danny and said that he'd like to give it a try. We set up rehearsals at Rainbow Studios across the street and taught him a few of the songs that we were doing. After a couple of run-throughs, the chemistry seemed so natural that we all were sold.

That night, Michael was scheduled to have a rehearsal with Family Scandal. But instead, he was going to tell them that he was quitting to join us. Since a few of the members had been working with him for a long time, they had a certain closeness and felt hurt and betrayed by his decision. One member was so pissed off that he hauled off and slugged Michael. With that as a farewell present, Family Scandal broke up.

We booked rehearsal time and spent hours fine-tuning the set with our newest band member. Things were falling into place quickly, and we were now playing with the precision of a well-oiled machine.

When the night of our next Whiskey engagement arrived, we

were ready to meet the challenge. Several people told us that San Francisco bands had an intense rivalry with L.A. bands and were pretty jaded. Armed with that information, we took the stage and were ready to decimate It's a Beautiful Day the same way we had destroyed Group Therapy.

In the short period of time between the last engagement and this, something wonderful had happened: We had gained a growing legion of fans and groupies. Among them were the GTOs (Girls Together Outrageously), who were the proteges of Frank Zappa. With the debut of Michael in the band, we went out and played like a house on fire. The audience was at a fever pitch, and their enthusiasm just drove us even harder. Michael confirmed on stage that he was the missing link in the band. We were now a complete seven-man unit.

When we came off stage, the leader of It's a Beautiful Day, David LaFlame, was standing there. As we walked by him, he didn't say a word, only nodded. Since they had just signed a recording deal with Columbia Records, they were feeling rather full of themselves. However, that night we took the wind out of their sails!

Once again, Bill and Burt were in the dressing room after the show with some wonderful news. They had arranged a showcase at the Troubadour for some of the major record label execs to come and check us out. They had already generated some interest with the people at Steppenwolf's label, ABC/Dunhill.

Dunhill was a relatively small label but had an incredible track record. It was founded in the mid-'60s by Lou Adler and some other business partners. Their first success was "Eve of Destruction" by Barry McGuire, followed by numerous hits by the Grass Roots and the Mamas and the Papas, whom Lou Adler personally produced.

Things happened quickly. We were so young and full of energy that it seemed we could do no wrong, and would soon have the world at our feet. When the night of our showcase arrived, we were slightly nervous, but confident enough to deliver an incredible show. The performance went well, beyond anybody's expectations.

Bill Utley went to the office early the next morning to start making phone calls. Later that day, he told Danny that everyone in attendance was so knocked out that there was a bidding war going on between the labels. Ultimately, Dunhill offered the strongest deal and won out. It seemed only natural, since we shared the same management with Steppenwolf, that we should also share the same label. Danny, Chuck, and Cory, along with Bill and Burt and their lawyer, set up a meeting with Dunhill president Jay Lasker to finalize the contract.

Upon signing, we started to receive our first national press in the music industry trade magazines. Our next concern was finding a suitable producer and selecting material for our debut album.

Dunhill had a stable of staff producers and suggested that we try Steve Barry, who had produced the Grass Roots. Steve was also a songwriter. Having co-written "Eve of Destruction" and the Grass Roots' "Where Were You When I Needed You?," he figured that he could not only give us material but would be right to produce us as well. He gave us a few demos of songs that he had, and we learned them. We then went into the Dunhill Studios on Beverly Boulevard, behind their offices, and began recording. After listening to the playback, and later going home and discussing it, everyone agreed that although Barry was competent, the material and his production were just too light for our raw, aggressive musical tastes.

The guys had another meeting with Jay Lasker, and they convinced him to scrap the material and look for a more suitable producer. While somebody more compatible was being sought, we continued to play dates at the Whiskey to packed houses. In this way, we fine-tuned our songs and got them ready for recording.

In June 1968, Bill and Burt really had something to celebrate, as their other group, Steppenwolf, had a runaway hit with their first single, the now-classic "Born To Be Wild." The sheer power of that song impressed Danny and the rest of the guys. They made a phone call to Jay Lasker, and after some discussion he suggested that we try out Steppenwolf's producer, Gabriel Meckler.

We set up a meeting at our management office to discuss with Gabriel the possibility of working together. He was an instantly likable, easy-going young man, who was Hungarian born and classically trained on the piano. Knowing that, he had my vote. Everybody decided to give it a try, and we agreed to meet at his house to listen to some demos. He suggested that if anybody had any tunes they especially liked, to bring them along. Everyone set about trying to find the perfect pop song. Although we knew that we'd keep some of the songs we were playing in the set, we also realized that some of them wouldn't make it on record.

For the next few months, we sat at Danny's or at Gabriel's house, going through numerous demos that had been sent to the management office. We continued to do more shows around the L.A. area and were starting to get bookings once or twice a month at the Earl Warren Showgrounds in Santa Barbara. There we would usually share the bill with two or three major groups. And every time we appeared, the same thing that happened at the Whiskey would transpire here as well. Pretty soon a lot of the bands didn't want to follow us because of our incredibly exciting stage performances.

While we were still searching for material, I began to bask in my sudden local rise to fame. Much to Lee's disdain, I was turning into quite the party animal and rock and roll social climber. I especially remember one night, when I was at Neil Young's place in Topanga Canyon, with Neil and Danny Whitten (a member of Neil's band, Crazy Horse). I had dropped some incredibly intense acid that night, and Neil and Danny were stoned on their own personal drug of choice. We sat around playing music and talking until after midnight. When I left Neil's place, I got into my car and headed for the Santa Monica Freeway to get back home. By then the acid was so intense that the lights on the freeway all seemed to be strung together. In my eyes, the glow became one long line; I couldn't see the individual lights. In addition to that, they cast incredibly long shadows. For the life of me, I couldn't see where the off ramp was!

I was scared to death that if I tried to exit the freeway, I might go over a guardrail and kill myself. So, I kept on going, down the Santa Monica Freeway, until it turned into the Harbor Freeway interchange. When I went back around, to the Hollywood Freeway over to the Valley, and then back to the Ventura Freeway until I once again reached the Topanga Canyon exit on the Valley side. I was afraid to get off anywhere. I thought to myself, *I'm going to do this until I either run out of gas or I come down from the acid trip.* Obviously, I ran out of gas first. I went to a callbox and phoned AAA, which was an experience in itself. Incidents like this were beginning to happen to me all the time.

The selection of material was coming along quite well, and with the holidays approaching we decided to take a break to be with our families. When we resumed work in early 1969, we had the songs narrowed down to what would become the best possible debut album. Gabriel came to rehearsals every day to lend his ideas, but basically he let us have free reign to arrange the songs ourselves.

Each of the three singers picked tunes that showcased their individual voices and varied musical backgrounds. Cory had already opted to do "Nobody," "Find Somebody To Love," and our showstopper, "Try a Little Tenderness." We also worked up a tune by one his favorite composers, Randy Newman, called "Bet No One Ever Hurt This Bad." Chuck brought in the debut album, *Aerial Ballet*, by a new RCA artist named Harry Nilsson. There was a song on it entitled "One" that he thought would be perfect. He also opted to do the Tim Harden ballad, "Don't Make Promises." To showcase the combined harmonies of the three singers, we of course included "It's For You," which — in a bold move for that time — was almost entirely done a cappella. Having an affinity for British rock, I suggested to Danny that we try another rather bold move and cover a tune that was currently on a hit album that I was into. With that we chose the Steve Winwood–Jim Capaldi song, "Heaven is in Your Mind," from Traffic's brilliant first album. Danny Whitten played us an impressive tune he had written, called "Let Me Go." We loved it, and decided to include that as a group song on the album.

Our only problem was that we didn't have a suitable tune to showcase Danny's fine pop voice. Although Danny was content to be part of the overall picture, he still needed a song to call his own. The opportunity quickly came our way one day while we were rehearsing at the Whiskey. Neil Young came down and played Danny a tune he had just finished writing, called "The Loner." He said that he was thinking of recording it himself, but that we were welcome to do our version of it.

In Gabriel's opinion, we were just one song short of a complete album. He suggested that since we had set up a pattern of taking current or previously established songwriters' material and reinterpreting it, that we try and cover a song on the Band's debut album, *Music From Big Pink*. After listening to the album, we mutually agreed to do a song that would showcase my talents. We chose the tune "Chest Fever," which opened with a lengthy, almost classical-sounding organ solo, by the Band's Garth Hudson. I took the album home, listened to it a few times, and came back to rehearsal the next day with my interpretation of the song. Everyone was knocked out, and the selection was complete.

We rehearsed day and night until the songs were second nature to us. Gabriel set up time at American Recording on Ventura Boulevard, where he had done the now incredibly successful Steppenwolf albums, and arranged for us to meet his engineers, Ritchie Podolor and Bill Cooper. On the first day of recording, we arrived there early in the morning to set up the equipment and start getting various sounds. Ritchie and Bill were buzzing around the place like flies on shit. Being in a studio was nothing new to myself or the three singers, but Floyd, Michael, and Joe, the rookies, found this whole initial process quite fascinating.

For the recording, Ritchie informed me that I would use his Steinway piano and the old Hammond B-3 organ that he had used on Steppenwolf's records. In a few hours everything was set, and we were ready to start recording the first track. Everyone was so excited, and things were progressing so well, that within two days we had literally finished recording. Gabriel went for an almost live sound. The band did only a minimal amount of takes on each song, and the singers sometimes recorded their vocal parts at the same time, thus creating a very spontaneous feeling.

After a few days of mixing the tunes, everyone, including management and record label personnel, was called into the studio to listen. From the moment the "play" button was pressed on the recorder until the time it stopped after the eleventh song, everyone sat motionless, totally mesmerized by what was coming over the speakers. When it was over, we all let out a hearty yell of approval!

We were convinced that we were on the verge of something really big. In order to rush the album out, we had to get the artwork and photography done as quickly as possible. Once again Jay Lasker came to our rescue, suggesting that we use photographer Ed Caraeff, who had already shot a number of the groups for the label. We met with Ed, and he decided that in keeping with the spontaneous feeling of the album, we should use performance shots. A few days later, when we were doing a show at the Whiskey, Ed came in and began clicking away throughout the entire set. By the end of the following week, after everyone's approval, he assembled a collage of live shots that were perfect for the album cover.

Dunhill's art department set about doing their job, while the finished masters of the record were rushed over to a company called the Mastering Lab in Hollywood. Within a few days, we had our first test pressing of the album and the finished artwork. With everyone's unanimous approval, it was completed and rush released. What had been a dream a few short months before was suddenly a reality.

As the first single, Dunhill chose the driving rocker "Nobody." Through our loyal legions of local fans, and Reb Foster's radio contacts, it became an L.A. radio staple, climbing into the local Top 10. Although we had been playing up and down the California coast and were rapidly gaining a large following, it wasn't enough to push the record high on the national charts. It only reached the mid-'70s before it began to fall off. We never became discouraged, because we had a wealth of other material on the album from which to choose. And besides, there weren't too many local bands that had achieved what we did in such a short amount of time and broke the Top 100 with their first single release.

As "Nobody" began to plummet on the charts, Dunhill immediately chose a second single, "Try a Little Tenderness." In order to service the record properly, we had to mount a national promotional tour. If we could get our music out to the masses, we were sure to gain wider acceptance. What resulted next only seemed like a natural progression.

Bill and Burt arranged for us to be the opening act on Steppenwolf's first major U.S. tour. As they were now a bona fide supergroup and were playing to audiences in the thousands every night, we jumped at this prospect. It seemed logical, since both Dunhill and Reb Foster and Associates had a vested interest in both bands. Things began to take off for us rapidly at that point. We now had to hire roadies and a tour manager — truly the big time!

The first night of the tour was in Portland, Oregon, at the 10,000-seat coliseum. To keep our costs low on the road, we had to sleep three to a room, which meant that someone always had to flip for the roll-away bed. We didn't seem to care, because this was all so new and fresh that we were just soaking up everything that was thrown our way. When we took the stage that first night, everyone was completely overwhelmed by the size of the audience. We had to realize that practically nobody in the Northwest had ever heard of us, except for the handful of people who had bought our first single. To make matters worse, almost the entire crowd had come to hear Steppenwolf, and seemed to be a rather rough bunch of people who openly embraced the "Born To Be Wild" credo.

Knowing that we had our work cut out for us that first night, we took the stage and ripped through our entire album with so much conviction and energy that by the time the set was over, we had gained the respect of Steppenwolf's crowd. They gave us a standing ovation. Although Steppenwolf was riding high with a hit single and album, I think that they were intimidated by our performance.

Suddenly, everything was falling into place for us. Groupies were everywhere. People were handing out accolades like candy. And the best part of it was that wherever we played, the reaction was the same. Within a few weeks, word had gotten back to Dunhill and the management that we were stealing the show from the star performers.

In virtually every town we played, our second single, "Try a Little Tenderness," would go on the local radio playlists the following day. While we were still on the road with Steppenwolf, the single made its debut on the national charts. Because of our continued exposure and high-energy shows, the record reached Number 29. For us, that was great — but still not good enough.

Halfway through the tour, we were dealt a temporary setback. It seemed that everywhere we went we were doing so well and left the audience in such a frenzy that by the time Steppenwolf took the stage, large numbers of people had already left. We were also getting incredible reviews in the local newspapers, while Steppenwolf was not.

John Kay, Steppenwolf's leader, got on the phone to Bill, and in what was probably a good artistic move, decided to have us dumped from the tour. We didn't have to worry, because we now had enough initial clout built up to secure a spot on someone else's tour. Burt Jacobs immediately got on the phone and began making several calls. We returned home, and within several days we were already scheduled to open for Vanilla Fudge.

The same thing that happened with Steppenwolf, Group Therapy, and everyone else we had opened for was destined to happen with Vanilla Fudge as well. On the opening night of the tour in Tulsa, Oklahoma, we played with such fierce energy that the Fudge, despite their loyal following and great songs, couldn't generate enough onstage energy to come close to the excitement of our set.

Nevertheless, we became instant comrades with all of the Fudge's group members, who initiated us into the real world of rock and roll with our first orgy that night in Tulsa. Practically everyone (except for Cory and Danny, who remained faithful to their mates) participated in the debauchery. It didn't matter to me that I had a wife waiting for me back home. All I could think about was partying and getting laid, and there was more than enough of that going on. There was something about hundreds of beautiful women throwing themselves at your feet nightly that tended to erase all inhibitions and concern for your apparent homelife.

After the show, both bands had arranged to meet at a club across town that was owned by B. J. Thomas. The great thing about having the opening slot on a tour was that you got to scour the audience for potential fun seekers and make your exit with them long before the headliners' set was over. On this particular night, everyone stayed to see the Fudge but had already spent a good portion of time setting up rendezvous with various groupies. We left before their last number, so that we could get to the club first with our newly acquired bimbos and start the evening's hedonistic revelry.

As soon as we drove up to the club, I knew that we were totally out of our element. About seventy-five percent of the vehicles in the parking lot were mud-caked pick-up trucks with gun racks. When we walked in, my suspicions were immediately confirmed. There was nothing but a sea of cowboy hats connected to pairs of cowboy boots with a redneck sandwiched in between. As we strolled in with our entourage, all eyes were upon us. We were already getting quite a favorable reputation on the road, and the club owner immediately came up to us and did everything short of kissing our asses. He ushered us over to a table where a group of locals were sitting with their girlfriends, and informed them that they would have to vacate the table because it was reserved for us.

As we sat down, I immediately snagged a waitress, sat her down on my lap, and promptly ordered a double Black Russian. The other band members placed their orders, and within minutes, the party was going. People started to get up and bump and grind on the dance floor, much to the chagrin of the cowboys. However, I noticed that some of their girlfriends were definitely giving us the eye. A few of them were exceptionally pretty, but I wanted to remain in one piece that evening, so I resisted the temptation to approach them.

About half an hour later, the Fudge came in and sat down. Carmine Appice and Chuck immediately started drinking shots of something and singing old New York rock and roll songs. They were obviously from the same area and had a lot in common. Mark Stein, the organist, was rather quiet and kept to himself, although he did have a girl on each arm. Their guitar player, Vinnie, wasn't there, but we were told that he was preparing a little surprise for us back at the hotel. The other band member, bassist Timmy Bogert, was as crazy as I was, and he demonstrated his ability with equal amounts of insanity and abandonment. In a very short time, the drinks were flowing freely, and clothes were being shed by the various partygoers.

All the while, we were totally oblivious to the sarcastic comments being directed at us from across the room. Before too long, various members of each band jumped up on stage and began to jam with the house band. We had the place turned completely upside down, and that was the only invitation that the locals' girlfriends needed. Soon several of them were at our table, joining our merry band of pranksters.

I remember it was getting quite hot in the club, and I moved my chair away from the table and close to the dance floor to get some air. Suddenly, a statuesque and obviously quite drunk blonde sat herself down on my lap and began to undress me. Not missing a beat, I stood up on the dance floor and started to undo her blouse. Everybody at our table was quite amused by my evident lack of inhibitions. Someone signaled that it was time to go back to the hotel, and as quickly as the party had begun, it was on its way out the door.

I was feeling no pain whatsoever. As I walked out the front door of the club toward the parking lot, I noticed that two huge cowboys were standing in front of me. They tried to block my way, and were saying something about the partially clothed tramp who was with me. In my current state, I couldn't comprehend anything that was going on, so I just pushed my way through them and suddenly felt something cold and wet on the back of my head. They had dumped their drinks on me, hoping to start a fight. But at that very moment, Floyd, who was quite intimidating and had arms like tree trunks, jumped in between me and the cowboys. He pushed me and the girl into the parking lot and said, "Get into the van, I'll take care of this." A few seconds later he reappeared with a smile on his face. "No problem," he said, "just a little misunderstanding." I didn't even want to know what happened.

We got back to the hotel and headed to our rooms. The doors to about three or four other rooms were wide open, and inside was the sound of a lot of female voices and loud music.

"What's going on?" I asked.

"Oh, those are our rooms, and we're entertaining a few of our close friends," Timmy replied.

Floyd, Joe, and I went back to my room and smoked a joint, and then freshened up. I had completely forgotten about the bimbo I had come back with. I figured she must have gone into one of the Fudge's rooms. At this point, Michael was looking a little blue. I discovered early on in our relationship that he really couldn't hold his liquor. All the way back to the hotel he had his head hanging out of the window, puking down the side of the van.

I lit a stick of incense to disguise the smell of the pot and then opened my door. As soon as I did that, two groupies invited themselves in. Before I knew what hit me, one of them was down on her knees, giving me head. The other one was servicing Joe. All the time this was happening, our door was wide open. After the girl was finished, she quickly disappeared into another room. I thought to myself, *This has fucking got to be heaven!* I pulled my pants up and went in search of her.

It seemed that every room I walked into, there were various sets of people engaged in any number of sexual acts. Naked bodies were everywhere — on the beds, on the floors, in the bathtub, on the toilet seats, and on top of the dressers. As I was walking out of one room and into another, I noticed a good-looking, delicate pair of feet sticking up in the air. I walked over to see who they belonged to and discovered one of the techs from Vanilla Fudge screwing the girl who had been with me at the club. "Just checking," I said. "Carry on."

I entered another room where a similar scene was being repeated. I walked up to one girl to ask her something, and realized as I was talking to her that she had obviously just taken on everybody in the entire room. Just then somebody yelled, "Switch!" in a loud voice. And, like a game of musical chairs at a nudist colony, male and female bodies were seen running in all directions, in search of new partners.

In a short while, the Fudge announced that they had a late plane to catch and had to leave. Within minutes, they were packed and had vanished into the night. The orgy was winding down, and my head was spinning. I barely made it back to my room, and passed out just as the sun was coming up. When I awoke some hours later, the events of that evening were just a memory. The only thing that remained were the disheveled beds, soiled towels, and the pungent aroma of sex. We had now been officially initiated into the world of rock and roll.

The tour progressed, and although nothing quite as outrageous as that night in Tulsa occurred again, the booze and women continued to flow freely. The tour ended two or three weeks later, and we headed home for some rehearsals before embarking on another cross-country trip.

As the chart life of "Try a Little Tenderness" was winding down, Dunhill announced that it was getting incredible airplay and response in the Northwest to another song on the album. The tune "One," which Chuck had picked, in the record company's estimation was destined to become a smash hit. They rush released it as a single, and we took off on another tour. Over the course of the next few months, we broke new ground and played so many incredible shows in so many incredible cities that it would be impossible to cite just one.

We went for the first time to San Francisco and played the Fillmore West and the Avalon Ballroom. We played the Kinetic Playground and the Aragon Ballroom in Chicago. From there we drove nonstop in two station wagons to play an early afternoon set at the Miami Pop Festival, held at Gulf Stream Racetrack. Although it was early in the day and we were tired from the long drive, our enthusiasm and energy were so high that, by all later reports, we stole the whole show.

On our first trip to New York City, we hit the club circuit and did Steve Paul's the Scene and Ungano's. While there, Chuck and I began to hang out with some of his high school buddies from the Bronx. The only hip place to be seen in New York in those days was a restaurant and bar in the Village called Nobody's. This would later be the scene of some outrageous antics. Also while we were in

New York, we headlined our first major East Coast show at the old World's Fair Pavilion in Flushing Meadows, Queens.

Dunhill's intuition proved correct: "One" was becoming a huge hit for us. We made our way back to L.A. and did a series of shows at a club in Torrence called the Bank. There we opened for the likes of Alice Cooper and Deep Purple. It seemed that every time we played we were getting tighter and tighter, and the crowd reaction was borderline hysteria. We continued playing the Whiskey-A-Go-Go with various groups. The most notable pairing was with a new band from Illinois, calling themselves Chicago Transit Authority. Soon after their debut album, they shortened their name to "Chicago." We became instant friends with them as well.

It seemed that we not only had growing legions of fans, but were also gaining mutual respect from our peers as well. A short time later, we took off for the Midwest. I will remember one particular night for the rest of my life. We were doing another festival, this time headlining in Sioux Falls, South Dakota. Just before we were about to go on, somebody came up to Joel Cohen, our tour manager at the time, and handed him a Western Union telegram. He called us over and then opened it up. Dated July 9, 1969, it read: CONGRATULATIONS AS OF TODAY WE HAVE SHIPPED 1 MILLION COPIES OF 'ONE.' IT WAS A LONG TIME COMING BUT THROUGH JOINT AND DEDICATED EFFORTS WE ARE ON OUR WAY." It was signed by Jay Lasker.

Everybody stood there in stunned silence for a moment and then let out a yell. "We've done it!" I said. "We've gone Gold!" I grabbed Floyd and we started dancing around backstage. Everybody else was exhibiting various forms of enthusiasm. We were so excited that we almost missed our cue to go on stage. When we walked out, the roar from the audience was deafening.

Halfway through the set, Cory was so overwhelmed by our accomplishment that he informed the audience what had just happened to us. With that, they let out an even bigger cheer.

We continued doing dates with an incredible new confidence and purpose. Bill Utley called one night and said that, due to our excellent shows at the Fillmore West and our rising superstar status, Bill Graham had called him and wanted us to headline at the Fillmore East. Everyone, especially Chuck — who was the hometown boy — was primed to win over the notoriously difficult and fickle New York crowd. The line-up for the show was to include Santana, Canned Heat, and an unknown local band called Sha Na Na.

The first night of the show we were all standing backstage, talking to various members of the other bands, when Sha Na Na walked in. As the stage door opened, I looked up and thought to myself, *These guys are going to get crucified.* Standing before me was an apparent gang of "greasers" and misfits. Everyone was wearing leather jackets and Chinos and had their hair combed into pompadours with enough "Butch Wax" and Brylcreem to grease the gears of the HMS *Queen Mary.* Not knowing what to expect from them, more than a few people backstage began to snicker. In a matter of minutes, even the most skeptical person would be proved wrong. Those guys went on stage and launched into wonderful cover renditions of every great rock and roll and doo wop song from the late '50s and early '60s. About halfway through the set, the audience was on their feet dancing.

Santana came on next, and it must have been quite a culture shock for them. They had just released their debut album, and despite New York's strong Latin community, the people in attendance that night weren't as responsive to them as they should have been. Still, Santana performed a blistering set of percussion-laden rock. The only low point that evening was having Canned Heat play between Santana and ourselves. Although their infectious blues/boogie tunes went over fairly well, they tended to bore people with their extreme and unnecessary solos and jams.

By the time we came out, the people had been roller-coastered for most of the evening. At first it was hard to get the response that we knew we were capable of getting out of them. But that just meant that we'd have to work a little harder to win them over. Chuck was in all his glory, strutting about the stage like some big man on campus. By the time I started the piano intro to "One," the crowd was ours. Barely taking a break between songs, we hit them with a massive left hook and did an incredible fifteen-minute version of "Try a Little Tenderness" that brought the house down.

As the song ended we stood there for a moment, drenched in sweat underneath the hot stage lights, soaking up that moment of glory, when suddenly from the wings Jay Lasker and some other record company execs walked out on stage carrying Gold singles for "One." We were in total shock. Although we had known about the single's million-selling status, somehow seeing it right before our eyes made it a reality.

Deep down I knew that I would have to alter my modest lifestyle, for things were happening to me way too fast. We returned home after that triumphant tour feeling like conquering heroes. The crowning glory of our initial success became apparent the following week, when I was driving my car down Sunset Strip. I pulled over to the curb near La Cienega Boulevard, and there before my eyes, in all of its splendor, was our very own billboard depicting the debut album. Right then I realized that there was no stopping us.

# 8 / Circle For A Landing

Less than a week after being presented with our Gold record for "One," everyone in the group was notified by the management office that our debut album, *Three Dog Night,* had gone Gold as well. I can't speak for the other members, but when I hung the phone up from receiving this news, I was so overwhelmed that for a few minutes I couldn't even relate to Lee what had happened. Then all of a sudden, as I had in Sioux Falls, I let out a triumphant shout. Suddenly, our name was appearing on a regular basis in the music trade magazines.

Our guarantee for live performances had almost tripled in a few short months. We were now ready to embark on a national headlining tour of our own. But the pressure was on from the record company to record another album before the end of the year. Since we had obviously stumbled across a hit formula, everybody once again went through the process of listening to hours and hours of demos that were now being sent to us by the hundreds.

After a few weeks, we weeded out all of the garbage and selected what we felt would be the strongest tunes for our sophomoric effort. We once again mined Traffic, and decided to do a cover version of Dave Mason's "Feelin' Alright?" Danny wanted to re-record a tune that he had written years ago called "Dreaming Isn't Good For You." Cory chose the Sam Cooke classic "A Change is Gonna

Come," as well as "Ain't That a Lot of Love," which was originally recorded by Sam and Dave. One of the biggest Broadway plays at the time was *Hair,* which sparked a lot of controversy for its frankness and unorthodox presentation. In addition, it contained numerous hit-quality songs. Chuck chose the beautiful ballad "Easy To Be Hard" from the show. A tune submitted by Don Preston, called "Circle For a Landing," was perfect for a group vocal, as well as a tune by the songwriting team of Bonner and Gordon. That song, "Celebrate," seemed to reflect everyone's apparent attitude about our success. With Chuck's affinity for New York songwriters, he one day brought in a tune entitled "Eli's Coming," from the second Laura Nyro album, which everyone felt was incredibly strong.

As a rather strange departure, we decided to also record an impromptu drum solo that Floyd had written called "King Solomon's Mines." This was because we now gave him the spotlight in our live shows to show off his unique talents. He would do a ten-minute solo that would wind up with him discarding his drum sticks and finishing with his bare hands. This would always send the audience into a frenzy.

To round out the album, we chose a song that was submitted to us by Dick James Music in London. The cover letter that accompanied the demo stated that here was a song by a new and talented British songwriting team that they thought would be perfect for Three Dog Night. We couldn't have agreed more and decided to record the song "Lady Samantha," by then-unknown Elton John and Bernie Taupin.

After weeks of intense rehearsals, we entered the recording studio and started work on the as-yet-untitled album. Every few days a Dunhill executive would come down to the studio to check our progress. They were getting such an incredible initial response for our new product that before it was even half finished, there were enough advance orders to virtually assure that it would be shipped Gold.

On two of the songs Gabriel decided that he wanted to use horns, so we tapped into our friendship with Chicago and called up their horn section — Walter, James, and Lee — to play on "Feeling Alright?" and "Celebrate." They came in and in a few hours had both written and recorded their horn parts. These guys were definitely pros. To give "Celebrate" more of a party feel, Gabriel also decided to call in a number of background session singers. The effect was perfect, and the end result sounded like opening day at Mardi Gras. The only other outside enhancement on the album was the use of strings on the end of "Easy To Be Hard."

This album was obviously taking a lot longer to record than our debut LP, which we had finished in only two days. Everyone was doing a lot of overdubs, especially myself. I was really getting into the arrangements and creating new keyboard sounds. Ritchie and Bill helped me in that respect, while Danny in particular kicked my butt and tried to get more out of me in a creative sense. At the time I might have resented that, but in retrospect I'm extremely grateful for his — and the other group members' — constant prodding.

Because of the demand, we had to rush release a single. Of the tunes that were already recorded, Dunhill wanted to capitalize on the overwhelming success of *Hair* and chose "Easy To Be Hard." There was an incredible race in the record industry to cover tunes from the play. "Hair" by the Cowsills had already been a huge hit, as well as "Good Morning Starshine" by Oliver, and the peace and love anthem for our generation, "Aquarius/Let the Sunshine In" by the Fifth Dimension. The latter song held the Number One position on the charts for an incredible six weeks — a feat reserved for only a handful of performers in the rock era, and one which many industry insiders felt would never be repeated.

The day the "Easy To Be Hard" single was released, it became the "most added" song on every playlist across the country. In a very short time it was a Top 10 hit. As the album was nearing completion, we selected the title *Suitable For Framing*, and spent a few days with Ed Caraeff discussing different photo ideas. For the centerfold, everyone decided to rent some bizarre costume that might reflect their current personality. Ed scouted some locations and found a lovely wooded area with a stream running through it called Coral Canyon, just off the Pacific Coast Highway, about five miles north of Malibu.

The day before the shoot, we all met in Hollywood at Western Costumes. The result was actually quite hilarious. Chuck picked out a flowing orange satin caftan with a matching orange velvet cape. To finish off the ensemble, he added what appeared to be his grandmother's doily as an ascot and a pair of rather worn moccasins. Cory chose a harlequin-like court jester's outfit with light blue ballet tights. Joe picked some mismatched rags that included a gold satin shirt, a vest that was obviously too big for him, and a pair of brown suede chaps. For the life of me I still can't figure out what Michael was supposed to be. All he had on was a wreath and necklace of plastic grapes and a pair of figleaf BVDs. Maybe this was supposed to signify Bacchus, the Greek God of Wine — on acid or something! Danny came off looking like an Edwardian minstrel, complete with puffy sleeved shirt, a multicolored embroidered vest, and a top hat with numerous feathers stuck in it. Floyd, sticking true to his heritage, chose a Zulu warrior outfit complete with ceremonial headdress and a lion's tooth necklace.

I was the only problem. I couldn't find anything in the extremely cavernous costume vault that suited the way I felt. I remembered that in my closet at home I had kept the infamous Coca-Cola stained toga from the show I did at the Family Dog in Denver with Superband. Suddenly, I spied a pair of ankle-high lace-up sandals. I told Ed not to worry, that I had something great in mind, and would show up the next day in full costume.

Ed was quite pleased with all of our eclectic choices, but informed us that there was just one missing element: we needed to have some female subjects also in costume. He suggested that we use the ubiquitous GTOs, whose various members from "day one" came to our Whiskey shows. We agreed, and after we left Western Costumes, Ed called them and made arrangements to meet him at the store later to select their appropriate attire.

When we all arrived at the designated spot on the day of the shoot, Ed had already set up the various lights, a rented fog machine, and other props that would prove necessary for the desired effect. A suggestion was made by someone that we use a little bit of make-up, so everyone except Joe and myself (who felt that our characters didn't require any cosmetic enhancement) applied liberal amounts of whiteface, rouge, and greasepaint to their faces and bodies.

The five members of the GTOs arrived looking equally as bizarre and sinister, except for the almost waif-like Pamela Des Barres, who resembled an anorexic Heidi. (Pamela became quite famous in the late '80s when she penned her tell-all book on rock and roll groupies, called *I'm With the Band.*) One of the members of the all-girl group was also obviously very pregnant, so we capitalized on this and opened up the bottom of her flowing top to paint the words "3 DOG NIGHT" on her protruding stomach.

The finishing touch came in the form of one last suggestion by Ed. We needed lots of fresh fruit that would be strewn all about the creek. In order to save time, everybody volunteered to drive back down to a market, not far down the coast highway. We were all so into character that we completely forgot, as we walked into the market amid the most shocked looks from the locals, that we were in complete costume.

With the album released, and the first single a major hit, we quickly rushed out the second single, "Eli's Coming." That began to ascend the charts and into the Top 10 even more swiftly than the previous one. The following week, the record company threw a private party for us at the posh Chasen's restaurant in Beverly Hills and presented us with the official RIAA (Record Industry Association of America) certified Gold records for our first two albums.

Everything that we touched seemed to be turning to gold. As soon as "Eli" began its descent on the charts, Dunhill rush-released yet a third single. This time they chose our party anthem, "Celebrate," which we were now playing on stage as our encore. That single followed its predecessors into the Top 20 as well.

We continued touring at a feverish pace, playing larger venues for incredibly larger amounts of money. My lifestyle and income were changing so rapidly that it was becoming difficult to keep a handle on it. Lucky for myself and the other band members, we now had attained enough star stature to afford the luxuries of our own personal accountants, lawyers, and other necessary evils. This also meant that my "party animal" status was growing at an equally rapid rate.

I could now afford more and better drugs. Since I hated the bulk and cumbersome messiness of pot, I quickly acquired an affinity for "downers" in large quantities. My favorites at the time were "reds" and quaaludes. Coupled with my excessive drinking, I was becoming an accident waiting to happen. Also around this time, someone had introduced the band to the yet-to-be-chic drug, cocaine. Since it was so expensive, and was only used by the elite in the entertainment world, which we were now becoming, it seemed only fitting that (speaking for myself) we try to indulge in its pleasures as well.

We were touring relentlessly, and almost everywhere we went, we began to break attendance records. Although we were gaining mass acceptance from our fans, the critics, who a short time before had loved us, now branded us as a slick, hit-making machine. To reiterate the point that we were becoming a "musicians' band," more and more hot players began to come to our concerts to hear us. It was really a testimony to our talent and star stature when members of our band would be invited to get up on stage and share the spotlight with the likes of Jimi Hendrix or Stephen Stills.

In August of 1969, while we were doing another show in Chicago, the news broke nationally of a heinous mass murder back in Los Angeles, in the Hollywood Hills. We later learned that a cult leader and casual acquaintance of Dennis Wilson from the Beach Boys, Charles Manson, had slaughtered a number of people in a house rented by director Roman Polanski and his beautiful wife Sharon Tate. People were shot, stabbed, and bludgeoned repeatedly in one of the most bizarre crimes of the decade. Sharon Tate was well into her pregnancy when her attackers showed no mercy and stabbed her repeatedly in the stomach. The news reports recounted that when the police arrived, the words "Piggy" and "Helter Skelter" were smeared on the walls of the house in the victims' blood. It was learned later that this was Manson's vision of the apocalypse.

A frustrated would-be musician, Manson had repeatedly tried to get his songs placed on a Beach Boys album. Because of Dennis Wilson's easygoing nature, and his excessive drinking at the time, he had even let Manson sleep on the floor of his home, as he did other drifters. However, when Dennis didn't express any interest in Manson's talents, or couldn't get his friend, producer Terry Melcher (Doris Day's son), to help him with his career, Manson became outraged. Apparently, this sparked his murderous rampage. It was Terry Melcher's house that was rented to Polanski and his wife, and on the night of the murders, the "Manson family" was probably sent there with Melcher as their intended victim — thinking that he still lived there. Unfortunately for those murdered, they were simply in the wrong place at the wrong time.

The savageness of this crime not only shocked the nation but freaked out everyone in our band as well. The main reason: We were often with Melcher, at his house or elsewhere, enjoying one party or another. And we had left our wives and girlfriends alone and vulnerable in our homes, which were only a few miles away from where the murders took place. We immediately got on the phone to comfort them and advise them to either spend a few days with friends or take precautionary measures. In my case, I told Lee to immediately go out and buy a gun. I told her that if anyone so much as set foot on the property unannounced, she should "blow their fucking brains out." Chuck's fiancée, Paula, wound up coming over to our house to stay with Lee.

In my mind, the nightmare vision of pregnant Sharon Tate's body being ripped apart hit a little too close to home, because at the time Lee and I were expecting a baby, and she was already four months pregnant.

We continued the tour but maintained constant contact with our families. The management office, looking out for the safety of our families, also offered to help them in any way they could. A few weeks later, the people responsible for the murders were arrested, and one of the longest and most complex court trials in history began. With that, everyone breathed a sigh of relief.

Finishing the tour, we returned to L.A., to what was to become one of our crowning achievements. Through the combined efforts of

Dunhill and our managers, it was arranged for us to once again share the stage with the slightly apprehensive Steppenwolf. In what was to set a precedent, in a rather bold move, we were to open for them at the 18,000-seat Forum in Los Angeles. There, on September 12, 1969, we would record a live album, our third LP. Dunhill wanted us to capture on vinyl what the rest of the country had been experiencing at our live shows. By now we had such an incredible legion of fans that even as the opening act it wasn't hard to completely decimate Steppenwolf. Although they still had numerous hits under their belts, it must have been awfully intimidating seeing the near riotous response we received on stage that night. Since we shared the same management, I don't know how they convinced John to agree to this arrangement.

The show was an unqualified success, and after a few days of rest, we once again convened at American Studios to listen to the tapes that were produced that night and prepare it for release. The resulting record, *Captured Live at the Forum,* was also shipped Gold and began its climb into the Top 10.

We finished off the year with a return engagement to the Northwest to what was becoming second nature to us: sold-out houses, standing ovations, wild parties, and plenty of drugs.

In a landmark show that took place at the Aqua Theater in Seattle, Washington, we were scheduled to go on before Led Zeppelin, whose debut album had just come out and was creating quite a stir. In what had to be one of the most bizarre concert bills in history, the opening act was an unknown solo performer who sat on a stool, playing folk-sounding songs on his acoustic guitar. His only claim to fame was that, although he was American, he was one of the first acts signed to the Beatles' newly formed London-based Apple Records. They had high hopes for him, but you couldn't tell by the performance that evening. The rock crowd, which had obviously come to hear us and Zeppelin, were so rude to him that halfway through his set they began pummeling the stage with anything they could lay their hands on. He finished the song he was playing, politely thanked them, and walked off the stage amid the debris. So much for the major concert debut of James Taylor.

On that night, Danny, myself, and several of our other band members struck up a friendship and mutual admiration with the various members of Led Zeppelin. Although we never worked together again, our paths would cross from time to time.

We rang in the new year of 1970 with plans to start our fourth album after a brief ten-day tour. Each release from this point on would take longer and longer to record, but would also be greeted with more and more anticipation from everyone involved. For me, the start of the new decade would undoubtedly hold the promise of many new things. However, nothing would compare to what happened early in the morning of January 10, 1970.

As I called Lee from some airport on the road, I found out that she was going into labor. When I landed at LAX, I phoned and discovered that she had already been taken to the hospital. Since I had been up most of the night, and needed some form of stimulation so I could comprehend this monumental event, I made a quick phone call and had my limo driver make a brief stop at someone's house so I could pick up some coke. I then had him drive as fast as he could to the hospital.

When I got there, Lee was already in the delivery room. Up to this point we were convinced that we would have a boy, so we had a number of male names picked out, without any thought toward a female one. As I paced nervously about the waiting room, I kept running through the different names in my drug-induced, sleep-deprived mind.

A few minutes later the doctor came in and said, "Congratulations, Mr. Greenspoon, you are now the proud father of a beautiful baby girl." He handed me a pink button signifying the same, which I haphazardly tried to pin to my jacket. It still hadn't sunk in that I had a daughter and not a son. "Would you like to see her?" he asked.

"Sure," I said, not really knowing what to expect.

As Lee was being wheeled down the hallway on the gurney, the nurse took from her this small, wrinkled bundle of flesh covered in blood. I guess to a mother that's one of the best sights in the world, although for me it wasn't quite like it is on TV. Picking up on my apparent confused look, the nurse quickly informed me that they had to take the baby to be cleaned up.

"Yes, of course," I said to her, quite relieved. I must admit that it was an incredible sight and a great feeling to know that that was the end result of two people's bond of love.

I was so tired that I told Lee I was going home to get some sleep, not giving any thought to how she must have felt having just pushed an object the size of a bowling ball through an opening in her body the size of a kiwi fruit. As I walked away, somebody was asking me the baby's name, so they could fill out the birth certificate. It finally became clear to me that "Aaron" and the other names we had carefully chosen wouldn't be suitable for a girl. As I walked out toward my waiting limo, I turned and said, "Let me sleep on it . . . I'll let you know tomorrow."

I went home, crashed, and woke up the next morning well before visiting hours were to begin. I think the shock of the previous day's monumental event wore off, because I was extremely eager and excited to get to the hospital, even though I knew they wouldn't let me in for several hours. As I drove to the Hollywood Presbyterian Hospital early on January 11, I kept repeating a new set of names over and over in my head. I thought I had the perfect one and, reflecting on my current favorite libation, I was dead set on calling her "Brandy." When I got to the hospital and was denied entry, I went around back and gained access through the emergency door, which luckily for me had been left unlocked. I snuck up the stairs to the room where Lee was sleeping and quietly woke her up.

As she wiped the sleep from her eyes, I kept repeating, "Brandy, Brandy."

"Don't you think it's a little too early to start drinking?" she asked.

"No, no. Not the drink. It's the name of our daughter," I told her.

"Nice try," she said, smiling, "but I think we should consider some other possibilities."

I sat down on the bed, and within a short time we had both agreed upon the name "Heather." I picked the middle name, "Lynne," because those two words just sounded so natural together. And so, when the birth certificate was being filled out later that morning, Heather Lynne Greenspoon had a name.

The song selection for our new album took a little longer than usual, because we wanted to be very careful not to disrupt our established hit formula. However, one significant change did take place. Everyone, after observing Gabriel in the studio, decided that even though he had a lot of input in the previous projects, it was actually Ritchie and Bill who were in control of the sessions. Through mutual agreement, it was decided that Gabriel would no longer produce us, and that from here on out, Ritchie would officially be our producer, with Bill as our engineer.

It seemed that more and more established songwriters were submitting songs to us, now that we had proved that we could interpret outside compositions and create commercial hit records out of them. So, once again, everybody met at the studio and after several weeks of listening to demos, we came up with yet another batch of soon-to-be classics. "Woman," written by Andy Frazer and Paul Rodgers from the English band Free (who already had a string of hits in Europe), was picked as a group song. Chuck decided to do the beautiful Randy Newman ballad "Cowboy" that would feature his vocal along with my keyboards and Michael's guitar. Cory chose the bluesy "It Ain't Easy." Another pop ballad, written by the up-and-coming team of Paul Williams and Roger Nichols, "Out in the Country," was also slated for a group effort. On this particular cut, I would give what in my estimation was one of my best performances on record. I was now becoming a virtuoso on the Hammond B-3 and was always striving to achieve unique and different sounds. To this day, people come up and ask me who played the flute solo on that song. I just smile and tell them, "It was me," knowing that it was just the unique sound I was able to get on the organ.

The next song we chose was also a group effort, and it became the basis for one of our more amusing stage routines. The song, "Good Feeling (1957)," was an ode to the wonderful rock and roll tunes of yesteryear. Wanting to mine Randy Newman's enormous songwriting talents, Cory chose to cover "Mama Told Me Not To Come." As another group song, we chose "Good Time Living" by the already established team of Barry Mann and Cynthia Weil, who had written numerous hits for other people. We once again turned to the enormous talents of Elton John and Bernie Taupin, who were just now starting to gain acceptance in America. We originally recorded a demo that they had submitted to us entitled "Take Me to the Pilot." In an unprecedented move for us, we extended the song, via various solos and intricate passages, to almost eight minutes in length. Elton's record company at the time informed us that since he had also recorded the song on his debut U.S. album, they were going to release it as a single. So instead, we opted for another tune that was submitted by Elton and Bernie, entitled "Your Song." However, within a short time, both that and "Take Me to the Pilot" were stateside hits which had established Elton as a true superstar. Somewhere in a vault, collecting dust, is our unreleased version of "Take Me to the Pilot."

At this point in time, when Floyd, Joe, Michael, and I would be getting ready to record a song, we would always launch into a wonderful impromptu jam that was fueled by various hit riffs. One particular tune that we came up with would end up being the first complete group original. Danny, Chuck, and Cory, along with some help from us and Ritchie, came up with the lyrics to the song. From that, "Rock and Roll Widow" was born. The tongue-in-cheek words definitely reflected practically everyone's philosophy about life on the road.

The initial artwork on the album depicted all of the group members sitting in an almost surreal setting that consisted of various movie props, including one of the talking trees from *The Wizard Of Oz*. We appeared to be completely nude, and our bodies were dyed orange from head to toe. In reality, everyone was wearing jockstraps that had been dipped into the almost indelible orange dye. To complete the picture, a totally nude girl somebody had found for the session was seated cross-legged in a large Plexiglas bubble. This proved to be not the wisest of decisions on our part, because during the shoot, we were locked in a studio with Ed and this nude girl until the early hours of the morning, somewhere in Hollywood. I don't know how it happened, but somehow Joe's wife, Jan, found out where we were, came down to the studio and, finding herself locked out, began pounding on the door. She thought we were all in there having at this girl, and although the thought did cross several of our minds, we kept it strictly professional. However, Jan wouldn't go away and was disrupting the photo shoot with her ranting and raving outside. So, Joe got up and excused himself for a minute, opened the door, and punched her in the mouth. He then closed the door and returned to inform us that the problem had been taken care of.

Because of the bizarre scene that we were trying to set up, the album was going to be called *Wizards of Orange*. However, when Jay Lasker and the other record company execs saw a mock-up of the photo session, they quickly nixed it, claiming that the middle-class, white-bread stores that sold our albums, such as Sears, J.C. Penney's, and K-Mart, wouldn't stock the record if it contained an apparent nude photograph on the cover.

In a rather hasty move, Danny, Chuck, and Cory met with Ed at Danny's house and used his music room as the background for the album cover. With the original cover shelved, the title *The Wizards Of Orange* didn't fit anymore, so we opted to use the name of one of the songs, "It Ain't Easy," as the album's new title.

For the centerfold and back cover of the album, we drove to the sand dunes outside of Palm Springs and once again donned some outrageous threads. The rather bizarre outfits that everyone (but Floyd) chose to wear were purchased at the trendy West Hollywood shop that was owned by Pamela Morrison, who was the wife of Jim Morrison of the Doors. She not only owned the shop but also made all of the clothes. They were constructed of leather, suede, and pieces of various fabrics that were sewn together patchwork style. Floyd, during this particular time, was stockpiling the towels from all of the various Holiday Inns that we stayed at on the road. The reason for this became apparent when he showed up the day of the shoot, wearing a jumpsuit made from the towels bearing the "Holiday Inn" logo. What an incredible marketing ploy!

Danny had contracted someone to make up some large Plexiglas props that could be used in our stage show. On the back cover of *It Ain't Easy,* which featured a photo of the four musicians, I was seated lotus-style on a Plexiglas "X" that, when placed in the sand, gave me the appearance of floating in thin air. We had already used the Plexiglas globe with the nude model for our ill-fated original album cover, so we brought it back and let Floyd hoist it above his head, like a black Atlas. A similar Plexiglas triangle was placed somewhere else in the picture to signify God only knows what.

For the gatefold shot, the three singers positioned themselves in the foreground, and on the sand dune in back of them, Ed had carefully placed a seven-foot-tall prop of some alien android that he borrowed from a movie studio. This had nothing to do with anything, but looked good in the picture.

The album was released in April 1970. Continuing in our already established pattern, it too shipped Gold. By now, everyone in the band came to expect that dubious honor. Due to overwhelming demand from radio programmers, the first single that was picked was "Mama Told Me Not To Come." It began to burn up the charts, and by June it became our first Number One single. It also sold a million copies and became our second Gold 45.

The demand for touring and more product was becoming almost unbearable. Some of the group members, especially Chuck, Danny, and myself, realized that to keep up this hectic pace we had to consume more and more quantities of drugs and alcohol.

With the record company's standard procedure of releasing a follow-up single as soon as its predecessor began descending, Dunhill immediately released "Out in the Country" as the album's next single. Although it sold well, it only got to Number 15 on the national charts. And following the Number One status of "Mama Told Me Not To Come," in the record company's estimation, that wasn't good enough. Their feeling was that there were no other hits to be pulled off the album, so once again the pressure was on to release new product. Unfortunately, the concert promoters were also demanding more and more of us on the road, which made it quite difficult to concentrate on recording. We decided to hold off on picking new material, even though everywhere we went we were constantly on the lookout for songs. After a much-needed two-week break, we embarked on yet another extensive tour.

At this same time, plans were also being made for a full-scale tour of Great Britain later in the year, since "Mama Told Me Not

To Come" was a Top Five record over there. Our records were already million-sellers in such places as Japan, Germany, Spain, Australia, and South Africa, but the U.K. seemed to have been a hard market for us to crack. We eagerly anticipated trying to repeat our stateside success there as well. Up to this point our only visit over there was for a short promotional tour in June 1969, when our first album came out. We received mixed reviews. Inevitably, this proposed second trip to England had to be shelved so we could work on our next album.

After our debut at the Miami Pop Festival, there was one music festival after another. Although we didn't play Woodstock in August 1969, because we were contractually obligated for other engagements that week, it seems that we played every other festival that sprang up. In L.A. we did the Devonshire Downs Festival with the Jimi Hendrix Experience. That was one of those shows where the bikers arrived, agitated the audience, and things became violent.

The next one was followed by the Denver Pop Festival, which was in the summer of 1970. It was a two-day affair, where we closed the show on one day and Jimi Hendrix and his band closed it the next. On the first day we played, a number of local bands opened the show. Among them was a Denver band, Zephyr, whom I had known indirectly from my Superband days in Colorado. Their guitar player, Tommy Bolan, was being touted as the new up-and-coming guitarist to watch out for. After a fairly inspired set, they were followed by the ever-popular but increasingly tedious Iron Butterfly, who spent the majority of their set playing their only hit, "In-A-Gadda-Da-Vida."

Frank Zappa and the Mothers of Invention went on before us. At one point in his show, Frank created what had to be the first "wave" at an outdoor event, with thousands of voices panning from left to right. For the ending to his little bit of inspired insanity, he instructed everyone by section to respectively stick their fingers down their throats and make a sound like they were vomiting. After 20,000 people faked "the technicolor yawn," which sounded utterly ridiculous, he told them "Thank you" and left the stage. Frank was always the innovator.

The next night the line-up changed slightly, with Zappa not performing, and us going on right before Hendrix. After our performance, which reached near riot proportions, everyone stuck around in anticipation of Jimi's set.

Jimi Hendrix was pretty much a quiet guy. He wasn't any more stoned than anyone else at the time, although his image led people to believe differently. He was obviously a genius, and his mind was always at work. His music was just one step ahead of the pack. Later, when he died, I could see that he was going to break out of that whole psychedelic mold. If he only had lived a little while longer . . .

I remember standing backstage in Denver with Noel Redding, the bass player for Hendrix. He was saying to me, "I wish we could do something special with the people in the audience, to get them more involved, like bringing them closer to the stage." He was obviously referring to the fences that were set up between the stage and the audience for crowd control.

I turned and said to him, "If you do that, you're going to cause a riot, and God only knows what the cops are going to do. A lot of kids are going to end up getting hurt."

On that night, unfortunately my prophecy came true. I don't know exactly who started it, but I think it was Hendrix, because he closed the show. Someone on stage said, "Come on and break the barriers down!" With that, the whole crowd came running down toward the stage en masse. The cops came out with their riot gear, complete with tear gas, and lobbed all of it into the audience. It turned into a real ugly scene.

I was amazed by the nightmarish battle that took place. The cops got way too rough with their clubs, and since this was probably the first time they were in a situation like this, a lot of the kids did get hurt. While the riot scene raged on, Hendrix got into his limousine and fled for the safety of his hotel room. He was back there getting high while he let the cops sort out the mess that had been created by the command from the stage.

We quit doing festivals after that debacle, until the Pocono Pop Festival on July 8, 1972, came along. And it took them paying us $200,000 for a half hour of work to lure us back. At that point, because of our superstar status, we were headlining over Rod Stewart, Joe Cocker, Humble Pie, Emerson, Lake and Palmer . . . and the list went on and on.

We were supposed to go on at 5:00 or 6:00 in the evening, but of course festivals always ran late. In those days especially, nothing went smoothly. There would be lag time between sets, with people arriving late and road crews scurrying around on stage changing equipment.

We flew into an airport somewhere in Pennsylvania, arriving late, a helicopter on the ground was ready to take off, with some guy standing next to it. Our road manager went over to him and said, "We're Three Dog Night, can we use this helicopter?" He said, "No, that's Humble Pie's, and it belongs to their manager, Dee Anthony." We were under a lot of pressure to get there, so our road manager lied through his teeth and told him that we were close personal friends of Mr. Anthony's. We convinced him of our dilemma, and although I did know some of the guys from Humble Pie, like Stevie Marriott, I had only met Dee Anthony once in my life.

The pilot finally relented and told us to get into the helicopter. It was really foggy that day, and it was starting to rain. The pilot was having a hard time seeing, and he couldn't find the hotel where he was supposed to land. This didn't exactly make us feel very safe. We ended up hovering over the freeway and following the road signs so we could find our way to the Holiday Inn. Eventually, we found the hotel, and the pilot landed the helicopter in the parking lot. Of all the places that he could have picked, we ended up landing right in front of Dee Anthony's hotel room. Anthony came running out of the room, screaming furiously. We ended up jumping out of the helicopter and running off in about ten different directions with our luggage.

By the time we arrived at our rooms, it was already 6:00 P.M. When we announced our arrival to someone in charge, he explained to us, "No problem, the show's been pushed back." They were still eight acts away from the time that we were supposed to go on.

I said, "You're kidding! What are you talking about?"

He said, "Well, what can I say? The show is running late."

Humble Pie was going on third from the last, followed by Emerson, Lake and Palmer, and then us. I went over to Stevie Marriott's room and said to him, "Well, let's go to the bar and get wasted!" I figured that we'd go on about ten o'clock at night, which left plenty of time to go to the bar, get drunk, sober up, and get drunk again.

Stevie always carried a big glass jar that was filled with assorted pills of different colors that some doctor had given him in London. They were probably from Dr. Robert (who was immortalized in song by the Beatles) or one of the other infamous doctors who supplied rock musicians with their drugs.

Stevie handed me a pill and said, "Here, take one of these." I asked what it was. "It's a Mandrex, the English version of a Quaalude." *Ah, my favorite downer,* I thought to myself. "It doesn't last too long and wears off quickly," he explained. To that I exclaimed with glee, "Oh, great! I'll take three or four of them then!"

So I did, and we took off for the bar and started drinking. I was getting more and more blitzed as the hours rolled on. One of the runners for the stage manager kept coming into the bar. "Is it time yet?" I would ask him. No, they were having problems. It would probably be another hour or two before Humble Pie went on.

Stevie and I were getting drunker and more wasted. Finally, Humble Pie got their call at one or two in the morning. By then everyone was tired. We had been waiting six hours, and I was pissed to the gills. A couple of the band members were off fucking their brains out, and I left the bar in search of some coke so I could try and get myself at least halfway awake for the show. I succeeded in my quest, and finally, at 5:30 A.M., we got the call and got into the waiting limos. I was wearing an expensive yellow velvet suit and a pair of custom-made snakeskin boots. It had been raining throughout the night, and by the time we got there, the place looked like a battle zone. As we arrived at the concert site, I stepped out of the limo and fell directly into the mud. So much for my expensive outfit.

The concert was held in a big vacant field. The fences had been torn apart, and people were making campfires with the wood. They were huddled in the rain around these campfires, trying to stay warm. The concertgoers had even dismantled the hot dog stands, chopped up the wood, burned it to stay warm, and then ate all of the remaining food.

Of course, the backstage food and deli trays had long since been trashed by everyone who could get their hands on them. There were people passed out everywhere. Out of half a million people, only a handful of them were still conscious. Two or three die-hard stalwart fans could be heard yelling, "Come on, let's party!"

We got out on the stage, looked at each other, and said, "This is nuts! Why are we doing this?" For $200,000, that's why! We went out there and gave them a half hour of music.

That fiasco was followed by the Rockingham Pop Festival in Rockingham, North Carolina, on August 18, 1972. This was the second time that, because of the massive size of the crowd, we had to be flown into the site by helicopter. This time, however, it was one reserved for us: an old army helicopter with the doors open and an incredibly loud engine. As it landed in back of the stage, dirt and debris flew everywhere. Even above the sound of the copter's rotor blades, we could hear the cheers from the assembled multitude. Although the audience was a little more conscious than the previous one, this would be the last festival we did in the '70s.

# 9 / Joy To The World

We now had obviously found the perfect hit-producing recipe, recording with Ritchie and Bill. After the incredible international success of "It Ain't Easy," and the Number One single, "Mama Told Me Not To Come," we decided to continue by making a near carbon copy (in song structure) for our fifth album. Although we had been recording hit albums for only a year and a half, it had become almost as second nature as breathing to us. By now, Dunhill would have enough advance orders to assure us that all of our albums would automatically be shipped Gold.

Because we had gone out on tour and were way behind schedule in starting this album, the orders mounted so quickly that before recording had even begun, it had already been certified Gold. This time around, there was an incredible amount of pressure from management and the record label to get the product out before the holidays.

Once again, everyone in the group was involved with the song selection. And, after the tunes had been rehearsed to the point of readiness, we entered the studio sometime in September. The first song that we recorded was called "One Man Band," submitted to us by one of its co-writers, Thomas Jefferson Kaye. It had a very R&B flavor to it, and on this particular song we opted for the live-in-the-studio sound that our first album had, without overdubs. For the second time we covered a Free song written by Andy Frazer and Paul Rogers. Their song "I'll Be Creeping" was also recorded in the same fashion. With these two songs out of the way in a rather short amount of time, the next song that we recorded was written by a band that was also signed to Dunhill, and our management company, called Bush. They were a talented quartet from Toronto, Canada. The drummer, Whitey Glan, and I had struck up a friendship years earlier when I was in the East Side Kids and he was in the Mandella. We decided to cover a tune from their debut album called "I Can Hear You Calling." Since we were on a roll, and pumping these tunes out so quickly, we also recorded this one with a live feel, in spite of a few overdubs.

At this point, Dunhill was under so much pressure that, after coming to the studio every day and listening to what was finished, they decided to rush release "One Man Band" before the album was even half-finished. As it made its way up the charts toward the Top 20, we continued recording.

In order to keep up with the pace, Danny, Chuck, and I were consuming large quantities of coke and other drugs just to keep going. We were also under the misguided illusion that the more substances that we ingested, the more creative we would become. It seemed that I was spending less and less time at home with Lee and more time partying and womanizing between recording sessions. The same thing was happening with Chuck and his wife Paula (they had gotten married earlier that year). Some nights I didn't even go home at all, having spent the evening in the arms of some adoring fan.

The fourth song on the album was again the result of one of our impromptu jams. The riff was so powerful that everyone decided not to put vocals on it, and "Fire Eater" became our first instrumental on a Three Dog Night album — written solely by Joe, Floyd, Michael, and me. As we had in the past, we also used the incredible songwriting talents of Steve Winwood. But this time around we went back to his early career with the Spencer Davis Group and recorded a tune that he had co-written with his producer, Jimmy Miller, entitled "Can't Get Enough of It." (Miller later went on to produce some of the Rolling Stones' best material, most notably their *Exile On Main Street* album.)

The next song we recorded was one that was very close to Chuck. "Sunlight" by Jesse Collin Young, from the San Francisco group the Youngbloods (who had recorded the late '60s anthem, "Get Together"), proved to be the perfect vehicle for his voice. This was recorded with an almost acoustic feel, sans drums and keyboards, although in a later version, which was intended as a single, I went in and overdubbed numerous keyboard parts.

The seventh song, "Heavy Church," written by Alan O'Day, took the longest time to record. For this one we decided to have layers of vocal and keyboard parts, reminiscent of a church choir. I personally did six separate overdubs on everything from the grand piano to an amazing pipe organ that Ritchie had at the studio. The result was an ethereal-sounding concept piece that was a complete departure for us.

Song number eight was one that I had brought to Danny's attention. It was originally recorded by one of my favorite English bands, Argent. I was a big fan of the group's keyboard player and co-founder, Rod Argent, who also was responsible for all of the Zombies' hits. After spending a week on "Heavy Church," for this song, "Liar," we went back to our straight ahead way of recording. Next on the agenda was another song written by an English band. We chose "I've Got Enough Heartache" by the British cult band Spooky Tooth. I was also a big fan of their keyboard player, Gary Wright, who later went on to record some brilliant solo albums.

With nine songs in the can, and the initial single already a hit on the charts, we thought that we were through with the album. However, when Dunhill came to the studio one last time to give a final listen, they felt that although the album was very creative and had a great overall rock and roll feel, there wasn't a monster hit on it. So, once again, it was back to the demo pile to search for an obvious hit single to add to the album.

A few days later, while we were at the studio listening to songs, Hoyt Axton wandered in with his guitar and sat down. He had been signed by our management company, and had opened for several of our shows. Knowing our dilemma, he said, "I've got the perfect song for you guys."

"Oh, really?" we asked, somewhat skeptically, although at that point we were willing to consider just about anything.

Without any intro he suddenly launched into the song, which began with "Jeremiah was a bullfrog . . ." We all glared at each other with one of those "What the fuck is this shit?" looks on our faces, while he continued singing the rest of the song.

When he was finished, he put his guitar down, and said, "Well, what do you think?"

Our collective reply was, "Well, it's different!"

He explained that he had originally written it as part of a treatment for a proposed Saturday morning cartoon show about a singing bullfrog named Jeremiah. Hoyt was such a lovable guy, and sang the song for us with so much conviction, that it made it hard for us to turn him down. He also had a fairly impressive track record throughout the years, having written songs like "Greenback Dollar" for the Kingston Trio, and "The Pusher" and "Snowblind Friend" for Steppenwolf. His mother, Mae Axton, was even more famous, having written the song "Heartbreak Hotel" for Elvis Presley.

The bullfrog song was a longshot. However, since we didn't have a lot of time to look around for other material, we decided to record it immediately. As was becoming the norm, I was required by the band to come up with some sort of hook-laden keyboard intro, as I had done with our previous hits. So, everyone took a break for dinner and left me alone in the studio to compose something, stating that they would be back in an hour, expecting "greatness." I didn't let them down. After a couple of drinks and a few lines of coke, I came up with the now-classic intro to that damn bullfrog song, "Joy to the World." When the rest of the guys returned to the studio, I played it for them and gained their approval. We began recording the last song on our fifth album before the sun came up the next morning.

After we finished recording the song that night, we all went home to catch a few hours of sleep, then returned later for the final listening session with management and record company executives in attendance. Halfway through "Joy to the World," Jay Lasker turned to Danny and said, "That's a smash!"

I thought to myself, *You've got to be fucking kidding me! This is a joke isn't it!?* It was no joke, and he went on to say that he wanted to press it as a single immediately.

Obviously, everyone in the group wanted a tune with more substance to represent us on the charts. The critics had been lambasting us for "selling out" and going commercial, so we had laboriously constructed an album featuring songs by respected bands like Free, Spooky Tooth, the Spencer Davis Group, and Argent. And now, this yo-yo wanted to release a spoof that was our last choice! We spent quite some time explaining to Jay Lasker that it was fine as an album cut, but it would never make it as a single. It was just too light for our "image." He still was relentlessly determined to release it and make it into a hit.

We left the studio that night wondering if he had lost his mind. Finally, we decided to let it rest for the time being, and figured that we'd talk him out of it later that week at a business meeting.

Danny, Chuck, and Cory had a meeting at Dunhill and found that Jay was as immovable as a brick wall as far as his decision was concerned. They reluctantly conceded, and went on to discuss other business.

As a reward for our hard work all year, the management company arranged for us to do a couple of concerts in Hawaii, and while we were there, we would shoot the album photos. Everybody brought their families with them, and we all set up temporary residence on the north shore of Oahu in various houses. The main party house was chosen as the site for the album cover photo. Wanting to keep things simple, we set up our equipment at the bottom of the drained swimming pool and wore casual clothing. For the back of the album, we set one of our road cases on a lava rock and shot it as if had been washed up on shore with the tide. The words "THREE DOG NIGHT; 211 SO. BEVERLY DR.; BEVERLY HILLS, CALIF." were clearly stenciled on it, as though someone would return it if they found it there! Because of our tropical location, and the overall feeling of the album, we decided to call it *Naturally*. For the centerfold, Ed used various concert and still shots and created a montage out of them, laid out like a contact sheet. There was also a perforated foldout poster that depicted everyone in the band, looking like stylized cartoon characters of ourselves.

While we were in Hawaii, Chuck and I continued to escalate our intake of drugs, and although our wives were there with us, we continued to flaunt our star status in front of them with other women. This was really beginning to piss Lee and Paula off. We played a sold-out concert at the HIC Arena in Honolulu, and then stayed on the islands for another week vacationing, while the album was being prepared for release before Christmas.

We returned home, and *Naturally* hit the album charts the week of December 12, 1970. After a few select concert dates, we took a break for the holidays.

The year 1971 started with Dunhill releasing our first "greatest hits" package, *Golden Biscuits,* and readying "Joy to the World" for release as our next single. Originally, we wanted to call the hits album *Dog Style,* but after the aborted nude cover for "It Ain't Easy," the record company flatly refused that idea. We, however, persuaded them to include one of the outtakes from the infamous *Wizards Of Orange* photo session on the inside of it. *Golden Biscuits* became our highest charting album ever, hitting Number Five in *Billboard*. It also became our sixth consecutive Gold album.

Because of our increasing fame, it became necessary for everyone to start acquiring all of the trappings that are befitting of a pop icon. My first move in this direction was to get rid of my two-year-old blue Camaro and search for a more suitable four-wheeled status symbol.

One day I went to my business manager's office, obtained a check for $10,000, cashed it at the bank, and drove to a Mercedes Benz dealer in Santa Monica. Since my red hair was down past my shoulders and I had on what would be politely termed as "casual clothing," I looked slightly out of my element as I walked into the showroom. As the salesman cautiously approached me he was probably thinking to himself, *What is this long-haired hippie doing in here?*

"Can I help you, sir?" he asked me with a rather condescending tone to his voice.

"How much is that one?" I asked, pointing at a new white 280SL roadster.

"It's quite expensive," he replied.

"How expensive?"

"Probably more than you're prepared to pay," was his curt answer.

Seeing that this conversation was getting nowhere fast, I reached into my pocket and pulled out my wad of $1,000 bills. Almost instantly his attitude changed and he began giving me detailed information about the car in question. After I learned that the price was $10,000 plus tax and license, I told him that I would take it. When he asked me how much I'd like to put down on it, I replied, "Nothing, I'll pay cash." With that, he put his arm around my shoulder as if he were some long lost relative, and he walked me into his office to draw up the papers. I got on the phone to my business manager and had him messenger over a check to cover the tax and license.

At this point in my life I was becoming quite impulsive, as I had just demonstrated. I embraced the philosophy that there was nothing I saw and wanted to possess that I couldn't instantly obtain. Everyone in the group was handling our star status differently, and with varying degrees of maturity. If I was low man on the totem pole, then Cory was at the top and seemed to be the most stable. He decided to move out of the small house that he was renting in the Valley and made the quantum leap to become a homeowner. He found a massive, secluded home somewhere in Malibu and purchased it for the security of his family. He quickly moved in with his wife, Mary, and their two daughters, Dawn and Coryann, and began furnishing his new investment.

Michael and his wife also purchased a home at the beach, but in the less pretentious section of Santa Monica. Since he was becoming increasingly more interested in the whole recording procedure, he decided, to the chagrin of his wife, to build a studio in the living room. There he would spend countless hours alienating himself from her, deeply entrenched in some off-the-wall project.

Floyd, who had been married long before he had joined the band, decided to move his family — wife Sandy and their two daughters, Tracy and Shannon — to a beautiful ranch-style house in the Hidden Hills section of Agora, California. There was plenty of wide-open space there, and since he liked to ride, he eventually purchased some horses from the home's previous owner, TV star Amanda Blake, who played Kitty on "Gunsmoke."

Danny retained his affinity for Laurel Canyon and bought a house only a mile away from where he was living. Although he was still seeing his girlfriend, June, on and off, he was the group's only confirmed bachelor, and was enjoying his status as the "party animal supremo." His place quickly became the social hangout, and on any given night you could see such diverse people as Brian Wilson, Dennis Hopper, Lowell George, Tommy Smothers, any English band that was currently in town, and an occasional Beatle or two, not to mention assorted groupies and thrill-seekers. Usually they would all converge over his pool table that never saw a game played on it, because everyone would lay out massive lines of coke and snort away until the sun came up.

Joe leased a house at the top of Lookout Mountain that was only half a mile away from where Danny and I first lived. Choosing not to purchase a dwelling, he instead used his money to secure large quantities of coke.

Chuck, Paula, Lee, and I were looking for suitable dwellings, but we couldn't seem to find anything big and pretentious enough. While the band was in Canada on a short tour, though, I received a phone call from Lee, informing me that she had just bought our dream house. I was incensed over the fact that she hadn't waited until I had gotten home. I kept shouting over the phone at her to try to find out how much it had cost. All the while she was trying to describe the home's strong points. As I proceeded to scream into the phone, I suddenly stopped when I heard her say something about an elevator. "Run that last part by me again," I said in a calmer tone.

She told me that it was a beautiful three-story home in the Hollywood Hills, behind the trendy Chateau Marmot Hotel, and it had belonged to the Belgian consulate. There were three bedrooms, three bathrooms, a sun room that we could turn into a playroom for Heather, a huge living room with hardwood floors, a large family room with fireplace and stone walls, and a massive kitchen on the center level with an indoor barbecue. The most outrageous feature of the house was the fact that an actual elevator ran through the middle of it to connect the three floors! There was also a large swimming pool that would be perfect for teaching Heather how to swim, and a large, fenced-in yard for Crystal. Also, there was a two-car garage with a separate one-bedroom/one-bath guest house situated above it (perfect for maid's quarters).

I was almost sold on it, except for the fact that she kept avoiding me every time I'd ask what the price was. Finally, she blurted it out: "Ninety thousand!"

There was stunned silence from my end of the phone. "How much did you put down?" I calmly asked her.

After another pregnant pause, she replied, "Thirty-five thousand."

At the time that seemed like an awful lot of money to me. But I was a rock and roll superstar, and as such felt that the house would be a suitable showcase for me.

"But wait," she said, "there's more."

"More?" I inquired, "What do you mean 'more'?"

"I was with Paula today, and she bought one for Chuck also."

"Oh, fucking great," I said. "How much did that set him back? And does he know about it?"

"A hundred twenty-five thousand . . . and no."

Just then I heard some screaming and an object hitting the wall in the hotel room next to me. "He knows now," I told her.

When we returned from the Canadian tour, Chuck and I moved into our respective homes, and our wives began to immediately tear everything apart. They proceeded to do what they did best: spend our money and redecorate.

As we were preparing for our spring tour, the single "Joy to the World" was released, and to our astonishment, it debuted higher than any of our previous efforts. It began an almost meteoric rise to the top of the charts, and in no time it repeated the success of "Mama Told Me Not To Come." Everyone in the band was obviously wrong in their estimation of the hit potential of the song, but we still thought that it was a fluke the first week it hit Number One. However, every week when we called up the office to check out the chart positions, we found much to our surprise it was still at the top. Everywhere we went we couldn't escape the song. It was being played constantly, and Dunhill was getting so many reorders that they were having a hard time keeping up with it at the pressing plant. The single eventually logged an incredible six weeks at the top of the charts, sold over three and a half million copies, and became the biggest-selling single in Dunhill's history and in our career. This became Three Dog Night's trademark song.

To capitalize on our incredible success, while "Joy" was still high on the charts, Dunhill released the third song off of the *Naturally* album: "Liar." It quickly climbed into the Top 10 as well. We seemed to have "the Midas touch."

The treadmill of album/tour/album/tour was beginning to run everyone down, and we felt that neither our management nor our record label was concerned about our personal health or well-being. Their only desire was to have us crank out more and more product in a steady stream.

My intake of drugs and alcohol was becoming alarming at this point. I was now a full-blown alcoholic, although I didn't recognize the warning signs — most notably my "blackout drinking." On more than one occasion I would hook up with various members of other bands and indulge in all sorts of excesses. This nonstop partying lifestyle had only one advantage: it resulted in lifelong friendships.

The group was now so huge that practically every major act of the early '70s opened for us. The list included Rod Stewart and the Faces, Humble Pie, Stevie Wonder, Jackson Browne, the Byrds, the Allman Brothers, the Doobie Brothers, Little Feat, Jethro Tull, Leon Russell, Jefferson Airplane, Kansas, the Steve Miller Band, Uriah Heep, Ten Years After, the Guess Who, Styx, R.E.O. Speedwagon, and Aerosmith — just to name a few.

We went into rehearsals for another marathon U.S. tour, this time with Uriah Heep slated for the opening spot. As the tour progressed we would indulge in the usual debauchery, but onstage food fights were becoming an everyday occurrence for us.

At one show in Greenville, South Carolina, Floyd, Michael, Joe and I, along with our roadies and Mick Box, the guitar player from Uriah Heep, arranged at a certain point to nail Danny, Chuck, and Cory with custom-made cream pies that were being created backstage. Not wanting to incur the wrath of the headliners, most of the members of Uriah Heep declined to engage in our shenanigans. As a break came between songs, the pies were brought out and carefully distributed among the musicians. At the appropriate time, we rushed toward the front of the stage, wielding the various pastries, and took aim at our intended targets. They must have sensed that something was up. When the pies were released, they ducked, and instead we nailed the front line of police officers who were guarding the stage! They were not the least bit amused by this childish prank, but we had a good laugh over it for days.

The food fights came to a head on the last day of the tour, as everybody by now was leery of everybody else, and consequently would be looking over their shoulders in anticipation of some sort of culinary delights.

I was having the time of my life on the road, screwing anything that walked, partying until I puked, and carrying on with my friends. In a way, I was apprehensive and a little sad to return home to what was supposedly my stable family life. But I made my bed — in a $90,000 house! — and now I had to sleep in it.

We arrived back in L.A. and prepared for our most critically acclaimed — and my favorite — album. Ultimately entitled *Harmony,* it ended up taking the longest time to record of any of our albums to date. Once again we spent an incredible amount of time picking the right songs to record, and when this process was complete, we began rehearsals.

Before we locked ourselves in the studio, our final concert dates that summer of 1971 produced three capacity audiences totaling almost 50,000 people, and represented a gross of over a quarter million dollars.

For the *Harmony* album, Ritchie Podolor wanted the lavishly produced layered effect that we had achieved on "Heavy Church" to run through all of the tunes. The first song we recorded was one that Danny found, called "My Impersonal Life," written by an unknown writer named Terry Furlong. It was very similar to "Heavy Church" in structure and execution. The recording of this song set the precedent for the entire album.

At this point in time, Danny would always go off into some time-consuming, drug-induced tirade about different sounds and recording techniques. On one particular overdub for "My Impersonal Life," Ritchie had a voice bag, which was an instrument that distorted and enhanced the vocal. Danny felt that Michael should somehow use it with his guitar and come up with a heavy-sounding riff for the intro of the song. We spent hours and hours playing the riff that Michael had finally come up with, in every possible combination, none of which Danny found acceptable. At one point, after we had been up for two days snorting coke, Danny was seen in the middle of the recording room, twirling the bag around in a metal garbage can, trying to achieve the sound he was looking for. After several days were wasted on a part that was intended for only a few seconds in the intro, we finally went back to the now-infamous "Garbage Can Theory," and once it was played back, we discovered that it really didn't sound any different at all. Subsequently, we used the sound on the entire song, proving that somewhere in Danny's inspired insanity there lurked a genius.

Since we had repeated success with proven songwriters, Chuck decided to record another Paul Williams composition, "An Old Fashioned Love Song." In an almost identical move from our *Naturally* album, I was again required to come up with the infamous "Greenspoon intro." As they had done before, the other band members left me alone in the studio to compose. When they returned, I had crafted — tapping into my classical roots — a very baroque-sounding intro that they immediately fell in love with. By now, we could smell a hit a mile away, and after this particular song was finished, we knew that it had to be a single.

Now that he was a commercially successful songwriter, and had no doubt gained our respect, Hoyt Axton played us a dub of a song he had written called "Never Been to Spain." Before it was even half over, we told him, "That's enough, we'll do it!" In keeping with the country feel of Hoyt's original demo, we decided to call in the album's only guest musician, Rusty Young from Poco, to play pedal steel guitar on the cut.

Next we recorded a song called "Peace of Mind," which featured just my piano and Chuck's vocal. The actual song was preceded by an intro poem, "Mistakes and Illusions," written by his wife Paula. I always felt it was a fitting ode to the marital status of most of the members of the band.

In a move that was calculated to raise some eyebrows, Chuck decided to cover a Stevie Wonder ballad, "I Never Dreamed You'd Leave in Summer." However, his performance was so convincing that it became the album's centerpiece. I also did some of my most inspired playing on that song.

Once again we included a group original, but this time we reached way back into our bag of tricks and pulled out the song we simply entitled "Jam." It was the one we first created on stage at the Whiskey when we were hard-pressed for material and received our first encore.

For Danny's spotlight song on the album, he decided to cover a Joni Mitchell song, "Night in the City," which would also garner favorable response from the critics. All the time that the group had been together, I had been trying to convince them to do a Moby Grape tune, since that was my favorite San Francisco band from the '60s. I found an ally in Cory, who was also a Grape fan, and got my wish when we did "Murder in My Heart for the Judge."

Chuck and Cory now had the lion's share of lead vocals, so it was no surprise when Chuck wanted us to rework the song "You," which was originally recorded by Marvin Gaye. That was the hardest song for me to try to be creative on. I had to literally take the original sparse Motown track and come up with something fresh and modern-sounding. After days and countless overdubs, I did some of my most intricate work that later (when we briefly included it in our live performances) had me literally running around my keyboards like a Tasmanian Devil, trying to faithfully recreate all of my parts. There were so many vocal overdubs that it was hard to reproduce on stage. Much to my relief, we eventually dropped it from the set.

The recording process was dragging on and on as we indulged each other's every whim in the studio. The last song that we chose on the album was also a Paul Williams tune, "The Family of Man," one that he co-wrote with Jack Conrad. (Conrad would later try out as our new bass player, in the early '80s.)

By now I had purchased a brand new $18,000 handmade 280SEL 3.5 Mercedes convertible to go along with the roadster. Again, I paid cash for this car. As I was bringing most of the group and Ed in with me to purchase similar vehicles, I was beginning to make a lot of friends at the Mercedes dealership.

During the recording of *Harmony,* I personally consumed more coke, booze, and pills than I had prior to this point. At times I would ask myself how it was even possible to do this and still be alive.

As the four-month recording marathon was now drawing to a close, Dunhill, in a well-orchestrated publicity move, arranged for the finished masters to the album to be picked up in a Brinks truck and hand-delivered to their office. To quote our press release concerning this landmark publicity stunt:

> Three Dog Night, the country's top rock group, must deliver its next album to ABC/Dunhill Records by 5:00 P.M. Friday (September 10) or lose a bonus totaling somewhere in six figures, called for by their contract.
>
> The group expects to finish recording sometime Friday afternoon (between 2:00 and 5:00 P.M.), at the studio it uses in North Hollywood. Three Dog Night has been at work there day and night for the past four weeks, with a special guard to keep out unauthorized visitors . . .

The only thing that was allowed to interrupt the recording was our taping of "The Glen Campbell Show." We performed the songs "Mama Told Me Not To Come" and "Joy to the World." The other guests on the show were John Wayne and Tim Conway. All of the group members were featured in several skits and dance routines, and for the finale of the show, Danny, Chuck, and Cory donned white spangled tuxedos and top hats for part of a Busby Berkley-style tap dance spectacular. The show, which was the premiere episode of the series, aired Tuesday, September 14, 1971.

Also that month, on Labor Day weekend, the group donated $38,000 to the annual Jerry Lewis Telethon to aid in finding a cure for muscular dystrophy. It was a nice gesture and a sizable chunk of cash on our part. We thought that Jerry Lewis would make a big deal about it when he announced it on the air, but we were quite mistaken. When he came to our donation, it was read in the middle of several others in an emotionless fashion, something like: "And here we have a donation from Mrs. John Doe for $5.00, one from Three Dog Night for $38,000, and $1.50 from Vicki Green. Thanks so much folks."

On the next to the last night of the final mix-down of *Harmony,* Joe and I were so exhausted that we excused ourselves and drove up to Stephen Stills' house. We sat with him and his drummer at the time, Dallas Taylor, snorting coke and listening to songs well into the next afternoon. When we arrived back at the studio the following day, it was as if time had stood still. Ritchie and Bill were babbling incoherently, working on the same song they had been on when Joe and I had exited.

When the fateful day arrived for the armored truck to pick up the master tapes, I was so burnt out that, having previously arranged a short vacation to London, I beat a hasty retreat back to my house to pick up Lee and drive to the airport. We left Heather with her grandmother, quickly packed, and were already on the runway by the time this ridiculous carnival was unwinding at the studio.

On the flight to London, I got quite drunk and started hitting on one of the stewardesses. Noticing Lee's obvious disgust, I cooled it — but not before I had obtained the girl's phone number. Once we landed and cleared customs, we took a limo to the Dorchester Hotel, where I proceeded to order massive quantities of alcohol. Fueled by the liquor and the obvious jet lag, I quickly passed out. When I awoke the next day, my head was throbbing, and I once again had the all-too-common hangover. Later that day, we went to Kings Road in Chelsea to do some clothes shopping. While we were there we ran into a few members of the South African band Osibisa, who had opened a few of our shows in the States. Sol, one of their percussionists, embraced me like a king and told me how happy he was that my wife and I had come to England to see him. He said the band was recording a new album, and asked if I would like to play on it, to which I quickly agreed.

The next day I somehow acquired some Mandrex and, coupled with numerous shots of Beefeaters Gin, I began to become quite belligerent and abusive toward Lee. I left the hotel and went to the session, not caring if I came back or not. As soon as I got there she called and started bitching to me on the phone, and I promptly hung up on her in midsentence. When she called back moments later, picking up where she had left off, I just said a hearty "Fuck you!" and slammed the phone down. Just then, Sol and Wendell, their guitar player, came in and asked me, "Any problem, mon?"

"Nothing I can't take care of," I tried to say in my obviously slurred speech. With that I reached into my pocket, produced the stewardess' phone number, and invited her down to the session. I was way too stoned to even get a hard-on, but I enjoyed flirting with her all night. As far as I was concerned, I would let Lee stew in her own juice until I decided to return to the hotel — in my own good time.

For the rest of our vacation, things were strained between Lee and myself, but I nevertheless made sure that I had a good time. We attended a Uriah Heep concert at the Lyceum and I got the star treatment from them, obviously in thanks for us letting them open our stateside shows.

The entire time I was in England I didn't care what was happening back home, and didn't want to know. As far as I was concerned, I was on vacation. The only transatlantic calls that I made were to my mother to see how Heather was doing. After only a few more minor confrontations with Lee and numerous shopping trips, we flew back to L.A. feeling only slightly rested.

For the first single off of the *Harmony* album, "An Old Fashioned Love Song" was picked, because it was obviously such a commercial record, and because Paul Williams was having incredible success due to his track record with the Carpenters. Their recording of "We've Only Just Begun" had made Paul *the* hot songwriter of the moment, and it certainly didn't hurt us to have two of his songs on our new album. "An Old Fashioned Love Song" was an instant hit and became our fourth Gold single.

To prepare for our upcoming concert tour I spent more and more time away from my house, hanging out at the Rainbow and other Sunset Strip bars. My home life was becoming for me quite the living hell. I was alienating myself from Lee more and more every day. And she continued to drink and use drugs at an alarming rate, but nowhere near my consumption level. When I did go home, the minute I walked in she would always try to start a fight and I would immediately seek the solace of some quiet part of the house. At times I would even sneak out of our bedroom in the middle of the night to go over to the guest quarters and screw our new maid.

I was truly becoming the consummate rock and roll scumbag. On more than one occasion, I would run through the house with Lee in hot pursuit, screaming at me over something that I thought was quite trivial. I was obviously insensitive to her feelings and didn't even begin to understand what it was all about. Not being able to find any solitude in the numerous rooms, one night I locked myself in the elevator with a vial of coke and a bottle of vodka. I then stopped it between floors and sat down to contemplate my next move, only to find that she had somehow found a way to override the interior control panel and bring me back to the top floor, screaming the whole way.

In a last-ditch effort to escape her incessant tirades, I donned some scuba gear that I had purchased from a friend of mine and took up the unlikely sport of "deep pool diving." There, underwater, with an hour's worth of oxygen and various amounts of drugs flowing through my system, I finally found the peace I had been seeking. But alas, even the tranquility of my newfound pool habitat was shattered by the rocks that Lee hurled at me from our bedroom balcony. Was nothing sacred?

Another time, I chose to meditate at the bottom of the pool. It was 5:00 A.M. and I was just coming down off of a seemingly peaceful acid trip that I had started miles away from home. I wanted to watch the sun come up from underwater, so this time, thinking that I was Jacques Cousteau, I donned full scuba gear, including a speargun and knife. That was just a precautionary measure in case I was attacked by the dreaded "floaties" (Heather's inflatable pool toys). I had been down there for about thirty-five minutes as the first strains of sunlight were making their way through the water. It was a surreal, almost Feliniesque vision of rippling beauty.

All of a sudden, a large unknown, shape pierced the tranquility and lurched for my head. I began to totally freak out and made my way to the surface, grasping my speargun. As I got close to the top, I noticed that the object that was terrorizing me was the tip of a "pool skimmer." The other end was firmly being held by my terrified pool maintenance man. Since it was still fairly dark outside, the pool man had no idea that anyone was resting on the bottom. Obviously, we scared the shit out of each other. We both let out screams at the same time. He dropped the skimmer and ran for his truck, and then he hastily drove off down the hill.

In the midst of our stateside tour, with Uriah Heap opening for us, we also made preparations to make our first appearance at the Cotton Bowl in Dallas, Texas. On the morning that we were preparing to leave for Oklahoma City, our road manager, Bob Tomasso, called Bill to tell him that Chuck was nowhere to be found. Paula was in a hysterical state because he hadn't come home that night, although that was becoming an everyday occurrence. Since he had been getting so fucked up lately, she figured that he might have been in an accident, or was passed out somewhere in an incapacitated state.

During this time both Chuck and I, and Danny to some extent, always seemed to be blacking out while driving our cars. Even so, none of us had a serious accident. We only ended up hitting inanimate objects such as parked cars, trees, and the dreaded "jumping curb" that was becoming an ongoing joke between me and the Mercedes dealer every time I had one of my cars towed in there.

Everyone was more concerned than usual about Chuck, since in the past Chuck would at least call to inform someone that he was still breathing. Everyone boarded the plane for Oklahoma, and we left Tomasso to comb the back alleys and seedy dives of Hollywood that Chuck was sometimes known to haunt. Still concerned when we arrived there, we all immediately went into Danny's room when he got on the phone to find out if anyone had discovered Chuck's whereabouts.

Bill Utley got on the phone to inform us that he was still missing, but that they now had people calling the highway patrol and the hospitals. Everyone went to sleep that night a little apprehensive as to the outcome of this latest charade.

As showtime approached, we had a major problem on our hands. Not wanting to face a lawsuit by canceling the show, we had to explain to the promoter somehow that Chuck had taken ill, had collapsed in Los Angeles, and was subsequently rushed to the hospital. We would then have to somehow do the show without him, obviously omitting all of his songs. We would give the audience our apologies and offer to make it up to them. This we did admirably and finished the concert without a major incident.

When we got off the stage, we found out that Chuck had been located and was in jail. Suddenly, our worst fears were confirmed. It seems that he had gone on one of his binges and had indeed passed out at the wheel, slammed into a parked car, and then promptly passed out. When the police arrived at the scene of the accident, he woke up and became quite belligerent, so they immediately handcuffed him and hauled him off to jail. There was no way to get him out of jail right away, as he was also being charged with possession of coke, which he had in his pocket at the time of the accident. We had to do some real tap dancing to pull this one off, because the next night he was definitely needed for the concert at the Cotton Bowl.

As we traveled the short distance to Dallas the next day, I thought to myself, *Chuck, you stupid shit, how could you possibly have done something so stupid and irresponsible?*—never dreaming that in the years to come I would far exceed his little joy ride.

Our managers decided that the only thing to do was to charter a Lear jet to get him to Texas in time for the show that evening. So, with an army of lawyers, Burt, Bill, and Joel Cohen went down and bailed him out of jail, assuring the authorities that he would come back later to be arraigned on whatever charges they had against him. Somehow they agreed, a bond was posted, and he was released on his own recognizance.

The management office guaranteed us that Chuck would be there in time for the show, but couldn't give us any assurance what condition he would be in. Knowing Chuck as well as I did, I knew that after spending a night in jail, and all of the other bullshit probably associated with the accident, that he would be one pissed off motherfucker.

For the show, the Cotton Bowl had been divided in half, with the stage set up facing the bleachers on the right side of the stadium. It was a sold-out show, with 20,000 people in attendance and a number of popular acts opening for us, most notably the Buddy Miles Express, Black Oak Arkansas, and the Texan singer named Lobo.

Everyone got to the show early to check out the other acts and to hastily restructure our set to accommodate Chuck in whatever condition he was in. However, nothing prepared us for how he looked when he arrived that night, just before it was time for us to go on. As he staggered out of the limo with Joel holding onto him, we saw that his arm was in a sling, and there was a large bandage across his nose. Both of his eyes were blackened, and he was obviously wearing the same clothes that he had on when the accident occurred. The blue "Chicago" T-shirt that he wore was ripped and had blood stains down the front of it. I took one look at him and thought to myself, *Oh my God, what a mess!*

Joel quickly ushered him into a backstage tent that had been set up for medical emergencies, and in a few moments a doctor carrying his ubiquitous "black bag" followed him in as well. We were genuinely concerned for Chuck's well-being, and Joel came out of the tent to assure us that Chuck would go on stage, but that he was obviously feeling like shit after his ordeal. Joel also informed us that the doctor was there to pack Chuck's broken nose with Novocain and to give him several injections of some painkiller that would enable him to at least sing long enough to get through the show.

At the time, everyone thought that his injuries were the result of the accident. However, I had my doubts. Knowing Chuck's violent temper, I figured that he had probably mouthed off to one of the arresting officers, and in his totally disoriented state of mind, had somehow gotten himself into a fight with them.

As we started the first song and the singers took the stage, I looked out into the audience to view the shocked expressions on their faces when they saw one of their idols the way he really was — battered and fucked-up. Somehow, when we played "Joy to the World" that night, it just didn't seem to fit the picture.

We had the next two days off, which was good, because Chuck definitely needed that time to nurture his wounds. For the remaining three or four dates on the tour, Chuck continued to get shot up with painkillers and other drugs from the local doctors so that he could perform. We barely made it through this one intact, and returned home to engage in some serious meetings with the band and our managers to discuss what our future would be if certain members continued this downward spiral.

It was decided that since Bob Tomasso could handle Chuck best, and really didn't give a shit what Chuck thought about him, that he would virtually become his babysitter. This meant going to his house when we were ready to leave for the road, packing his bags, and physically putting him on the plane if he had to. The same thing would be done on the road as well.

We finished another tour in the fall without a major incident, and then made plans to finally do the full-scale tour of Great Britain. Because we had to abort the proposed British tour of 1970 that would have capitalized on the success of "Mama Told Me," we had rescheduled it for the end of 1971. It would coincide with the success of "Joy to the World," which was our only other hit in England. Because of their star status in the U.K., we would open a series of shows for Uriah Heep. The tour was scheduled to last a little over two weeks, with us spending the holidays over there and returning on New Year's Day.

When we arrived in London, it was apparent that the star stature that we had attained in the U.S. had been somehow ignored by the British audiences. What occurred over there was the exact opposite of what had happened in the States. In the U.K. the critics loved us, and the audiences only gave us a lukewarm response. Thus, even when we played with all of the energy that we expelled on stage, we couldn't seem to win over the British crowds.

Danny, Cory and I continued to roam throughout London looking up old friends we had met on the first promo tour. We would frequent many of the trendy bars there at the time, most notably the Speakeasy, where we had done our debut show in 1969. That was the elite hangout in London where all the musicians would get together to socialize and jam. I was also buying all the trendy clothes from the various stores on Carnaby Street and Portabello Road. While I was there, I managed to look up some girls that I had met earlier, and even hooked up with the stewardess from a few months earlier.

I also wound up one night getting incredibly stoned with some members of Uriah Heep and wound up at a wonderful jam session that lasted well into the next day. It was an incredible scene, and I found out that it was a birthday party for Paul Kossoff, the guitar player for Free. I was quite excited when I met the various members of his band and found out that we had gained their respect by our interpretations of their songs. Also in attendance at this jam was another of my keyboard idols, Brian Auger. It was a real kick in the butt playing next to him.

Throughout the course of the evening, a succession of Britain's best musicians filtered in and out of the room. Among them was Eric Clapton, Steve Winwood, and so many others that I had trouble keeping track of who was who. The whole event was taped at the studio we were in, and somewhere in some deep, dark vault somebody has a priceless album just begging to be released.

I continued drinking and sleeping my way through the British Isles, stopping only occasionally to call Lee and wish her and Heather a "Merry Christmas."

Three Dog Night at the height of our fame, in the early 1970s. (Standing): Joe Schermie, Floyd Sneed, Michael Allsup, Jimmy Greenspoon. (Seated): Danny Hutton, Cory Wells, Chuck Negron.

My father and I. (Photo: Private collection of Jimmy Greenspoon)

Mom and I, my first year. (Photo: Private collection of Jimmy Greenspoon)

In Hawaii with Michael Lloyd (left) in 1962, with unidentified groupies. (Photo: Private collection of Jimmy Greenspoon)

One of my first groups: The Alleykats. (Left to right): Danny Belsky, David Doud, Art Guy, me (with guitar), and Michael Lloyd. (Photo: Private collection of Jimmy Greenspoon)

The first Three Dog Night public relations shot (left to right): Joe, Floyd, Cory, Chuck, Danny, me, and Michael. (Photo by Ed Caraeff courtesy of MCA Records)

My first wife, Lee, our daughter Heather, and I at our Lookout Mountain home. (Photo: Private collection of Jimmy Greenspoon)

The infamous elevator house, high in the Hollywood Hills. (Photo by Jimmy Greenspoon)

Me stoned after recording "Prelude to Morning." (Photo by Bill Cooper)

Leaving the NASA Space Center after our guided tour. I'm in the far right background. (Photo: Private collection of Jimmy Greenspoon)

Chuck at the Cotton Bowl after his "accident." (Photo by Bill Cooper)

My dad and I at "the elevator house." (Photo: Private collection of Jimmy Greenspoon)

The definitive Laurel Canyon party house: 8901 Wonderland Avenue. (Photo by Jimmy Greenspoon)

Three Dog Night live in concert. (Left to right): Michael, Floyd, Chuck, Joe, Danny, me, and Cory. (Photo by Michael Putland/Retna Ltd.)

Me, in the studio, stoned. (Photo by Bill Cooper)

Chuck . . . awake. (Photo by Bill Cooper)

(Left to right): Lee Carlton, our roadie; Michael and myself. (Photo by Bill Cooper)

(Left) Floyd in the studio. (Photo by Bill Cooper)

(Below) Ed Caraeff (Photo by Bill Cooper)

Backstage at Pocono with a fan. (Photo by Bill Cooper)

Backstage with bodyguard and assorted personnel. (Photo by Bill Cooper)

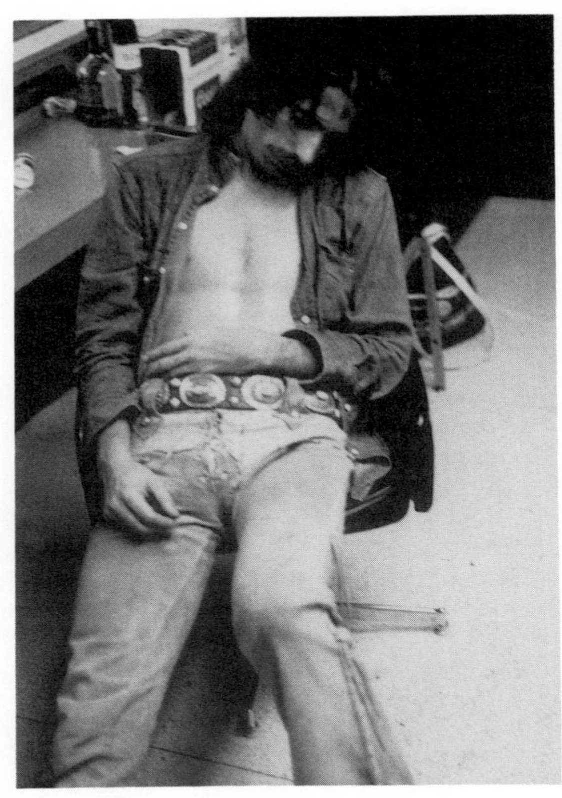

(Left) Chuck after a marathon recording session. (Photo by Bill Cooper)

(Below) Danny conscious in the studio. (Photo by Bill Cooper)

Me during my "Elton John phase." (Photo: Private collection of Jimmy Greenspoon)

Early 1980s group and personnel shot. (Back row from the left): Floyd, Cory, Chuck, Danny, and Michael. (Seated): Jerry Cooney, Al Thomas, me (obviously wasted), Mike Seifrit, and John Meglen. (Photo: Private collection of Jimmy Greenspoon)

At the *Malibu* magazine party, October 1983, Baja Cantina, in Malibu, California. (Left to right): Laurie Hutton, Richard Grossman, me, Cheech Marin, and Danny Hutton. (Photo by Wendie Kohn)

Karen and I on our wedding day. (Photo: Private collection of Jimmy Greenspoon)

Me, on stage, New Year's Eve 1989. (Photo by Karen Greenspoon)

Chuck during a 1989 solo tour. (Photo by Hattie)

Danny on stage in 1989. (Photo by Jude and Gary Yarber)

Cory, 1989. (Photo by Jude and Gary Yarber)

Me, during the 1989 summer tour—clean and sober! (Photo by Diane)

# 10 / Easy To Be Hard

We boarded the plane back to the States at Heathrow Airport in London and landed at LAX in just enough time to ring in the new year. I had only been home three hours when I heard a knock at the door. Since I was having my own personal New Year's Eve party with my family, I figured that it was probably a neighbor coming to help me celebrate. With a joint in my mouth and a drink in my hand, I walked over to the door and opened it.

For one brief moment I panicked when I saw a gentleman in a black uniform standing before me.

"Mr. Greenspoon?" he asked.

"Yes . . ." I said as I took the joint out of my mouth.

"I'm your limo driver," he replied.

"That's nice," I said to him and continued to stare, not knowing what he was doing there. "I'm here to take you to the parade site," he explained. With my jet lag and everything else that was going on, I had completely forgotten that our road manager had told me that the pick-up time would be quite early, but I never realized it would be 3:00 A.M.! I somehow had to find some suitable clothes and get myself together enough to pull this fiasco off. I thought to myself, *Whose fucking idea was it for us to be in the Rose Bowl Parade, standing on a float, freezing my ass off, and waving at people like I was the Pope?*

In reality it was our publicist Bob Levinson's idea, and in retrospect it was nothing short of brilliant.

To capitalize on our incredible popularity, Levinson had arranged for us to appear on the FTD (Florist's Transworld Delivery) float, appropriately themed and entitled "Joy to the World." We would ride in the parade and wave to the people while lip-synching several of our hits. Also, we would be viewed by countless millions of people on television, who would help to make Three Dog Night a household word.

I told the limo driver that I would be down in a few minutes, and politely slammed the door in his face. I took a quick shower and put on anything I could find, not really caring what I looked like. Remembering how cold it was, I decided to wear my full-length wool and suede coat for the parade. Since I knew that all we had to do was stand there and wave and move our lips, I decided to cop a healthy New Year's buzz. I finished off the joint, ate the roach, and washed it down with the remainder of my double vodka gimlet. I then went over to my sundry bag, which was still unpacked, rummaged through it for a minute, and produced two Mandrex that were given to me by someone in London. I chased those with another vodka gimlet, put on my coat, and was ready to party!

We arrived at the prearranged meeting spot, which happened to be a nuns' sanctuary that was rented for us by the City of Pasadena. Since being in the Rose Bowl Parade was a "first" for any rock group, I'm also certain that we were the first rock group to meet at a nuns' sanctuary! When I entered, however, I found that there were no nuns in attendance — only the other extremely tired members of the band.

We remained at the sanctuary until it came time to board the float for the early morning judging, which would at that time determine the prizes of "Best Float" and all of the dozens of other categories.

When we arrived at the float, I took one look at it, and in my current state of mind thought to myself, *This looks like an out-of-control acid trip in a flower shop!* Upon closer examination I realized that it looked more like some sort of bad 1950s "B" horror film like *Attack Of The Killer Chrysanthemums*. For the people who made it, however, it was obviously a labor of love. To quote the official parade program, it was: "A psychedelic free-form float depicting an enchanting song of astrology. Water flows from vase held by Aquarius. Vase is pink gladiola, carnations, and vanda orchids. Sun is yellow mums. Moon is gold mums. Aquarius is blue iris petals, pink carnations, gladiola, and vanda orchids." I was done up in Acapulco Gold, Gimlet Green, and Mandrex White.

Immediately everyone realized that there was going to be an incredible logistical problem about where to position ourselves on this massive artistic nightmare in buds. In a second the rush was on, with Cory and Floyd obtaining the most secure positions, on the right side of the float. There they could rest their arms on the float's structure. Michael positioned himself on the far left side, leaving Danny, Chuck, and me to stand in the front, without any apparent support. Realizing that we'd have to hold this position for hours, I knew this just wouldn't make it. On top of that, it looked like Danny already was doing the "slow fade." Seeing this, one of our quick-thinking roadies ran over with a couple of Michael's guitar stands and put them behind Danny and Chuck. He then secured their bodies to the stands with duct tape to ensure that they would remain upright through the entire parade.

We would soon find out that this was a brilliant move on the roadie's part, because shortly after the parade had started, we began to smell pot and realized that the float driver was getting high. When we began to move down the parade route he would speed up and slow down, causing the float to lurch violently.

Somehow we finished the parade without falling off of the float. In the final analysis, the whole fiasco ended up being quite a coup for us, as our float ended up winning the Grand Prize.

As the 1971 year-end issues of the music industry trade magazines — *Billboard, Cash Box,* and *Record World* — hit the newsstands, we were unanimously proclaimed "Group of the Year" in both the albums and singles categories. In addition, "Joy to the World" was also named "Record of the Year."

When the Grammy nominations were announced, "Joy" was up for two awards: "Best Vocal Performance by a Duo, Group or Chorus/Pop, Rock and Folk" and "Record of the Year." We had already appeared on the live telecast from Hollywood the previous year, when the single was first a hit. In 1972, when they announced the winners, we were in New York at the Felt Forum performing the song again on the Grammy telecast. Right after we did the song, a stage hand came up to us and told us not to go anywhere. At the same time, another person was walking toward us, carrying an armful of the awards. Immediately, everybody assumed that we had won, and we all became extremely excited. When the envelope for "Record of the Year" was opened, and the winner announced, we were in total shock: "And the winner is . . . Carole King for *It's Too Late.*" Earlier in the evening we had lost in the other category to the

Carpenters. After the initial shock wore off, I quickly realized that it was an honor just to be nominated, and for that I was extremely grateful.

Later we attended the post-Grammy party at one of New York's posh restaurants, and I proceeded to drink myself into a coma. I vaguely remember going back to the Plaza Hotel where we were staying. As I started to walk toward the elevator, Karen Carpenter was standing there with her award, saying, "I'm so sorry you lost." As the elevator doors were closing, I flipped her the bird and said a hearty "Fuck you!" Fortunately for me, the doors had closed too quickly for her to witness my rather immature outburst. It's a good thing for Carole King that she wasn't staying there too.

Just prior to this, at the end of 1971, Dunhill had released the second single from the *Harmony* album, Hoyt's "Never Been to Spain." They had hoped to capitalize on the incredible success of "Joy to the World," and although "Spain" was a number one record, nothing would ever come close to the bullfrog song.

With the Rose Parade under our belts, it seemed that our publicist was always searching for another "first" for the band to pull off. In a well-calculated move, our management arranged for us to play a series of twenty-two outdoor ballparks and stadiums in an eleven-week period from June 16 to August 22. Because of the massive undertaking and the sheer size, we dubbed it "The Tour of Tours." Until then, the only group to play venues of this size were the Beatles, who had disbanded in 1970. Also, plans were made for us to tape our first network television special, to be produced by Dick Clark and featuring Roberta Flack as our special guest. The U.S. tour would be followed by a month-long European tour, with a short break and a Pacific/Asia tour slated to finish off the year.

As the concert itinerary was being published, we were still in negotiations for our opening acts. However, several popular or up-and-coming acts had been confirmed for the shows. For the show in Bloomington, Minnesota, we had the Electric Light Orchestra open for us, and at the Sports Arena in San Diego we had the Allman Brothers. At both the Cotton Bowl and Atlanta Braves Stadium shows we had Rod Stewart and the Faces as our opening act. Two Northwest dates would open with the Doobie Brothers, who were promoting their first hit single, "Listen to the Music," and a late addition for the Three Rivers Stadium show in Pittsburgh was the lineup of the Buddy Miles Express, Seatrain, and Leon Russell.

Since we were obviously doing everything on a grand scale, we decided that our travel arrangements would also have to reflect our stature in the business. We therefore decided to charter our own jet.

The Lears proved to be too small and costly, so we finally settled on an eight-passenger Falcon Fanjet that we had custom painted with our logo on the side of it. This made it extremely easy to get in and out of airports, and since we could pretty much dictate our own departure and arrival times, we didn't have to punch any clocks. Once we had arrived at the designated private airfield, our limos would be on the runway waiting to meet us and whisk us to our hotel suites. To insure our security, and not piss off any other hotel guests (with food fights, all-night parties, and orgies), we would now rent an entire private floor.

My partying and excessiveness were getting out of hand, and besides taking a toll on my family life, it began to change my whole way of thinking. I perceived myself as some sort of invulnerable Superman who could consume any quantity of dangerous substances and still emerge unscathed. There was a little "in joke" going around at the time, where certain people would be warned, when they met me, not to try to keep up with my drinking and drugging . . . because it was impossible. It seemed that no matter how fucked-up I got, I would rebound the next day, and somehow appear to be functioning at a normal rate.

A lot of the people in the business whom I knew, respected, and partied with, had already snuffed out their lives unnecessarily. Within a one-year period, three of rock's most promising stars met an untimely death at the height of their success because of drugs and alcohol. On September 18, 1970, Jimi Hendrix was found dead, having suffocated on his own vomit after ingesting a number of barbiturates. On October 3, 1970, Janis Joplin died of a heroin overdose, in a Hollywood apartment/hotel (where, coincidentally, years earlier Joe Schermie had lived). And on July 3, 1971, Jim Morrison, while in Paris, reportedly died of a heart attack, which was never proven or disproven, because his body disappeared. There were many people who speculated that he had "faked" his own death just to obtain some much needed rest, but those of us who knew him suspected that his lifestyle had finally caught up with him.

The ironic thing is that all three of them died at the age of twenty-seven. I figured I was safe, since I had at least three more years until my twenty-seventh birthday. Plenty of time to have fun in the meantime.

It seemed that out of those three stars, Janis Joplin was the most inapproachable. Janis was a lot of things, but feminine wasn't one of them. She had a voice that could melt the chrome off of a trailer hitch, a personality as abrasive as number-four grade sandpaper, and an onstage appearance straight out of *The Exorcist*.

The first time that I saw her was in December of 1966, when she was the lead singer of Big Brother and the Holding Company. It was the night that Superband shared the bill with her at the Family Dog in Denver, Colorado. I was awed by her abrasive singing style, but I didn't like Janis at all as a person back then. She was surrounded by a bunch of Hell's Angels, and she always had her trademark bottle with her. I had always felt that girls were supposed to be girls, and Janis wasn't. Her attitude was always very aggressive.

The next time that I saw her, she and Big Brother were among the headliners at the Monterey Pop Festival in June 1967. At the time I was tripping my brains out on acid. When I was at the show that day, under the influence of the drug, I thought that the whole festival was an incredible "cosmic experience," and surprisingly I wasn't as turned off by Janis' singing voice, which sounded like the uncontrolled shrieking of a banshee.

Years later, when I rented a video of the documentary called *Monterey Pop,* I discovered that not one performer on the bill played or sang on key that day. Otis Redding's horn section seemed to be playing a totally different song than he was singing, the Jimi Hendrix act was mesmerizingly visual — so that the music was secondary — and only the Mamas and the Papas came across as professionals. The crowd was so fucked up that they cheered and screamed for everyone on the bill. They even applauded for the people who introduced the bands. The whole scene at the festival was more important than the music. That was one of the pluses to taking acid.

In the late '60s, when Three Dog Night was the house band at the Whiskey-A-Go-Go, Janis would come in at all times to hear us play. She had a mad crush on Cory and loved the way he sang. She also liked the fact that he was one of the few white people who could sing "Try a Little Tenderness" and do real soulful songs.

One night she came backstage at the Whiskey to meet the band, and was obviously putting the moves on Cory. He was happily married and wasn't into Janis on a sexual level, and when he let it be known that he wasn't interested in her, she got really pissed off.

The next time that we ran into Janis was at the Atlantic City Pop Festival in 1970. I was standing backstage with Cass Elliot, and Janis came reeling in with her obligatory bottle of Southern Comfort that she was always swigging. (Although everyone assumed that it was filled with Southern Comfort, we found out later that it was actually a bottle full of codeine cough syrup.) Cass had dropped some acid that day, and as we were about to go on stage, she wanted to know if I wanted to drop some too. I said, "No, I'll wait until after the show." She was great like that, always sharing her drugs. "Oh come on, Jimmy," she argued, "it'll make the show better." I told her, "No problem, I'll do it later — OK, Cass?"

Janis came in totally blitzed. Cory saw her coming down the hallway, so he split. He knew that she would probably say something about their feud at the Whiskey. Chuck was in rare form that night. Since he grew up in a tough neighborhood in the Bronx, he didn't take any crap from anybody. I don't know exactly what was said wordwise, but he said something to Janis, and she said something rude back to him. With that, the two of them really got into it. Chuck ended up embarrassing her by sarcastically saying back to Janis, "Oh, Miss Imagemaker. Miss White Rock Singer trying to sound black, with your bottle of Southern Comfort as your crutch." It wound up being a verbal fighting match, which heated up to the point where he called her "an ugly slut." Finally, some of the guys from Big Brother and the Holding Company came in and dragged her off into the dressing room, and I got to Chuck and told him that it wasn't worth it to argue with Janis because she was so screwed up.

The last time that I saw Janis she was appearing on "American Bandstand" with her new group, the Full Tilt Boogie Band. Three Dog Night was also on the show that day. We just exchanged polite "hellos" and went into our respective dressing rooms.

I had heard that she was trying to clean up her act, and get off of drugs. I remember following the progress of the recording of her last album, *Pearl,* when I heard the news that she had died of an overdose of heroin.

Janis lived so hard and fast that it's really a wonder she survived as long as she did. Although our personalities clashed, and her music wasn't always the tightest, I thought that nobody should have to go through so much self-inflicted pain and die so needlessly. In the end, she became just another rock and roll casualty.

Since 1972 was obviously going to be our busiest year ever, in terms of touring and media exposure, we had to make sure that we had enough product on the market to sustain us throughout the year. We also didn't want to incur the wrath of Dunhill, and risk losing a bonus. With this thought in mind, we set out to record our sixth studio album and eighth consecutive LP release. As we entered the studio to do this, a third and final single was picked off of the *Harmony* album. The song "The Family of Man" marked the third time that we had a hit with a Paul Williams song, and it peaked at Number 12.

The first song that we recorded for our new album was a reggae tune that Danny had found when we were in London. The song "Black and White," co-written by David Arkin (actor Alan Arkin's father), was originally recorded by a Jamaican group called Greyhound, and had been a hit some years earlier in England. For the almost nursery rhyme-like feeling of the song, all of the band members who had children brought them to the studio to sing on the chorus. Heather was only two years old at the time, and couldn't have cared less about this. The song was finished quickly, and the resulting product set the tone for the rest of the album, in that it was almost a throwback to the recording technique that we used on our debut album. It was once again very spontaneous, with very little overdubbing. The fact that we had to get this out before "The Tour of Tours" started meant that we couldn't fool around with garbage cans and other time-consuming devices as we had with *Harmony*.

Once again, Cory chose a Randy Newman tune, "My Old Kentucky Home (Turpentine and Dandelion Wine)," that both he and Ritchie Podolor played guitar on, to achieve a rather backwoods feel. The next song that we recorded was picked by Chuck and written by songwriter Dave Loggins (who later scored with "Please Come to Boston"). The song "Pieces of April" became a crowd favorite at our later shows.

The night we finished recording "Pieces," I stayed in the studio, listening to the playback with Ritchie and Bill. I had a brilliant idea swimming around in my drug-soaked brain. Since I wanted some time to formulate it, and wasn't needed in the studio, I told them I was going home. Instead, I went to the house of my good friend and fellow party animal, Whitey Glan from Bush.

I arrived at his house late that night, and after consuming mass quantities of drugs, we both decided to drop some sort of unknown and unnamed new psychedelic. It wasn't as intense as any of the acid that I had taken years earlier, and therefore afforded me a very mellow yet long-lasting trip. I remember watching the sun come up, floating on a raft in Whitey's pool, when I heard the phone ringing up at the house. Whitey poked his head out of the window and said, "Hey Spooner, they need you down at the studio right away!" I wondered how that could be, since they told me that my presence wouldn't be needed. Nevertheless, I got out of the pool to phone the studio and see what was really going on. When Ritchie answered he instantly apologized and said there had been a minor accident in the control room, and that I would have to come back and redo a small part on "Pieces of April." I didn't want to explain to him that I was too busy tripping to come back down and do my part, so I reluctantly got into my car and drove back to the studio.

After one runthrough, I repaired the damage that had been done to "Pieces" and was ready to go back to Whitey's and resume my acid trip. But as I heard the playback of the song, I got wrapped up in the moment and decided to run into the studio and bring to life the idea that I had previously formulated. I sat down at the keyboards and started playing a beautiful little melody and chord structure, when Ritchie pressed the "talk back" button and asked, "What's that?"

"Just a little something I came up with," I answered.

"Give us a minute and we'll roll tape. I want you to play that again."

I proceeded to lay down the piano part on one runthrough and then went back in to listen. We all agreed that I was on to something, so I went back to the studio and began dubbing various keyboard parts. Within an hour we had a completed tune. For that little something extra, Ritchie suggested that I pluck and strum the strings of his Steinway grand piano like it was a harp. With a lot of echo, the finished product was the perfect lead-in to the passage I had just recorded. In a brilliant bit of splicing, Bill Cooper tagged the instrumental piece that I had just recorded onto the beginning of "Pieces of April."

The following day, when everyone came in to listen to "Pieces," we didn't tell them what I had done the day before. As my composition (which I entitled "Prelude to Morning," in an obvious reference to the time that I was distracted from my acid trip) came on the speakers, everyone was immediately knocked out.

"What's that?" Chuck asked.

"Just a little something I came up with," I replied.

Everyone liked it so much that we decided to include it on our new album.

The next song that was recorded was a power ballad entitled "Going in Circles," which was used in the closing credits of the forgettable movie *X, Y and Zee,* starring Elizabeth Taylor, Michael Caine, and Susanna York. This was an attempt to make up for an opportunity that we royally blew earlier on, when we turned down a song for another movie. After the incredible success of "Joy to the World," everybody and their brother was coming to us with projects and ideas. One day at a meeting, a new and talented director named Robert Altman presented us with the song "Suicide is Painless" that was to be included in his forthcoming film. Everyone figured that with a title like that, it just didn't fit our current image. Also, after hearing the synopsis of this movie — about a team of medics in the Korean Conflict — we figured the subject matter wasn't strong enough or funny enough to be accepted by the general public anyway. *M*A*S*H* was released, and the rest is history. We had high hopes for "Going in Circles" because of this blunder. Unfortunately, neither the film nor the song received much notice.

For the album's no-holds-barred rocker we picked another Argent tune, written by Russ Ballard (who had penned "Liar" on our *Naturally* album). We did our interpretation of his composition "Chained," which wound up being a vocal tour de force. The next song, "Tulsa Turnaround," required a piano intro from me that would come off sounding like it was played by a sloppy drunken honky-tonk piano player in a saloon. For this song we rented an upright piano and put thumbtacks on all of the pads to achieve that sound. However, the execution would have to come from me and, drawing on my vast musical background and well-stocked liquor cabinet, I prepared to record it. The end result, complete with unintentional missed notes and other glitches, more than yielded the desired effect we sought.

A group effort entitled "In Bed" seemed to me to be the weakest song on the album. Allen Toussaint's "Freedom for the Stallion" was recorded with only my piano, Floyd's marching drum, and several off-the-wall overdubs on different instruments. The end result had an almost anthem-like quality.

The brilliant guitar player from Bush, Dominic Troiano, submitted another one of his songs, this one entitled "The Writings on the Wall." (Previously we had recorded his "I Can Hear You Calling.") We instantly agreed to include "Writings" on the album as well.

For the last tune, we decided to give a nod to the studio's janitor, Gary Itri. To our surprise we had discovered he was a talented songwriter. His composition, "Midnight Runaway," became the closing song on the album.

Throughout the whole recording process, everyone's individual personality had been developed and tapped fully. Therefore, we came up with the very apropos album title, *Seven Separate Fools*. Immediately, the ideas began flowing for a packaging concept that up to that point was unprecedented. Since we were Dunhill's "golden boys," cost was no object. What resulted was one of the most lavish album packages in music industry history.

The concept was to package the album like it was an elaborate twelve-by-twelve deck of playing cards. An intricate graphic design on the front cover looked like a nineteenth-century card box. On the inside of the package, which had a flap that had to be opened, were seven full-color playing cards with a concept photo of each of us depicted on them.

Ed Caraeff had a field day doing the photography for these. Everybody individually met with him to discuss how they wanted their persona to come across to the public. Cory, being the nature lover and naturalist, was depicted as the consummate sportsman, complete with shotgun, fishing gear, stuffed pheasant, and other outdoorsy props. Chuck came off as the suave riverboat gambler, dressed in a beige Bat Masterson-like suit complete with string tie and an eyepatch. He carefully held the cork to an open decanter of booze, while seated next to a kerosene lamp.

Joe, in keeping with his rather dark and morbid mood, situated himself inside an iron maiden (a seventeenth-century spiked instrument of torture) in front of a fireplace. On the mantle were various other instruments of pain and destruction, including a mace and skull spike. For Michael, Ed achieved a double image of him holding one of the rare guitars that he collected, against a plain red background. On the top and bottom corners of the card Ed, positioned three guitars to simulate a "club" symbol.

Floyd's card depicted him as the "Ace of Spades," and it was truly the most elaborate one. In a dingy basement gameroom, amid numerous props, Floyd was seated at a long table that had garbage strewn all over it, as if he was the victorious croupier at an all-night card game. Empty hands of cards were left on the table, along with empty bottles, shotglasses, half-eaten food, wads of money, and ashtrays full of cigarette and cigar butts. Somewhere in this mess, if you look carefully, you can also pick out a hash pipe and a vial of cocaine, which Floyd had obviously used to get him through the photo shoot. Again in whiteface, and wearing a rather outrageous embroidered orange shirt, Danny was depicted as the deck's "Joker." Ed used the same split body effect here that he had on Michael's card.

For my card, Ed wanted to somehow capture my hyperactivity and the fact that I always seemed to be racing through life. I arrived at the photo shoot wearing the most mismatched outfit I could find, considering the fact that I didn't want to spend too much time at home fighting with Lee. I wore the same shirt and vest that I had on the back cover of *It Ain't Easy,* augmented with a pair of beige pants that segued into fire engine red velvet bellbottoms with stars painted on them. Ed had me climb atop an antique bicycle, a highwheeler with the seat situated on top of a huge main wheel. As this was extremely difficult for me to maintain my balance on, Ed tried to secure it with two thin guy wires. To simulate motion, he turned on a fan to blow my hair. Shortly before the wires broke, and I came toppling to the floor, he got the necessary photo. To complete the picture, he placed the bicycle in front of a blue backdrop and then airbrushed the photo to give the illusion of movement.

With the album completed, we went into rehearsals for our television special. When the day of taping came, we had a specially selected (by invitation only) studio audience. Although the special was to be aired on ABC-TV, it was taped at the NBC-TV studios in Burbank, California, down the hall from where "The Tonight Show" is filmed.

The special was structured very much like a live performance. We also shot a backstage dressing room scene complete with snappy banter, and at one point someone made a reference to the infamous groupies, the Plaster Casters, when someone's empty cast was brought in to be autographed by the group. Also as part of the dressing room sequence, we were introduced for the first time to Roberta Flack, which gave the whole show a feeling of spontaneity. She was currently riding the success of her song "Killing Me Softly," which she performed on the show, and then she joined Danny, Chuck, and Cory to sing her hit "Where is the Love."

Later we got together with the Dick Clark executives to edit the show and prepare it for the airdate. Then it was time to sequester ourselves on a massive soundstage at Studio Instrument Rentals in Hollywood and begin to preparing for "The Tour of Tours."

As the kick-off date in Milwaukee on July 7 approached, I had to stockpile enough drugs for the tour. However, I knew that if the supply was depleted, certain members would not be adverse to flying in our various dealers. I went on a massive shopping spree and bought all new stage clothes and luggage. That was the least I could do for myself, considering the fact that Lee had spent so much money redecorating the house and securing her own personal possessions.

During this time in my marriage, I was quite unhappy. Lee and I were constantly at each other's throats over seemingly trite and insignificant bullshit. I was now becoming quite blatant with regards to my womanizing. Besides the obvious groupies on the road, I was also having affairs with various women right in my own backyard. The cement that once held together our marriage was progressively dissolving. Although the thought was in the back of my mind, I was far too selfish to get a divorce, knowing that half of my precious accumulated wealth would be sucked from my bank account.

I started an ill-fated affair with one of the secretaries at the Whiskey that would soon mark the disintegration of my already less-than-happy union with Lee. It seemed that every time I came out of this girl's house, I would see a man sitting in a parked car, pretending not to notice me. Since it would usually be in the early hours of the morning, I could only surmise that Lee had hired a private detective, but I later found out that was my own paranoia. On more than one occasion I walked up to the car and tapped on the window to inform the gentleman seated inside that I was "through fucking," and that he could write that in his report.

The straw that broke the camel's back came when the group did a short tour of warm-up dates on the East Coast. We had checked into the Holiday Inn in Roanoke, Virginia, when I called up the girl I was having the affair with and informed her that I had arranged for a plane ticket for her to come and meet me. At the same time that I was talking to her, and because the front desk manager was new and obviously didn't know anything about the switchboard system, and didn't inform me that Lee was on the line, and he wound up patching all three of us on the same line. It turned out that I thought I was talking to my mistress, inviting her to come on the road, when in reality I was talking to my wife. When I called the girl by her first name, and instead heard Lee's irate voice, I knew my goose was cooked.

As I recall it, the line went dead, and I immediately slammed down the phone and ran out the door toward the lobby to crucify that stupid son-of-a-bitch at the front desk. I stormed into the switchboard room, screaming at the top of my lungs. Fortunately for me — and him — I was restrained by two of our roadies who happened to be there. In another instant I would have lunged over the front desk and strangled the little creep with my bare hands.

After trying to calm down and explain to him what he had done, I decided to return to my room to attempt to repair the damage that this blunder had caused. When I got Lee on the phone, I could tell that she was completely fed up with my extracurricular activities, and by the tone of her voice, I knew that it was all but over. Nevertheless, in a last-ditch effort to patch things up, I apologized and began pleading with her. At that moment my mistress, who apparently was not aware of what the hell had happened, was calling me back to find out if she was still invited. In what had to be the most ridiculous comedy of errors, the lame-brain at the front desk put us together for the second time. When I heard Lee scream, "That's it!" I knew right then and there that my marriage was officially over. I was so outraged that I ran down to the lobby again and hurled a chair at the motherfucker who was running the switchboard.

After the tour was over, I flew home. When the limo pulled up in front of my house, I noticed that a number of cars were parked outside. When I went inside, Lee invited me to move out, and told me that she would agree to divide up some of our belongings.

On the flight all the way home, I prepared myself for such an event, so it came as no surprise to me when I walked in the door and found her glaring at me. She stepped forward and informed me that she was fed up with my constant bullshit and wanted a divorce.

"Fine," I told her, "let me get a few of my things, and I'm history."

"You can say that again," she said.

By that time Three Dog Night had made several wise investments, one of them being the purchase of our own apartment building, located at 718 Kings Road in West Hollywood. Since Floyd was going through a similar experience, and even though he and his wife had never gotten a formal divorce, he had moved out of his house and into the Kings Road building. I called our business manager and told him what was transpiring in my life, and that I would also be moving immediately into one of the apartments. I then called up one of the roadies and had him come to the house with his pickup truck to help me move my TV, clothes, and some small pieces of furniture to the apartment. Since it wasn't furnished, and I wouldn't be able to purchase a bed and other items until the next day, I naturally found a substitute bimbo to spend the night with.

I went to various furniture stores the following day and bought the required necessities to make it my very own home. I also arranged to have the money in our joint bank accounts transferred to just my name, and then proceeded to call a good divorce lawyer. Since there was a lot of community property and a child at stake, I knew I was going to have to give up a lot. But I was ready for a fight.

Once I was settled into the Kings Road apartment, I discovered that, besides Floyd, several members of other groups were also living there. My eventual neighbors became Butch Stone, the manager for Black Oak Arkansas; a few of his band members; Gerry Beckley and Dewey Bunell from the group America; and actor David Joliffe, from the TV series "Room 222."

A week later I found out that one of our managers, Burt Jacobs, had been fighting with his wife and had moved in there. My apartment became one big party and orgy center. I quickly dubbed the place "Three Dog Night Arms."

Even though I was wallowing in my newfound freedom, there was a void in my life. Almost immediately, through the girlfriend of our road manager, I was introduced to and began dating a friend of hers, model and part-time actress Christine Forbes. She was a number of years younger than I was and had an incredible zest for life. She was also extremely beautiful and possessed the kind of figure that men would kill for. Being with her somehow lessened the pain and trauma of my divorce.

While my divorce raged on, my lawyer was preparing me for the worst. However, since he had a good track record, I wasn't worried. The main thing Lee wanted was a healthy alimony, adequate child support, half the equity in the house, one of the cars, half the furniture, half of my record and concert royalties — as well as any future compensation, the money from half of my investments, a few pints of blood, and my left testicle. *That's reasonable,* I thought to myself, *No fucking way!*

When everything was said and done, we made a deal to give her sole ownership of the house allowing me to keep my royalties and investments. I also would pay $1,000-a-month alimony until such time as she could find a suitable job, or remarry, plus $500-a-month child support. We also split all of our possessions equally, along with the court and lawyer costs. To put the icing on the cake, our side also offered her a $125,000 cash settlement. After reviewing her options with her lawyer, and being continually beaten down every time we went to court, she finally agreed to the settlement.

The day that the decree became final, we left the courthouse in Santa Monica and were greeted by a flurry of reporters, photographers, and newscasters. That night, as I sat in my new apartment, getting head from one of my girlfriends, I knew that I had made the bigtime when I watched myself being talked about on TV by Rona Barrett.

As a testament to our incredible popularity, on the day that we were supposed to leave for the tour it was arranged for us to have a photo shoot that would ultimately be the cover of an upcoming issue of *Rolling Stone* magazine. Along with our group photographer, Ed Caraeff, *Rolling Stone* photographer Annie Lebovitz would take pictures for the feature story the magazine was doing on us.

When the article ran in the September 14, 1972, issue of *Rolling Stone,* the cover shot was a photo of us with our own jet. The headline read: "More Gold Than the Stones! Bigger Crowds Than Creedence! Fatter Purses Than Elvis! Three Dog Night: See How They Run." We were being acknowledged as the highest grossing rock and roll band in the world — and that's exactly what we had become.

# *11* / Never Been To Spain

Now that I was a confirmed bachelor, I didn't have to worry about bringing home misplaced panties in my luggage, or about crossed lines on hotel telephones. As "The Tour of Tours" progressed, everyone in the band, although very aware of their star status, was never overwhelmed by the response we were getting. Screaming fans, near riot receptions, food fights, orgies, drugs, booze, and other forms of debauchery were being played out to the hilt. We were on top of the world, and we thought we lived like it.

On the night of July 15, 1972, after finishing our show at the Metropolitan Sports Center in Bloomington, Minnesota, we returned to the hotel, where I immediately set up camp in the bar with various members of Electric Light Orchestra, our opening act. Shortly after Michael came down to join us, we began to innocently toss around pretzels, peanuts, and various other bar condiments at each other. In a short while we were also joined by our pilot and copilot, who weren't drinking (because they had to fly the next day), but who nevertheless joined in on the merriment.

Within minutes, this had all the earmarkings of a full-blown food fight. I had thrown a glass of water at Michael and at the same time had dumped a bowl of dip on his head. Fearing retaliation, I ran for the elevator and the safety of my hotel room above. Michael and our two pilots were right behind me in hot pursuit.

Since we occupied the entire floor of suites, almost all doors to connecting rooms were left open. I ran into my room and quickly filled up the wastepaper basket with cold water. I then emptied about four or five icetrays into it, from our various refrigerators, and stood by the door, poised and ready to strike. When I saw the doorknob turn I didn't waste a second. No sooner had it opened than I hurled the bucket of ice water at whoever happened to be standing there. Fortunately for me it was Michael, who, vowing revenge, took off after me as I ran from room to room. All the while he was doing this, our pilot and co-pilot were also chasing Michael, who was chasing me. Fearing for his safety, he figured that at least the odds would be even if he joined forces with me. In a second we had closed and locked the door to one of the adjoining rooms and were quickly mapping out a fiendish plan of ambush against our two aeronauts.

We armed ourselves with some fruit and more water-filled trash cans, and then went out into the hallway to circle the rooms and come up from behind them with the element of surprise. The plan worked perfectly, and as they were pounding on the connecting door, trying to entice us to come out of the room, they never realized that we were sneaking up behind them. Suddenly, we let loose with a blinding volley of destruction. Realizing they had been had by us, they turned and began to chase us out of the room. With them almost breathing down our necks, I quickly grabbed the door behind me and slammed it shut, feeling a slight resistance. Michael then turned and deadbolted it, and almost immediately we heard screams coming from the other side. It was our pilot yelling, "My hand, my hand!"

"Don't open it," Michael said, "it's only a trick," as we held the door tightly shut. The screaming continued and we heard our co-pilot's voice informing us that his friend's finger was caught in the door. I could tell by the tone of his voice that he wasn't bullshitting us, and at that very instant I saw a small trickle of blood coming through our side of the door. I quickly undid the deadbolt and cautiously opened the door to find the pilot sitting on the floor, holding his hand, while a lot of blood was flowing freely from the stump where one of his fingers had been. With two and a half joints of his finger missing, he was laughing and almost in shock.

The co-pilot's face was as white as a sheet, and he was on the floor holding his injured companion. Just then, hearing the screams, several of the other band members and our road manager came down the hallway to see what had happened. With the ambulance on its way, we wrapped the pilot's hand in a towel and got him downstairs so he could be rushed off to the hospital.

Everything had happened so quickly, we didn't see where the severed finger had landed. We knew that if we found it in a reasonably short period of time and packed it in ice, we could rush it to the hospital, where it could probably be grafted back onto his hand. As the elevator door opened and more and more partygoers started to spill out onto the floor, they were immediately turned away from the area so that we could carry on a thorough search for the missing finger. At one point everyone was lifting up their feet and looking at the bottoms of their shoes, to see if they had stepped on it. We spent what seemed like the longest time combing the area — both in the vicinity of the accident and away from it. The strange thing about the whole situation was, except for the small amount of blood on the door, there wasn't a drop of it anyplace else. As time was running out, our road manager in a calculated hunch reached into the doorjamb and brought it out of the space where the deadbolt fits into. It seems that our pilot had his finger in the door the precise moment when I closed it and Michael deadbolted it. Because of the swiftness and force we used, the cut was so clean that the flesh and the bone were both relatively unmangled.

By now I was so shaken up that I couldn't even talk. I went back to my room to take a few downers, knowing that I had ruined the career of a friend. Our road manager took the wrapped finger to the hospital and me along with it so that I could at least see the outcome of my childish prank. Seeing him lying there made me feel even worse. Although by now he had been shot up with so much Demerol he didn't care, I was crying as I walked up to his bed and told him how sorry I was.

"Don't worry about it," he said to me. "It was an accident. It could have happened to any one of us."

As the doctor was leaving his room, our road manager asked him if he could write out a prescription for a sedative for me, seeing how I was more shaken up than the pilot. The doctor agreed to give me the pills, and in a second I was saying my goodbyes, as our pilot was rushed off to the operating room. Before he was wheeled out of the room, however, he motioned for me to come over. As I bent down he whispered in my ear, "Payback is going to be a bitch!"

Miraculously, the doctors grafted the severed finger back on in time, and he was able to continue the tour. Although he couldn't fly the plane (the co-pilot took over those duties), he was still able to navigate and use his uninjured right hand for various controls.

With the new album and initial single, "Black and White," released simultaneously to coincide with the tour, we continued to break hearts and hotel rooms across the country. The album, which of course shipped Gold, quickly climbed into the Top 10, and the single became our fourth Number One hit. It too was certified Gold, becoming our fifth song to do so.

The tour was progressing quite nicely, with the usual fantastic crowd response, wild parties, and excessive behavior from several band members. By the time we got to Chicago for a show at the International Amphitheatre, we had fine-tuned our performances both on and off stage. That night our opening act, Lee Michaels, spiked the punch in our dressing room with acid, causing Chuck, me, our lawyer, and a policeman to see God in various stages. Aside from that minor setback, nothing out of the ordinary happened, except for the fact that, in keeping with true rock and roll acceptance, we were introduced later that evening to the infamous groupies: the Plaster Casters.

Michael and I were sharing a two-bedroom suite at the Astor Towers and were holding court for several of our friends and adoring fans. I was walking from room to room, trying to scrounge up some more drugs and another drink, and hitting on one of the girls who had been following us for some time. When I reappeared in the living room, I saw what can only be described as two extremely overweight and unattractive girls, sitting on one of the couches and holding a small suitcase. I thought to myself, *Did somebody lose a water buffalo?*

At that point they introduced themselves as Cynthia and Diane Plaster Caster.

"Nice to meet you, Miss Caster," I sarcastically said. Michael was on the floor, rolling with laughter. They then proceeded to open up the suitcase and launch into a sales pitch that would have made any Fuller Brush man proud.

For those who are totally unaware of the legend of these two beached whales, let me give a brief explanation of their operation. After one of the duo performed fellatio on the intended castee (who had to be a rock star of prominent stature), the other would immediately smear fast-drying plaster of paris on his erect genitals. This was done in order to construct a mold of the "love torpedo." Their favorite subjects were rock stars such as Jimmy Page and Jimi Hendrix. They would then take the finished molds home and cast a phallic statue, which was immediately displayed on their wall, in some bizarre trophy room.

After the Plaster Casters expressed profound interest in "doing" any of the members of Three Dog Night, I politely declined, but told them that I was sure there would be another suitable taker lurking in one of the rooms. Then, having wasted precious time listening to their pitch, I returned my attention to the girl I was initially trying to pick up, by saying simply, "It's getting late. Do you wanna fuck?" She agreed, and we were off to the bedroom, leaving the Plaster Casters to find their way out and fend for themselves. Although nobody would ever cop to it, I suspect that someone in our ranks that night ended up with his member as a member of their elite little collection.

Next on our agenda was our date at Cobo Hall in Detroit on August 6. We were staying across the street at the lavish Ponchartrain Hotel, which was being overrun by various groupies and fans. I ducked out a service entrance and ran across a parking lot to Cobo early on the evening of our show to catch the opening act, Johnny Winter. By the time it was our turn to hit the stage, I was feeling quite ripe. Although I was careful not to get too fucked up before a show, I still managed to slam down several glasses of wine and other mixed drinks that were brought to me on the stage. Also, Danny and I had a little ritual of taking our downers at the appropriate time during the encore so that we could come on to them when we arrived back at the hotel.

On this particular night, however, we made a grave miscalculation. The enthusiastic crowd wouldn't let us leave, and going back for an unscheduled second encore, I could tell that Danny's 'Ludes had hit him a lot quicker than mine. As everyone was leaving the stage and walking back to the dressing room, we suddenly heard a muffled voice coming from the arena. Every few seconds it would be punctuated by some intense cheers. As we ran for the waiting limos, our road manager took a head count and discovered that Danny was missing. Several of us accompanied him back in the direction of the stage, and as we got closer we could make out the mumblings as belonging to Danny. We got to the side of the stage and looked up to see Mr. Hutton in all his glory, rambling incoherently about his love for Detroit and the people, and God only knows what else.

Suddenly, as if shot by a sniper, he dropped the microphone and fell forward as if he were a tree that had been cut down by a logger. With a resounding "thud" he hit the stage and received a standing ovation. We quickly got him out of there, into the limo, and back to the hotel. He was drifting in and out of consciousness, so Burt Jacobs, who was with us, quickly sent in the paramedics. They administered whatever medical care was deemed necessary, and Danny was carried back to his room so that he could sleep it off.

With the night coming to a grinding halt somewhere around

3:00 A.M., we all retired. Around 3:30, Danny came out of his drug-induced coma and decided that it was time to party. When he knocked on my door I tried to explain what had happened and that everybody needed some sleep. Besides, the bar had long-since closed. Luckily for us, we had a four-day break before the next show in St. Louis, and everybody could get some R&R in Detroit.

On the morning of our show at the Houston Coliseum on August 13, we achieved another "first" when we were invited to tour the NASA Space Center. Since some of us had partied pretty heavily the night before, we weren't up to walking around looking at a bunch of moon vehicles. But after some gentle persuasion by the management, we conceded that it would be a unique experience. When we got there, Chuck was just too out of it to move from the limo, so, after being locked up by his keeper, the remaining members set off for the tour.

Once inside, we were greeted by several of the astronauts and given the "star" treatment. There we got to see the lunar landing module and other fascinating space and exploration items. Danny and Floyd in particular were so fascinated by the place that they arranged to come back the next day, which we had off, to partake in some of the demonstrations and to see more of the facility that they had missed on the initial tour.

Immediately after the Rockingham Festival, we boarded our private jet and flew to Dallas, Texas, to prepare for the Cotton Bowl show the next day. Unlike the previous time we appeared there, where they blocked off half of the stadium, this time we had sold out the entire stadium well in advance and established a house record. This show was also going to be a major media blitz. The entire group was sequestered at the Fairmont Hotel, and at our expense we flew in various members of the press from all over the country to view the spectacle. Also in attendance was science fiction writer Harlan Ellison, who was there to write a series of feature stories on us for various magazines, including *Playboy*.

After holding a press conference in the afternoon, everyone readied themselves for the show that evening in various ways. Of course, I spent most of the time prior to the show making a dent in the hotel bar with members of the press and Rod Stewart's band, who would open the show. When we arrived at the Cotton Bowl, we found out that the police had set up barricades completely around the stadium and had positioned themselves in full riot gear about every twenty yards or so. My first thought was, *Oh shit, another Denver!* But ultimately, everything would go so smoothly that even the newspapers and the local authorities would comment on the relative lack of trouble for a concert of this magnitude.

Rod Stewart and the Faces' staging reflected their hard-drinking attitude. Their set was constructed to look like an English pub, complete with a roadie dressed as a bartender, who served the band drinks throughout the show. I thought this was a rather brilliant idea. After a set of loose but crowd-pleasing rock and roll that had made them famous, Rod and the Faces left the stage to a standing ovation.

I remember standing backstage with our two main roadies, Jerry Sloan and Freeman Bachelor (who were third-degree black belts in Hop Kido and instructors to several members of the band), thinking, *This is going to be one hell of a party!* As soon as my thought was formulated, Jerry turned to me and said, "Fuck! This is going to be one hell of a night." I nodded my approval and made the long trip from the backstage area to our dressing room, in search of a refill for my empty glass of Pouilly Fuisse. There were hundreds of people around the dressing room area, congratulating Rod, Ron Wood, and the other lads on their performance. Between the two dressing rooms there were enough groupies, lawyers, managers, and other hangers-on to fill a small auditorium.

The PR that we were receiving for the tour was unprecedented, largely due to our new publicists Bob Gibson and Gary Stromberg. Continuing with the Three Dog Night tradition, we literally brought the house down. The audience would not let us leave the stage. Throughout the show, every band member shined in his individual and collective glory. Every time a vocalist or musician would take a solo, another thunderous ovation would erupt.

For the finale of the show, one of our stage techs came out dressed as a bullfrog, and at the same time a massive fireworks display was set off, culminating with the words "Joy to the World" spelled out in blazing rockets over our heads. Without a doubt, this was our finest hour to date.

I was so pumped up that I didn't want the night to end. I was bound and determined to go back to the hotel and make sure that it didn't. At one point our hospitality suite was so crowded with both bands' various members and collective entourages that I could hardly make my way over to the open bar. It seemed that the only place to find peace was in one of the bathrooms. I noticed that Danny had ducked into the john, closely followed by Rod and Ron Wood. I immediately knew what was transpiring, and since my vial of coke was empty, and Danny obviously had the fresh supply, I would grace them with my presence also. We all stood in the bathroom with the door locked, sipping from our various drinks and snorting lines that were laid out on the counter.

The concert scenario was repeated the following night at the Atlanta Braves Stadium, the only difference being that we played the entire show in a torrential downpour. Even though we were completely protected from the rain, it was amazing to see thousands of fans soaked to the bone, standing and cheering with their fists in the air, trying to flick their lighters in flaming approval.

After another four-day break we flew to the Northwest for two shows, in Portland and Seattle, with the Doobie Brothers opening. On the night of the Seattle show, as I was coming off the stage, our pilot, who had now seemingly recovered from his injury, was standing on the stairs and holding a large bucket. As I walked by him, trying my best to retain my balance in my eight-inch-high, platform-heeled stage boots, I saw a volley of ice cubes coming at me. Alternately trying to duck and stay upright, I slipped on one of the cubes and did a swan dive off the last step, onto the floor, where I landed face down on a large chunk of ice. Embarrassed, I jumped back up to my feet and started to run after him when he grabbed me and said, "Oh shit, Spooner, I'm sorry." I had no idea what he was referring to, but at that very moment I looked down and saw blood all over the front of my shirt that was obviously running from an open wound in my forehead. A roadie and a backstage hand quickly came over and escorted me to the first aid room, where the resident doctor, upon examining me, and sticking his finger into the wound, proclaimed, "That's worth at least ten stitches."

Our road manager came over and, along with the pilot, put me into the limo and rushed off to the hospital. All the way there I was holding the towel to my head, thinking to myself, *Didn't we just go through something like this at the beginning of the tour?* The tables were now turned, and it was our pilot who was consoling me and giving his apologies. When we got to the hospital, I sat in one of the emergency rooms, awaiting the doctor's arrival, and thinking of how this was really going to mess up my looks. I didn't want to have a bunch of stitches sticking out of my head like Frankenstein.

Even though the cut was quite deep, and required over ten stitches, it was situated right on my eyebrow, so that when it healed the scar wouldn't be visible. However, when the doctor came in and started to give me various shots of Novocain in the forehead to numb it, I discovered that he was the cousin of our pilot. He wasn't exactly pleased with the little premature surgery that I had done on his cousin's finger. As he was suturing me, it seemed that he was going that extra little mile to apply unnecessary pressure. Our pilot was right: Payback *was* a bitch!

Various other members of our entourage had been injured in

stupid and careless accidents. Jerry Slone had broken his leg when an equipment case rolled off a loading dock and hit him; Floyd sprained his thumb while playing football on a day off; several of our roadies had various cuts and lacerations from handling different pieces of equipment; and I had a huge bandage over my left eye.

On August 27, the last day of the U.S. tour, when we returned to L.A. for a sold-out show at the Long Beach Arena, I remember my parents walking up to all of the injured members backstage, saying, "What the hell happened to you guys?"

"What can I say, Mom? The road's a bitch, but somebody's got to do it."

Following this date we took a well-deserved monthlong break. I continued dating the model, Chris, and at the same time began seeing some of L.A.'s finest groupies. Also during this break we arranged for Ritchie and Bill to accompany us, along with Ed Caraeff, on the upcoming European portion of the tour. They would make preparations and secure a mobile recording unit in the various countries for an upcoming double live album (which would include the European and Asian part of the tour).

We resumed the tour on October 1 and flew into London a day early to recover from the effects of jet lag. The next two days would be spent taping our BBC-TV special and the immensely popular "Top of the Pops." Accompanying us as special opening act on this leg of the tour was a new all-girl band that Dunhill had signed and was trying to break, called Bertha. Although quite competent, they somehow weren't taken seriously by the crowds. Nevertheless, we became friends with all of them. Joe, who had just gone through a divorce, began sleeping with their drummer, who was known only as "Liver." They seemed to be the perfect pair.

Chuck, because he continually flaunted his womanizing in front of Paula, had decided to send for her to meet him when we arrived in Frankfurt, Germany, on October 18. He figured that having his wife there would keep him in line, and she could see how faithful and devoted he was. However, during the early part of the tour, Chuck started a relationship with Bertha's bass player, Rosemary Butler, who later became one of the most respected and sought-after background singers in the business. After we finished a series of dates in England, which had been reshuffled to accommodate further Scandinavian dates, we arrived in Frankfurt two days early. Paula was already at the Intercontinental Hotel, where we were staying, waiting to meet Chuck.

That night we all went to a private Russian restaurant and were treated like kings at a feast held in our honor by our European booking agents and the German promoters. During the course of the dinner, we dined on fresh venison, more potatoes than I really wanted to see, and enough vodka to embalm half the people in Moscow. As a matter of fact, I don't think our water glasses contained any water. Every time someone finished their drink and was about to set the glass down, some Russian waiter would be standing right behind him, waiting to fill it back up again. At the end of the dinner, Danny and I decided to pop a couple of Mandrex, just to take the edge off of the booze. By then, I was completely blinded by the vodka and was having a hard time walking.

I mumbled my goodbyes, thanked everyone involved, and set out to find the hotel by myself. After what seemed like hours in my drunken state, I realized that I was totally lost in this foreign city, and began to panic. But I was also so tired that I just wanted to lie down someplace and sleep it off. As I was walking through a beautiful park, I spied a suitable bench that would have to make due as my temporary bed. The next moment I was passed out cold. I awoke to the sound of people speaking in German, and quickly sat up to find someone sitting on the other end of the bench, feeding the pigeons. I had the most horrendous hangover that I could remember in a long time. All I wanted was to get back to the hotel, take a hot shower, and go back to sleep.

As morning was breaking, I pulled myself off the bench and started walking up a hill that was in the park. No sooner had I gone fifty yards than there in front of me, big as day, was the hotel. Now I was good and pissed at myself. I had spent the night on some hard cold park bench, thinking I was lost, when in reality I was right in front of the hotel the whole time!

The concert was sold out. Afterwards, we went into the recording truck to listen to the playback of the recording Bill and Ritchie had made from that evening's show. Although there were a few mistakes, it definitely had a spontaneous feel, so we decided to make it a "keeper." We would continue recording various shows until we had enough tape from which to chose.

That night after the show, in what had to be a moment of totally insanity, Chuck arranged to meet Rosemary back at the hotel. I thought this was going just a bit too far, considering Paula was there, and it would be hard to keep her away from the situation. While Chuck was busy in the hotel room with Rosemary, we were trying to keep Paula busy in the bar. Suddenly, she got up and announced that she was heading for the room. Realizing we couldn't make up enough bullshit to keep her there, we immediately got on the phone to try to warn Chuck. Unfortunately, the asshole had taken the phone off the hook. Paula was already on her way up the elevator, and there was no time to run up the stairwell to intercede. We decided to just let nature run its course. A short while later, Paula reappeared in the bar completely red in the face and obviously quite furious.

"That's it for the asshole!" she began screaming. "He's done this one time too many." With that she checked her purse to make sure her passport and credit cards were intact, then headed for the airport to fly home. As she stormed out of the bar she shouted, "Just send me my luggage."

Apparently, Paula had gotten to the room, opened the door, and found Chuck and Rosemary engaged in something on the couch, although she couldn't see what it was that they were doing. Chuck would later recount to me that he was so wasted that all he could do was look up into Paula's shocked eyes and say, "It's not what you think it is."

With another divorce imminent, and Paula on her way to the airport, Bill Utley went after her to try to smooth things over, while various band members tended to Chuck. When he arrived at the airport, Bill, through his wisdom, calmness, and bullshit, convinced Paula that it would never happen again. He asked her to reconsider what she was doing, as this would definitely disrupt the entire tour. She agreed to come back to the hotel with him and give Chuck yet another undeserved chance.

Meanwhile, Chuck was feeling quite remorseful. After finishing off a few more drinks, he apologized to us for his actions, and genuinely seemed to be sorry about the whole episode that had taken place. We left him alone in his room, after finding out that Bill was returning from the airport with Paula to try to patch things up. We then returned to the bar to order a few more drinks.

Unknown to us, however, at that very moment, Chuck was on the phone to Rosemary to tell her what had happened. He was obviously so spaced out that he completely forgot that Paula was returning. Figuring that his marriage was over, he invited Rosemary back into his room to console him. Although nothing physical was going on between them, just the fact that they were sitting together on the couch when Paula entered the room was enough for her to throw in the towel. This time she did leave Frankfurt, and we had to call an emergency meeting to figure out our next move, as Chuck — despite everyone's pleas to stay — flew home the next morning to make one last stab at saving their marriage.

With Chuck missing, the only thing we could do was cancel the Scandinavian portion of the tour (which I was looking forward to with great anticipation) and fly home ourselves while Chuck sorted out his personal life.

We had over a month until the Australian and Japanese leg of the tour was to begin, and would make sure that in that time — no matter what the outcome — Chuck would finish off the tour. Also, we had to record virtually all of those dates now, because of the ones that we had just canceled.

We found out later that revenge was in full swing, for as Chuck was pulling up to his house, Paula and one of our former road managers, whom she had been secretly seeing toward the end of their marriage, were loading all of the furniture into a moving van. As the van pulled away, Chuck went in to find a completely empty house, save for his bed, a TV, and a small couch. Immediately after that, Paula began divorce proceedings and announced to Chuck that she was taking up residence with our former employee, which was the final slap in the face — and his just desserts. This whole episode sent Chuck on what would become one of his longest binges of drugs and drinking.

During this short break Dunhill released the second single, "Pieces of April," from our *Seven Separate Fools* album, which had hit the Top 10. A month later we left for our Far East tour according to our original schedule.

Our first stop was Sydney, Australia, and after a horrendously long flight, crossing the international date line, everybody was completely wiped out. When we landed at the airport, we were all ushered into private rooms, where everyone was strip-searched (apparently because Joe Cocker had been busted a short while earlier). We purposely didn't bring any drugs with us, for just this reason. The next day after we rested, we held a press conference and did some media interviews, then took the day off.

The following morning we boarded a plane for a massive outdoor concert in Auckland, New Zealand, with our special guests, the Guess Who, who would accompany us on most of the tour. Danny and I had become friends with various members of their band years before in Canada. We were especially close with Burton Cummings, who, when in the presence of Danny and myself, would virtually insure us all to be "86-ed" from wherever we happened to be at that given moment. The concert was a huge success that came off without any incident — unlike the rowdy scenes that occurred at shows in America.

The next day we flew back to Sydney and were dealt our first major setback of the tour. We had apparently arrived on the mainland just in time, for at noon that day there was a massive transportation strike that affected the entire continent. All airlines and buses suspended service for an indefinite time. We had to hastily make the only other preparations we could, and we booked passage on the wonderful Australian rail system. This wouldn't have been so bad, except for the fact that after doing several concerts in Melbourne, Adelaide, and Brisbane, with Gerry and the Pacemakers, we were supposed to come back and do two shows at the Sydney Opera House with the Guess Who, and then travel to Perth. Perth is literally thousands of miles on the other side of the continent from Sydney.

We performed all of the dates up until Sydney, and then geared up for what everyone described to us as "an incredibly long and boring journey across the Outback." How right they were.

Danny, Burton and I, along with several other band members, had been raising quite a bit of hell in the various towns we were in. Shortly after departing from the train station in Sydney, we hit the dining car and began to drink our dinner. A few hours later we were cut off by the bartender — not because we were so drunk and obnoxious, which we were, but because we had depleted the bar's supply of liquor. There was absolutely nothing else to do on the train, and boredom soon set in. There wasn't even any scenery to look at — only miles and miles of nothing but miles and miles. No trees, no people, no towns. Not one fucking thing but dirt.

About an hour after being cut off, Danny and I went back to our bunks to stare at the ceiling, and we left Burton passed out on the floor in the middle of the narrow hallway. About two hours later, no doubt completely rested, I heard Burton banging on Danny's door. I looked out into the hallway and discovered that he was somehow obviously revived and ready to party again. Since it was difficult to sleep anyway, Danny and I decided to join him, and soon the Three Musketeers were off on their quest to find something suitable to drink.

Since the entire train trip was going to take well over three days, we needed to put our heads together and quickly come up with a solution to our dilemma. As we walked by the kitchen, Burton stopped suddenly and exclaimed, "I've got it!" He then forced the kitchen door open, and once inside, we discovered a stash of cooking sherry. Each of us grabbed a bottle and went off to drink ourselves — we hoped — into a coma. Fortunately, the mission was accomplished long enough to miss at least part of the grueling trip.

Then something wonderful happened when we were about six

hours out of Perth. We came across a little desert border town that contained some crudely constructed small huts, complete with animals that were indigenous to that part of the country. There were also shrubs and an occasional spindly dead tree trunk. *My God,* I thought to myself, *Everyone get your cameras . . . this is a photographer's dream!* Since everybody on the train was just sitting and staring out the window, we all saw this desert oasis at the same time, and as we pulled into the station to take on a few passengers (and hopefully more booze), all you could hear was the clicking sound of cameras.

But the best thing that the town contained was a whorehouse. Although we were only scheduled to stop for a short while, Tomasso managed to get off, get fucked, and get the clap. (A shot of penicillin cleared up his problem before we left the continent.) Hours later we pulled into Perth, relieved to see that people really did live in this part of the world. Besides the Great Barrier Reef, home of the great white shark and miles of pristine white sand, not to mention beautiful bikini-clad women, Perth resembled Hawaii without the foliage.

We were scheduled to play two concerts there with four days off. Of course, Cory went fishing, Joe stayed on the phone calling the States, Michael and Floyd went shopping, Chuck continued his post-divorce binge, and Danny was never seen. Every time we walked past his room, there would be room service trays of nothing but empty shot glasses. Occasionally, there would be rumors of a sighting, but only his arm would be seen either pulling a full tray into his room, or pushing an empty one out. Naturally, during this time I was doing everything in my power to keep the rock and roll fire burning.

On the night of our show in Perth, some words were exchanged backstage between Joe and the singers. I walked in, heard them arguing about business, and immediately left the room. It was common knowledge within the organization that Joe was into the company for a lot of money in advances to pay for his drug use, outrageous phone bills, and other excessess. That night on stage, he seemed really distant, and had a blank stare on his face. Right before we started "Joy to the World," he walked up to me on stage and said, "What key is this in?" I thought he was kidding and ignored him. A second later, when we started the song, I realized that he wasn't joking. We almost had a train wreck on stage because of his major faux pas.

We clearly had a big problem with Joe, not only because of things like this, but because his overall attitude was starting to drive everyone crazy. I didn't know it at the time, but I think that's probably when the singers decided that when the tour was over, they were going to fire him from the group.

Two days before we were to leave the country, the plane strike was over. Next stop: Hong Kong, with a brief layover in Jakarta in the South Pacific.

When we arrived in Hong Kong, we were met by our Asian promoter, who was trying to secure a concert date there. Unfortunately, through some sort of bureaucratic red tape, we were unable to do so at that time. However, since we were already there, we would make the most of it and go sightseeing and shopping. We checked into the Hong Kong Hilton, and Danny, Chuck, and I assumed our positions at the bar. The next day everyone went off in different directions, then we met up and had an incredible meal at one of the floating restaurants in the harbor. Later that evening, Tomasso, after meeting a lovely Chinese girl in a bar we went to, disappeared into the night. Before he left, however, he wrote down the flight information for us, for our departure to Tokyo the next day—in case something happened to him. Of course it did. The next morning, when everyone was packing their bags and getting ready for the airport, there was no Tomasso. We got a pass key to his room and saw that he hadn't even come back the night before. Not knowing where or how to start looking for him, we decided to be our own keepers. We would simply board the plane ourselves and leave him to fend for himself—although we would leave his plane ticket at the front desk.

Meanwhile, Tomasso had woken up feeling like a stranger in a strange land. He later described a rather comical scene to us. When he awoke in this girl's apartment, she had already left for work, and the phone was ringing. Since he couldn't speak Chinese, he was unable to ask the caller to help him out of his dilemma. He also didn't have a clue as to what part of town he was in. Everywhere in the apartment there seemed to be live chickens running around, having come in from an open window. Somehow he managed to escape from this Hong Kong Colonel Sanders and caught up to us the next day.

Japan was especially ripe for our drunken antics. We could get away with more in foreign countries because they hadn't experienced our lifestyle, and for the most part, couldn't understand English. I remember on this, our first Far East tour, Danny and I had a day off in Tokyo. We started drinking hot saki in the Hilton Hotel bar, and by nightfall we were pretty well gone.

Danny came up with the brilliant idea to take the express train to some other city and see the sights. Not speaking or reading Japanese posed a slight problem. Boarding the train in Tokyo was easy. Where to get off was entirely different.

We rode for about an hour until we got tired of the train, then got off in some sea coast fishing village that looked as if it belonged in a Godzilla movie. It wasn't hard for us to find a place to drink. We wandered into a brightly lit bar with the sound of laughter coming from the front door. The people inside had never seen anything like Danny or me before. I thought they were on loan from Central Casting. Nobody spoke English or anything even remotely resembling English.

We walked straight to the bar and with very crude hand gestures tried to order a drink. It's funny how, when there's a language barrier, you tend to slow down your speech and shout everything. "MAY . . . I . . . HAVE . . . VODKA?" Low and behold, it worked. The bartender poured me a shot, all the while looking at me like I had just stepped off a spaceship.

Danny, on the other hand, was into some strange new drink he found at the Rainbow Bar and Grill back in L.A. called a Bishop's Cap. Watching Danny with his drunken sign language slowly shouting, "Bishop's Cap!" was quite a sight. The bartender just kept shaking his head, signifying that he didn't know what the hell Danny was talking about. Finally, I could see Danny was getting tired and he ordered hot saki. By then, I had put quite a dent in the vodka bottle and gladly switched to saki as well.

Then I saw it over in the corner of the bar. A big, beautiful, fire engine red piano. Before I knew what hit me, I was sitting behind it, pounding out old Drifters songs, with Danny singing along at the top of his voice. After a rousing version of "On Broadway," I noticed out of the corner of my eye that we had sparked some interest in the locals. These guys were Japan's answer to the redneck. Everyone in the place was now turned toward the piano and burning holes in us with their intense stares. All sounds had ceased in the bar except the out-of-tune piano, Danny and me singing "Needles and Pins," and the fog horns from nearby ships in the harbor. It's true that music is the universal language. Within five minutes, we had everyone singing "Twist and Shout." The place was once again filled with the sound of laughter. Above the chorus of "Surfin' USA," you could hear Danny, now with renewed confidence, shouting, "Bishop's . . . Cap!"

God only knows how we made it back to Tokyo. The next morning, I woke up in my bedroom at the Hilton. My clothes were on the floor in a direct line from the door to the end of the bed. On the nightstand lay two used train tickets and a matchbook that I couldn't read.

Since Japan is a country bathed in culture, it seemed only natural that we indulge in one of its oldest traditions: the bath house. After some inquiries, Mr. Udo and Tats, our promoters, were more than happy to oblige us. They suggested a place called "#1 Bath House." This was clean and run by an older family. Most importantly, it was free of hookers who roamed the Ginza area of Tokyo and the local hotels. Mr. Udo instructed us not to pay any money. The cost would be taken care of; we were to just go and have a good time.

We all took cabs from the Hilton to the bath house. None of us knew what to expect. When we walked in, it was quite surprising. I was greeted by a lovely Japanese lady who took me to the bar, poured some hot saki, had me change into a silk robe, and told me to meet her in one of the three hot mineral tubs. I went through various salt rubs, saunas, hot tubs, herbal wraps, and the most thorough massage I've ever had in my life. I later found out that everyone had similar experiences. When we all left there, it was with a feeling of complete euphoria. I was clean in places I never knew I had.

As I was walking to the waiting cab, I noticed that Bob Tomasso was a little too relaxed. I didn't think anything of it at the time, but when we returned to the hotel, he promptly passed out. I had seen this before. He was holding out some downers. This made me mad, simply because of the intense lecture made by our management before we left the States: "No drugs! Don't get busted in a foreign country!" Somehow he had snuck some in.

I was even more angry now, because I wanted some too. How to get even? He looked so peaceful, so clean, so relaxed, lying there on the bed. Then I noticed a full tray of food that he had obviously ordered earlier but hadn't finished eating. What better form of revenge than to make him into a "human salad"?

First I poured all of the salt and pepper out around him in bed. Then I carefully placed pieces of meat and various condiments in his ears and over his eyes. Lastly, the mask. I made a foul concoction of mayonnaise, mustard, split pea soup, and any other liquid that was available. This I spread liberally over his face, hands, and feet. Then I quietly snuck out of the room.

I went back in the morning to find him still asleep. *He's slept long enough,* I thought to myself. *Time to face the day.* I saw a maid coming down the hallway and stopped to ask her if she would make up my room right away. Of course, I sent her to Tomasso's room. I then picked up the house phone to ring his room so he would be sure to be awake when she arrived. When he answered, I hung up and hid around the corner. By then the maid was knocking at the door. I could hear him mumbling as he went to answer the door. When he opened it, the maid took one look at him and let out a piercing scream, which in turn took him by surprise and he also began to scream. I could see that the goo I'd put on his face the night before had dried to a sickly yellow-green crust. There were two dried pieces of roast beef hanging out of his ears.

I was on the floor laughing so hard that my sides hurt. He ran back in the room, looked in the mirror, and then came after me. I ran down the hall, all the time hearing him screaming in the distance: "Greenspoon! You asshole!"

It would not be the last time that the recipe for "human salad" was used, but it was certainly the most effective.

Chuck and I became quite close on this tour, since we now shared the same common bond: divorce. In our quest to deplete the country of all available liquor, one night we set out for the trendiest spot, a club called Biblows.

Once inside we were quickly escorted to the VIP table. People were coming out of the woodwork, asking for autographs, since we were the biggest thing to hit Japan since the Beatles. Wanting very much to live up to our status as rock and roll goodwill ambassadors, Chuck and I started to order "doubles" of our current favorite drinks. Within seconds there were suddenly several Tequila Sunrises in front of me, and gin and tonics in front of Chuck. When we ordered "doubles," they assumed that we meant we wanted two of everything. As we finished one drink, they would return with two more of each. In what resembled some bizarre ritual, this went on for about an hour. At some point later in the evening, the disc jockey would announce to the assembled clubgoers that two members of Three Dog Night were gracing them with their "honorable presence." As a spotlight swung over to the table where Chuck and I sat, slumped over numerous empty drink glasses, I could barely hear the DJ as he began saying, "Ladies and gentlemen, Chuck Negron and Jimmy Greenspoon." At that point, with the spotlight burning a hole in the back of our heads, Chuck and I simultaneously raised our hands and gave a feeble wave before we dropped them back down on the table.

Later on in the tour, we traveled to Sapporo, which had been the site of one of the Winter Olympics, for a series of concerts and a few days of R&R. One day, while the rest of the band members were off sightseeing, Chuck and I decided that after spending some time in the hotel bar, we would do some sightseeing of our own. Quite drunk on our midafternoon saki, we got into a cab and began a personal guided tour of the area. After about two hours, we arrived at the ski run that was used in the Olympics. At the top of the mountain was a quaint little restaurant and bar that we *had* to try out. After some tempura and more saki, it was time to find a cab and return to the hotel. Unfortunately for us, when we went out into the parking lot, we found out that the cabs, through some bizarre custom, weren't allowed to pick up customers, only to drop them off. One of the locals informed us that we could walk down the long road to an area below where they did stop. Thinking that this was utter bullshit, Chuck and I walked over to the edge of the parking lot, ducked under the railing and, ignoring the numerous signs that were printed in Japanese, began walking down the side of a steep mountain toward the road below.

Every few feet there would be barriers set up with more signs we couldn't read. Since the incline was extremely steep, we began to gain speed as we went stumbling down the side of the mountain. All the while we were unintentionally trampling the neatly manicured Bonsai trees that we were encountering. At one point, from behind us, we heard the combined voices of many people. When we stopped to look back up at the top, we saw a large crowd pointing and screaming at us. I immediately flashed to one of the Japanese monster movies where the assembled crowd announces the arrival of Mothra, Godzilla, or some other atomically mutated creature.

In all this confusion we didn't notice that, at the same time, somebody was yelling to us from the road below. We turned and saw a cab driver standing next to his parked vehicle with the door open, waving frantically for us to get in. We trampled the last few trees and jumped in the backseat of the cab as he sped off down the hill. On the ride back to the hotel, the cab driver told us that we had committed a great sin against the Japanese people. It seems that the signs and barriers were there to keep stupid Yankees like Chuck and myself from destroying their sacred Bonsai forest. How were we to know? Had we brought along our Japanese/American symbol dictionary, we might have known what the signs had said!

At the remainder of our shows in Japan, Ritchie and Bill recorded more than enough material to complete our live album. They flew home to begin the long editing process, and on December 24 we left Tokyo to spend the holidays in Hawaii, where we were scheduled to co-headline two shows with our old friends, Chicago.

# 12 / The Writings On The Wall

The live album *Around the World With Three Dog Night,* was released in March 1973. After immediate Gold certification, it became our ninth album in a row to achieve such status. On the final product, the performances that were used consisted of the Frankfurt show and one of our shows at the Budokan in Tokyo, where we set a house record. The album featured one of my five-minute organ solos as well as new versions of several of our greatest hits, and other assorted album cuts.

It too was one of Ed's elaborate packages, complete with fold-out cover and photos from the tour on the individual dust sleeves. As an interesting side note, since Ed was there taking pictures seemingly every minute of the day, one of the pictures that made it on the inside sleeve was a shot of me "mooning" Danny at close range, aboard a South African mining plane that we had leased for part of the tour. We affectionately named this bucket of bolts "Rodan," since it was so terrifying to fly in and was so old that they couldn't pressurize the cabin.

The live album proved to be our last one with original bass player Joe Schermie, as we did fire him from the group when we returned from Hawaii. After holding a few weeks of auditions, we found a suitable replacement in Jack Ryland, who had previously played in Helen Reddy's band.

During this time I moved out of the Three Dog Night Arms and back to my old neighborhood in Laurel Canyon, into a house that Chris had found for me. We rented a beautiful English Tudor cottage that had belonged to actress Susan Oliver. It was located at 8901 Wonderland Avenue, and quickly became *the* party house of Laurel Canyon. I instantly got a good feeling from the house — numerologically — when I learned its address, because 8901 Sunset was where the Whiskey-A-Go-Go was located.

That spring we recorded our tenth Gold album, *Cyan,* which contained our sixth million-selling single, "Shambala," written by Daniel Moore. Aside from another Moore tune, "Lay Me Down Easy," and Jimmy Seals' (from Seals and Crofts) "Ridin' Thumb," the only other memorable song on the album was the second single release, "Let Me Serenade You," written by our friend John Finley, from the short-lived but popular Elektra recording group, Rhinoceros.

Also on the *Cyan* album, as a departure, Michael ended up contributing three songs he had written, which reflected his philosophy on religion and his home life. They were entitled "Happy Song," "Storybook Feeling," and "Into My Life." Obviously, unlike me, he was happily married.

This was also the first time that Ritchie and Bill brought in an outside keyboard player to enhance some of my parts. Skip Konte was one of the founding members and principal songwriters of another group that Ritchie and Bill had produced, called the Blues Image. (Their only hit was a tune called "Ride Captain Ride," a song based on the infamous *Pueblo* incident.)

My drug use had escalated to the point where things didn't have the same appeal that they did for me in the beginning of Three Dog Night. Everybody from management, producers, and on down to the group themselves were becoming far too complacent. We were getting stuck in a rut at the top and needed a change of some sort to kick us into gear. Although *Cyan* was a certified Gold album, it became the first time that a Three Dog Night album didn't make the Top 20, having peaked at Number 26.

That summer we mounted another massive tour to try to maintain the public's fickle interest in the band. Although most of this year was the same routine of play, party, puke, get up and start all over again, there were only a few shows and instances that were unique. One that stood out involved my old friend Don Johnson, later the star of "Miami Vice."

I remember Don when he was hanging out with Chuck and Chuck's new girlfriend Julia Densmore (who had just gotten a divorce from her spouse, John Densmore, who was the drummer for the Doors). Don lived up in the Canyon. This was during the period when he was with Melanie Griffith for the first time. We had indirectly known some of the same dealers and would score coke from several of them. Since we all lived in Laurel Canyon, we would often meet down at the County Store and chew the fat for a while. We'd all go up to either his place, mine, or Julia's place, and sit around snorting and drinking all night.

We used to keep tabs on each other's careers. Don was a big fan of the group. We ran into him again when we were doing a concert in Lafayette, Louisiana. At that same time Melanie was filming *Drowning Pool* in Lafayette, with Paul Newman and Joanne Woodward.

Melanie and her mom, Tippi Hedrin (who starred in the classic Hitchcock movies *The Birds* and *Marnie*) came to the show, and afterwards, Paul, Joanne, Melanie, Don, Chuck, myself and several other band members went to a great Cajun restaurant that they kept open afterhours for us. After a fabulous meal, Paul and Joanne went back to their hotel room. Returning to our hotel, Chuck, Don, Melanie, and I went back to one of the rooms to get high. We sat up all night smoking, drinking, snorting, and talking about all sorts of topics, like how we were going to save the world.

Don wasn't happy with the way that his career was going at the time of our tour. Even back then he was talking about trying to pursue a singing career. His movie *The Harrad Experiment* had just been released. I didn't know at the time that he was serious about music. I just thought of him strictly as an actor back in those days. I lost contact with him shortly after that. In 1975 his cult movie *A Boy and His Dog* was released, and I was happy for my friend who was on his way to what appeared to be a successful acting career. Then, as quickly as before, he vanished from sight, and out of contact. Years later I turned on the TV to catch the premiere episode of "Miami Vice," having seen his name in *TV Guide*. The rest became history.

When "Let Me Serenade You" was released that fall, and peaked at Number 17, we knew for sure that things had to change rather quickly if we were going to try to capture the success that just a short time before had come so easily to us. After the tour ended, everybody took off in separate directions to rest and give serious thought to what our next move was going to be.

For our particular form of R&R, Danny and I decided to make a trip to South America with our current girlfriends, Chris and Gretchen. The first stop on our itinerary was a week in Rio de Janeiro, where we set up camp at the lavish Palace Hotel on Ipanema

Beach. I immediately knew we were in trouble, because virtually everyone on the beach was so tan that they even made George Hamilton seem anemic. Also, all the women, of course being of Latin descent, had jet black hair. Here were four obvious *gringos,* two of which were tall, fair-skinned blondes. We definitely stood out and attracted a crowd wherever we went. Immediately we began roaming the streets on a shopping spree that was occasionally punctuated by an incredible meal and drinks at some local bar.

Later that night, at one of these bars, we met a German fellow named Werner who offered to be our guide the entire time we were there. We became quite chummy and proceeded to paint the town red. One night we all went to a disco to witness the latest dance craze that was acted out to a song called "Macumba Love." As it turned out, Werner explained to us that Macumba was the Brazilian form of voodoo, and was deep-seated in sacred religious belief. He told us that one night, if we were very careful and quiet, he would drive us to the hills just outside of Rio where they held their sacrificial rituals. On the night that we were to be the only people from a western civilization to ever witness this, we found we had missed the festivities by only a short time. However, I was still quite fascinated as I viewed the large clearing that contained numerous burnt candles around a circle. At the center of the circle were some mutilated animals that obviously had the blood drained from their poor bodies.

We went back to Rio, where I settled for second best and bought a copy of "Macumba Love" from the DJ at the club. Danny, the girls, and I continued our shopping spree and holiday for a few more days. In the middle of all of this partying, we managed to score an ounce of the most incredible coke that I have ever had the privilege to shove up my nose.

The night before we left Rio, Werner called up to invite us over to his house for a home-cooked Brazilian meal, and to meet his wife, whom we had never seen. Once we had arrived there, he told everyone to get comfortable and then poured us a round of some incredibly potent Brazilian liquor that, if left alone long enough, would no doubt have turned into rocket fuel.

Throughout the dinner Werner kept staring at the girls, all the while making subtle references to his wife. After we were through eating whatever it was that they made for us, we retired to the living room for another round of cleaning solvent. In a short while, Werner's subtle innuendos were becoming quite blatant. At that point, feeling quite uncomfortable, Danny and Gretchen excused themselves, saying that we had an early flight to catch the next day. Werner then turned his attention to myself and Chris, who was also becoming quite disturbed at his obvious advances. Chris and I got into a small fight that ended up with her returning to the hotel alone, leaving me there with Werner and his wife.

"Well, I guess it's just the three of us," I said to Werner.

"Not quite my friend," he said, at the same time walking to the back door of their apartment to let in the biggest fucking German Shepherd I had seen in quite a while. The dog immediately ran into the living room, came up to me, and began licking my nuts. I stood up and matter of factly said, "I'll pass," and in a matter of seconds was heading back to the hotel.

The next morning, when I went to get Danny up to go to the airport, I found that Gretchen had taken ill during the night. She had all of the symptoms of the dreaded Montezuma's Revenge. She was so weak and dehydrated from throwing up all night that she could hardly move. To top it off, Danny couldn't find his passport or visa, and told Chris and I to go on ahead to Peru and to have a great time. They would catch up to us the next week in Acapulco.

We left them behind at the hotel and flew to Lima. Once we arrived there we checked into the Sheraton and, after getting a good night's sleep, went on to the mountain village of Cuzco. That was the village where Dennis Hopper and Peter Fonda did many of their post-*Easy Rider* films, because the coke was cheap and legal. To prove that point, when we checked into the hotel, we were immediately sent to the bar while the rooms were prepared, whereupon we were presented with a hot cup of coca tea. On the side of the saucer was a coca leaf. After I began to chew on it, I started to feel like I had just spent a year Novocained in a dentist's chair.

We went shopping the next day, and everywhere there were wonderful old ladies sitting on the street, weaving intricate blankets and other Peruvian crafts. As a result of the altitude and intense sunshine, their skin resembled hundred-year-old leather. Every one of them was chewing on a large bunch of coca leaves and had wonderful, shit-eating grins on their faces.

The following day we took a train to the top of the 13,000-foot mountain to see the ruins of the famed walled city of Machu Picchu. This was truly an architectural wonder, and had both Chris and me spellbound. We discovered that at this altitude, if we drank anything alcoholic or chewed on a coca leaf, we instantly became twice as high as we would have at sea level.

We took off for Acapulco the next day, with about half a dozen intermediate stops at what seemed like every Latin American country in between. Due to some government regulation, we had to change crews and planes in Panama, and it was only after we had arrived in Acapulco that I realized that my luggage didn't successfully make the switch. But that wouldn't be a problem, since I had already put more than $10,000 on my Diner's Club card and knew that there were some wonderful boutiques in and around the Las Brisas Hotel where we were staying.

We checked into our private bungalow that had its own individual swimming pool, and, of course, headed for the bar. I was relieved to find that the Mexicans had civilized drinks — like tequila and Coronas! The next day what appeared to be the tail end of a hurricane swept over the Mexican Riviera and definitely put a damper on our sun and fun. Danny finally called from Rio to say that he had just found his passport, and that it was so late in the trip that they would just fly back to Los Angeles. Chris and I returned home the following day.

Our relationship became slightly strained after that trip because of a jealous streak that I had. Wherever we went, every guy in viewing distance would have his tongue hanging when he laid eyes on her. This made me feel very uncomfortable, so she and I went through a series of break-ups, and finally we just called it quits.

During this whole time after my divorce, I found myself alienated from my daughter. After Lee sold our house for a lot less than it was worth, she moved herself and Heather back to Colorado. Wishing to avoid any confrontation or an ugly scene with her, I chose to simply not call them at all. I regrettably began ignoring Christmas and Heather's birthday as well.

I had kept my "little black book" throughout all of my relationships and break-ups, so consequently it was no problem for me to come up with a suitable female companion to help me with my quest for the perfect party. On one particular occasion, as I recall it, when Lee came to town to take care of some business with the house, I had picked up someone at the Rainbow, after attending a concert next door at the Roxy. I took the lady back to my house, which I had purchased for the then wonderfully-unheard-of price of $60,000. After a Jacuzzi and enough drugs to ensure that she was primed, I made my move, and we retired upstairs to my bedroom.

While we were in the middle of our actively passionate lovemaking, I distinctly heard the sound of someone opening the back door to the house, and then footsteps coming up the stairs. The next thing I knew I was looking up at the glaring face of my ex-wife, who began screaming some tirade of senseless bullshit. I started to scream back at her, "What the fuck are you doing here? This is my house, get the fuck out of here!"

As I got out of bed, I put my robe on and covered up the girl I was with. The whole time, Lee just stood there yelling at me. It was totally beyond comprehension. As I backed her out into the hallway at the top of the stairs, we continued screaming at each other, when all of a sudden she started to go for one of my framed Gold records hanging on the wall.

"Don't even think about it, you bitch!" I shouted at her. With that, she grabbed the record and smashed it on the stairs. There was broken glass all over the floor, and my blood was boiling. She took a step down two of the stairs, plucked another framed Gold record from the wall, and smashed that too. Because of all of the screaming and commotion, my neighbors had already come up to the house to see what was going on. At that moment, as she went for yet another record, I gave her a swift kick, and down the stairs she toppled.

In an instant I was at the bottom and we were rolling on the floor, engaged in a totally ridiculous brawl. We had gathered quite an audience in the living room. Completely undaunted by their presence, Lee and I continued to battle. The guys who were my friends were obviously rooting for me, and the girls (excluding my appalled date upstairs) who had known Lee were rooting for her. After knocking over chairs, tables, and other furniture, the living room was beginning to resemble a battlefield. At that point someone had to physically separate us so that they could get her out of the house before I killed her.

During all of this mayhem, one of my neighbors had called my mother. As everybody was clearing out, she came up the walkway and into the house, exclaiming, "Just what the hell do you think you're doing?"

"Right now I'm cleaning up this mess," I explained.

We then sat down over a stiff drink and had a serious mother-to-son talk. I admitted to her that marrying Lee was a big mistake, and that I would think before I ever made that mistake again.

She helped me pick up my various broken possessions and then drove back home, leaving me to do some quiet reflecting on my own. When I went back upstairs I found that my date had long-since vacated the premises. Downstairs, underneath a broken flowerpot, I found my little black book, chose a name in it, and picked up the telephone.

Another time I was locked in my upstairs bedroom, snorting a vast quantity of newly purchased coke. Since there were always people coming and going, and I heard music coming from downstairs, I knew that it wouldn't be long before they would be able to have "an audience" with me. When it was appropriate, I donned a long red satin smoking jacket, grabbed the bag of coke and a spoon, and threw open my bedroom door. I then dipped the spoon into the bag and, as I slowly descended the staircase, began tossing coke into the air, proclaiming, "This is for my loyal subjects." As the assembled multitude below witnessed me performing this totally outrageous act, they rushed to the foot of the stairs at the same time and began trying to snort the coke off of the floor. In retrospect, I don't know what looked more insane: me wasting hundreds of dollars of cocaine, or a half dozen people wiggling on the floor like epileptic worms, attempting to snort up any trace of that ludicrous drug. Just another fun day on Wonderland Avenue.

We had decided to bring Skip Konte on as a full-time second keyboard player in the group, which would give me more room to stretch out on stage and in the studio. He owned a Chamberlin (an instrument that contained tape loops of various other instruments), so we could achieve several new and different sounds.

In a highly calculated move, we decided to change producers in hopes that it would give us a much-needed spark of inspiration and return us to the winning streak that had suddenly eluded us. After numerous meetings with producers, we finally decided on New Yorker Jimmy Ienner. He had produced hits for the Raspberries and Grand Funk Railroad, and he seemed to understand the current trends in pop music. Also, at his suggestion, we would change the location of our next recording. Everybody agreed that if we got out of town we wouldn't be subject to the temptations and pitfalls of L.A. After spending a short time discussing possible sites, we decided upon the Record Plant in Sausalito, California. That particular studio had been cranking out hits for various groups for a number of years and contained all of the current state-of-the-art recording equipment.

We would rehearse for a short time in L.A. and then fly to San Francisco, where we would all get a hotel room somewhere near the studio. In a manner that was completely different from what Ritchie and Bill had done, Ienner chose to rehearse less and work out everything in the studio. Although it was a little more costly, we didn't have so many preconceived ideas about how we thought the songs should sound. We also found that listening to a rough version of it on tape made it easier and quicker for us to arrange the song.

Once again, everyone picked material that they thought would be suitable for themselves or strong as a group effort. We locked ourselves into Studio "A" at the Record Plant in the fall of 1973 and began recording our eleventh album. Although there were only eight songs on the album, we tried to keep a central theme running through all of them. We went for a more R&B feel in our performance. Having already had a major hit with a Daniel Moore song, "Shambala," we picked two more of his compositions: "Put Out the Light" and "On the Way Back Home." Chuck picked another ballad, entitled "Anytime Babe," and he also covered the tune "I'd Be So Happy," which was written by Skip Prokop, the drummer for the multitalented Canadian horn band, Lighthouse.

Ienner, realizing that Danny hadn't had a real song to call his own since "Black and White," was quite pleased that he had decided to cover Jimmy Cliff's "Sitting in Limbo," with its infectious reggae beat. He had high hopes that the record label would see it as another hit for him. Cory firmly sank his teeth into another Allen Toussaint song, "Play Something Sweet (Brickyard Blues)." As the album's gimmick tune a la "Joy to the World," in a bold move to get the jump on another record company that was going to release the original version, we decided to cover the Leo Sayer song "The Show Must Go On." Sayer's version was already Number One in England, and his label, Warner Brothers, had spent a considerable amount of money on advance promotion in the United States. After our version was finished, complete with circus calliope, banjo, and other unusual instruments, everyone was so knocked out that Dunhill decided to rush-release that as the first single. Ultimately, our version won out, and it became our seventh Gold 45, and our sixth Number One hit.

The decision to record outside of L.A. turned out to be a very justified one as our consumption of dangerous substances was held to a minimum. The only time that someone got a little squirrelly was one night after we were through recording, and Danny decided to stay behind to do something. Stephen Stills was recording in the next studio with his group Manasas and came over on his break carrying a full bottle of Jack Daniels. Danny whipped out his ubiquitous bag of cocaine and proceeded to dump it out on top of my organ. When I left the both of them in the studio, I could see that Stephen wanted to turn on my B3 so that he could play a tune for Danny but was having trouble finding the switch, which I had positioned in a rather unobvious place. I flipped it on for him and then left the studio to go back to my room at HoJo's, where we were staying. Later that night I got an idea and decided to go back down to the studio just to fool around for a while. When I walked in, Danny and Stephen were still seated at the organ, drinking and tooting, and engaged in the exact same conversation they were amid hours earlier. I quickly turned around and went back to the hotel to leave those two Rhodes Scholars to finish their deeply introspective conversation.

We finished mixing the album without any further interruptions and returned to L.A. to discuss our ideas for the album artwork. Since we had worked so hard at coming up with a totally new and different stageshow, and that change was also reflected in this album, we decided to call the whole effort *Hard Labor*. Ed came up with the idea of an almost surreal delivery room scene, where some sort of creature would give birth to a new piece of vinyl, signifying the emergence of a totally new Three Dog Night. Instead of featuring us on the cover, it was decided to use other people, including black actor Don Pedro Coley (who had starred in one of my all-time favorite science fiction movies, George Lucas' *THX 1138*). Ed used an actual delivery room, complete with all the various instruments, and between them placed three microphones. The creature giving birth was actually Danny's old girlfriend June Fairchild, wearing a bizarre baby mask and huge lizard feet. Her legs were spread, with a sheet draped over them, and Dr. Coley, holding a pair of forceps, was extracting the newly born record. Standing around him were other various shocked medical personnel. Also placed in the background was a mannequin molded in Chuck's likeness, left over from one of Danny's earlier disastrous stageshow ideas.

The inside of the album was made to look like a foldout medical file, complete with prognosis sheet and other bits of unrelated Three Dog Night information. For the inside record sleeve, everyone was shot from above, lying face down in a circle with outstretched hands, pulling at a large orifice. Also on the inside was a live shot in the studio, depicting the new line-up of the group. For the back cover, Ed shot a beautiful antique merry-go-round that was located on the Santa Monica pier.

When the album was released in March 1974, once again Dunhill's censors felt that we had gone a little bit too far with the delivery room scene and the afterbirth-covered record. So after only a few pressings (which are now collector's items) they decided to slap a large Band-Aid over the offending part of the cover.

The album was certified Gold, made the Top 20, and spawned two more Top 40 hit singles: John Hiatt's "Sure As I'm Sittin' Here" and "Play Something Sweet." However, the latter song only made it to Number 33 on the *Billboard* charts, and signified our weakest charting single since "Nobody," in the very beginning of our career. The fire was starting to die, and everyone began to realize that maybe this dream wouldn't last forever.

We prepared for one of our more elaborate tours, in the sense of production. With Skip now a full-time member of the band, we could work up various routines, including our '50s segment, at which point we came on stage with pompadour wigs and lamé suits to perform "Good Feelin' 1957" a la Sha Na Na. Every time we did this, people would think that a difierent group had come on stage. After that skit, we would leave Skip on stage to do a long keyboard solo, dressed in a long, flowing black robe and Kabuki make-up. We then would return to the stage with yet another costume change, and we'd do some more hits. We repeated this procedure two or three times, with Floyd and I doing long solos, to give the appropriate members time to make their costume changes. Each member had his own wardrobe custom-made by Billy Whitten in Hollywood. Nothing that we wore was sedate or understated, since Billy was also responsible for Elton John's stage wardrobe. Everything was coordinated by our wardrobe and make-up man, Ron Berry, who had been with us since we first worked with him on "The Glen Campbell Show" in 1971.

I think at this point we must have really confused the fans, because several of the members — most notably Danny and me — took to experimenting with outlandish make-up. For one week he'd come out in whiteface, and I would try different color combinations of eye shadow, rouge, and colored lip gloss. Our competition on the concert road must have inspired this experimentation. This was the era when Elton John was at his most outlandish, and Kiss and David Bowie also helped to perpetuate a Halloween image.

The stage was also quite elaborate by our standards, as we used three large mylar platforms — one for me, one for Floyd, and one for Skip. We were also carrying double the amount of sound and light equipment than we had on previous tours. With our lead-off tune in the set, "The Show Must Go On," the entire show had a bizarre, carnival atmosphere.

The usual excesses prevailed, and the tour dragged on without any major incidents. Despite the costumes and make-up, it had become quite routine for us by that time.

Somehow, repeating the success of that "Joy to the World" single kept eluding us. We came close with "The Show Must Go On," but not close enough. Since we had already made changes in other areas, the next one to take place would be a change of management. While the musicians took a short break and went off to do various individual projects, the singers held a number of meetings and announced that the group had signed with Jim Guerico's Caribou Management. Guerico was the man responsible for producing all of Chicago's hits, and before then had a string of successes in the '60s with the Buckinghams. The only three groups he handled were the Beach Boys, Chicago, and us, so we felt that we would be getting a lot more exposure. Bill and Burt had done wonderful things for us, and literally made us what we had become. Unfortunately, though, they were running out of new ideas and things were getting stale.

For our upcoming album project we would go to the Caribou Ranch recording complex outside of Boulder, Colorado. If we liked what we saw, and Jimmy Ienner felt comfortable there, then that would be our second change in recording locales since our inception. Caribou had an impressive track record, as Elton had recorded two highly successful albums there — *Caribou* and *Rock Of The Westies*. Also recorded there were Supertramp's *Even In the Quietest Moments*; the last two Beach Boys albums; virtually all of Chicago's albums; and several of Earth, Wind and Fire's albums.

After we finished our tour that fall of 1974, everyone took a short time off, and then we headed for the ranch to give it the Three Dog Night inspection. We found that the various group members who recorded there stayed in a series of beautiful rustic log cabins with stone fireplaces. There was a large dining room up the hill, with some smaller cabins in back of it, and about fifty yards away was a huge renovated barn that served as the studio. It had every conceivable state-of-the-art recording device in it. This whole complex was situated on 3,000 wooded acres of the Colorado Rockies, complete with a huge stocked lake, stables, a ghost town, and numerous hiking trails and other activities. It got Cory's vote right away, and in no time the rest of us fell in love with the place too. Plans were then finalized to return early the next year to work on our next album.

In the meanwhile, Dunhill released our second "greatest hits" package, appropriately entitled *Joy to the World*. It contained fourteen of our most successful songs, continuing from where the *Golden Biscuits* album had left off. In the December 14, 1974 issue of *Billboard*, the album was the "Spotlight Pick" of the week, and to quote the review, "One of America's true supergroups comes up with what is a true 'greatest hits' package. Three Dog Night has been criticized in the past for not writing their own material and for taking cover versions from others — in short, for lack of originality. On the contrary, they are a highly original group. Whatever they take immediately becomes their own, and they hold down one of the most distinctive sounds in the business. And, as a commercial unit, skilled at making the best possible AM singles, there is no better. From the softest ballad to the most frenetic rocker, Three Dog Night knows how to make hits, and that's what really counts." The album became our twelfth and last consecutive album to go Gold, and made it to Number 15 on the charts.

After completing a short tour the next spring, we began to realize that not only were our record sales in decline, but our concert attendance was on the wane as well. Although we still had sell-outs, they weren't as numerous or as swift as they had been in the past. For me, and very possibly the rest of the group, this year — 1975 — marked the beginning of the end.

The group had become a revolving door for personnel at this point, as both Floyd and Michael were becoming more and more disillusioned with everything. Although they would appear on the next album, *Coming Down Your Way,* it would mark their last one recorded with Three Dog Night. We would also bring in various other musicians to augment the already lackluster performances that we were now giving. Of these new musicians, we would use a number of them in various combinations for the touring band, with me and the singers being the only originals left in the group.

In an attempt to recapture the early magic of our hit albums, we tried to mine the talents of songwriters who had previously given us hits. Although we had recorded Randy Newman's "You Can Leave Your Hat On" (long before Joe Cocker's version), Daniel Moore's "Lean Back, Hold Steady," and Allen Toussaint's "Mind Over Matter," the only memorable song and Top 40 hit was Dave Loggins' "'Til The World Ends." The only other exception possibly was "Kite Man," written by a good friend of ours, Jay Gruska.

Some of the outside musicians on this record included Mickey McMeel (drums and percussion), who succeeded Floyd in the touring band; Ron Stockert (keyboards), who eventually succeeded Skip; Dennis Belfield (bass), who succeeded Jack; and James "Smitty" Smith (guitar), who briefly succeeded Michael.

Recording the album in Colorado proved to be harder than we thought, since everyone wanted to go off and partake in some outside activity. Usually on the day of recording, Jimmy Ienner would get really frustrated when he had to send someone up to the lake to get Cory, to the top of the Continental Divide to retrieve Skip, some bar in Boulder to extract me and Danny, and usually one of the maid's quarters where Chuck was holding court. Rarely was anyone in the studio with the other group members at the same time.

About halfway through recording, my coke supply ran out and we called the local dealer down in Boulder to make a delivery. One night, while we were in the screening room where Guerico would show 35mm prints of current movies, the dealer arrived with his girlfriend. The buy was made, and when the two were ready to leave, I remember getting up from the screening room and running after this guy's girlfriend to get her phone number. I was quite drunk and obnoxious and all she said was, "I don't think so." After spending several moments expounding upon my finer attributes, I blurted out one of the dumber things that I have ever said in my life. She was already out the door and into her car when I ran out after her and shouted, "If you stay, I'll buy you a Rolls Royce!" She looked at me and then back at her boyfriend, and then at their rather modest vehicle. After a moment of contemplation, she said to me, "Nice try." With that they sped off down the dirt road and back down to Boulder.

Of course, never being one to take rejection that well, I was determined to give this my best shot. A few nights later, I had someone call the dealer's house. Upon finding out that he was making a delivery out of town, and that his girlfriend would have to come up to the ranch to do the deal for him, I started to formulate a plan to impress her.

When she arrived, we immediately went up to the dining room and, over a bottle of wine and some coke, began to talk. I found out that her name was Trisha Kroos, and that she was from a small town in Wisconsin. She shared a house across the street from the university in Boulder with two other girls. Later that week she would bring one of her friends to the ranch with her, who would end up briefly dating Floyd.

From that point on, I began to spend more time in Boulder with Trish and less time at the ranch, doing what I was supposed to do. Although I loved all of the guys in the group dearly, my heart just wasn't in this album. As its completion was drawing nearer, I decided to briefly move in with Trish and her other two roommates and stay in Colorado to party while the singers, Jimmy Ienner, and engineer Carmine Rubino flew to the Record Plant in New York City to mix it. The following week, in what later can only be described as a moment of sheer desperation and stupidity, I decided to have Trish accompany me back to L.A. and move in with me.

To show what a basically selfish and insensitive scum I was at that time, the girl who was currently sharing my house with me back home was told via my answering machine to vacate the premises because the king was returning with a new queen.

In June 1975 the album *Coming Down Your Way* was released and received critical acclaim. According to *Cash Box* magazine, "One of the major factors behind Three Dog Night's rise to top of the pop heap has been their almost uncanny ability of giving new life and stature to other people's songs. This mastery of other people's material continues on *Coming Down Your Way,* as the dog put their own brand of pop polish on the likes of Randy Newman's 'You Can Leave Your Hat On' and Allen Toussaint's 'Mind Over Matter' . . . there isn't a dog in this musical litter."

However, this album marked the first time that one of our LPs did not go Gold. And, after peaking at Number 70 on the charts, it quickly vanished. Obviously, the critics were wrong, and at this point maybe we should have all been taken back to the vet and put to sleep, like any terminally ill dog.

The future of the group was in question now. To interject some form of stability into my life, being compulsive, I asked Trish to marry me. She accepted. With only a few friends in attendance, at a church that we found in the Yellow Pages, we tied the knot.

When the group went out on the road, we tried to resurrect the old spark with the new and constantly changing line-up of musicians, but came up short. Our performances were, at best, lackluster, and by now we had been doing these songs for so many years that the original remaining members seemed to have become caricatures of themselves. Danny was so heavily into drinking, and his input in the group was practically at "zero," that the decision to replace him was inevitable. During this period, Chuck had been busted for possession two or three more times, one of which, in Louisville, Kentucky, made the national news. But the cases were dropped for insufficient evidence.

I was disillusioned with the whole music scene and wasn't getting anything out of the drugs that I was doing. Maybe it was because of that, or just the fact that I needed to spice up my own drab life, that I began dabbling in heroin. I had known that Chuck had tried it, and for a while he had been offering it to me. But, up until then I had always declined, thinking that it was the ultimate evil. My perception of a junkie was some lowlife who would sell all of his own possessions, and even steal from his own mother, to get a fix. I swore to myself that I would never wind up like that, even if I did try heroin.

Finally, curiosity got the best of me, and while on the road with our opening act, Johnny Winter, I succumbed to it. Everyone was sitting around the hotel room, snorting some brown heroin and trying to keep from throwing up — with little success. Someone laid out a line for me and told me not to worry about the immediate wave of nausea that would probably hit me. "That happens to everyone," I was told. I did the line and sat back in my chair, waiting for something to happen. A few seconds later, I thought to myself, *Hey this is no big deal. I feel like I have just taken a couple of 'Ludes.* To their surprise, I asked for another line. Once I had done that one, I sat back once again and announced, "Hey, I kind of like this shit."

"Don't you feel sick, man?" someone asked.

"No," I replied.

A few minutes later we all got up and left the room to go to the hotel restaurant, where we all ordered large bowls of chili. I was really getting behind eating this slop, but noticed after a few minutes that some of the other guys were face down in theirs. I thought that they were just drunk, not realizing at the time that they had nodded out behind the smack. It was a wonderful high, but to me didn't seem all that it was cracked up to be. However, the next day when I woke up, I felt like I was coming down with a cold. All of my muscles hurt, and my head was plugged up.

Later that night I did a line with Chuck, and found that with more heroin, these symptoms quickly went away. I was feeling quite good at that point, and I asked for a few more lines. The more I did, the better I felt. The better I felt, the more I did. Again, the next day when I awoke, I felt like I was coming down with something, only this time I felt worse. I didn't do any more heroin for a week or two, but when I did, this same cycle was repeated: Feel good — wake up — feel bad — do some more.

When I returned home, I found out that Chuck's sister-in-law, Connie, was dealing heroin, so I decided to make my first real purchase. I selfishly did the whole thing myself and felt fantastic. But it wouldn't be long before I would also drag Trish into this nightmare world with me. Soon I found myself at Connie's house every day, buying more heroin so that I wouldn't feel bad. Like any other dealer's house, there was the usual succession of people coming and going, and you would inevitably end up running into someone you didn't want to see or be seen by, and vice versa. It seemed that Greg Allman and Danny Sugarman (roadie to the Doors and author of the book *No One Gets Out of Here Alive*) always were either arriving or leaving when I was there.

Since our concerts and records were in a tailspin, my income also dropped considerably. I found I was spending more and more money on heroin, but still thought that I had it all under control. At this point I only snorted it, and defiantly rejected the idea of putting a needle in my arm. I thought that was taking a good thing too far.

After spending the holidays in Wisconsin with Trisha's parents (most of the time completely out of my brain), we returned home and I went through the now-tedious ritual of preparing for yet another Three Dog Night tour. In the spring of 1976, because of Danny's problems, the decision was finalized to oust him from the band and replace him with Jay Gruska.

We had already started work on what was to become our last album: *American Pastime*. Danny's only input consisted of lead vocals on one tune: Andy Fairweather Lowe's "Mellow Down," which seemed ironically apropos. His vocals were nowhere to be heard on any of the other unmemorable eight cuts. By now the "disco" craze was in full swing, and because we had once again changed producers — to Bob Monaco (who had recorded hits with Rufus) — this album was intended to capitalize on that genre. Unfortunately, it seems that none of the stalwart Three Dog Night fans could accept this radical transition. Even with songs by our old friend Hoyt Axton, and proven songwriters such as Alan O'Day and Dobie Gray, nothing could turn this album into anything closely resembling a Three Dog Night record. The sessions were marked by uninspired singing and playing, save the impressive drum tracks by Jeff Porcaro and disco king Ed Green.

The album was recorded at Quantum Studios in Torrance, California. I was more concerned with getting my parts done as quickly as possible so I could go home and do some more heroin, than I was with trying to give it my best. At this point I just didn't care anymore. I figured that I had a big enough reputation in the business, and since the ship was obviously going down, I could bail out and find something else that suited my talent.

When the *American Pastime* LP was released in April 1976, it was a major disappointment. It peaked on the album charts at Number 123 and became a sad way to end Three Dog Night's once-brilliant recording career.

On May 9, 1976, Chuck and Julia officially tied the knot at the Bel Aire Hotel in Los Angeles, with me as best man, Trish as one of the bridesmaids, and what seemed like half of L.A.'s music community in attendance. There were also several drug dealers present — just for insurance. It was a rather lavish affair with plenty of drugs and champagne. Chuck and Julia bestowed upon me the honor of giving the best man's congratulatory toast and a brief speech. The toasting part was no problem, since I already was toasted, but the speech was another thing entirely. Since this came hours into the wedding reception, I was already so far gone that all I did was stand up in front of all those people, babble incoherently, and totally embarrass myself. I vaguely remember trying to find the coatroom, because I knew somewhere in someone's pocket there had to be a vial of coke. Instead of a formal coatroom, I discovered all of the guest's coats piled onto a bed in one of the hotel suites. About halfway amid my search of everyone's pockets I passed out on the mound and was found in that position as the various guests were leaving the reception.

When it came time to tour, Chuck, Julia, Trish, and I had now become quite strung out on heroin. After a series of backstage fights between Chuck and Cory, over Chuck's escalated drug use, we wound up doing a few shows without him. We had again changed managers, and had retained Joel Cohen, our first tour manager, who now had his own company, Kudo III. Chuck was so sick at this point that the management office had to make sure that a full-time nurse was on the road to accompany us and to administer Methadone to him and his wife.

Although I was quite sick as well, and I knew that Trish was back home spending my money to ensure that she felt better, I thought that I could handle it out on the road and wouldn't need help. I was very mistaken. On an unscheduled break in the tour, to fly Chuck and Julia home and enter a Methadone program in Century City, I made the painful decision to tell Cory and the rest of the band that I had a problem as well. Everyone was incredibly sympathetic and urged me to accompany Chuck so that I could get help also. In an emotional hotel scene, I agreed and for the first time admitted to myself that I had a problem.

Unfortunately, Methadone is every bit as addicting as heroin, and although it replaces your craving for heroin, you quickly find yourself hooked on this substitute. So, with a two-week supply of 'Done, Chuck and I returned to finish off the remaining concert dates.

As our dose of Methadone was gradually decreased to practically nothing, I began substituting downers and more booze for the heroin that I craved. Although I had successfully been weaned off of the heroin, I was indulging in other things at a frightening rate.

Chuck and Julia couldn't — or wouldn't — handle how they felt, so they began chipping at heroin again. In a very short time, they were at the same point in their addiction as they were when they had left the tour.

I managed to stay away from heroin for several months, and just prior to what was to become Three Dog Night's final show, I was actually feeling quite good about myself. Although Trish and I were constantly engaged in fights, usually stemming from financial problems and her chronic illnesses, we still somehow kept our marriage alive.

Our last concert that year was scheduled on a warm summer night at the Greek Theater in L.A. By then the various promoters and other insiders were well aware of the group's internal and drug problems. We had tried to hide this from the fans as well, but to no avail. When I arrived with Trish backstage at the Greek, the first thing I noticed was a complete lack of guests, media, or various other personnel. The final blow came when I walked into our dressing room and saw a couple of cans of soda and a towel. No deli tray, no flowers, no notes, not one thing that had marked our glory days.

As Cory, Chuck, and I wandered around backstage, we somehow managed to keep our distance from each other. The other musicians, who were unfortunate enough to be caught up in our decline, witnessed this sad conclusion to a once great rock and roll institution. I knew that this was finally the end.

When the house lights came on, we left the stage without so much as saying a word to anyone, and got in our individual cars to drive home. I couldn't accept the fact that after all we had been through, and how much we had achieved, that it was going to end like this. Trish and I drove out to our bass player, Dennis Belfield's, house in Woodland Hills, and I remember standing alone by his pool looking out at the lights of the city. The events of my entire life started flashing in my mind, and a second later I found myself sitting on the edge of the hill, crying.

Maybe it was a testament to our talent, or a desire not to milk our once-loyal fans, but we declined having the usual highly publicized "farewell tour." There was never any mention in the media of the break-up of Three Dog Night. We simply ceased to exist. In a business where you're forgotten as quickly as you are discovered, our star was silently extinguished.

# 13 / Somebody's Gonna Get Hurt

The first thing I did the next day was to go to my business manager's office and make arrangements to receive the money from the Three Dog Night pension plan. My share came to a little over $225,000. Of course, being so compulsive, I requested that the entire amount be given to me all at once, not realizing that the IRS would take 50% of the money right off the top. Had I waited to get the pension money doled out to me, it would have accrued interest, and ultimately I would have paid less in taxes.

Trish and I immediately went on a massive spending spree. I called up my old friend John Nelson, a very chic antique dealer on Melrose Avenue that Lee had turned me on to when we were married. Within a few days, all of our old furniture was out of our house and replaced with very costly antiques. I didn't go into the shop and buy antiques from one period; instead, I arrived stoned and picked my furnishings from every conceivable era and country — except Oriental. Of course, we both spent a small fortune on clothes. Trish started shopping at Holly's Harp on Sunset Boulevard, and I began to acquire a rather expensive taste for custom-made clothes at a store called Maxfield Blue.

Naturally, we had an open charge account at Greenblatt's Delicatessen on Sunset. At one point my business manager called to inform me that our monthly bill there had exceeded $4,500. I didn't seem too surprised since we had been ordering cases of the finest wine, imported vodka, caviar, and other expensive gourmet foods.

Aside from redoing the kitchen and the bedrooms, Trish and I decided that the most obvious way to increase the value of our property was to install a pool and Jacuzzi. Because of many logistical problems and delays, the cost was slightly higher than the original estimate, and when the final bill was presented to my business manager, he was less than excited about the $26,000 price tag. Of course, the first thing that I did when it was completed was to turn the water heater thermostat up to ninety-five degrees, and to permanently leave it there — thus assuring me an incredibly huge monthly gas bill.

Trish and I continued to make at least three or four trips a day to Julia's sister's house to score heroin. We also had found out something wonderful: Julia's brother-in-law, Dan, worked for a pharmacist, so after hours we would sneak in and steal countless pills. These he would pass on to us at an incredible "rock and roll discount."

Day in and day out the same routine was repeated, and after a while I began to feel a void in my life. Trish and I were arguing like cats and dogs, mostly about our rapidly dwindling finances and the fact that she was getting sicker and sicker with her ongoing colitis problems, which were becoming very costly. I turned to a couple of old friends for comfort and help during the times that I felt my marriage was in danger. One of them was a lady named Barbara Shore, whom I had met through our former publicist, Bob Levinson. She was an incredibly honest person who would usually tell me exactly what she thought of my situations. The other friend, Wendy Busig, I had met early on in our career backstage in Baltimore, Maryland. Throughout my various marriages and career projects, Wendy and I would keep in touch and confide in each other our deepest secrets and frustrations. She proved to be a valuable friend, especially in times of my great depression.

But the main thing I found that I missed was life in the spotlight. Passing out on your living room floor with your own records blaring on the stereo, under a 75-watt bulb, just doesn't cut it. One day I got really stoned and drove down to my favorite spot at the beach. I just sat on a rock, stared out to sea, and recounted my entire life up to that point. I knew for me that death was out of the question, because I was now twenty-eight years old and had passed the fatal "twenty-seven" that Joplin, Hendrix, and Morrison had succumbed to.

Images were now dancing in front of my brain, and I began to play a word association game. I would think of a city and immediately recall someone or something connected with that place. When I thought of Dallas, I remembered the infamous groupie, the Butter Queen, and the Stoneleigh Hotel. Little Rock was Connie; New York City was Linda and Devon, the Sherry Netherland, and Nobody's; Detroit was Chris, Ann, and "downers"; Chicago was Cinnamon, Rush Street, and jam sessions; Miami was Vivica, convertibles, and beach parties.

Cleveland (yes, I even remembered Cleveland!) was Joan, Karen, Reggie, Colleen, and downer contests with Danny; Seattle was the club the Trolly, and all of the models; Tulsa was my first orgy; Pittsburgh was the first time a show had to be stopped because all of the girls were taking off their bras and panties and throwing them up on stage at us.

As I sat on the rock, remembering all of this, I literally went through every city and state, and began to feel a certain sadness that this whole thing was over. I knew that my money wouldn't last long, and neither would my marriage with Trish. We hadn't made love for over a month because of all her physical problems. I had to find another group or something else to do that would help get me back in touch with all of the missed feelings and people.

I continued to do session work with various artists, through the end of 1976, and always seemed to show up at the right places to jam, using my celebrity status as carte blanche. Unfortunately, I also found out that that status was also a curse to me. When I let it be known to people that I was available for other tours and work, it seemed that they thought I was far too important and expensive to take whatever they had to offer — so they never offered. In reality, I would have been happy playing in a club band, as long as it brought in steady income, to pay the mounting doctor bills Trish was running up and our combined drug debt.

Then one day I received a phone call from my old friend Michael Lloyd. It seemed that he would soon be my salvation, when he asked me if I wanted to play keyboards in a band he was assembling for teen idol Shaun Cassidy. Shaun, the younger brother of "Partridge Family" star David Cassidy, and the son of Shirley Jones, had suddenly become an incredibly huge star due to his success with his TV series "The Hardy Boys Mysteries" and his Number One Gold single, a remake of the Crystals' "Da Doo Run Run." Michael had already assembled some very impressive players. Besides myself, there would be Carlos Vega on drums (who was one of the most respected session drummers around) and Ritchie Zito on lead guitar (also an incredible session player, who later became a hit producer). Michael would alternate between rhythm and lead guitar, as would Joey Newman (who later played in Sheena Easton's band). As a second keyboard player, Michael hired my old friend Jay Gruska, who had most recently replaced Danny in the last incarnation of Three Dog Night. He also hired Three Dog Night alumnus Dennis Bellfield on bass. On vocals and percussion he used Shaun's good friend David Joliffe. Also on vocals was Shaun Harris, a West Coast Pop Art Experimental Band alumnus. To round out this rock orchestra, Michael used the sax player who had played on Shaun's records, George Englund (Cloris Leachman's son).

Since both Shaun and his management knew that the life of a teen idol is relatively short, we had to get out and do a concert tour before he grew up, his voice changed, or teenage girls stopped buying his records. The incredible thing about Shaun was that since he had the cream of the crop as a touring band, he was willing to pay handsomely. Everything was first-class for us, from accommodations to group limousines, to special people assigned just to carry our bags. He compensated every member of the band with a $2,300 a week salary, plus a $50 per diem and a healthy retainer when we weren't on the road. This would more than adequately cover my mounting bills and drug habit, at least for the time being.

We went into rehearsals late in the spring of 1977 in a massive sound stage at the Culver City Studios. Shaun had an elaborate stage set-up, complete with a trap door, where he could disappear and reappear. There was also incredibly intricate computerized lighting, along with the usual pyrotechnics. After a few weeks of rehearsal we assembled all of our friends to present the final show before we took off on an extensive summer tour. The night of our run-through, somebody started passing around what I thought was just a normal joint. Since I already had numerous drinks, a few Valiums, and some coke in me, I accepted a hit to take the edge off of my high, although I had long since graduated from smoking pot to bigger and better things. To my — and everyone else's surprise, the joint was laced with Angel Dust. Of course, Shaun, Michael Lloyd, and several other members were unaware that I had snuck off with the more party-oriented band personnel. As we tried to find our way back to the soundstage, we realized that this was going to be difficult.

Out of all of the drugs that I had ever done, Angel Dust was one thing that I knew I would never have any problem with: I hated it with a passion. It is the most insane and physically debilitating substance known to man, since its original use was intended as a animal tranquilizer. The only other experience that I had with "Dust" was when I was married to Lee, and mistakenly bought an ounce of grass laced with it. After smoking half a joint, I crawled on all fours with the Baggie clinched tightly in my mouth, toward the bathroom, where I flushed the entire thing.

This same feeling was now coming back to me, and God only knows how the other guys felt. I knew that if we made it back into the studio, there was no conceivable way that I could run down the show in front of all of these people, feeling as I did. But, not wanting to blow this golden employment opportunity, I knew I had to do something, so I ducked into the bathroom and did the remainder of my gram of coke.

When I finally found my way back to my keyboard riser, I quickly discovered that this was a dumb idea. Not only was I incredibly stoned, but because of the coke, I was incredibly paranoid at the same time. I thought that everyone there was looking at me like I was wearing a sign that said, "This Man Is On Drugs!" Somehow I managed to get through that nightmare evening, and swore to myself that I would never take a hit off of anything unknown again . . . Who was I kidding?

Within a couple of weeks, we left for the extended summer tour. I had cut myself off from heroin, knowing that with this particular entourage it would be impossible to score — or get laid — on the road. Instead, I substituted massive quantities of alcohol, downers, and cocaine, while Trish stayed at home and carried on the tradition single-handedly.

The night of the first concert was a culture shock and an incredible learning experience for me. We quickly realized that the thousands of pre-teen fans had come for one purpose: to see, and not necessarily hear, Shaun. The screeching sound of their teeny tiny shrill voices completely drowned out anything we did. Even though the band was incredibly tight, it really didn't make a difference what we played on stage. And, as the tour progressed, several of the other band members and I began experimenting with the songs and arrangements, inserting strange unrehearsed passages here and there. It was our own private joke, because you couldn't hear us from the stage anyway.

Shaun kept to himself and stayed in his hotel suites, watched over twenty-four hours a day by his personal bodyguards to ensure that one of the thousands of screaming pre-pubescent fans didn't tear him apart. I remained close with my small circle of hell-raisers in the band: Ritchie, Carlos, and Joey.

Although I was being handsomely compensated for the easy and fun task I was performing, I longed for the comfort of old friends. I didn't dare phone up any of the groupies from Three Dog days, for fear of being laughed out of the city. So, instead Joey and I began hanging out at various college bars in the towns that we played in. If somebody asked us who we were playing with, we would make up some lame story about assembling a supergroup for some future project.

At one particular bar, someplace in the South, Joey and I met two beautiful co-eds who were attending college and just happened to be roommates. After a brief stop at the local liquor store, they took us back to their house, where we proceeded to listen to records and get good and fucked up. It really didn't take any effort on our part to get both of these girls into bed. Joey took his down the hall into one of the bedrooms, while I was escorted into another one with my *bimbo de jour*. After some brief required foreplay, I quickly discovered that my date was uniquely vocal. All of a sudden she let out with what became the tour phrase: "Whip me! Beat me! Tell me you're Jewish!"

"O.K. — I'm Jewish!" I said to her, and proceeded to turn her over and spank her.

As this was happening, I heard a thud coming from the room down the hall, followed by Joey's hysterical laughter. Ignoring any outside sounds, we kept at it until moments later when she came up with "Tour Phrase #2": "Fuck me with your big rhino cock!" This time I had to laugh. I never did know her name, but from that point on she was known as "Mountain Woman." I was so thrilled by her strange outbursts of apparent affection — or anyone's at this point in the tour — that I invited her to meet me a week later in Washington, D.C. Of course, by then she had discovered who Joey and I worked with, but that didn't seem to bother her.

After I relayed the events of that evening to the other band members, they told me that I had to get everything down on tape from our next "big game hunt." And so, while Mountain Woman was being entertained in the hospitality suite, at a posh D.C. hotel after the concert, I was in my bedroom preparing the Sony tape recorder under the bed. I walked back into the party, slammed a couple of drinks down from the open bar, looked at the other band members for their nods of approval, grabbed Mountain Woman, and took her back to the room.

Within minutes, we were at it again, and as soon as she blurted out the now infamous phrases, I could hear the combined sound of laughter from out in the hallway. She was oblivious to this whole thing; her only thought was to take down this savage beast. When she fell asleep, I turned off the tape recorder and hid it in my suitcase. The next day we said our goodbyes and I expressed an interest in seeing her somewhere again. I listened to the tape and got a good laugh out of it, then turned it over to some of the other guys so that they too could experience the wisdom of the big game huntress.

After that, I forgot about the tape and went off in search of the bar. A few days later, when we assembled for a soundcheck at the Civic Arena in Pittsburgh, I was talking to a couple of reporters and a good-looking TV anchorwoman, when all of a sudden, over the PA system, came blurting out: "Whip me, beat me, tell me you're Jewish!" and "Fuck me with your rhino cock!" Everyone involved was doubled over with laughter, while I was quite embarrassed and pretended not to know what any of this was about.

Life on the road with Shaun was trouble-free, and because of the nature of the shows, it enabled me to do some of my most serious drinking without fear of repercussions from anyone. Who cared if I couldn't find my own piano keys, or didn't remember a song? Nobody could hear anyway. The entire time I was on the road, I was into blackout drinking on a regular basis. It became a little disturbing to me, and should have been a warning sign that I had to be told daily of my escapades — and/or performances — of the previous evening.

Meanwhile, back on Wonderland Avenue, Trish just kept spending what little money we had left in our bank account on her own supply of heroin. Although the bills were being taken care of by my business manager, the money I was making with Shaun was quickly being eaten up with Trish's doctors and drugs. On the side, to supplement what money she thought we had, Trish began dealing small quantities of heroin, which she usually had cut the shit out of, to various friends. One of these people, Danny Sugarman, always seemed to be at my house every time I called from the road. In my paranoid state, I began to suspect Tricia was having an affair with Sugarman. Of course, I never found proof that they did.

On several occasions, Michael Lloyd would report back to his mother about my escalated drinking on the road. Since she was a good friend of my mother's, and felt that it was her duty to inform her of this problem, I found myself in a rather awkward situation. It's hard to get chewed out by your friends and your own mother when you're twenty-nine years old, and take seriously anything they're trying to tell you. My mother's main point was that because of my drinking, I was in danger of losing this rather lucrative, if rather short-lived, employment opportunity. I thanked her for her concern for my well-being, but curtly informed her that the situation was under control and that I was well aware of it — which I wasn't.

While on the road with Shaun, we recorded several of the shows for a live album, and while I was still part of his band we taped his network television special. The TV show was out of the musical variety mold. The guests included Jack Albertson and the Crystals, who came on stage at our Anaheim concert and performed the song that they and Shaun both made a hit: "Da Do Run Run." The incredible thing was that when they had gotten up on stage with Shaun, they had somehow forgotten the words to the song.

The whole time we were taping the TV special, I was warned repeatedly to be on my best behavior. *No problem,* I thought to myself, and surprisingly, I was. But not for long.

Shaun received a Grammy nomination for "Best New Artist" in early 1978, and we appeared on the telecast. The day of the rehearsals, which were held at the Shrine Auditorium in downtown L.A., I was already well on my way to being totally shit-faced drunk. For rehearsals, the entire band was set up center-stage, and for some unknown reason, they put me way off on stage left — so far off that I could barely see or hear anything. As soon as we started our first number, I stopped playing and began throwing a complete tantrum. I was ranting and raving about how "fucked" the whole thing was, and how dare they put me — "the great and powerful Jimmy Greenspoon" — in a situation like that!

Michael Lloyd came over and tried to calm me down by explaining that this was just a temporary mix-up and for showtime I would be in my normal position next to everyone else on stage. We started the tune again, and after a few bars, I flipped out once more. This time the director's voice came over the monitors, explaining to me that he was well aware of the situation, but to please bear with him. To this I promptly said, "Fuck you!" and stormed out of the auditorium.

Michael rushed out after me and told me in no uncertain terms to get my shit together and calm down. I apologized and told him that I just couldn't work under those conditions, and that I would be all right at showtime. After the rehearsal, everyone went home to relax and to change for that evening. Everyone, of course, except for me.

I quickly contacted one of my many dealers, who happened to live close to the Shrine, and asked him if anything was available immediately. He said he was waiting himself to score, and all that he had were some 'Ludes. *Well,* I thought to myself, *if 'Ludes is all he has — then 'Ludes it'll be!* I left his place, and without any sort of liquid, except for my own saliva, I swallowed two "714s." I then drove the short distance to the downtown Holiday Inn and assumed the now-all-too-familiar position in the bar. I started drinking double vodka gimlets, and in a while graduated to double Kamikazes. All the time I was doing this, I made sure to keep checking my watch so that I wasn't late for the show. Since I had hours before I actually had to be there, I decided to go home and clean up for the evening. As I was driving home, I suddenly remembered that I had ordered a limo that was supposed to pick up not only me, but Joey Newman as well.

When I walked into the house, Trish was on the phone with a rather serious look on her face as she handed the receiver to me. On the other end of the line was my mother, who had apparently heard "through the grapevine" about my totally unprofessional behavior earlier in the day. She wasn't so much concerned about my saving face in front of Shaun, but didn't want me to alienate myself from Michael Lloyd, since he had become a powerful and respected person in the record industry and could help me whenever I needed it. Once again, I thanked her for her concern but told her that the problem was well under control, and that I had just gotten a little pissed off. Knowing my volatile temper already, she actually agreed that if she were in the same position she would actually have done the same thing herself.

After getting ready, I ran to the neighborhood coke dealer to secure a couple of grams to get me through the evening. Before the limo arrived, I had already done most of it myself, just to get me back on an even keel. Trish and I got into the limo, and all the way to Joey's place — in grand old rock and roll tradition — we sat there in the back snorting coke and drinking from the stocked bar, as we passed the "little people" on the streets.

By the time we picked up Joey and his date and drove to the auditorium, I was actually feeling seminormal — for me. As a matter of fact, I was getting a little too edgy on the coke, and as soon as we got out of the limo, past the paparazzi and screaming fans, I headed directly for — where else? — the bar. As I was walking toward the dressing room, I apparently said or did something to Steve Martin, who was seated in the hallway talking to some people. Unaware that anything was wrong, I kept on walking when suddenly he started yelling at me. Just then, everything snapped: the booze, the coke, the 'Ludes, that afternoon, the pressure, the situation — everything. I stopped dead in my tracks and turned with a look on my face that probably was a cross between Anthony Perkins in *Psycho* and Jack Nicholson in *The Shining*. With that I uttered my favorite retort, a hearty "Fuck you." I quickly turned to walk away from the shocked and suddenly silent multitude.

Luckily for me, none of the other group members were there at that moment, or I probably would have been thrown out of the auditorium on the spot. By showtime I somehow had regained enough composure to pull off what was required of me, without any further incident.

The last thing I did with Shaun was to play on his *Under Wraps* album that generated the hit single, a remake of the Lovin' Spoonful's "Do You Believe in Magic?" Interestingly enough, all four of Shaun's Top 40 hits were cover versions of other people's songs. Actually, Shaun was quite a talented songwriter as well, and his albums contained the bulk of his compositions. After 1978, Shaun's musical career dissipated just as quickly as it had appeared. Like so many teen idols, Shaun could never shake the image of singing fluff to a bunch of screaming teenage girls. Even though he really is a talented singer and actor, no one can ever seem to take him — or other former teen stars — seriously.

I had managed to save up over $60,000 while working with Shaun, but I needed to find something more substantial, both financially and artistically. My marriage was in a complete nosedive. Although I had managed to abstain from heroin while on the road with Shaun, whenever I got back around my old friends and my wife, I started using it, and subsequently became addicted to it all over again.

In 1979, after a series of unforgettable sessions with some fairly important people, I received a phone call from my old friend Lowell George of the group Little Feat. He was doing a solo album and wanted to use both me and Floyd on it. Having already cut three or four songs over a five-month period, he was either a meticulous craftsman or a wasteful fool. I found out that the latter was the case.

The album contained virtually the "who's who" of rock and roll, including Bonnie Raitt, David Crosby, piano player Nicky Hopkins (who worked with the Rolling Stones), and many others. Usually we would start a song and halfway through it, Lowell would take a break, leaving Nicky slumped over the piano, while he and I would make a trip to a liquor store. From there we would either go to his coke dealer's house or in search of some heroin.

Through hanging out with Lowell, I began to acquire a taste not only for fine brandy but for fine heroin as well. Since Lowell had written a song about his love of "China White" heroin, we made it almost an obsession to try to score some at least nightly during the sessions. Needless to say, the recording dragged on for weeks and weeks. When the album was finished, however, it turned out to be an incredibly diverse and exciting first solo effort. I think that his label, Warner Brothers Records, had a little trouble finding a market for it, as they were looking for that elusive "pop hit." Consequently, no singles were released.

Sometime later, Lowell assembled a road band to go out and play clubs, in support of the album. He asked me if I wanted to play with him, and although flattered, I had to decline, as my own heroin habit was already so bad that I couldn't stay away from home — or my dealer — for more than a couple of hours. Nevertheless, I stayed in contact with him out on the road. The last time I talked to Lowell was the night before he played a club in Washington, D.C. The next day I heard on the news that he had died of an apparent heart attack. Again, drugs had claimed the life of one of my friends, and again I failed to heed the warning that their demise had foretold.

For me the decade of the 1970s ended on a rather depressing note. During the first half of it, Three Dog Night had been the largest grossing group in the world of rock and roll and had afforded me things that were previously unobtainable. At the same time it had thrust me into the nightmare world of drugs and sex. Although it started out innocently enough, by the end of the '70s I was broke, floundering, and on one particular evening found myself in Chuck's bathroom shooting up for the first time. No matter how much heroin I had snorted up to that point, I kept telling myself that I would never go that extra mile and use a needle.

After being constantly told by devotees of the drug how much money and smack I was wasting by merely snorting it, and how much longer the high lasted when you shot it, I hesitantly gave in. Since I had hated hypodermic needles — a fear that had dated back to childhood visits to the doctor and dentist — the first time around I had Julia shoot me up while I turned my head and grimaced in pain. Everyone was right, for as soon as the needle was withdrawn, I immediately felt a warm rush in my veins and throughout my body. I dared not tell Trish about it, for fear of what she might think — not that I gave a shit about her opinion. Besides, this meant that I could now get higher than she could.

I didn't want to make this new practice of shooting up a constant thing, so I only occasionally had someone do it for me. The rest of the time I used the conventional nasal method. The visits to Julia and her sister's house were becoming more and more frequent, and in time Trish and I realized that we weren't getting that high anymore. Everything that we purchased was being used just to make sure that we could maintain and not become sick. This was a vicious cycle that would repeat itself over and over again.

When the new decade dawned, I was once again in Chuck's bathroom, doing lots of heroin.

With both of our addictions, Trish's medical problems, and the obvious financial situation that was caused by the above, it was only a matter of time before the inevitable happened. Although I was prepared for it, the blow was still heavy, mostly to my ego, when one day Trish came into the living room and announced that she was divorcing me. She cited any number of obvious reasons for leaving, and although somewhere deep inside I was relieved, my initial response was that of complete rage. In fact, I got so pissed off and became so violent that, knowing my temper, Trish immediately called up her friend Jill and got out of the house as fast as she could. Dwelling on the impending situation, I instantly called up one of my dealers and got him to front me a large quantity of heroin, which I promised to pay for the following day.

I sat in my living room alone and, fueled by the heroin, numerous drinks from my liquor cabinet, and whatever drugs I could scrounge up at the time, I began to get both depressed and outraged at the same time.

The first time I had experienced divorce, I more or less called all of the shots, and it was I who walked out of the house. This time, however, someone was telling me that I had failed. I just couldn't accept the fact that I couldn't make it work out, even though inside me I knew that was the case long before this day ever came.

Suddenly, it dawned on me: *I'll get her back, where it hurts.* I went to the kitchen, opened up a drawer, and pulled out a large pair of scissors. I then went upstairs, opened the closet door, and very methodically began cutting in half every piece of her expensive clothing. I then took all of the decimated articles back downstairs and threw them outside the back door. Next I went into the bathroom and retrieved every possible trace of her make-up and cosmetics. What I couldn't break in half, I took a hammer and pulverized. This too was thrown onto the mounting pile outside the back door. I returned to the living room and sat down after I poured myself another strong drink. *That'll teach the bitch,* I thought to myself. A few hours later, I heard a car pull up in the driveway, and got up from the couch to see who it was. Trish, Jill, and some unknown man emerged from the garage.

Trish was horrified when she saw all of her destroyed belongings lying in a pile in the yard. She ran into the house, screaming at me, while Jill and their friend stayed outside, trying to calm both of us down. What resulted next was a ridiculous game of cat and mouse. At one point I went back outside and told Jill and her friend to shut the fuck up and to mind their own business. As soon as I stepped outside, Trish slammed and locked the back door and stood there grinning at me through the window. In a rather dramatic move, I turned around and, with all of my might, kicked a hole through the door. This took Trish completely off guard. I reached inside the broken door, unlocked it, and threw it open. Trish ran off into the bedroom, locking another door after her. Of course, now I was good and pissed, so I put a hole in that one also. No doubt fearing for her life, and rightly so, Trish made a swift exit out of the side door from our bedroom and ran out into the street to jump into Jill's car. As she sped off, she was screaming, "I'll get you for this! . . . I'll see you in court!"

"I can't wait!" I screamed back at her. I returned to my living room and continued to drink until I passed out.

The next morning I woke up, snorted the remaining heroin to get rid of my hangover, and then called my divorce lawyer, Michael Dave, who had done so well for me with Lee.

After I relayed all of the events of the previous day to Michael, the first thing he told me was to try to get a grip on my temper, and secondly, he would issue a restraining order so that Trish wouldn't be allowed to come and harass me. He then pointed out a very interesting fact to me. Although I probably had gotten great satisfaction out of destroying her possessions, which were technically "community property," I failed to realize that the joke was on me: I had paid for all of the expensive clothes and cosmetics that I had just maliciously destroyed!

We set about the tedious and involved task of taking depositions, talking to lawyers, and getting all of the ridiculous requests from both sides. It seemed that all of 1980 was taken up solely by this messy divorce. I was really taking it hard, and my work and creative output were reduced to zero. The only thing I could do was borrow money, sell some of my possessions, and get high. Of course, the higher I got, the more I would dwell on how my life was becoming a complete shambles.

We played "The Waiting Game" for a number of months and flatly rejected every offer her lawyer came up with. Finally, in September, we had our first court date. Of course, I showed up wasted. Michael Dave pulled me aside and told me to get my act together if I wanted to win this case. Throughout all of this, my mother was incredibly supportive and made sure that I knew how she felt about this whole affair. After I had married Trish she told me it was a mistake, and that I would wind up getting hurt again. Somehow that phrase "I told you so" kept popping up in our conversation.

When I got on the witness stand on the strong advice of my lawyer, I admitted to the judge that I had been at fault when I destroyed Trish's personal property; however, under the circumstances I was coerced into it. Another strong point that was brought up in the initial hearing turned out to be in my favor. My lawyer, through documented reports and witnesses, showed the judge that Trish in less than a six-month period had spent over $17,000 on prescription drugs alone. Although she couldn't be faulted for her medical problems, the fact that she used that as an excuse for her escalating and excessive drug use, and the source of our daily fights, was brought up.

To everyone involved, it was a clear-cut case of irreconcilable differences, and after a brief recess in the judge's chambers, with both lawyers, I was granted a continuance until late that year. Time was on our side, as the longer we waited, the more desperate Trish would get financially. Finally, in a preliminary agreement, I conceded to giving her half of the furniture, the car, and $25,000 in cash. She would not get the house, any future royalties or investments, or anything else involved with income. She would have to surrender all charge cards, and would be asked to pay for all of her lawyer's fees, which they originally had wanted me to do.

Her lawyer strongly advised her to take this deal, because the longer she waited, the less she would get. She agreed and we immediately tried to set up another court date to finalize the whole mess. Unfortunately, due to bureaucratic red tape and a full judicial calendar, the only date that was open was on the morning of Christmas Eve. Since my Christmas was already ruined by the fact that I had spent most of my money allotted for presents on drugs, I figured, *Why not go for it, and screw up my entire holiday?*

The night before I was to appear in court I spent with my friend and coke dealer, named Roger. We stayed up until about 5:00 A.M., drinking and tooting with our friends Don Stroud and Huntz Hall (of "The Bowery Boys" movies). When I looked at my watch and saw the time, I freaked out. I drove home, took a shower, changed clothes, poured myself two strong "doubles," and snorted the last of my coke on my way out of the door. I then got on the freeway and proceeded to drive downtown to the courthouse.

When I arrived there, it was apparent to both Michael Dave and my mother that I was in no shape to take the witness stand. So, Michael and Trish's lawyer met briefly behind locked doors and emerged with a decision to settle everything out of court. The judge was informed of the final decision, and after reviewing the circumstances, he called Trish, me, and our respective counsel in front of him. As long as I didn't have to say anything more than "Yes, your honor," I knew I was safe.

In a few short minutes it was over. The divorce was granted. After thanking Michael Dave and wishing him a "Merry Christmas," I told my mother that I would be over later that evening to celebrate with the family.

However, I was so drained both emotionally and physically from this ordeal that I stopped at a few bars on the way back home. By the time I got back to my house at 8901 Wonderland Avenue, I was quite drunk. I passed out on the couch in front of a warm fire, with the stereo going. When I woke up it was well past midnight. *Oh shit,* I thought to myself, *I missed Christmas!* I phoned my mom, who was still waiting up for me. She told me she understood how I felt, but that a phone call would have been nice. I told her that I would make it up, and that I would be over on Christmas Day. Now, totally pissed at myself for letting this happen, I somehow scrounged up a little bit of money to buy a small quantity of heroin. By 4:00 A.M., I was again alone in my living room with a drink in one hand and a mirror of drugs in the other.

Christmas morning I poured myself into my car and drove to my mother's house without a single present for anyone. Just before I got there I stopped off and bought a pint of vodka, and as I sat parked in front of the house, swilling it down, I began to write out a series of rather tacky IOUs to my family members. I then put them into envelopes with everyone's name on them and went inside. My mother, father, and sister were all there reheating the dinner from the night before, so that we could at least have that much together as a family. When I handed them the envelopes, they must have thought that there was money inside. As they opened them and pulled out the IOUs, I could see the disappointment on their faces. I apologized, but told them that under the circumstances that was the best I could do, and would make it up in the not-too-distant future.

I finished off the year 1980 smashed out of my mind at someone's New Year's Eve party. Surrounded by a bevy of new bimbos, I was once again single and in the market for a new woman in my life. The last thing I remember about that evening was lying face down on the floor at my friends' house, nuzzling the pile in their living room carpet.

In early 1981, I came to the conclusion that it was now time for me to seriously get back to work. Then one day I received a phone call that was to put my life back on track and reunite me with some old friends. Nick St. Nicholas, the original bass player from the group Steppenwolf, phoned to tell me that he was now into the management end of the business. He said that there was a rather prominent producer with a lot of money who would pay to get Three Dog Night back together. Through repeated but failed efforts to contact either Danny or Cory about the proposed reunion, Nick suggested that the original four musicians and Chuck go out and work under the name "Three Dog Night." That seemed entirely logical, as it represented the majority of the group. However, the name was collectively owned by Danny, Chuck, and Cory, and if they didn't mutually agree on what we were doing, we couldn't use it. Nick set up a series of meetings with Floyd, Michael, Joe, Chuck, and me at the Beverly Hills house of Hong Kong producer and financier David Chow. David would put up all of the money needed to get this new version of Three Dog Night off and running.

Although Chuck and I had remained constant companions throughout the group's five-year hiatus, I had lost contact with the other members. However, once we started playing together again, we quickly discovered that we still got along and had something musically creative to offer. Things were going along quite smoothly until, through Danny and Cory's individual lawyers and accountants, they found out our intentions. Immediately we were thrown into a "Catch 22" situation. Danny and Cory were not about to let us go out as Three Dog Night without them being involved, and they didn't want any part of it. Things quickly turned into a stalemate.

After a couple of weeks, Danny, Chuck, and Cory agreed to meet with their lawyers to discuss the disbursement of the group's old "slush fund." When the three singers sat down in the same room together and started discussing old business, they quickly realized that they all still got along fairly well. Somehow they agreed to give Three Dog another try, with a couple of stipulations: (1) that David Chow and Nick St. Nicholas weren't involved; and (2) that Joe Schermie wasn't involved, since Cory still did not like him.

The one minor problem we had was that Chuck, Joe, Floyd, Michael, and I had signed contracts with Chow and St. Nicholas. But after a few phone calls from Danny and Cory's lawyers, saying that they would sue them if they used the name Three Dog Night, we quickly determined that the contracts we had signed were null and void.

With this matter out of the way, we told Joe once again that he was not with Three Dog anymore, and set about holding auditions for a new bass player. Within a few days we found a suitable replacement named Mike Seifrit, who had just left Tina Turner's touring band, feeling certain that she was going nowhere in a big hurry.

Once we all got down to the business of rehearsing for the first time in five years, it was readily apparent that the old spark was still there. Although a few members were a little rusty on chords and words, everything quickly came back to us. After some group meetings, Danny, Chuck, and Cory decided to enlist our old friend Tom Hulett from Concerts West as the group's manager. We then set up a series of club dates, along with a few small venues. We wanted to start off on a small scale to see if the public still wanted us, but most of all to show the industry and promoters that all of the bad blood between us and the drug problems were now things of the past.

Our initial tour was small but successful. It seemed that we were back on track and would soon become a powerful music force once again in the '80s.

Now that my creative void was being filled, it was time to take care of my personal life. Although I outwardly reveled in my new bachelor status, I secretly felt the need for someone to help stabilize my personal life. After sleeping with a succession of mindless bimbos, I one day received a phone call from my old friend Terry Pierce, who was a movie extra at Paramount Studios. She told me that one of her bosses, an assistant director on the TV show "Laverne and Shirley," named Linda McMurray, had just moved in up the street from me and was looking for someone who had some good coke connections. Always wanting to help a fellow druggie in need, I called Linda up and introduced myself. We made arrangements to meet later that night, after I went to the neighborhood coke dealer's house and bought a quantity for her to sample. As I was into keeping my house as meticulously clean as possible, I also purchased a small quantity of heroin, so I could do the job right.

Linda's first introduction to me was when she pulled up in my driveway to find me standing in my short Japanese robe, drunk and stoned on heroin, sweeping the driveway and dusting the plants. She thought that was a rather odd thing to do, but didn't say so at the time. We went inside, and after a few drinks and a couple of lines, she decided the quality of the coke was good enough for us to strike up a business relationship. At the same time, we both realized that we had a lot in common, and knew a lot of the same people in the business. I invited her to a band rehearsal, and in turn she invited me to the Paramount lot to watch them tape an episode of "Laverne and Shirley."

Almost immediately we began dating and hanging out at each other's houses for days on end. Since she only lived at the top of the hill, it became a very convenient situation. She still had her friends that she dated, and I still had mine. But in a short time it seemed that we were constant companions. We would stay up laughing and talking all night: drinking, snorting, and doing amyl nitrate.

In the beginning, I didn't tell her about my love for heroin, and every time I wanted to do some, I would sneak off into the bathroom. Finally, one night in a violent rainstorm, her house suddenly got flooded out. She grabbed whatever possessions she could and took them down to my place, where she set up temporary housekeeping while her insurance covered the damages. By the time her house was repaired and ready to be lived in again, we had come to the unanimous decision that since we got along so well, and were actually falling in love with each other, that she should move in with me and sublet her place.

Things worked out beautifully. The fact that I would go out on the road with Three Dog Night, and she would spend sixteen hours a day at the studio taping the show, seemed to bring us much closer. There were always people over at the house getting wasted and sunbathing in the nude or taking a Jacuzzi. It seemed like this was finally the perfect relationship for me. I had found someone who not only was extremely intelligent and sensitive, but who also had a well-paying and respected job.

While Linda was with me on the road one night, Danny announced his engagement to his girlfriend, Laurie Gaines. He had been the last bachelor in the group, and I was so pleased for him, as he now was getting his life completely in order. He wanted very much to have a family and already had a headstart, because Laurie had a son from a previous marriage. Also, sometime long before this, Danny had cleaned up his act by going "cold turkey." He was now "drug free" and a complete health nut. On any given morning you could see him jogging up the steep roads in the Canyon, toward Mulholland Drive.

I vowed that I too was going to settle down and try to lead a healthier life.

All I actually wanted to do was to gain approval from my friends, and I did this by my increased drinking and drug use. It wasn't long before I turned Linda on to heroin for the first time, and although she really didn't care for it that much, we still seemed to do our fair share of it. Of course, it was especially useful the morning after one of our all-night parties, to erase any of the effects of the abuses of the night before.

One weekend when we were both quite drunk and stoned out of our minds, we decided since we loved each other so much, and got along so well together, that we should get married. In a rather impulsive spur-of-the-moment move, we set up a mock wedding in the living room. It was performed by one of our friends who was some sort of self-ordained minister in some nondenominational church. Actually, a few words were exchanged over some drinks and laughter, and we then considered ourselves "married." The next morning we awoke, reviewed the events of the previous day, and came to the conclusion that if we were serious about this, we would have to do it legally and right. Content with living together, we then started going through all of the pros and cons of marriage, and decided to put it on the back burner for a while. The relationship was fine the way it was, and we mutually agreed that marriage would only screw it up. Since nothing was legally done or signed, we quickly undid what we had so impulsively and hastily done.

The one thing that Linda did do, for her protection, due to the mounting palimony suits in California, was to have me sign a piece of paper stating that if anything was purchased jointly, it would be distributed as such if ever we broke up. Also, because of my mounting bills and dismal financial situation, Linda agreed to loan me several thousands of dollars with some of my furniture as collateral.

Meanwhile, things were going progressively well with Three Dog Night. On the concert trail we were becoming more and more successful at filling concert halls and selling out shows. My drinking was still way out of hand, but although Linda joined me, she always seemed to know when to quit. Never once did she jeopardize her work. On the other hand, I began to adopt the attitude that I really didn't care about the music anymore — all it was now was a source of income to fuel my addictions.

As Three Dog Night prepared for another tour in 1982, we learned that our new bass player, Mike Seifrit, wanted to spend more time at home with his family, and consequently would be unable to tour with us. We held auditions again, and within a few days selected Richard Grossman, who had played in Rick Springfield's band. We had, prior to this, done a TV show, once again from the ship the *Queen Mary,* with the Beach Boys, Rick Springfield, and Pablo Cruise. It was there that we were informally introduced to Richard and our future guitar player, Paul Kingery, who also was with Springfield.

After a succession of short tours, the group decided that it was time to once again enter the recording studio. We tried to generate some interest from major labels, but it seemed that they were very short-sighted. They felt that all of our popularity was in the past, and that we couldn't generate any current chart hits. We therefore turned to an independent label, Passport Records, based in New Jersey, and secured a small amount of front money to cut a five-song mini-album.

We chose material carefully, as we had done in the past. And, hoping to capture the feeling from our earlier hits, we once again enlisted Ritchie Podolor and Bill Cooper as our producer and engineer, respectively. The songs we chose were the reggae title tune, "It's a Jungle Out There," by the unknown songwriting team of Bill Moloney, Paul Pilger, and Denny Polen; "Shot in the Dark," co-written by Barry Devorzon (who had a string of hits with TV and movie themes) and Michael Towers; "Livin' It Up" (Chuck's theme song) by Bill Labounty, Cynthia Weil, and Barry Mann; and "Somebody's Gonna Get Hurt" by Charlie Black, Richard Feldman, and Marcy Levy (a background singer in Eric Clapton's band).

The fifth song on the EP was a tune called "I Can't Help It," which was previously recorded in San Francisco by Danny and Cory, without Chuck, me, or the rest of the band. It was a leftover from the period before our reunion. Though the sessions took a long time, we were quite pleased with the outcome and the new sound that Ritchie and Bill achieved with us. However, despite incredible reviews from the critics who once loathed us and because of the record company's complete lack of distribution and promotion, the majority of the records remained in a warehouse in New Jersey. To this day, the five-song EP of *It's A Jungle* remains a little-known Three Dog Night collector's item.

My heroin use was becoming more blatant, and although I tried to disguise it from the other band members, I was continually being lectured to by my concerned friends. Also, sometime shortly after the ill-fated EP's release in 1983, Linda and I began to grow mutually apart. We finally decided, in a move that was best for both of us, to go our separate ways but to remain close friends. It was the first time in my life that the break-up of a relationship didn't send me into a tailspin of drugs and drinking. But I would use my third "divorce" as an excuse when things later got out of hand.

# 14 / Bet No One Ever Hurt This Bad

The years 1983 to early 1985 represented the lowest points to which I would sink in my self-induced drug sleaziness. It seemed that every day was taken up with plotting and scheming new ways to come up with money to support my habit. Before it was all over, I would lose everything I owned, deplete every possible source of money, and alienate not only my close friends but my entire family as well.

Even though Three Dog Night continued to tour steadily, thus affording me a comfortable income, I was running up such huge drug tabs that I needed to find alternate sources of income. I was not above theft, deceit, lying, cheating, or whatever else it took to ensure that my needs were met.

At this point most of my friends were a small circle of addicts and dealers. My every waking thought was geared toward how, when, and where to get the necessary drugs it took to maintain a daily existence. Drugs were rapidly replacing music as my number-one obsession. I was now on my way to becoming a junkie, in the truest, most depressing, dangerous sense of the word.

One of my many flirtations with death came when the band went to Hawaii for a series of concerts and a vacation in May 1983. We were winding down an Alaskan tour with four sold-out shows in Anchorage. After the last show, we were to catch the "red eye" flight to the islands. There were still three or four hours before the plane took off, so as usual, I was holding court in the hotel bar. My main drink for that trip was alternating "shooters" of Wild Turkey and Yukon Jack. By the time we got our hour call to leave for the airport, I had already run up a $125 bar tab. To call me shit-faced would have been a gross understatement. I had a small quantity of very expensive and very bogus coke that I had bought from some Eskimo in the hotel. I think it was more speed than the pure coke that Nanook claimed it to be. I was so drunk that I didn't bother to test it.

The rest of the band members were already in the limos waiting for me. They were quite anxious to get to Hawaii and meet up with their families. I, on the other hand, was single again, and was in no hurry to leave.

If we were going to make this flight, I would need to leave immediately. My clothes were strewn all over my hotel room. Sundry items covered every possible space. There was only one solution to the problem: Leave it behind. *When I arrive in Hawaii,* I thought to myself, *I'll buy new stuff.* I threw my stage clothes and anything else within ten feet of the bed into my suitcase, grabbed my tote bag, and ran for the elevator.

In the lobby I was interrupted by a waitress from the bar. She wanted to know if I meant to give her a $200 tip for a $125 bar tab. Had I left it alone, she probably would have been my best friend for life.

I poured myself into the white stretch limo and made my apologies to the rest of the band, who at that point didn't care about my financial faux pas with the bar maid. Several members voiced their condemnation for the current state of disarray I was in, to which my sweet alter ego replied, "Fuck you."

As soon as we got to the airport in Anchorage, I made a beeline for the bar. Once there, I carved out a permanent spot for myself and continued to down shots of Wild Turkey and Yukon Jack. At one point the bartender told me I had had enough and threatened to cut me off. I pulled out an almost empty vial of what passed for coke, and when nobody was looking, poured the remainder on the back of my hand. In one swift, piglike snort, I finished it off.

I couldn't possibly have known, at that point, what a mess I looked like. Large rocks of coke dotted my mustache. My hair and clothes were unwashed. If anyone within five feet of me lit a match, I probably would have gone up like a Roman candle.

The bartender returned to where I was now standing at a forty-five-degree tilt, took one look at me, and promptly threw me out. *Shit! Eighty-sixed again,* I thought to myself. *He just didn't understand me.*

It seemed that nobody did when I got this out of control. All I wanted to do was unwind after a successful tour and "have a few drinks."

One drink, one line, one pill was never enough for me at this point in my life. I didn't drink for the social comfort it afforded, but rather to get what I call "Stinking, shit-faced, puke-in-the-gutter, falling down drunk." This was now true with whatever I took, be it cocaine, pills, or heroin. I just couldn't seem to stop until I either fell down or passed out, which usually happened at the same time.

I knew, however, that if I didn't demonstrate some reasonable knowledge of the English language without slurring, I wouldn't be allowed to board the aircraft. I realized that waiting for me on the plane was a fresh supply of booze and people who hadn't seen me in my present condition. Clearly, a "Catch 22" was in effect. I couldn't drink anymore in the airport bar, yet I couldn't go on the plane and continue my binge if I appeared intoxicated — which I did. To make matters worse, I had done the last of the coke, and even washed out the bottle in hopes of getting that little bit that always clings to the rim.

One thing could bring me around long enough to fool the stewardesses: lots of coffee. Seemingly out of nowhere the solution hit me! I sat down in the waiting area and proceeded to tear through my sundry bag with all the zeal of a kid at Christmas. At the bottom of the bag, among the lint and other debris that had collected there, I saw it — one lone black pill. *I'm saved!* I thought to myself. I pulled it open slightly to see if there was any of the precious cargo still inside of the capsule. Most of the time I had already taken out whatever drug was there and left an empty gelatin capsule in my bag. But this time it was whole. What a beautiful sight: a perfectly good, unused Black Beauty. If I took it then, even with coffee, it wouldn't hit me for over half an hour. *Not quick enough,* I thought to myself. *I'll snort it!*

I went into the bathroom and found a vacant stall. Pouring the contents of the capsule onto the back of the toilet tank, I began to pound this powerful upper into a fine powder with my stolen hotel room key. Sounds easy, but it wasn't. You see, inside a Black Beauty are hundreds of tiny time-release capsules. With every swing of my room key, large numbers of the tiny beads would fly off in all directions. At the end of this bizarre ritual, however, I did manage to save enough to make a long line of the crudely crushed-up powder.

I rolled up a dollar bill. In one, uninterrupted movement, I managed to cram it all into my nose. The pain that immediately followed this stupid act was of no real concern to me at the time. I put my hand over my mouth and made a muffled sound closely resembling that of someone who just had his balls caught in a mouse trap.

As the bathroom door swung open, I caught a glimpse of myself in the mirror. I could have passed for *The Exorcist* poster child. If I was going to continue this facade of normality, something would have to be done quickly. I filled the sink with warm water, washed my face, and at the same time managed to get most of my hair wet. *No problem,* I thought, *I'll just grab some paper towels and dry myself off.* As luck would have it, this was an airport restroom with a blow-dryer mounted to the wall. By now I was starting to feel the effects of the Black Beauty. I bent down and tried to dry my face and hair under the blower. To anyone walking into the airport bathroom, this probably looked totally absurd.

Despite insurmountable odds, I managed to pull myself together long enough to make it past the gauntlet of security and onto the plane. As soon as we were airborne, I rang the call button and requested a few doubles. Since the plane wasn't equipped with a fully stocked bar, I had to switch to Bloody Marys. Not a bad choice, except that I was wearing all white clothes.

As mentioned several times before, I am and always will be a hyperactive person. As a child, I was diagnosed as such and Ritalin was prescribed. Ritalin is a strong upper that is supposed to, somehow, work in reverse and calm a hyper person down. With this information, it doesn't take a Rhodes scholar to figure out that a Black Beauty, or any other amphetamine, is the last thing that I should take as an adult. I later realized that my hyperactivity was the reason that I had switched to downers and heroin.

But for now, on this particular flight, I couldn't sit still. I was running up and down the aisles, talking a hundred miles an hour to anyone who would listen to me. A friend of mine later told me that when I got in this condition, I looked like a Benzedrine parakeet.

It had been a while since I had snorted the Black Beauty. Consequently, I drove everyone on the plane nuts. Between asking all the stewardesses out and talking in a slurred fashion to total strangers, telling them my entire life story, at one point one of the stewardesses threatened to cut me off. I realized that I had too much "speed" in my system, and I needed to nosedive in the opposite direction.

In my quest for someone's ear to bend, I ran across a lady in her mid-thirties who looked like a willing subject. It didn't take long before we were drinking and laughing together. Then she turned to me and asked if *perhaps* I needed a valium. "Sure." I said, "how many do you have?" She pulled out eight or ten blue Valiums from her purse and gave me half of them. Never doing anything in moderation, I took them all. By this time it was morning and the stewardesses began serving breakfast. Shortly thereafter, I was face down in it. To the rest of the band, this erratic behavior only confirmed that I still had a severe problem with drugs and alcohol. To me, it simply meant that people who fly shouldn't eat and take Valiums.

Somehow I survived that flight, but when we landed, a greater fate was awaiting me. Never having been known for getting large amounts of sleep — unless it was drug and/or alcohol induced — and with two or three hours of slumber under my belt, I was ready for the day. In my present condition, and in my own mind, I arrived in Hawaii several hours ahead of the plane.

We landed, got our luggage, and went straight to the hotel. Richard Grossman and I decided to rent a jeep and head for the north shore of Oahu. When we started out, it was 7:00 A.M. We took our time getting around the island so that we could take in all the sights, and most importantly, wait for a bar to open. On our way to Sunset Beach, a sign caught my eye: "Pat's Bar . . . OPEN."

It was time to switch drinks again and go for some local island color. I ordered a Scorpion, and Richard chose a Mai Tai. Since I had been up most of the past two days drinking and taking various drugs, I was not quite ready to be out in the intense Hawaiian sun for that long. The cool drinks afforded Richard and me a much needed break. After two more rounds, we decided to find a surf shop and buy some skin-diving equipment. We were feeling no pain whatsoever.

We found a little shop in Haliewa on the north shore. From there we headed for the Turtle Bay Hilton to put an edge on our ongoing buzz. After some more exotic drinks, we were ready to go scuba diving and play "Sea Hunt."

The ocean is beautiful and mysterious when you are straight. In my state of mind, it offered more stimulation than I was ready to accept. The explosion of colors and various life forms was completely overwhelming. I had to surface every few minutes to reestablish the fact that I was still alive.

I hadn't had that much exercise in years, and the sun and surf were beginning to take their toll on me. Richard was getting tired too. Around 2:00 P.M. we decided to call it quits with the Jacques Cousteau crap and head for the west side of the island. Along the way we stopped at a few more bars and began to play a game I call "Drink By Color." We drank blue drinks . . . red drinks . . . green drinks . . . yellow drinks . . . orange drinks . . . purple drinks. I felt like the flags flying in front of the United Nations building. By 5:00 we were ready to head back to our rooms at the Waikiki Sheraton.

I had been in and out of the sun for over ten hours. On the way back, I started to feel the effects of everything I had been bombarding my body with for the past forty-eight hours. When I got back to the hotel, I took a nap for a few hours, and woke up around 9:00 P.M. that evening. I wanted to "kick back" in the worst way, and knew that my heroin partners, Chuck and Julia, had a Federal Express package of drugs arriving sometime that evening. I phoned them up and, much to my excitement, found out that it had just gotten there.

In less than a minute, I was standing in the living room of their hotel suite, talking to Barry and Chuckie, their two sons. As soon as Chuck and Julia were through shooting up in the bathroom, it was my turn. Julia saw how sunburned I was and knew I had been drinking . . . but she had no idea how much. I assured her that I just had a few drinks all day. We went into the bathroom and she measured a tenth of a gram, got it ready, and proceeded to shoot me up.

As soon as that warm rush hit me, I knew it was a good batch. I did an about face, walked three or four steps, and fell like a tree to the floor. What happened next was told to me after I returned from a trip to the emergency room at Kaiser Hospital.

It seemed at that point, since my face was turning blue, both Chuck and Julia thought I was dying. They screamed to Barry to call the front desk and request an ambulance at once. Then Chuck, himself not in the best shape, began to give me mouth-to-mouth resuscitation.

The paramedics came quickly and brought the police, who were told that a member of Three Dog Night was either dead or dying.

Coming out of my drug-induced stupor, I couldn't help but notice the mass confusion in the room. Although I was semiconscious, I couldn't move. While Julia was in the bathroom getting rid of any evidence, Chuck was standing over me trying to divert the attention of the policeman who was questioning me. Chuck hoped that the officer wouldn't see the needle marks on my arm.

After what seemed like a lengthy interrogation, the paramedics hoisted me onto the gurney and the police called hotel security to clear the way in the service elevator. They thought that if they went down the back way, they could avoid a scene in the hotel lobby and keep this OD a secret.

Chuck and Julia rode down in the elevator with me to make sure that I would be all right. As we headed out the back way to the waiting ambulance, I sat up on the gurney and said, "Hold it. I need to take my stage clothes with me in case I meet someone." Julia laughed at this seemingly absurd statement and knew I would be OK.

On the way to the hospital, however, something strange happened. I started to cough up a large wad of gum. It seems that when Chuck was giving me mouth-to-mouth back at the hotel, he was chewing gum. He wound up blowing it down my throat. To the paramedics, this was the evident cause of my blackout and not the drugs. I knew differently. At that point, I told them I didn't need to go to the hospital and thanked them for all their time and effort.

Chuck, who was following the ambulance in his rental car, took me back to the hotel. I went right to bed to forget about the events of the last two days.

From the moment I woke up, I knew that something was very wrong. I was scared like I've never been before. I didn't have any feeling in my left hand. It wasn't paralyzed, but it was numb, as though shot with Novocain. *My God,* I thought to myself, *after all the close calls I've had with drugs, it all comes down to this?* When we flew to Maui the next day, I was silent on the flight for the first time in years.

Chuck and Julia knew I didn't feel well after the night's ordeal. They had no idea, however, that I had lost the feeling in my hand. Richard was hung over and didn't ask me what was wrong. Thank God. I don't think I could have made up a lie for this one.

When the plane landed in Maui, we went to the hotel and I headed for the beach. I thought that if I could get some fresh air and swim a little, then maybe, just maybe, this would go away and I would be back to normal.

The day went by slowly with no changes. It was the first time in my life, but not the last, that I would drop to my knees and pray to God to pull me out of a drug-induced disaster.

The drive to the Lahaina Civic Center was breathtaking. But the feeling I had on that ride was one of total acerbity. Dozens of self-pitying thoughts went through my head: *Why was this happening to me? Why did God turn his back on me once again?* It became painfully clear later that I was the only one responsible because of my total disregard of my mind and my body.

Before our show, Tower of Power was just finishing a kick-ass set that left Danny slightly paranoid to go on after them. I just kept thinking to myself, *I know our songs inside and out. Shit, I've played them for fifteen years, most of the time on auto pilot." This wouldn't be that hard.* However, I was still unable to feel anything with my left hand.

The lights dimmed. John Meglen, our tour manager, announced the band and we bounded onto the stage. From the opening chords of "One Man Band," I knew I was in trouble. "One Man Band" is structured so that all of the musicians hit the downbeat of the song together. I hesitated slightly, only because of the fact that I couldn't feel anything with my left hand though the fingers were moving. I was scared shitless but tried to hide it. I had a big tumbler of wine on stage, and I must have had the roadies refill that five or six times on stage.

Miraculously, I made it through the set without any major mistakes. I was extremely relieved when the show ended. I went right back to the hotel after the show and went directly to sleep. I didn't party with the rest of the band that night or for the rest of the tour. Neither did I tell anyone for several years what really happened that evening.

Although I survived the night, I figured that the heroin was at the core of my problem, and I didn't take any more for the rest of the trip. However, I continued to drink at a frightening pace. I figured that if I stayed drunk, I wouldn't experience the effects of withdrawal.

Our next stop was on the big island of Hawaii. We had one show to do and then three days off in Kona. There were no major problems, except that when I checked out of the hotel, my three-day bar tab exceeded everyone else's combined total. I about hit the floor when they presented me with a $625 bill! On one of those nights off I must have bought a round of drinks for everyone within a two-mile radius of the hotel.

I continued my habit of black-out drinking. The drinks were merely a temporary substitute for the drugs that my body craved. Unfortunately, nothing would take the place of the heroin to which I was addicted. I couldn't wait to get back home to L.A. I even called my dealer from Hawaii and placed my order so that it would be waiting for me when I returned — and it was.

By Christmas I was in a state of depression stemming from resentment I felt from my own lifestyle, although I had created it for myself. It was becoming a lot of work to get high now, with little or no rewards. It wasn't fun anymore, but at this point it was much harder to quit than to continue.

I rang in the New Year with a resounding crash. Once again I spent New Year's Eve on center stage at a party, and ended up out cold on the floor. This was it, folks. 1984. Big Brother. I remember back in high school, reading George Orwell's book and wondering what life would be like in 1984. As far as I was concerned, the reality was a big disappointment.

In February of 1984 my mother came to me with a very interesting business proposition. Once again, we sat in the kitchen, drinking Bloody Marys and plotting my future. Since I was so far behind in my house payments, and the bank had already foreclosed on it, she had the idea to loan me the money for the back payments and to place the house with an agency so that I could lease it out temporarily while entertaining the idea of selling it. I was on the road most of the time with Three Dog Night anyhow. If I had the extra income from leasing the house, I could make my monthly mortgage payments and still have some money left over. I could also move back into my old room at my parents' place and not have any bills to pay.

I readily agreed to her proposal. She called up a few friends of hers who were real estate agents and property managers. They came up to the house and looked around, and we agreed on a monthly price of $2,300. Then came the tedious routine of getting the house fixed up and in tiptop shape.

The only major thing that I did to improve it was to rip up the carpets and to sand and varnish the hardwood floors. We put out the "For Lease" sign, and waited.

I went back on the road for a few weeks with the band, only to return and find that just a few people had inquired about the place. Figuring that maybe my mother's agents just weren't that good at presenting the house, I called up Mann Realty once again and immediately placed the house with them. They said the house would be leased almost instantly, if we just lowered the price. I brought the price down to $1,600 per month. That very day we had four callers. None of the people, though, struck me as being the kind of tenants I would want to have.

The next weekend, the agent told me that a couple of musicians who knew me were interested in leasing the house almost immediately. As they drove up and got out of the car, I didn't recognize them right away. We walked through the house, and I showed them all of the finer points of it. The Jacuzzi pretty much sewed up the deal.

Then came the most important point, to me. I asked them who they played with. The quieter of the two guys turned to me and said, "Oh, we're the guitar players for Rod Stewart's band." *Oh, my God!* I thought to myself. Having worked with Rod in the past, and knowing his current drummer, Carmine Appice, I knew that they were notorious hell-raisers. I didn't want to take any chances. I made up some lame story that I had to ask my business manager before I approved, and that I'd call them back in a day or so. I turned to my agent, who was looking at me like I was some kind of idiot for not grabbing the opportunity right away. I said quite simply, "No fucking way." I knew that if they were anything like me, all they would want to do was to have wild parties, and destroy the place. I had already spent a fortune on renovations. The idea of having my place destroyed by some shit-faced rock and roller and their friends did not appeal to me in the least.

About a week and a half later, my real estate agent informed me that she had found a suitable person to lease the house — one whom everybody would approve of. It turned out that the person was a single elementary schoolteacher who was recently divorced. She would gladly pay the first and last month's rent up front, plus a $2,000 security deposit. Also, I would go through the entire house and inventory every piece of furniture and other personal items, and have her sign a paper stating if anything was broken or damaged, she would pay the full replacement value on the item. She agreed to that also, so I thought that there was no reason on earth why I shouldn't lease the house to her.

The next day we met at the real estate office, signed the papers, and I promptly received a check for $5,200. At my mother's insistence, I opened up a separate checking account for myself at her bank. I also made sure that both my parents and I could sign on the account, the reason being that if I was out of town, my parents could pay any or all of my bills, thus relieving me of any responsibilities.

I made the first deposit, and then went on the road. Once again, before I left for my short trip, I managed somehow to have one of my dealers, Lenny, front me some more drugs. I told him that I had leased my house and now had a steady source of income. When I returned a few weeks later, I had Lenny meet me at the airport with my usual bindle of heroin. Just to make him happy, I gave him $300 that I had saved from my per diem money, and told him that I could give him at least $1,500 the next day, to go toward my mounting tab (which was in the $3,000 vicinity by now). The sudden change in my financial status gave Lenny enough encouragement to continue fronting me dope whenever I needed it.

The next morning I went down to the bank and cashed a check for $2,500. Obviously, I didn't want my parents to find out that I was dipping into the lease money to pay off my drug debts, so whenever the bank statements would come into the house, I would do my best to intercept them and hide them in my room. If my mother ever questioned me about them, I simply told her that everything was paid and up to date.

I drove to Lenny's house that night, paid him the $1,500 I had promised him, and also gave him the extra $1,000 toward another supply of drugs. He made me a great deal on an eighth of an ounce and told me if I cut it, I could make it last a lot longer. I thanked him for his advice, but I paid no attention. My rationalization was, "Why have mediocre shit for three days, when you could have a killer high for one night?"

I went home, went into my room, closed the door, and started to snort until the sun came up. Around 7:30 in the morning I nodded out for a while. When I woke up, around 11:00 A.M., I immediately went to the place below the TV set where I kept my drugs. The night before, it had been piled high with heroin. Now there was hardly anything left. I knew that all I had to do was to finish off what was left on the plate, clean myself up, and go to the bank to draw out some more money. If I exceeded what I had in the account, I knew that in another two weeks I'd be receiving another rent check, and I could use that as collateral.

This seemed like the perfect situation. I was being paid for letting a sweet little schoolteacher live in my house. However, that was not the case. Within the first three months, my tenant had already started to screw me on the rent checks. Sometimes she wouldn't pay me on time, sometimes the checks bounced. My father, being the businessman that he was, was concerned about the poor business ramifications. However, my only concern at the time was the fact that I couldn't afford to pay my dealer on time so that I could do more drugs.

Once again, I found myself in the kitchen with my mother, having another of our little talks over a couple of Bloody Marys. She suggested that I just sell the house, liquidate my things, and pay off all of my back debts in one fell swoop. It sounded like an excellent idea, mainly because it would give me immediate access to a lot of cash — and a seemingly unlimited new supply of drugs.

I once again left for the road, and when I returned, my mother had wonderful news. Only a few weeks after they had put the house on the market, a young lady who appeared regularly on the television show "The Price Is Right" wanted the house, and was willing to pay the asking price — $250,000 — in cash. Within 24 hours I had a cashier's check for the total amount. I drove immediately to the bank, and this time — at my father's insistence — put it into a thirty-day money market account. This worked to my advantage, because it meant that at the end of each month, all I had to do was roll over the money into another account and live off the interest.

Any normal person could have lived quite comfortably this way. But what my parents didn't know was that I had a *major* drug habit. And the other thing that they didn't know was that I was going down to the bank daily and withdrawing anywhere from $500 to $2,000 every time. Even though the bank told me that there would be early withdrawal penalties to pay for each time I dipped into the account, I didn't care. As long as I had the money to buy the drugs, I was avoiding my own withdrawal problems.

Knowing that I had this sudden new supply of money in the bank caused me to adopt the attitude that I was once again rich. After I got high every day, instead of watching mindless TV, I would go out on extravagant shopping sprees, pick up girls, take them out for expensive dinners, and generally throw money around like it was growing on trees. The only responsible thing that I did was set aside $12,000 to purchase a new car later that year. Since I had a surplus of money, I also loaned Chuck $10,000 for his drug habit. Needless to say, during the next few months I had a lot of new and instantly devoted friends. I was so wrapped up in my own little world that I couldn't see the inevitable approaching.

By late October, I had gone through almost all of that money and was down to my last $500 (excluding the $12,000 earmarked for a new car). In November, I was once again going to the bank, but this time it was to gain access to my mother's safe deposit box, in hopes that there would either be money or pawnable valuables.

I had received the check from the sale of the house sometime in early June, and later that month, Three Dog Night embarked on an extended concert tour. It was while on the road that my spending really escalated. My only goal was to stay high and to have as much fun as possible. I didn't care how my performance on stage was. As long as I got through the gig, and knew that I had a fresh supply of drugs waiting for me at the hotel afterwards, everything was perfect.

On July 4, 1984, Three Dog Night played at a huge festival-like concert with the Beach Boys in Washington, D.C. It was called "The D.C. Beach Party." Due to the scene that took place, Secretary of the Interior James Watt banned rock and roll music on the Capitol Mall the next year, and Wayne Newton played instead. The show we did also featured John Lodge and Justin Hayward (of the Moody Blues), America, Hank Williams Jr., Ringo Starr, LaToya Jackson, and even Julio Iglesias. There were 750,000 people gathered on the grounds in front of the Washington Monument.

We did the show in D.C. at 10:30 in the morning, and the same day flew in the Beach Boys' chartered 727 to Miami. That evening we did the same show with a duplicate set of equipment. In D.C., Chuck and I were waiting for a Federal Express package full of heroin to arrive backstage. We couldn't — and wouldn't — go on stage until it arrived. I was standing there shouting, "The stuff's not here yet!" I was drinking like a fish just to try and keep myself together enough to go on. The package finally came five minutes before the show started. We would have kept all of those people waiting just to get a fix.

When you're heavily addicted, being high is the only priority in your life.

Occasionally, I would trust a total stranger to find the coke and heroin I needed. It was this complete trust in people that led me to one of the most insane and frightening experiences of my life.

At this phase of my addiction, whenever I would leave for one of our tours in the United States, I tried to make sure to take enough drugs along to at least get me through three or four days before I would have to call my connection to send a Federal Express package. This time, however, I did nearly all of my supply the first day. It was during a break in our 1984 tour that I went to New York City to hang out and attend the television taping of the first annual "MTV Awards" with a girlfriend who lived there. Up to this point, she didn't realize how strung out on heroin I was.

During the first two days of my trip, we drank way too much and stayed up freebasing coke. To come down, I knew I needed heroin. My body was starting to ache all over. I'd scored some 'Ludes the night before, so in the morning I took four of them to try to keep myself together. This worked only for a few hours. By that night, I was in extremely bad shape. I broke down and told my friend that I needed heroin real badly. Not being into this particular drug, the only comfort that she could afford me was a few words of encouragement, a bottle of vodka, and some pain pills. By then I was practically begging her to find me a connection. As a last resort, she turned me on to a friend of hers who told me that the only place in town to get good quality street heroin was Harlem.

At 3:00 A.M. I phoned for a cab to come to her apartment in midtown. When it arrived, I got in and calmly said, "Take me to Harlem, please." I might as well have said, "Take me to the moon." The look he gave me was one of complete astonishment.

"You want to go *where?*" he said.

"Harlem. You know, it's the bad part of town."

"You got that right asshole," he snapped back. "There's only one thing that would take you to Harlem at three in the morning: *smack*," he said with authority.

"You got that right, asshole!" I responded. Clearly, there was a situation here that had to be rectified right away. I reached into my pocket and pulled out a roll of bills. I peeled off a fifty and gave it to him. "Drive!" I commanded.

He looked at me for a moment and said, "You're either the dumbest motherfucker to walk the face of the Earth, or the baddest."

"Neither," I said, "just the sickest." He took the $50, turned off the meter, and said something about not wanting to take a fare from a dead man.

Not another word was said the whole way there. As we drove past the bombed-out looking buildings and street gangs on the corners, I began to think this wasn't such a good idea. *Too late to turn back now,* I thought. I was going through excessive withdrawal pain, and I was getting sicker and more scared by the minute. In my condition the drive to 125th Street seemed to take hours. We turned the corner past some vacant buildings and pulled up in front of a dingy little bar.

"This is as far as I go," the driver said. I stepped out of the car and, as I turned to thank him, puked all over the side of his cab. Needless to say, he was history.

Now I was alone. I took a deep breath, cleared my throat, and walked into a bar that seemed to be a likely place to score. There was loud music, lots of smoke, and a sea of black people. What happened next was right out of one of those E. F. Hutton commercials. I stood there in the doorway and said, "What's happening?" At that moment the entire bar became silent. All eyes were fixed on me.

A rather tall gentleman in green pants, a purple shirt, and a large pink felt hat walked up to me. He looked like he just stepped out of the movie *Superfly*. "You're in the wrong part of town, honky," he said.

"No shit," I replied.

By now I was soaking wet from fear and shaking from withdrawals. He could see that I wasn't there for Black Awareness Week, so I wasn't at all surprised when he asked me if I needed some "downtown."

"Yes, I would like about five hundred dollars' worth," I told him.

"I take it you've got the money on you?" he asked. I pulled out my roll of hundreds — not a smart move, considering where I was. "You're either the dumbest motherfucker on earth, or the baddest," he said.

Quizzically I replied, "Funny, you're the second person to tell me that tonight."

He motioned for me to follow him into a back room. When we

got there he turned to me and said, "Look, I know who you are. I've seen you guys play before and I like your music. If it were anyone else, I'd kick the shit out of them and take the money."

Before I could thank him, he grabbed me by the shirt, threw me up against the wall, and said, "Man, you're a junkie. You're in a junkie's world now. There's no right or wrong — good or bad. I'll take care of you, but it will cost." I told him that all I had was the $500 and wanted to use that for the heroin. "You'll just have to buy less shit, and cut me in on it."

I couldn't believe that I was standing in this broken-down bar in Harlem, arguing with some pimp about what his cut would be. After a short debate with him on the pros and cons of staying alive, I reluctantly agreed to give him $100. I'd just buy four bills' worth. He said he'd cut me a deal: half a gram for $400. I knew that this was way overpriced, and the quality probably wouldn't be that good. However, I was in no position to bargain with him.

He led me out of the bar, down an alley, and into one of the hundreds of bombed-out, vacant buildings I'd passed on my way into the combat zone. We crawled through a window, down a dimly lit hallway, and up to an apartment in the rear of the building. The place was rat-infested and smelled of rotting garbage and human waste. I thought to myself, *This is right out of a bad movie*. But it was all too real. My new friend turned to me and asked for the money. He told me that when we got inside to shut up — he'd do all the talking.

It seemed that his friends didn't trust too many people, let alone a honky. He told me that he'd have to take a test shot first, to see if the shit was any good. I was feeling so bad by now that I didn't have the strength to argue.

After a secret knock, the apartment door opened to reveal an honest-to-God shooting gallery (a room where people gather to shoot up drugs). Everyone in there eyed me cautiously. I remembered what he said about keeping my mouth shut. These weren't exactly the kind of people I'd invite to my home. This was, without a doubt, the sleaziest thing I've ever done, and I've done some pretty sleazy things.

At that very moment I was confronted with the fact that I was no better than anyone else in the room. I had sunk lower than I ever thought possible. Another thing I noticed was that most of these scumbags were armed and extremely dangerous.

A rather large man of Spanish descent walked up to my pimp friend and whispered something to him. After a few seconds they exchanged the money and drugs. He then told me to stay put. Even though I didn't know this guy from Adam, when he walked out of the room, I felt all alone. I just stared at the people around me who were getting off on the drugs. I was getting a "contact high" myself. There's a span of time before you shoot up that you go through all of the symptoms of doing the drug. Psychologically, I was setting myself up for what I knew was only moments away.

After about five minutes, my inner-city tour guide returned with that telltale look about him. His eyes were pinned to the max. He could barely stand up. "Good shit?" I asked him. He turned and looked me straight in the eyes with a stare that almost burned a hole in me. "Man, I thought I told you to shut the fuck up!"

"Yeah, but I only wanted to know if—"

He cut me off in midsentence. "Don't ever question these people. You'll do the shit here, and I'll drive you back downtown."

He could tell that I was scared to death. When one of the guys motioned for me to come over and roll up my sleeve, he whispered in my ear, "Real good shit." I held out my arm as the guy searched for a good place to hit me. When he found a suitable vein, he had me pump it up by making a fist repeatedly.

Even before the needle went in, I could taste the heroin. Seconds later I was in heaven. Somehow this whole night of madness was worth it in that instant.

They walked me over to the corner of the room and sat me down. Everything was now moving at a much slower pace, and that suited me just fine. I was content to stay where I was for the time being. In fact, I was feeling so good from the heroin that I wanted to strike up a conversation with everyone in the room.

As soon as I stood up to say something, a firm grip was applied to my shoulder. "Sit the fuck down, man," someone said. I didn't look to see who it was, but from the smell of his aftershave, I knew it wasn't Calvin Klein.

I didn't question anyone as to why they wanted me to do the stuff there, but later when I retold the story at a party, I was told that most dealers of that caliber don't trust anyone. They probably thought I was a narc. What better way to find out than to shoot me up to see if I could handle it. I passed the test with flying colors.

My fashion-conscious friend indicated that it was time to go, so I cautiously said good-bye, and commented that the smack was good. I knew, however, that it wasn't good enough to hold me through the next day. I'd have to call L.A. and have a fresh supply sent out.

We slowly made our way out of the building and back to the

bar. By now there were only a few people in there. My heroin buddy bought me a shot of vodka and introduced me to a few of his friends. "This is my man, Jim. He's OK."

For the time being I was "OK" But tomorrow I knew this madness would start all over again. I swore to God, no matter how bad I felt, I would never do something this stupid again.

# 15 / Tulsa Turnaround

November of 1984 once again found me standing in the doorway of my parents' house, saying good-bye to my mother, ready to embark on yet another adventure. In one hand I had a small suitcase crammed with clothes and sundries (I always overpacked). In the other I had a cashier's check for $12,000, a gram of heroin, a cassette copy of the new Don Henley album, *Building the Perfect Beast,* and a one-way ticket to Tulsa, Oklahoma. I was going to fly there and stay with my friends, Henry and Becky Freeman. I would also pick up a brand new 1985 Nissan 200SX Turbo with every option available on it. Since there is no sales tax in Oklahoma, I would save a lot of money on the car. Also, the fact that Henry was a car dealer himself, and could negotiate a deal with the Nissan people to have me pick up my vehicle for "cost" (if I paid cash) was a strong selling point.

It was a simple plan: get there and party till I puked! Then I would pick up the car the next day, get a good night's sleep, and drive back home. If I took it easy, and kept to the southern part of the U.S., as to avoid any snow or bad weather, it should take only three or four days to reach Los Angeles, allowing for food and fuel stops and two nights of staying in a hotel somewhere to rest.

I must have been real stupid to think that one gram of dope would last me the whole trip. I shot up a healthy hit before I left my mom's, and not wanting to take my needle with me on the plane, I then proceeded to snort a fair amount in the back of the cab on the way to the airport.

By the time the plane took off, my stash was nearly gone. Somewhere over New Mexico, I was in the bathroom washing out the vial and scraping out the cap to get every last bit of the precious drug. The only thing to do was to start drinking heavily, and then call my dealer, Lenny, back in L.A., and have him Federal Express some more to me when I got to Henry's in Tulsa.

When I arrived in Tulsa, Henry was there to meet me. I was pretty well plowed by then, and knew that as the smack wore off I would be feeling real rough. My first instinct was to walk right past him and phone Lenny immediately. But, having slightly better manners than that, I tried to hide the fact that I was going through withdrawals and was obviously in a lot of pain. I suggested that we hit the airport bar while I waited for my bags. I knew that Henry shared my lust for life and was always on the lookout for a good time. A friend of mine who was a drug dealer for over 14 years had first introduced Henry and his wife to me.

Avoiding moderation at all costs, I ordered two double vodka gimlets and downed them in a matter of seconds. This produced a slight temporary rush, but nothing close to my craving or need for the heroin. We went and picked up the bags, then drove to his house. I greeted Becky and their little girl, Danielle, and immediately went to take a hot shower — which was extremely uncomfortable. As any junkie will tell you, when you're experiencing withdrawals, your nerve endings are so sensitive that something as simple as water hitting them will send you crawling up the wall. This is coupled with the fact that virtually every joint and muscle in your body aches to the degree that even walking becomes difficult. To top all of this fun, you also tend to puke a lot, usually bringing up nothing more than stomach bile, and at the same time you have uncontrollable bouts of diarrhea.

Just like a boy scout, I was prepared and did bring a back-up high with me, just in case something like this happened, and I couldn't contact Lenny right away. This alternate high came in the form of my father's prescription drug, Dalmaine.

Not satisfied with merely swallowing them, I pulled the capsules apart and snorted the vile-tasting powder inside, till my nose burned and I started to dry heave. This at least temporarily gave me the required strength to get through the shower and carry on the facade that nothing was wrong.

When I got out of the shower, I had Becky pour me a tall glass of straight vodka, which I took back to the guest room and chugged. Then I called Lenny and told him to Federal Express me some more "downtown." He told me that a new batch had just come in, and that he'd get a good-sized gram off to me that evening. I told him to just put it on my tab, and I'd pay him when I returned in a couple of days. I hung up and thought, *Will one gram be enough?* I somehow rationalized that it would, and that I didn't want to spend too much of the money that I was saving on the car, in order to buy drugs for the return trip.

I knew that I could get good and drunk that night, because the package would arrive the next morning before 10:30, with my life-saving heroin inside of it. One of the main attractions for me about the drug was that it was the only thing that I had ever known to completely get me over a hangover. However, I had to be careful not to use up too much of it for that purpose, because I needed it to last all the way back to L.A. Luckily for me, we all went out for dinner, and then went over to one of Henry's friends' houses for a quiet night of videos, fueled by some coke, a few 'Ludes, and only a couple drinks.

I got tired and Becky drove me back early, leaving Henry there to watch the sun come up. I figured since I wouldn't have a bad hangover, I could snort another Dalmaine until the package arrived. Then Henry and I could drive the short distance to the town of Broken Arrow, Oklahoma, where the Nissan dealer was, and pick up my new toy.

I slept in until 11:15 A.M. I looked at my watch, and then crawled out of bed. I knew the package was sitting on the coffee table, and the anticipation was so high that I went out there totally nude to retrieve it. To my horror, I discovered that the table was as bare as I was! I went back to the bedroom, put on my robe, and went looking for signs of life in the house. No one was around. Henry either hadn't come home, probably having crashed at his friend's, or he had gone to work early. Becky might have taken Danielle someplace. Just then the back door opened, and their maid, who could hardly speak any English, walked in. Talking as slowly as I could and using sign language, I tried to ask her if she had picked up a package from the living room table. She shook her head from side to side, indicating that either she hadn't or she didn't understand what I was talking about.

"Plan B" had to go into effect immediately. I went back to my room and took out the last two Dalmaines. I opened them, poured the yellow powder out on the nightstand, rolled up a bill, and snorted the whole hideous pile. My head jerked back violently, my eyes watered, and I started to gag. This meant that the desired effect was being achieved. I went into the kitchen, ignoring the freshly waxed floor and the maid's apparent rambling, and poured a small amount of orange juice (for color only) into a tall glass. Then I went to the liquor cabinet and filled the rest of the glass with vodka. I went back to my room and practically inhaled the drink. Then I sat on the edge of the bed, contemplating my next move.

When I heard Becky's voice in the living room, I came running out of the bedroom, anticipating finding her holding my package. But luck was not with me that day. Regretfully, after giving her the third degree, I discovered that no package had arrived that morning. I was in deep trouble now. I quickly picked up the phone and called L.A. to see what had happened. Once again I was out of luck. There was no answer at my dealer's house.

By now I was feeling pretty toasty around the edges, and I began to panic. I called up Federal Express and told them that a package containing important contracts was somehow lost. But, once again, it was I who was lost, because without the airbill number, they couldn't trace it.

I didn't want Becky to know what bad shape I was in, but at the same time I didn't give a flying fuck who knew or what they thought. I got dressed and went back to the kitchen for a refill of O.J., making sure once again to put only enough in the glass for added color. This procedure was becoming quite tedious, but once more I filled it to the top with vodka. In the time it took to walk from the liquor cabinet back to my room, the drink was gone. I suddenly realized that my Dalmaine was gone as well, and that I was on my way to that final state as well.

I think Becky sensed my dilemma, because she suggested that we go out for lunch and have a few drinks. I was more than ready. I tried L.A. once again, and was only temporarily relieved to find the answering machine on at my dealer's house. This meant that he had come home, turned it on, and then left again, I presumed, to score.

I left one of my wonderful coded messages, and told him the "contracts" had not arrived, and to *please* call as soon as possible. Henry met us for lunch, looking absolutely hammered. We got our table, ordered lunch and a round of Kamikazes, and settled back for some idle chatter. In the time span of about one hour, I downed a half dozen Kamikazes. I didn't feel much like eating, because my stomach was understandably tied in knots.

After we finished at the restaurant, Becky went home, and Henry and I drove out to Broken Arrow. He had a small amount of coke that we did to take the edge off of the booze. But I needed something else.

As we drove down the road to the showroom, Henry pointed to a new white car in the window. "There's your baby," he said. It was beautiful. All I wanted to do was get in it and go. After signing the necessary papers, and giving the salesman the check, I followed Henry to his house. All the way there, I had the incredibly powerful stereo cranked up to the max, blasting out the new Henley cassette that I had brought for just this purpose.

When we pulled up in his driveway, Becky and Danielle came out to see the car. I got out of the car and walked right past both of them to go pour myself another drink. I was almost inside when Becky told me that Lenny had called and wanted me to call him back. I was inside and on the phone in a flash. I was only slightly at ease to find out that he hadn't made it to the Federal Express office the night before and would make it up by putting "a little something extra" in the package. He then guaranteed that it would arrive by 10:30 the next morning.

I now breathed a sigh of relief when I hung up the phone, and then poured myself another drink, which I sipped slowly instead of chugging. Now I was between hangovers, on my way to the next one, not to mention being deep in the throes of heroin withdrawal. Taking a cue from my obvious actions, Henry made a call and an hour later we were on our way to a friend's party.

I knew that after the smack arrived the next morning I would have to get on the road, as I had a very long drive ahead of me. But, using the excuse that it was the last night with my friends, I stayed out late drinking, snorting, and taking various downers.

When I woke up in the morning, I had great difficulty remembering anything from the night before. I must have had a good time. Becky was already up cooking breakfast for Danielle, and Henry was still crashed out. She asked me if I wanted something to eat. I declined, saying, "No thanks, I'll just drink my breakfast."

After about a half hour, Henry came wandering out of his bedroom, looking almost as bad as I did — if that was possible. We mutually decided that what we needed was a hot Jacuzzi, so we took off whatever clothing was left on our bodies, put on our bathrobes, went outside, and climbed in the water. In a few minutes, Becky came out carrying two strong screwdrivers. I thanked her, took a long gulp, and sank back into oblivion. I was almost asleep in the Jacuzzi when she reappeared, carrying my package. I was so excited at the prospect of instant physical and mental gratification that I forgot I was stark naked and started to stand up in the hot tub to take the package from her. Henry shot me a disapproving look, and I quickly sank back into the swirling water. I grabbed my robe and put it on, took the package and, dripping wet, made a beeline for my room.

I proceeded to tear open the package like a kid at Christmas time. Inside I found a note from Lenny, apologizing for the delay. Taped to the back of it was a large bindle. I opened it very carefully and saw what must have been at least a gram and a half of the only wonderful-looking white powder that I had seen since I had left L.A.

I took a razor blade from my sundry bag, cut out a long line, rolled up a bill, and snorted. I just stood there in total silence for a while, savoring every feeling that was returning to my body. I repeated this process one or two more times until my headache and body pains were gone. Keeping in mind to save enough for my long journey back to L.A., I quickly jumped into the shower, which, now that I was under the influence, felt like heaven. I then packed up my belongings and went out to say my good-byes. I thanked Henry and Becky for everything, kissed Danielle, and went back into the bedroom for one more good-sized hit for the road. With my suitcase, bindle, and Don Henley cassette, I was off.

The day was practically shot, as it was well after 1:00 P.M. and it had now started to rain quite heavily. I got about a half a block before I realized that I didn't know how to turn on the windshield wipers. It was then that I pulled over and got the owner's manual out, figuring it might be wise to learn the functions of everything in the car. Once I had mastered what all the buttons were for, I looked at my map and headed for the freeway.

I decided to drive till about eight or nine o'clock that night, since the storm was getting quite intense. I could find a Holiday Inn, or other suitable accommodations, have a few drinks, do a line or two, and get a good night's sleep. The next day I could get up at the crack of dawn and get an early start.

I found a Holiday Inn, checked into my room, ordered room service, took a hot shower, and then went looking for a nightcap. The bar was totally deserted. For some insane reason, I decided not to go to the bar, but to the state owned liquor store next to the hotel. To this day, only God knows why I did what I was about to do.

Not satisfied with merely buying a bottle of vodka or some other suitable liquor, I was compelled to go to the furthest extreme. I saw a bottle of Everclear sitting on the shelf. Having had the opportunity many years ago, in a Houston club called The Cellar, to experience the effects of Everclear, I wanted a repeat performance.

Everclear is the closest thing to moonshine that you can buy legally. Simply put, it's 190 proof wood-grain alcohol. It is so strong that it could remove the chrome from a trailer hitch. Unlike conventional liquor, you have to mix Everclear with something to even swallow it. I bought a pint of it and a six-pack of 7-Up, and headed back to my room. Once there, I poured myself a tall drink and started to chug it. I did it only once more before I blacked out.

When I woke up the next morning, it felt like someone had cut off the top of my head with a machete. Words can't even describe the pain. I immediately reached for my bindle of heroin, opened it up, and snorted everything that was there. Within seconds, I was back to "normal" again. I looked on the floor and saw the empty bottle of Everclear, and thought to myself, *Oh my God, I drank the whole thing. That was real stupid. It's a wonder I woke up at all.*

But then the reality hit me: here I was, only about six hours out of Tulsa, in a hotel in some town in Texas, and I had just done the last of my heroin. What was I going to do now?

The bars weren't open, as it was early in the morning, so I had to drive as far as I could, until either I found an open bar or liquor store, or the heroin started to wear off and it became too painful to drive.

Surprisingly, I made it for about six or seven hours on the road. I decided to get another room for the night. And, as my money was running out, I had to look for some super-cheap accommodations. I found a Motel Six in some little backwater town in Texas (damn, is it a big state!), checked in, and called my dealer. Unfortunately, I wasn't anyplace Federal Express could deliver it to the next day. And, if I waited for the regularly scheduled delivery, I would be totally out of money. I told Lenny just to sit tight, and I'd either drive to someplace that he could send it to or make a suitable substitution. The latter is exactly what I did. Trying to conserve my funds, I went next door to the drug store and bought a bottle of Nyquil Nighttime Cough Syrup. The main ingredients are 25% alcohol and belladonna. I took it back to the room, opened the bottle, and drank the entire thing.

The following morning, I woke up feeling worse than I did after the Everclear episode the previous day — if that was possible. The only difference was that this time I didn't have any heroin to help me out. I found myself on the telephone again, calling Lenny, only to find — to my horror — that he had gone away for a few days. Now I was totally alone and rapidly becoming quite sick. I mustered up all the energy I could, got into my car, and drove on down the road.

Quite a while later, I saw a liquor store that was just opening for the day. Having only a few dollars left on me, which I needed for gas, I knew that I had to buy some cheap booze just so I could contemplate what my next move would be. I resigned myself to the fact that I would probably once again have to have my mother bail me out and wire some money to me someplace. I walked into the liquor store, looked around, and realized that the only thing that I could afford was a gallon bottle of Thunderbird wine for $1.98. My hands were shaking so badly that I could hardly hold the money. I paid the man for the wine, got into my car, and drove down the road a ways to a rest area. There I unscrewed the cap and sat on my car, drinking the wine until it was almost gone, stopping only to throw up occasionally.

As I drove I would lean my head out the window, but still puke all over the door of my brand new white car. I drove on a little further until I couldn't take it any longer. By now it had started to snow. *Where in the hell am I?* I wondered. I pulled into a convenience store and found out that I was sixty-five miles northeast of El Paso, Texas.

I got on the phone, called my travel agent in L.A., and told her that I needed a one-way ticket from El Paso back to Los Angeles. In my mind I had formulated this plan that I would drive to the El Paso airport, park my car, fly home, score some drugs from someone, get some money from my mother, and fly back and pick up my car. I made it to El Paso in my puke-streaked new car, parked in the short-term parking lot, went to the ticket counter to pick up my prepaid ticket, boarded the plane, and continued to drink.

When I arrived in L.A., I felt unbelievably fucked up. I called my dealer, who had returned from his trip, and told him of the ordeal I had been through since our last conversation. He told me to sit tight, and that he'd be down to pick me up in about forty-five minutes with some "relief." Just knowing that I was going to feel good suddenly made it better.

When we drove out of the airport, he handed me a bindle containing some Mexican Brown heroin. This was greatly inferior to the China White that I was used to, but at this point, I didn't care — I would just do more of it. He told me that there was $250 worth there, and that he'd put it on my ever-growing drug tab. Before we got on the 405 freeway, heading back toward Hollywood, it was all gone. However, I didn't care about my drug tab, the puke-stained car, or the ordeal that I was going through to maintain this suicidal lifestyle.

We went back to Lenny's house, where I put yet another gram on my ever-growing tab. I promised him that I would get some money from my mother and at least pay him for the heroin I just bought, and also the stuff he had sent to Henry's house. We talked for a while, and then he drove me back to my mom's house. At least when I greeted her this time, I was already sufficiently high and not suffering from withdrawals or the "shakes" it causes.

My mom fixed me a bite to eat, and I went in and talked to my dad just for a minute, only to tell him — after he gave me the third degree — that I was caught in the middle of a raging snow storm and had to leave the car in Texas. I told him that I would fly back in a few days, pick it up, and return. As usual, he was more concerned with my finances than he was with my well-being.

I went back into the breakfast room, poured myself and my mother a strong Bloody Mary, and sat down and talked for what seemed like hours. Before I was ready to go to bed, I asked my mother to loan me some money once more, so I could finish off the trip. As usual, she gave it to me without question. I took advantage of the situation by asking for $750, knowing full well that $500 of it I had promised to Lenny the next morning.

This is where the addiction really takes hold of a person. It controls his every thought, not to mention his every move. I knew that the gram that I had picked up from my dealer probably wouldn't even last me until I got to the airport the next day. And, if I gave him the money I owed him, I would be right back where I started. So, as any devious junkie would do, I waited until my mom was asleep, and went into her wallet. I knew that the woman who rented the upstairs apartment from them had just given my mother that month's rent. Being greedy — but not entirely stupid — I only took half of it. I knew I would be long gone by the time my mother discovered the money missing, and that there was a chance she would blame herself for misplacing it.

I called up another dealer that I knew and told him my problem, saying that I needed a gram of heroin, but only had $250 to spend. I would pay him that now, and settle the balance when I returned to L.A. Of course, I had no intention of paying him the remainder of the money, but since I could "tap dance" around town easily, I would avoid him like the plague if he tried to track me down at my mom's house. Stupidly, he agreed to this, and sometime around midnight I was on the freeway, heading for Tarzana to consummate the deal. Now I had close to two grams.

The next morning I got up bright and early, mixed a drink, and called the airport to book a one-way flight to El Paso. I shot up a healthy dose, jumped in the shower, and then packed a few extra belongings, for what I thought would be a short trip back to Texas. Nobody was awake in the house yet, so I quietly slipped outside to wait for the cab I had just called to take me to the airport. I wanted to be out of the house, because I knew that any minute Lenny would call looking for his money.

After boarding the plane, I waited for the take-off so I could go into the bathroom and do some more drugs — being careful this time not to deplete my supply. I only did a small amount, and as we were flying over New Mexico, I chuckled to myself, *This time I did it right!*

When we landed in El Paso, I went immediately to the parking lot to retrieve my vehicle. Somehow it didn't quite look like it did when I first saw it in the showroom window. About two inches of dirt covered the car, along with my three-day-old puke, and there was some fresh bird shit on the windshield. Under normal circumstances, the first thing I would do would be to go and get it washed. Instead, I drove to the airport Hilton and got a room for the evening.

After I checked in, I called up Domino's Pizza and then went to the bar to buy a bottle. I stopped and got a couple of 7-Ups, and settled in for a relaxing evening. I put on my robe, turned on HBO, ate the entire pizza, polished off a fifth of vodka, and snorted a fair amount of dope. In the back of my mind, I heard a little voice telling me to conserve the drugs for the long trip back to L.A. Being my usual belligerent self, I told the voice, "Mind your own fucking business!" Then I promised myself one of the great lies of rock and roll: "One more line, and I'll go to sleep."

With a hangover the next morning, I instinctively reached for the dope, stuck the rolled up bill into the remaining pile, and took a healthy snort. Relief was just a "toot" away. Although my supply was greatly diminished, I surmised that I still had enough to get me back home.

Somewhere around Las Cruces, New Mexico, I pulled over for a bite to eat. I ordered a cheeseburger, and then went into the bathroom to have yet another snort. By now, it was slim pickins in the smack department, so I thought I might as well go all the way and finish it off. Somewhere in the back of my mind I knew that the buzz this small remaining amount would produce couldn't possibly get me home. I got back on the road and drove as far as I could before I started feeling shitty.

By nightfall the pain was becoming increasingly more intense. From the road signs I saw that I was only about twenty-five miles east of Tucson, Arizona. I drove to the sign marked "Downtown" and got off the freeway, hoping to find a liquor store or a quiet out-of-the-way bar. I drove down Broadway past the Holiday Inn, and proceeded to get lost, even though the downtown area is probably only eight to ten blocks long.

I was strung out on heroin, sicker than a dog, looking for a bottle for a substitute buzz, and all of a sudden I found myself wanting to buy another cassette tape. This was probably due to the fact that I couldn't seem to find a good radio station, and I was sick and tired of listening to the same Don Henley album — over and over again. I pulled into a record store and, even though I was feeling like death warmed over, I still managed to spend quite a while shopping for just the right cassette to orchestrate my mood. I picked out Foreigner's latest release, *Agent Provocateur,* and went back to my car to preview it.

Spotting an all-night supermarket, I pulled in and headed directly for the liquor department. Not wanting to buy a fifth of liquor, because I'd just wind up drinking the whole thing, instead I opted for one dozen pre-mixed daiquiris. Before I was out of the parking lot, two of them were already gone. I then drove a little further, to the Inn Suites, and got a room for the evening. I was too sick to eat anything, and too tired to go out, so instead, I polished off another six cans of daiquiris. That left four for my breakfast buzz.

The next morning I woke up with some serious heroin withdrawal symptoms. I knew that I had to somehow make it straight home from here. Seeing as how it was only 7:00 A.M., I thought that I could do it. I knew that Lenny was probably pretty pissed off at me again, for skipping town without contacting him. Instead, I called Chuck and Julia, who had probably scored anyway. I knew that once they discovered the ordeal that I was going through, they would be more than happy to front me something. True friends that they were, that was exactly the case. However, there was only one drawback: Chuck informed me on the phone that they were taking off for the weekend, and would be leaving the house around 6:00 that evening. That gave me roughly eleven hours to drive 500 miles.

I got behind the wheel of my car, found the freeway, and started to drive like a man possessed. With a single goal in my mind, I pressed the car at times to ninety miles per hour. I wouldn't stop until I got back to L.A. At one point, just outside of Indio, California (125 miles from L.A.), I had to pull over to dry heave and run into the bathroom of a nearby service station. I repeated this procedure about six or seven more times, and also was frequently changing my sweat-soaked tee shirts.

As soon as I hit the downtown L.A. area, traffic was practically at a standstill. *No time for this shit,* I thought to myself, *I've got to get up to the Canyon before Chuck leaves.* Lucky for me that I knew practically every back road and surface street in Southern California. Getting off the freeway, I zigzagged around the Hollywood Hills and made it up to Mulholland Drive. From there it was only a matter of minutes to Chuck and Julia's.

As I pulled up in their driveway, they were in the process of pulling out, with the kids and suitcases in the car. Fortunately, Chuck was very trusting. He told me that the front door was open, and that he had left a good amount in the usual spot. "Just lock up when you leave," he said, and he was off.

I went inside, found the bindle, and proceeded to snort half of it. I then made myself quite at home. I cooked myself dinner, and then settled back to watch some T.V. When I was feeling in tip-top shape once again, I drove back to my parents' house.

As I was driving down the street, I began to get a sick feeling in my stomach — not caused by the drugs, but by the fact that I suddenly realized something very important. Throughout this whole insane nightmare, I had thought only of myself, and no one else. When I had originally flown to Tulsa to pick up my new car, it was the middle of November. By the time I arrived back in L.A. with the car, it was the end of the month. The realization hit me that I had completely missed Thanksgiving with my family. I never once even called them from the road to tell them what was happening. I deeply regretted having put my parents through all of this shit.

When I got home, I went into the house. Not hearing any sounds, I figured that they were asleep. As I was trying to quietly slip into my room, like some sort of weasel, I heard my mother crying in her bedroom. I put my bags down, went into her room, and sat on the edge of her bed. I put my arms around her and whispered, "I'm so sorry," and in a few moments, I too was crying.

Late that night, I found myself once again sitting in the kitchen, with a drink in one hand and a rolled-up bill in the other, thinking to myself, *How can I keep on doing this?* Somehow I would find a way.

# 16 / One Is The Loneliest Number

After missing Thanksgiving because of my car episode, I knew that I had to do something extra at Christmas to make up for it. Unfortunately, I had a slight cash flow problem, since I had gone through the entire $250,000 from the sale of my house in a six-month period! All of the wonderful new friends I had made that year when I had money suddenly vanished into thin air.

I now launched into what I referred to as my "Let's Make a Deal" period. I started to sell off every material possession that I owned. Instead of spending my time at the shopping malls and expensive night spots, my new hangouts became a succession of pawn shops on Santa Monica Boulevard. The most famous of these was a place called Elliott Salters. There I could exchange expensive items — like my stereos, cameras, and watches — for cash. The stereo equipment, which cost hundreds, only yielded $50. My TV only brought me $20. After I went through all of those items, I began selling my musical equipment for any amount they would give me. At one point, I even got into my father's jewelry box and stole a ring that had been in his family for years. Something of sentimental value like that you don't even put a price on, but I did: $65. I was sinking so low that I would do anything just to stay high enough to avoid the torture of withdrawals.

Once I ran out of things to hock at the pawn shops, I found a record shop on Melrose Avenue called Aaron's, where they would buy used albums and tapes. I immediately dumped my entire record collection — which at the time consisted of about 100 albums and 500 cassettes — into large trash bags, and took them down there. The sad thing about that is the fact that, at one point in my life, those albums represented everything to me. Piece by piece, I was selling off my entire life — for drugs. My complete record collection, which I spent years amassing, was wiped out in moments, and supplied me with only enough drugs to sustain me for one evening.

Also at this time, Chuck was going through the same thing. However, he took it a step lower and pawned his Gold records in order to get a fix. That was one thing I swore I would never do, no matter how desperate I got. And I was getting desperate.

I had to immediately find a new source of income. The money from Three Dog Night wasn't nearly enough to carry on this lifestyle. Usually, I would be so far ahead of myself, advancing money from them, that by the end of the tour, I wouldn't have anything left. I asked our accountant not to deduct any money for state or federal taxes, assuring him that I would deal with the government myself. Naturally, I spent all of my earnings, and decided that the government could go screw themselves.

Suddenly, one morning, it dawned on me that I had an untapped cash flow right under my nose: my unsuspecting mother's bank account. My junkie personality started to plot the following scenario:

I would obtain the latest canceled check from her bank statement. Then I would get the next blank check in the book, paperclip it to the canceled check, hold it up to a lamp, and gently trace my mother's signature. I went through two or three checks before it looked pretty convincing. I knew that my mother's handwriting changed now almost daily, because her hands would shake slightly when she held a pen to write anything. I knew that the bank tellers would compensate for this penmanship variation and probably wouldn't question a slightly different looking signature. I also knew that she was becoming increasingly more bed-ridden, due to her own escalated alcoholism. I told her that I was so concerned about her conserving her strength that I would gladly do all of her banking for her. She agreed, and the very next day, I went down to her bank with the upstairs rent deposit. I also tried out my forgery plan, being careful to start off with a small amount — under $500 — so they wouldn't call for verification.

I carefully made out a check for $250, dated it, and wrote on the "memo" line, "medical expenses." I made the deposit first, and then, with sweaty palms, apprehensive eyes, and some nervous small-talk for distraction, handed the forged check to the teller. I closed my eyes just for a second, and thought, *Please God, let this work.* Almost immediately the teller said, "How would you like that, Mr. Greenspoon?"

"Like what?" I said, surprised at the astonishing success of my latest act of deception.

"Your cash."

"Oh, that . . . small bills will be fine."

I had pulled it off. I got the money and calmly walked out of the bank. When I reached the street, I let out a loud victory cheer.

I thought to myself, *If it worked once, it will work again.* That afternoon I was on the phone informing my various dealers that once again I had an unlimited cash flow.

The very next day, I tried my scam again. Only this time I pushed the amount to $600. Before I left the house, knowing that the bank would be calling, I took the phone off the hook. When the bank did call my mother, and informed me that the line was busy, I simply said that my mother was way too sick to talk to anyone and had probably taken it off so she could get some sleep. Everyone at the bank knew her, so this didn't seem too far out of line. Seconds later, I had the money in my hands.

Every day for the next couple of months, I would escalate the amount I forged on the checks, and subsequently my drug intake would grow as well. The more I cashed, the more I snorted or shot up. By the time this little escapade was over, I wound up stealing over $50,000 from the only person in the world who unquestionably loved me.

With Christmas just a short time away, I had to make sure that I would not only buy presents for everyone, but that I had enough cash to do it. A normal person would simply get an extra job around Christmas time. I, however, chose to have one of my girlfriends ripped off, so I could go out and hock her belongings. I knew that she had full insurance to cover a theft, so I called her up and suggested that we go down to Palm Springs for the weekend. The night before we left, I stayed at her house, drinking, snorting, and having sex. The next morning, when we were loading the car up, I made sure that I left the latch on one of the back windows of her house open. On our way down there, I stopped and made a phone call to an anonymous party, whom I informed, "Everything has been taken care of." That was his cue to rob her apartment, sell everything, and we'd split the money.

When we returned from Palm Springs after the weekend was

over, I acted totally shocked to find that, when we walked into her place, she had been robbed. Little did she suspect that I had set her up. Her insurance policy paid her to replace everything, and I turned a nice little profit.

Unfortunately, by the time Christmas rolled around, the money that I had planned to use for presents had already gone up my nose and into my veins. Once again I found myself sitting in my parents house, surrounded by the entire family — except for Heather, who was in Oregon with Lee. When it came time to open presents, I sat my drink down and produced a number of envelopes with everyone's name on them. With an anticipating look in their eyes, they thanked me, assuming that, since I had sold my house that year, I was giving everyone cash — an accepted family tradition. However, this was not the case. Once again, in each envelope was a handwritten IOU. I made up some lame story that I had so many extra bills that I simply hadn't enough time to shop for them properly, but I would make it up to them in a week or two. I then poured a stiff drink, excused myself, got into my car, and went in search of more drugs, which I would purchase with the money that I should have used for Christmas presents.

Things had to be better in 1985. But they didn't get better — only worse.

I was on a constant treadmill of lies and deceit to maintain this charade. I owed money to everyone, which I didn't have. My only remaining possession was my new car, but I needed that so that I could get to the dealers' houses to score more drugs.

I didn't care about anything but getting high and watching TV. If I didn't have the dope to get high at that particular moment, I would drink myself into oblivion, or raid my parents' medicine cabinet. At this point I had gained twenty-five pounds and didn't give a shit what I looked like. The furthest thing from my mind was the spring tour with Three Dog Night. Instead of looking forward to it, I dreaded it. I knew that I would be sick without my drugs.

Chuck was the only person, other than my parents, that I saw. Since his life paralleled mine, I knew that he was having an equally tough time making ends meet. Finally, by April, both he and Julia couldn't take it anymore. I went up to do my daily fix with them one day and found out that they were both going to check themselves into a detox unit. I commended Chuck for his bravery and told him that I hoped it worked for him. I never even gave a second thought to the fact that I also needed help. Chuck informed me that Three

Dog Night would postpone the upcoming tour to accommodate him going to the hospital. Through all of our scheming and constantly doing drugs together on a daily basis, my only thoughts about this situation were totally selfish: "Who will I get high with?" and "How can I get the stuff now that I don't have any money, and no one else will front it to me?"

I had decided to halt stealing money from my parents, and tried to go it alone. Chuck told me that he knew things were going to be rough for me, and that I could stay at their place for a while. I thanked him for his hospitality and pondered my own fate.

Chuck's two sons had gone to stay with their grandfather, so my obligation would only be to go up to the house to water the plants and feed the cats. In return I had my own private place away from my parents' place to do drugs — if I could find them.

Chuck and Julia checked into the hospital, but a day or so later, a strange thing happened. When I got up to his house, I found a message on his answering machine for me. It was Chuck, almost whispering like he didn't want to be heard. I turned up the volume and was quite surprised to find that he wanted me to go to our manager's office and pick up a check that was waiting for him. Then he wanted me to drive to a dealer's house that he knew in the Valley, score some drugs, and smuggle them into the hospital.

Being the good friend that I was, I went along with this latest folly. On the way out to the Valley, in my devious little mind I formulated my own plan. Whatever the dollar amount that the check was for, I would tell the dealer that it was for $100 less. This way I could insure that I could buy some for myself. At the same time, I would take the remainder that was supposed to go to Chuck and Julia, skim a little off of that, and cut the shit out of anything left over. My plan succeeded brilliantly.

I made the long drive on the Ventura Freeway from the dealer's house to the hospital out in Glendale. Just before arriving, I stopped and bought a few magazines, so that I could tell the head nurse I was delivering them to the Negrons. When I arrived at the hospital, I announced myself at the nurse's station, where I was signed in. I then proceeded to Chuck and Julia's room — high as a kite, as a result of the drug-skimming scheme I had just pulled off.

They weren't handling life on the inside too well, and they were happy to receive anything. Therefore, when I handed over the drugs to Chuck, and he shot them up with a "rig" he had smuggled in, he didn't even question the quality. This arrangement worked quite well, so we continued doing it on a daily basis. Every time I went to deliver something to them, I would look a little more disheveled than the day before. This was due to the fact that I wasn't able to skim as much as I needed each time I purchased.

Although I was doing a portion of Chuck and Julia's drugs before I delivered them each day, it wasn't enough to keep up my habit. I was starting to go through withdrawals, and I looked simply horrendous. I hadn't shaved or showered in days, and I would be dressed in a long coat and a hat. This probably seemed quite peculiar, seeing as how the temperature outside was hovering around ninety degrees.

On one particular day, Chuck asked that I take with me one of the rigs that he had left back at the house, when I went to score. It seemed that the one he had smuggled into the hospital had broken. He instructed me to have the dealer fix him up a strong dose and put it in the syringe. Then I would carefully wrap it up and hide it someplace on my person so I could smuggle it in.

Deep down I was thinking to myself, *The only reason that Chuck is having me do this is that he doesn't trust me. And this is his way of assuring himself that he is getting the full amount.*

After the next purchase, I placed the loaded syringe in my glove compartment and once again made the long drive to the hospital. When I got there, before I entered the building, I stuck the "works" down the front of my pants, and then walked in. Being very nervous about this latest method of deception made me act suspicious to the nurses on duty. I signed in, and after a few moments of some very doubting looks, I walked down the hall. I was certain to take small steps as I walked down the hall to their room, so that the syringe wouldn't fall through my pants and onto the floor.

Just then, I felt the cap come off of the end, and a second later I felt the needle piercing my skin. The weight of my expanded stomach and the action of walking pressed the plunger down, and I unintentionally injected my penis. As the rush came on, I leaned against the wall for momentary composure. Just then, Chuck came out of his room. He took one look at me and knew that somehow I had again managed to do his drugs.

Needless to say, with his attitude of really not wanting to clean up, it was hard for me to take Chuck's attempts at drying out seriously. This only reassured my belief that I was caught in a trap from which there was no escape.

The drugs that I was doing at this point came from anywhere I could get them. One night I managed to rip off several Quaaludes from a girl I was staying with.

On the afternoon of May 23, 1985, I took a number of the 'Ludes and, before night had fallen, I also managed to polish off a bottle of vodka. This in itself would have been lethal enough to kill a drug novice. But even so, something was still missing. I was addicted to heroin, and nothing else would take the place of it. I also knew that deep down inside I was crying out for help, but I was just too scared to ask for it. That evening, somehow I managed to convince Lenny to front me a gram of China White. I took this deadly combination, fully aware of the consequences.

When I left Lenny's house, I intented to drive back home and sit quietly in my room. I hoped that this would be the night when I got enough nerve to finally make the life-saving decision to seek help. Unfortunately, this plan was cut short when I slammed into the police car on Fountain and La Cienega. The scene of flashing lights and paramedics declaring me dead, which I have described earlier in detail, is like a hellish dream to me now.

The morning after my accident, I was not only feeling bad physically, but my emotional state of mind had sunk to an all-time low. *How could they have done this to myself and my family?* I thought. However, up to this point I still thought my mother was unaware that I was hooked on heroin.

When I checked out of the hospital, I went immediately up to Chuck and Julia's house. I knew there was virtually no one in town who would give me what I needed. I had all of $1.25 in my pocket— not even enough to buy a bottle of booze. The first thing I did when I went into the house was to go into the bathroom, where we spent all of our time doing drugs, and began searching for any drugs or drug paraphernalia that might have been left behind. I found some, but it was hardly enough to make it worthwhile. The pain was becoming so great that I knew I had to do something fast.

I went into the kitchen, hoping to find some liquor in their cabinets, even though I knew that they weren't really big drinkers. To my relief, there were two bottles — one of vodka, the other, vermouth. I opened up the icebox to see if I could find something suitable to mix with them. The only thing in there besides some month-old Pop Tarts and sour milk was a bottle of prune juice. I immediately began mixing up some stiff prune juice and vermouth cocktails. When the juice ran out, I was stuck with the dilemma of what to mix with the vodka. After going through the rest of the shelves, I found a half-empty bottle of ketchup. I opened up the bottle of vodka and poured the remaining ketchup in it. I closed the bottle back up and shook it a few times. Abracadabra: instant Hunt's Bloody Marys.

After that, I went into the bedroom to lie down. I tried desperately to get some sleep, but I was kept awake by the sound of the alarm clock ticking and my own heart beating. Suddenly, I felt myself about to throw up. Too weak to stand up, I just puked in the bed. Then I passed out for a short time.

When I woke up, I was not only surrounded by my own vomit, but I found that my left hand was peppered with broken glass and was bleeding. Apparently, in my sleep I had broken the crystal on my watch and dragged my hand through it. Also, the cats who were free to roam around the house had defecated on the bed, only further adding to the mounting stench.

I rolled over onto my side and saw my own reflection in the mirror. I began to cry. There once was a time when I would look in the mirror and see a person who was on top of the world, who had an unlimited supply of money, cars, clothes, and the love of thousands of fans. Now, looking back in the mirror among the puke and shit was a pathetic, pitiful, strung-out, overweight junkie and alcoholic. I had finally hit bottom.

With all the strength I could summon, I picked up the phone and called the very hospital where a short time ago I had been delivering drugs to my only friends. "Somebody, please help me," I said when they answered the phone. They put me on hold for a second, and then a woman who identified herself as a drug counselor came on the line. She asked me a few questions, and I told her in a nutshell about my years of addiction. I gave her my AFTRA insurance number, knowing that they would cover the whole care unit stay. However, I wasn't prepared when she told me that she would have to get verification that the insurance was valid, and could I hold out until tomorrow?

I got extremely pissed off and began to shout at her. I didn't realize that she was only trying to help me. She then told me that if I could come up with $500 to cover the admitting costs, I could come in that night. "Look lady, if I had the five hundred fucking dollars, don't you think I would have used it for drugs already!? That's why I'm calling you! I'm just sick and tired of being sick and tired!" I yelled. She told me not to hang up, and she put me on hold for another couple of minutes. I just lay there on the bed, with the phone propped up to my ear, wanting desperately for someone to take away the pain.

Just then, Julia came on the line. Once again, my friends came through for me. It seems that Julia guaranteed that the insurance was fine, because it was the same company that covered Chuck. All of a sudden it felt like the entire weight of the world had been lifted off of my shoulders. The counselor came back on the phone and asked me if I wanted them to come and pick me up. "No," I said, "I've come this far by myself, I may as well finish the job by myself."

She informed me that once I got there, somebody would meet me at the admitting room door with a wheelchair. Before the counselor hung up, both Chuck and Julia got on the phone and told me not to worry about anything, because the pain would be over soon. Then we all started to cry.

I hung up the phone and, a second later, dialed another number. This call was harder than the one to the hospital. When my mother picked up the phone, I was crying so hard I could hardly talk. She asked me if I was in trouble and needed help. Through the tears I said, "Yes, a lot of it." I just simply said to her, "Mom, I'm a heroin addict and I need to go to a place where there's other people like me, to get help." What she said next totally caught me off guard. "I've known about it for a long time, son," she told me. I then tried to tell her about the house money, and all of the things that I had done to her, at which point she cut me off in midsentence to tell me that everything would work out and to thank God that I was at least alive. She said that she would come up to Chuck's house and stay with me until I was ready to go.

I knew there was nothing I could do about the way I looked, until I felt better. But I had just enough dignity left in me that I didn't want her to see me lying in the puke and shit. It took me about ten minutes to get from the bedroom to the living room, where I collapsed on the couch, waiting for her arrival.

When she arrived, she let herself in, as I was too weak to get up off the couch to greet her. We just sat there for a while, hugging and crying. Soon we were drinking Bloody Marys and laughing. After about an hour, I had enough temporary strength from the alcohol to make the journey to Glendale. Mom helped me downstairs to my car, and I kissed her good-bye and told her not to worry. Then I headed toward my salvation.

I felt a certain sadness and security from the minute I entered the doors of the Care Unit. I knew these people understood the way I felt. They had been there and somehow managed to turn their lives around. Why couldn't I? My life truly did have a purpose that didn't include any mind- or body-altering chemicals. It would take a little while longer for me to fully see the light, but when that moment of clarity hit, everything would fall into place.

In the twenty years of my addiction, this was the first time that

I actually took hold of my life and did something useful. All it took was one phone call. The cost previous to the call was a number of failed marriages, more money than most people make in a lifetime, and more pain than I ever thought possible. I would have to learn how to live free of drugs and alcohol and deal with life's problems with a clear head.

The first step was "detox." I had, at times in the past, tried a form of self-imposed detox with little or no results. This was largely attributed to the fact that if I went too long without one substance in my body, I became violently ill. Of course, any addict knows that to avoid this, you have to substitute your DOC (drug of choice) with something else.

Detox usually lasts only two to seven days, depending on how severe your habit is. They kept me for over ten days. I had to taper off the heroin slowly. The usual method is to use Methadone, which, I've explained, can be just as addicting as what you're taking it for. Since I had such a severe habit, the doctors decided to try a new drug on me. It was called Klonidene, and it also acted as a blood pressure medicine. My blood pressure was so ridiculously high to begin with, it seemed only natural to experiment with this new drug and take care of two problems at the same time. It worked well beyond the medical staff's expectations.

The only frightening thing about the whole detox phase was the day they cut me off from everything. It was now time to stand on my own two feet and face life as it was meant to be. I didn't think, at first, that I could do it. I felt safe with the knowledge that I was being given drugs in a controlled environment to curb a habit in a non-controlled one.

When Dorothy, the nurse in charge of medication, said to me, "OK, Jimmy, today is the last of your medicine. From here on out you'll do it straight," I felt a mixture of panic and relief. Panic because I didn't know what to expect from life without that crutch I'd used for all those years, and relief because I was glad the pain and suffering were finally over.

I was like a baby learning to walk for the first time. I didn't venture too far the first day: from my bed to the nurses' station and to the shower.

After that I was ready to enter the mainstream population and attend my first group. What a sobering experience: sitting in a room full of other addicts just like yourself and pouring your heart out to total strangers. The beauty of the whole thing was that they didn't remain strangers for long. Everyone shared a common bond. We all had some demons to exorcise, and in the four short weeks we would be together in the unit, lasting friendships would be made.

From the onset, the other people were amazed at my honesty and humor considering all that I had been through. I quickly became their daily outlet for laughter and a shoulder to cry on when they were feeling down.

The hospital director and other staff members had such complete faith in me that I was called upon to try to keep some of the first-timers from bolting. This was especially gratifying to me because I didn't have a clue as to what I was doing. All I knew was that they listened and could sense that I was sincere. More than once, I found myself sitting on the edge of someone's bed, telling them of the living hell I'd gone through for twenty-three years and assuring them that their lives would get better.

With each passing day in the program, I became stronger both in body and, most importantly, in mind. I did come to truly believe that a power greater than myself had restored me to sanity. God was working small miracles through me. And, in return, I was helping others. They looked to me for guidance and inspiration and I generously gave it. This was why my life was spared that night as I rode in the ambulance to the hospital.

A typical day on the unit began at 6:00 A.M. Out of bed, shower, clean your room, and head down the hall to take your morning vital signs. Then breakfast. Ah, wonderful Care Unit food! It appeared that someone in the Dietary Department was trying to poison us. To make matters worse, this was a Seventh Day Adventist hospital, so they didn't believe in meat. Instead, they substituted tofu for everything that once roamed the land.

Everyone in the unit made waves about the food, but nobody wanted to get out of the water. The only logical thing to do was let Greenspoon handle it. And handle it I did. I started what was later called "The Greenspoon Food Rebellion of '85." When we were served green tofu eggs one morning, I promptly turned my dish upside down on the table. I instructed the other patients to build a large mountain out of their eggs. While they did that, I took the soy bacon and tofu cakes and tacked them to the bulletin board with push pins.

About five minutes later, the unit director came in and asked to see me. He wanted to know what it would take to stop this foolishness. I told him, "Better food and some time off the unit at a real restaurant." The next day before breakfast, we all met with the staff from the Dietary Department and tried to come to a mutual agreement about the food quality. There was a slight improvement. However, nothing could take the place of a Big Mac and fries.

After breakfast we would have a morning walk off the hospital grounds supervised by one of the nurses. It felt great to get outside and see with a clear head what the world looked like, although some of the patients felt a little insecure away from the womb, so to speak. The more time we had out, however, the easier it became for them. Someday they would have to leave the nest. But for now, they were safe.

After our morning walk, we would start group therapy. There were various groups in the program that ran up until dinner time. Some groups would just involve reading. Others were geared to work off of each other's emotions. We would tell our stories of how it was before we got to the unit. The common bond was that everybody had the same disease — no matter if you were doing coke, heroin, grass, booze, or pills. We were all addicted and couldn't manage our own lives. The group sessions would always end the same way, with a lot of emotions being poured out. Crying was followed by laughter, love, and respect for each other.

There were numerous writing assignments, the purpose being to strengthen our images of ourselves. Some people grumbled at this. I found it richly rewarding. One of the most effective written exercises was to list all our character defects on one side of a piece of paper, and on the other, list all our strong qualities. The sicker people would have one or two defects and ten or fifteen positive things. At first, I was harder on myself than I should have been. By the third week, my list was pretty well even.

My counselor was a lady in her early thirties named Gloria Champlin. She knew I took recovery seriously and gave me extra writing assignments. I think I drove her crazy with my hyperactiveness and compulsive cleaning. I made sure that my room was neater than anyone else's. I had a roommate named Steve, who was just in his early twenties. He was a dear person, but somewhat of a slob. Every morning when he would go to have his vital signs taken, I would make his bed and fold all of his clothes. Gloria and the rest of the staff, as well as most of the patients, were aware that I was doing this. One day Steve came in and caught me making his bed.

"Hey, Jim, you don't have to do that," he said to me. "The maid takes care of everything."

"Steven, there are no maids here. I've been doing it for you for weeks now!" I told him and broke out laughing.

I was the last one to go to bed at night and the first to rise. For a while the staff thought I never slept. I would wait by the elevator in the morning to greet Gloria with my latest assignment completed. "What next?" I'd say. I don't think she truly believed my seriousness toward the program until around the second week of group.

Three times a week after dinner we would attend an AA or CA meeting. The first time I ever set foot in one of those rooms, I knew I was among friends. Everyone was happy in spite of all they had been through. I was scared to be out in public without my crutch but was curious as to why everyone always laughed. I quickly found out. For the next two weeks, I attended the meetings but sat in the back of the room and didn't say a word. I began to feel more at home as time passed. My introduction was a meeting called "The Gong Show." After a month, I was on stage. I had spent half my life entertaining thousands of people but never got to know them — and I never did it straight.

A month passed and people were graduating from the unit. The average stay was thirty days. However, some people required more time — if their insurance covered it. Some, unfortunately, only checked into the hospital to dry out. They were discharged in anywhere from two days to two weeks time. The recovery rate among short-timers was very low. Many returned again and again. Some we only heard about. They had gone back to their drug of choice at the same amount as when they stopped, usually with fatal results. In the short time I was in the Care Unit, many people I had become friendly with became a statistic. It was driven into our heads, especially after someone died, that if we thought we could go out and drink or use drugs again, we were wrong. It would kill us sooner or later.

Sometimes in the hospital I had nightmares about shooting up and death. I would wake up in the morning soaking wet, with my arm in pain where I used to inject my deadly companion. All this would pass with time, I was told.

The days wore on in the unit. The food got better. Our group got stronger. And I was staying well beyond the normal thirty days. I was experiencing a whole new flood of emotions. One of them, which I thought was love, turned out to simply be infatuation. I developed a crush on one of the nurses who worked there. I must have been doing something right, because the old Jimmy from years ago was coming through, and I charmed her off her feet and — when I got out of the hospital — into her bed.

Finally I got my notice that I was graduating. It had been forty-six days since I made the decision to put my life in God's hands. When I walked out of those double doors at the front of the hospital, I knew I was on my own for the first time in my life. I couldn't look back. I didn't want to spend too much time thinking about my past and wondering what the future would hold. Out of all the slogans in the program, the easiest to live by was "One day at a time." My priorities had been so screwed up that I couldn't see the simplicity of those five little words. It may sound like a cliché, but when I left the unit, it did feel like it was the first day of the rest of my life.

The love I shared with everyone was given back in spades. At my graduation, there were so many guests that we had to move it downstairs to one of the large meeting rooms. My manager, ex-girlfriend (whom I had set up for the robbery), and other important and supportive people in my life came to wish me luck. This was one of the most emotional moments of my life. There wasn't an empty seat in the house. At one point I said to Gloria, "Maybe we should have rented the Hollywood Bowl. This room is sold out!" Always the entertainer — thinking of the next show.

When it came time to say good-bye, each member of the unit held a brass coin with the Serenity Prayer on it and said a few words about the departing patient. Of course, these were recovering addicts and short speeches were few and far between. I never knew the love and respect I commanded from these people until that day. There wasn't a dry eye in the place.

Slowly I made my way to the parking lot to climb into my dirty car. I had resisted in the room, but now tears were streaming down my face. I knew there was a possibility that some of the people I left behind wouldn't make it. Some would go back to their families. Some would return to waiting jobs with sympathetic employers and co-workers. Some would die. That's the way it is with this disease. They would go back out and, for whatever reason, wouldn't be able to handle life straight. They would turn to the only comfort they knew.

I was crying hard now, for I realized I'd have to deal with all this shit. I knew I could do something to help these people. Everyone had commented on the wonderful rapport I had with them. I made up my mind to come back to the hospital as a volunteer worker. It seemed so natural. Was this what God had planned for me all along? Whatever it was — call it a miracle, or just common sense — I knew I needed these people and they needed me. Tomorrow I would set the wheels in motion, and by the end of the week, the student would become the teacher.

I knew before me lay the greatest challenge, and I was prepared for it. My journey would provide me with more highs and lows than I've ever experienced in my life.

For now my priority was Jimmy Greenspoon. The old me did, in fact, die. He was left somewhere in one of those rooms at the Care Unit. With a lot of pain and humility, I shed that old persona. Now, for the first time in my life, I had the task of really living before me.

# 17 / An Old Fashioned Love Song

When I got out of the hospital, I immediately had a meeting with the rest of the members of Three Dog Night, and the management. They saw how well I was doing and welcomed me back with open arms. In the interim, when I was in the hospital cleaning up, the group had to hire a different keyboard player when they went on a three-week tour. This was the first time in seventeen years that I didn't perform with the band. From what I gathered later on, it was sheer hell without me.

I was more than willing to get back to work, and after finding out that we had a tour with the Beach Boys lined up, I became both very excited and very nervous, for I would have to play in front of those thousands of people — for the first time in my life — totally straight.

Chuck had come and gone not only from the Glendale hospital but from Cedars of Lebanon as well. It seemed to take him a little longer to comprehend just what this whole sobriety thing was all about. But from all outward appearances, he was ready too.

We had a few weeks to get ready for the tour, and I divided my time between going to AA meetings and trying to comprehend the vast wealth of emotions that I was now carrying. I also briefly continued my affair with the nurse from the hospital, but that turned out to be a big mistake for both of us. The one thing they stress in the hospital is to not enter into any kind of relationship for the first year. This is simply for the reason that you can't comprehend all the new emotions you are feeling, because you are drug free, and you will probably end up hurting yourself or someone else. Luckily, we were both mature adults, so the lovely nurse and I decided to cool it and just remain friends.

There was one particular AA meeting that I frequented on Monday nights. It was called "The Musicians Meeting," and it included people in the business, friends I hadn't seen for years. There was so much warmth and love in that room every Monday night that it is almost impossible to describe. You could say and do things and let all your feelings out, and everybody would understand because, being entertainers, they had done exactly the same thing and knew exactly where you were coming from.

Every time I went into the meeting, I got there a little early, waiting for Chuck to arrive. There was a girl who always sat in the same seat at the end of the row. She was very short but drop-dead gorgeous. As I blatantly stared at her, on occasions she'd shoot back an admiring glance toward me. Finally, one night I introduced myself and found out that her name was Sheila. I asked her if she and the friend she was with wanted to go have some coffee with me and a friend of mine from the meeting. For some reason I was anticipating rejection. But, almost without even thinking, she accepted my offer. After the meeting, we went over to the local hangout, which was the Howard Johnson's on Vineland Avenue in Studio City.

We sat there for about an hour, describing our various backgrounds, addictions, likes, dislikes, and other pertinent information that might lead to a full-fledged date. After that we said good-bye, and I went home to begin preparing for the upcoming tour with the Beach Boys.

The first thing I had to do was to buy some new clothes, because now that I was becoming health-conscious, I had lost most of the weight that I had gained before I went into the hospital. The next thing that I did was to buy a brand new cassette player to take out on the road. This time I would hang onto it and wouldn't have to hock it. I even had an Anvil case custom made to carry my stereo and all of my tapes for the road. I then went to the drug store and spent about $150 on every sundry item known to man. I was going to be the cleanest and most well-equipped person on that tour.

Ever since I had gotten out of the hospital, my mother's attitude changed in a way that's hard to describe. We'd sit up at night now and talk about all the things that had happened to me, and how lucky I was to be alive. She would still have her Bloody Mary, but I would be cradling a glass of juice or Perrier. I began to see, through clear eyes, that my mother really did have a drinking problem. I suddenly did little things to get her to stop. It seems that everywhere in the house she had these little "stash" places hiding her bottles of vodka. When I thought about it, it was not any different from me hiding my drugs.

My father's health had begun to deteriorate rapidly, and his mental state was also in a downward spiral. I thought for sure that he would be proud of me for what I had accomplished. But instead he could only find fault with the way I was living my life now. It seems that he didn't believe I was clean and sober. And nothing that I did or said could convince him otherwise.

It was around this time that we got some of the worst news possible. Dad went in for one of his weekly visits with the doctor, and while he was still in the examining room, the doctor called my mother and me into his office. He came right to the point: my father had terminal lung cancer, and at best he probably only had six months to a year to live. It was too late to try chemotherapy, or any of the other treatments, so all we could do was to make his life at home as happy as possible. The one thing that the doctor could do was to prescribe some strong painkillers, which he warned my mother about and gave her strict instructions on how many to administer to him.

I couldn't believe that my dad had developed lung cancer so suddenly, since he didn't even smoke. Apparently, it was from the pillow factory. Not only was there asbestos insulation all over the place, but the polyurethane and countless other chemicals used to manufacture plastics and foam rubber had gradually infected his lungs.

We took my dad home and began the long process of caring for a terminally ill person. Unfortunately, the entire burden would have to fall on my mother's shoulders because I would have to leave for the road in a few days. My mother expressed to me her concern about not being able to handle the situation by herself. I suggested to her that we hire a nurse for dad, and I made a few inquiries. We found out that it was very expensive, because it would require a nurse to not only take care of my father's needs, but also help my mother out. This meant that the nurse would have to live in the house full-time. We went ahead and hired one.

With my bags packed, I took off for the Beach Boys tour and told my mom not to worry, that everything would be fine. I checked in daily from the road and found out that my father's condition was deteriorating rapidly. Also, my mother wasn't pleased with the attitude of the nurse that she had hired. She went through two more nurses before she came to the conclusion that it was not only too expensive but that nobody could care for him like my own mother. She ultimately enlisted the help of a family friend name Fay. Fay was a wonderful black woman who used to clean our house, and she was a good friend for my mom to have around. They talked for hours, and could relate well to each other. When my mother took up the hobby of making beaded flowers, she even got Fay involved in that, and the two would sit there for hours in the breakfast room, working and laughing. Fay even agreed that on certain nights of the week she would stay overnight to make sure that everything was all right with my parents.

With me being on the road, my sister would usually have to come by once a week and do the grocery shopping for my mom. I know this was difficult for her, because she lived on the other side of town, was trying to hold down a job of her own, and was also experiencing some medical problems. However, she did it and never complained.

Meanwhile, I was on the road having the time of my life. The first night of the tour, in mid-July, was about as hectic as it could be. We were playing in Charleston, West Virginia, and for some reason our connecting flight got delayed. When we arrived in Charleston, we literally jumped into a waiting van, drove to the show, and walked right on stage, wearing the clothes we had on. The one thing that I hate the most is working under pressure, and this day there was plenty of it. Not exactly the way I wanted my first sober show to turn out. I was also feeling strange physically. My stomach was tied in knots, and I felt like I was on the verge of throwing up. What it turned out to be was a simple case of nerves. For the first time in my life, at least that I could remember, I had stage fright.

When the lights went down and I heard the roar of the audience, my heart was beating a mile a minute. I closed my eyes, assumed my position behind the keyboards, and as I had done countless other times before, I hit the downbeat to "One Man Band." A few seconds later, I opened my eyes and looked at the sea of people in front of me. I suddenly got the warmest feeling of love from the audience. At the same time, even though I had played these same songs for what seemed like eternity, I was really hearing everything for the first time. *Damn that's good!* I thought to myself. I was really having a ball up on stage, watching the reaction of the audience and of the other band members watching me. When the show was finished, I came off the stage feeling higher on what I had just done than any drug I had ever taken before.

The one thing that I had worried about being on the road was not being able to go to AA meetings. The tour schedule was so hectic that it became impossible to try to find meetings. So, the management office suggested that we bring the meetings to the hotels at which we were staying. Two or three times a week, we would arrange to use an empty banquet room and set up some tables and chairs and a large pot of coffee.

After a concert was over, Chuck and I would get cleaned up and go with our road manager at the time, fellow AA member Dwayne Taylor, to the prearranged meeting room. The support we got from total strangers was unbelievable, and we made a lot of friends. I could sense at the time that Chuck was not handling his sobriety very well. We figured that these meetings while out on the road, coupled with the support from the rest of the band, would help to strengthen him.

I, on the other hand, was having no problem adjusting to life beyond drugs. My whole philosophy was that I never did anything half-assed or in moderation. Since I had spent over two decades of my life getting as fucked up as humanly possible on a daily basis, I figured that I had to work hard not to reverse that way of thinking, and stay as sober as humanly possible, on a daily basis.

Time passed so quickly that, before I knew it, the tour was over. When I got home, I found the situation there was slowly getting out of hand. I suggested to my mother that we put Dad in the hospital, where he could have constant supervision and they could administer the painkillers to him when he needed them. The situation was taking a toll on my mother. Even though I was gone for only three weeks, it looked to me like my mother had aged years. She was also becoming very irritable and was drinking way too much. One day Fay took me aside and told me that at certain times, late at night, she would hear my mother crying in her room. Fay knew that this was too much of an emotional strain for one person to handle. She agreed with me about putting Dad in the hospital. And since Medicare would pay for it, there wouldn't be any financial burden on my mom. All we had to do was convince her.

Besides trying to take care of the family business when I got back from the tour, I also continued going to as many AA meetings as possible. Of course, my favorite one was the Monday night musicians' meeting. I was usually so excited to be in a room full of my peers that I would show up an hour early, looking for something to do. Thank God, they didn't have a broom or a dust mop lying around, or I would have cleaned everything in sight.

Sheila kept coming to the meetings, and in my own subtle way, I was trying to get up enough nerve to ask her out on a date. After so many years of being a rock star, and having girls throw themselves at me, I couldn't believe that I was intimidated by this woman. Finally, one Monday night, one of Sheila's friends asked me if I wanted to come over to her house for a party that Friday night. She told me that a lot of people from the meeting, including Sheila, would be there. I accepted the invitation without hesitation. All the way home, though, I kept thinking to myself, *What will I do, and how will I act in a room full of sober people?* I also thought to myself, *How is it possible that a group of straight people can have fun without drugs and alcohol?* This was going to be a real challenge.

On the road it had been easy for me to stay sober because I had the support of people I had known for years. But now I was going to be surrounded by people I had just met or didn't know at all. One thing I learned in the hospital was to not dwell on anything too long. So, I just let it go until Friday night.

When I got to the party, early, of course, the hostess greeted me, introduced me to her family, and then pointed me in the direction of the tables that contained various soft drinks, juices, and appetizers. Slowly but surely, people began to arrive. I felt slightly out of place because I didn't know anyone, and I was trying to keep this reserved attitude about myself. In the old days, I would have been dancing on the tables (probably with half of my clothes off) or pissing in the punch bowl.

I was introduced to another musician, which made me feel comfortable. After talking briefly, we found out that we shared similar interests, many of the same friends, and on various occasions in the past had even been introduced. Rudy Sarzo had just left one of L.A.'s top metal bands, Quiet Riot. He was looking to either do something on his own or to get into another group that had a greater longevity.

After about an hour, Sheila arrived, looking absolutely radiant. I offered to get her a glass of juice, and then we both went into the living room and sat down on the couch. After only a few minutes, not knowing what to say, the conversation began to go totally blank. I could sense that she was as nervous as I was. Every few minutes, when someone new would arrive, I would excuse myself with the pretense of going to greet them. What I would do instead was go over and talk to Rudy. Since he was a big Three Dog Night fan, and up to this point I wasn't even sure if Sheila knew what group I was in, Rudy and I had much more to talk about.

Our tour manager, Dwayne, arrived at the party, and after a few minutes informed me that he had four tickets for the following week to the Thompson Twins concert at the Universal Amphitheater. We both agreed that it was time to make a move, on someone, and utilize the tickets. Of course, my intended target was Sheila. She accepted. Dwayne chose the easy way out, by asking the hostess. Since her husband, who was a record producer, was leaving for England that week, he encouraged her to go ahead and have a good time. With plans for the double date made, I informed Sheila that I had to be getting home. Sheila said she was leaving also.

Being the suave, debonair gentleman that I was, I walked her to her car first. Then things all of a sudden got awkward. We were like two kids on our first date. I didn't know whether to kiss her, shake her hand, or pat her on the back. So, amid some flying arms, bumping noses, and misplaced lips, I kissed her. She drove off into the night, and I thought to myself, *I'm going to get her in bed.*

The following day, Dwayne and I formulated a plan to make the upcoming date an evening to remember. We made reservations at one of the trendiest French restaurants in the Valley, Le Seuir. We also ordered a white stretch limo to take us around for the evening. When the night finally arrived, we both let all of our inhibitions go totally out the window. I was trying hard all through dinner to keep my hands off of Sheila, even though I was mentally undressing her. In retrospect, I was being a complete asshole — but a sober one.

At the Thompson Twins concert, it was interesting to look at the kind of audience that this techno-British band drew, compared to the wide demographic variety that Three Dog Night attracted.

It wasn't that bad sitting in the audience not being stoned, except for a few girls in back of me, who kept hitting me on the shoulder and squealing at Tom Bailey, the lead singer. Afterwards, we got back into our awaiting limo and decided to go someplace to have some coffee. This, of course, replaced the once fashionable "night cap."

Later that evening, Dwayne took me aside and said, "Hey, Bud, I paid for the car until 2:00 A.M., so after they drop us off, why don't you two just drive around and have a good time?" Never being one to turn down a free limo ride, I thanked him for his generous offer, and thought to myself *That will be the opportune time to make my move on Sheila.*

After we dropped Dwayne off at his place, I instructed the driver to go over Benedict Canyon and take Mulholland Drive back to the Valley, where Sheila lived. On Mulholland, I told him to pull over to the side of the road, and Sheila and I got out to look at the liquid sea of pulsating lights down below. Somehow it took on a whole new meaning, looking at everything through clear eyes. I didn't tell Sheila, but I had been to this point many times before, with different girls, fucked up on various drugs. We stood there for a little while, and I noticed she was shivering. This was my cue to put my arm around her and pull her closer to my warm body. Then, without another word being said, we launched into a long kiss. Taking a cue from me, she took me by the hand and led me back to the limo. "Drive," she said to our chauffeur.

"Where to ma'am?"

"I don't care, just take your time getting there," she replied in a determined tone. Suddenly, I was all over her like a wet blanket.

Although no article of clothing was shed, our combined animal magnetism and sheer lust far exceeded any erotic movie I've ever seen. As we approached Sheila's house, almost two hours later, I found out that she was in possession of old-fashioned values. She said that she would like to invite me in, but she knew what would happen if she did, and didn't want to rush anything. One small part of me commended her for this very lady-like attitude, while the other major part said, "Is this bitch for real?"

I continued to see Sheila on a regular basis and finally wound up sleeping with her. We were becoming more and more attached to each other, and I was spending more time away from the house. This left my mother alone to deal with my father and her own mounting problems. I realized that this wasn't fair, but I had a life to live, and in essence I was trying to start all over again.

Finally, one day I came to my mother and — in what had to be an exercise in incredibly bad timing — I informed her that I was moving out of the house and would be moving in with Sheila. I could see that she was deeply hurt by this move, and probably thought that I was abandoning her and my dad. Up to this point, she hadn't even met Sheila, so I set up the obligatory dinner, with only my mom, Sheila, and I going. Fay stayed with my father at the house that night.

My mother has always been a pretty good judge of character, and although she had always told me that I would eventually learn from my own mistakes, I could sense that she didn't like Sheila at all. That didn't matter to me at the time. Right or wrong, I'd always done as I pleased — with or without my mother's blessing.

Shortly after that, my mother had to concede that putting my dad in the hospital was the best thing for everyone concerned. It was a hard decision, but she knew that when the final time came for my father, she wouldn't be able to handle it if he were home. Suddenly, it looked as if everyone was deserting her.

Later that week, as I was in my room packing up my things, I heard my mother crying, and I went in to see what was wrong. She practically begged me to stay. I told her that this was something that I had to do for myself, and that she should be happy for me. I didn't realize it then that she was just afraid of being all alone.

I had our bass player, Scott Manzo, come by with his van to take some of my furniture over to Sheila's house. As we drove away, and I saw my mother standing in the doorway crying, I flashed back to the day I had left for Colorado. I was still causing my mother pain, even in sobriety.

I set up housekeeping at Sheila's newly purchased condo in the Valley and proceeded to go about conducting my life. By fall, I was gearing up for another Three Dog Night tour. Before I left for the road, I made arrangements for Sheila to fly out and meet me in a few cities where I knew I would have some time off.

The first of these was in Tampa, Florida. The other guys left immediately after the show, in the tour bus, and headed for St. Louis, where I would catch up with them the next night. Sheila and I went back to our hotel, and across the street to a nice little restaurant for some late dinner. I don't know how it started, but halfway through dinner, we were in the throes of a horrendous fight. Suddenly, a side of her that I hadn't seen before became quite apparent. I should have seen the handwriting on the wall. But ignoring what my counselor at the hospital, my mother, and everybody else told me, I entered into this relationship anyway, knowing damn well that it was too soon in my sobriety to get involved. The fight lasted until the next morning, and I got on my plane to meet the guys in St. Louis, feeling drained.

When I got to the hotel, I called Sheila and tried to apologize to her. I still wasn't sure what this whole thing was about, but I detected a real cold attitude toward me. Basically, if I had had a few more years of sobriety under my belt, I would have seen at that very moment that we weren't compatible.

Every time I called her, I got the distinct feeling that she didn't have time for me and would rather have been doing something else. I chilled out on the phone calls for a few days, and this only brought temporary relief.

All during this time I was still continuing with my meetings on the road. On many occasions, Chuck and I would venture out to a meeting together and take "chips," which signified the amount of sober time that we had. I was having no problem keeping my life on an even keel. I was also pleased to see that Chuck was apparently trying to do the same. Therefore, it came as a complete shock when, one night before a show in Houston, Chuck sat in the back of the tour bus shaking and looking like death warmed over. Cory and Danny, thinking that he was clean, thought that something was medically wrong with him. I, however, knew immediately when I saw him that he was going through heroin withdrawals. My first reactions were anger and resentment. Obviously, he had been "chipping" this entire time, and trying to keep it a secret from everyone. How could he have expected to keep up the masquerade of being sober, going to meetings, when the whole time he was "dirty"? He was obviously in no shape to go on stage that night, so we had two problems confronting us. The first one was that our road manager had to get him to a hospital, where he could get some methadone or another suitable substitute for the heroin. The second one was that we had to drastically alter our set with various band members, covering Chuck's vocal parts. A few of the songs we would have to drop all together.

While Dwayne took Chuck to the hospital, the entire band held an impromptu rehearsal in the back of the bus. I agreed to handle a lot of the falsetto parts, if Scotty and Paul Kingery, our guitar player, would handle the other missing parts. We were left with no choice. We told the club owner that there was a medical emergency, that Chuck had collapsed and had to be taken to the hospital. He wasn't pleased, but the club was packed, and in order to avoid an ugly scene from the drunken patrons inside, he agreed.

Halfway through the first song, people started screaming, "Where's Chuck?" We got through the first two tunes before Cory told the audience the same lame story that he had told the club owner. With a lot of guts, and sheer persistence, we finished the show, and actually did quite well. That was when all of us realized that, if necessary, we could get along without Chuck.

The next day, many phone calls were exchanged between our managers, agents, and various promoters. We were now faced with the problem of rearranging the tour. We gave everyone the option of canceling the dates once they found out that Chuck wasn't with us. To our surprise, no one did. We then launched into what we later called "The Mystery Hang Tour," so nicknamed because we hoped that if we got to a town and somehow got a doctor to administer something to Chuck, he would be well enough to sing. However, this was never the case. Dwayne would usually end up flying with Chuck to the next town, in hopes of conning a doctor there out of some medicine. The rest of the band would stay in the previous town and just hang out. Then we'd fly to the next city, do the show without Chuck, and hang out for a few days more.

Finally, the management agreed that Chuck would have to be readmitted to a hospital to dry out. He flew home and we continued on the tour, doing the rest of the shows without him. All along the way, we kept telling the press, fans, and promoters the same bullshit story that Chuck had collapsed with an unknown ailment, but would be back with us as soon as he was better.

That was the last time I saw Chuck for quite a while. I wondered how a person with such incredible talent could throw his life away, when he was given every opportunity to turn it around. The entire band felt betrayed. He had deceived and lied to us, and that's what really hurt. Amid all of this nonsense with Chuck, I tried not to get too involved, because I was waging a war with my own sobriety as well — one that I was determined to win.

Sheila and I made plans to hook up again in Denver. It worked out so that the group had a day off right after Thanksgiving. I arranged to stay at the Park Suite Hotel downtown, so Sheila and I could spend time away from the other guys.

I remember the night before I was to meet her in Denver, we were in Wichita, Kansas, in the middle of a severe snowstorm. I was so concerned that the roads would be closed and we wouldn't be able to make it there in time, but I was ready to fly out at any cost. I must have gotten two hours of sleep on the bus that night. As I watched the sun come up, all I could think about was spending a few relaxing days with Sheila, trying to make up for whatever went wrong in Tampa. I arrived at the hotel in Denver on Friday, about two hours before she got there. When she arrived, I made sure that I was on my best behavior. Everything worked out well.

The previous evening, I had tried to get hold of my mother to wish her "Happy Thanksgiving." However, each time I phoned, there was no answer. That seemed a bit strange. I figured that maybe my mother was at the hospital, spending Thanksgiving with my dad. I was always missing holidays with my family.

The next morning I woke up with the strangest feeling that something was wrong. I picked up the phone and dialed my mother's number. She answered it immediately. I knew right away, from her distant and disorganized tone, that something had happened. The doctor had been preparing us for the inevitable for quite some time now, but when the time comes, you're never really ready for it.

"Mom, what's wrong?" I inquired.

"Oh, did you have a nice Thanksgiving?" she asked, almost as though she hadn't heard what I said.

"Mom, is everything all right?"

"Where are you?" she asked, once again ignoring my question.

"Forget that shit, and tell me what's happening!" I said, wanting to cut to the chase. There was a long silence, and I knew what the answer on the other end of the phone would be.

"Your dad died last night," she said, almost in a whisper. Never having dealt with death, either stoned or sober, I really didn't know what to say to comfort her. I felt totally helpless. I knew that she had made previous arrangements with an organization called the Neptune Society, which would pick up the deceased, cremate them, and then sprinkle their ashes over the ocean. Right now, that was the least of my concerns. When I did speak, I wanted to know if it was painful, or whether he died in his sleep. She told me that he had been in a lot of pain for the last few months, even with the pills, but tried not to complain too much to her, knowing that he was a burden on everyone. She told me that he had died peacefully in his sleep. I asked her how she was, and she told me not to worry, that she would be all right until I got home.

Now I did feel like a heel for moving out and leaving her alone. I hung up the phone and sat there for the longest time, trying to cry, but nothing would come out. Granted, my father and I were never that close, but he was a part of my life and did the best that he could. Now he was gone. I was thankful that he didn't have to suffer any longer. I knew that my mother was still in shock, and that my sister and I would have to be extremely supportive of her.

Just then Sheila woke up and asked me what was wrong. I didn't say anything for a moment, then I turned and put my arms around her, and the floodgates burst open. I began to cry uncontrollably. I could sense this was awkward for her, since she had never met my father. Basically, she didn't know anything about my family — or me, for that matter.

Dwayne called and Sheila answered the phone, telling him what had happened. Within fifteen minutes, he arrived at the hotel to help comfort me. I thanked everyone for what they were trying to do, but told them that I just wanted to be left alone. Had I not been strong, and building a solid foundation for my newly discovered sobriety, I probably would have gone down to the bar and gotten shit-faced right then.

The next night, before we went on stage, Danny came up to me and said, "I heard what happened, I'm very sorry." I thanked him for his concern, and went off to psych myself up for the show. I could have dwelled on the situation long enough that it would give me another reason to want to go and have a drink. But, once again, I proved to myself just what I was really made of. As the house lights dimmed, and the D.J. announced us, everyone patted me on the back and said, "Let's go kick some ass." As I was walking onto the stage amid a thunderous ovation, I looked skyward, and said, "This one's for you, dad."

That night we played what was probably our best set in years. When it came time for me to solo, I was playing like a man possessed. We got off the stage and came back to do our usual encore. Upon leaving that time, the people were now standing and cheering and stomping their feet so loudly that I thought the ceiling was going to cave in. We went back to the dressing room, and after a couple of minutes we realized that they weren't going to let us leave without playing another song. This only posed one problem: we hadn't rehearsed another song. So, we went out on stage and launched into a massive jam session, with Cory just making up lyrics and everyone joining in whenever they felt so inspired. This sudden spontaneity fueled the band even more and drove the audience to new heights of frenzy.

The whole time this was going on, Sheila was taking a back seat, realizing that I needed my space to get my head together. The next day she flew home and I continued with the rest of the tour.

We finished off the remaining dates without Chuck, who had now checked himself into a hospital, along with Julia, whom he also brought down whenever he slipped. I returned to L.A. and prepared to celebrate my first sober Christmas. I knew that this would be a particularly hard time of the year for my mother, seeing as how she had just lost her husband and was becoming more and more depressed every day. Her drinking problem approached the point where she nearly eclipsed my addiction when it was in full swing. I knew that it was infeasible to have a full-time maid or nurse stay with her, and it was hard for me to divide my time. So my sister and I agreed to find a suitable rest home for her. That was something that I hated to do.

I found that there was an opening at the Edgemont in Hollywood. This was the same place that my dad had been in and out of the last year that he was alive. However, the atmosphere there was one of a prison, as it was basically a mental institution with bars, locked doors, and screaming people. Every time I visited her there, I thought of the way I felt when I went to see my father in the same situation. I phoned up Lyla one day and said, "We have to get her out of there." We both agreed to find someplace where she could come and go as she pleased, and not be put behind locked doors like some nutcase.

After making a few inquiries, I discovered a convalescent hotel in Beverly Hills only about a mile and a half away from her house. It was basically an apartment with supervision and a full-time nurse on call. Mother moved in there, informing my sister and me that it would only be temporary, until she could get her health back. But I knew differently. She was still grieving over the death of my father, and her condition seemed to be getting worse. Whenever I would go over to visit her, she would have a drink in her hand and a bottle stashed somewhere in her tiny room. Every time someone came to visit her, she would ask them to bring her a bottle of vodka.

My sister and I consulted the same psychiatrist who had treated my father over the years for his chronic depression. We explained our concern over her increased drinking, and that we were worried that she might hurt herself. He agreed to see her on a regular basis, to try to get her to stop drinking, as she was too old to admit to a detox unit.

As Christmas approached, I was making up for lost time, buying presents for everyone. Suddenly, one night I got a panicked phone call from my sister. "Mom's escaped!" she said hysterically into the phone.

"What do you mean 'escaped'?" I retorted.

Lyla explained that the doctor had gone over to see her and discovered that she wasn't anywhere around. No one knew of her whereabouts. I told my sister to stay where she was, in case anybody called with information, and I would go check it out. When I pulled up at the home, I saw my mother sitting on the couch with two nurses, obviously chewing her out for the stunt she had just pulled. Apparently, she had gotten so drunk that she went downstairs, became disoriented, and wandered off down the street.

Everybody concerned knew that this wasn't working out. We decided to take my mother back home and hire a full-time nurse until the holidays were over. I knew my mother was in no shape to have any kind of Christmas gathering at her place, so I made arrangements to pick up some food at the Chalet Gourmet and take it to her. I could then give both her and Lyla their Christmas presents and return back to my place with Sheila for more food and gifts. This worked out perfectly, and everybody seemed to be in good spirits.

However, in no time at all, Sheila and I were once again engaged in a fight over something completely inconsequential and stupid. It was apparently obvious to everybody but me that we couldn't get along and maybe shouldn't be living together. But I was quite stubborn. The relationship had become such a crutch for me that I thought I had to make up for lost time and prove my stability to everyone. I did this the only way I knew how: I proposed to Sheila. She accepted my offer of marriage, and the next day we went downtown to a diamond wholesaler and I bought her a $1,200 engagement ring.

It was on Christmas Eve that I told my mother about my engagement. She told me what a stupid ass I was being, and that this would probably be the biggest mistake of my life. I thanked her for her concern but ignored her warning.

Early in 1986, Three Dog Night was once again gearing up for a few sporadic concert dates, prior to our full-blown spring/summer tour. It was acknowledged at this point that Chuck was not returning to the band unless he cleaned himself up. He had now been in and out of a dozen various hospitals, usually only to get the medication and detox, and then he'd bolt. By now he'd almost used up all of his AFTRA insurance.

I drifted in and out of town for the shows but managed to be back for my thirty-eighth birthday. Sheila was giving me the old standard line that she needed her space and wanted time to go out "with the girls." Even though I was sober, my worst character defects — jealousy and insecurity — were rearing their ugly little heads. Basically, I just didn't trust her.

I left to go out on the road, anticipating looking up some old girlfriends. I went along with Sheila's plan and gave her all the space she needed. I also only called her a couple of times a week, figuring that this would patch things up between us. The whole time this was going on, I was still planning to marry her, but in the back of my mind I knew that it was wrong.

The night before I was to return to L.A., I kept calling the house and getting no answer. Finally, at 2:00 A.M., Sheila picked up the phone and got pissed off at me for giving her the third degree about her whereabouts. When I came back the next day, she told me to meet her at a restaurant close to the house. I drove from the airport straight there.

When she walked into the restaurant and sat down at the table, I knew something was wrong. She got right to the point: things weren't working out the way she wanted them to. She said that it would be better if I moved out, we called off the marriage, and just became friends. This shouldn't have bothered me, because I wasn't happy either. But I was suddenly devastated, and felt like I did every time another of my relationships broke up. I couldn't admit to myself that I'd failed again. (I learned later on that failure is not a character defect, and that everybody has to experience rejection — even in sobriety.) I sat at the table and began to cry. Then Sheila became very diplomatic. Without showing any emotion, she told me that I could stay with her at her condo until I found a new place.

The next day I began calling my friends to find out if there were any vacancies where they lived. When I talked to Julia, I discovered there was a one-bedroom apartment in the complex where she resided, since she had recently left Chuck. She had grown tired of him dragging her down, and she was serious about rediscovering sobriety, even if he wasn't. I looked at it, liked it, and rented it. The only problem was that the apartment wouldn't be ready for another week. And, to put it mildly, the air was thick around Sheila's place. To top it off, when I asked for the engagement ring back, Sheila refused, saying that it was the least I could do to let her keep it.

Not wanting to stay there another minute, I checked myself into the Hollywood Holiday Inn. But I realized that in a hotel stay for over a week would end up being quite expensive. I was just getting back on my feet finanacially. So, I called up Linda, who was working at least twelve hours a day, now that she was the production manager for "Cheers." Since she already had some of the belongings that I sold her after we broke up — and my two cats — I thought that it was only natural for me to spend a couple of days there, if we kept it strictly platonic. She agreed to let me stay there.

At the end of the week I gathered up my suitcases from Linda's and called a moving company to go over to Sheila's to pick up the rest of my things. I met the movers over there and began loading the truck. When we were almost finished, Sheila came home, probably just to make sure that I wasn't taking any of her possessions. Then, almost as if we were business partners, she shook my hand, put her arm around me, gave me a little pat on the back, and said, "Good luck."

As I was driving over to my new place, it hit me that once again I was single and free. In retrospect, I know it was an insightful decision. If we hadn't broken up when we did, we would have only ended up hurting each other more.

I moved into the new place, and within twenty-four hours was off on the road with the band. One of the first dates that we did was a concert set up in the parking lot of the Camelback Raddison Hotel in Scottsdale, Arizona. I knew the promoter of the show, Charlie Johnston, who had done a number of shows for Three Dog in the past. After the concert, Charlie introduced me to his secretary and a few friends who were there with him. One of them was a woman named Mary Margaret. We immediately hit it off, and amid our conversation I found out that she owned a hot air balloon. She asked me if I'd like to go up for a ride in it the next morning. I told her that I had never done that, and would love to.

The balloon flight was one of the most incredible things I have ever done. It was the highest I had ever been without drugs. I knew then what a bird must feel like.

M. M. (as Mary Margaret's closest friends addressed her) gave me her phone number and told me to call her whenever I came back into town. She was very supportive of my sobriety and gave me the names of a few of her friends who had logged a lot of time on the program. I flew back to L.A. for one day to deposit some dirty clothes, and then met up with the guys on the road.

When I got the upcoming itinerary, I noticed that there was a concert date set for Tucson, Arizona, after a softball game at the Toros Stadium. I called up M. M. and asked if she would like to come to the show and bring some people with her. She was really excited about the idea. She had a friend who worked in the sales office of the Westward Look, a resort down there, and said she would try to get a couple of rooms "comped" for me and anyone else in the band. As it turned out, the rest of the guys had their rooms "comped" by the promoter, at the airport Ramada. Not especially wanting to stay there with them, and looking forward to spending some time by myself at this resort, I eagerly waited for M. M.'s reply. A few days later, a letter arrived from M., saying that her friend could only "comp" two rooms. That worked out perfectly, because I took one of them, which gave M. the other one for herself and whoever she brought with her. When we landed in Tucson, I informed our tour manager that I had another place to stay that evening, and I would meet them back at their hotel room before the show.

M. was at the airport to pick me up, and we headed for the Westward Look. On the way there she told me that Karen Walden was the one who had gotten the rooms for us, and that she had invited her to the show. I told her, "No problem. The more the merrier." It was the least I could do in return for her hospitality.

When we were driving to the hotel, I recalled seeing the same scenery a couple of years before, amid my infamous drive from Tulsa. But, this time Tucson struck me as being quite relaxed and pleasant. The mountains, which I hadn't been at all impressed with on my last visit there, looked quite majestic.

M. had brought two of her girlfriends to Tucson with her, and her friend Karen from the hotel was to join us in time for the concert. When I got there, she informed me that Karen was busy and didn't know whether she could make it to the show. I was quite adamant that Karen attend the show, and pressed M. to convince her to join us.

I didn't know at the time that Karen thought M. was trying to set me up with either her or one of the other girls, and she wanted no part of it. Finally, M. convinced Karen to at least come along to the concert. We met in front of the hotel, and drove over to the Ramada, to hook up with the rest of the guys. Karen looked beautiful that evening, and although I had just briefly met her, I could tell immediately that she was unlike any other girl that I had met. For one thing, she was totally unimpressed with my rock star status, and she was just going along to placate M.

After the concert we all went out for some late-night breakfast. Karen knew of a place over by the Westward Look, so I rode with her, and M. followed. As Karen and I drove to the restaurant, we got to talking about things, and I found her to be a very honest and open person. The one thing that impressed me the most about her was that her family came first on her list of priorities. I found that quite admirable, since I had done such a great job of fucking mine up.

At breakfast, Karen and I ordered the same thing: an avocado omelette. After a few more inquiries, I discovered several similar likes and interests. This was becoming more and more interesting by the minute. I couldn't take my eyes off of her throughout the meal. But a little voice was telling me, "If you want to get anywhere with her, treat her with respect."

As Karen drove me back to the hotel, I turned to her and nonchalantly said, "You know, I'm a little tense after the show. I could sure use a Jacuzzi." I paused for a moment, giving her time to respond.

She replied, "There are several at the hotel."

I thought to myself, *That's not quite the enthusiastic response I was looking for.* So, I forged ahead, and came right out with it, "Would you like to take a Jacuzzi with me?"

"I don't think so, but thank you for asking," was her curt reply.

I let it go right there, and was quite impressed with the fact that she was refusing my blatant advances.

What I didn't know was that years earlier, Karen had worked as a sales director for the Holiday Inn chain in Wyoming. Three Dog Night was doing a concert in the ballroom of the Cheyenne hotel property, and her job was to promote the show. Of course, I was drunk and drugged out, and chasing anything that was moving in a skirt. After the concert, she had come into the private dining room to make sure that everything was all right. I don't remember anything that I said or tried to do to her that night, but years later she informed me that she thought I was the most obnoxious jerk she had ever met. I probably was.

At the Westward Look the next morning, she called up the room and invited me down for breakfast, which I thought was a very nice thing for her to do. I went into the restaurant and sat at the table waiting for her. When I saw her walk in, I thought to myself that she looked even more beautiful than the night before. This is when my famous plan, as I would later refer to it, went into effect.

For some strange reason I felt compelled to tell her my life story and all of my problems in a nutshell. I don't know the reasoning behind that. Maybe if she knew about all of the sex and drugs and rock and roll, she wouldn't be interested, and I wouldn't have to pursue this challenge any longer.

After listening to my escapades involving groupies, heroin, cocaine, booze, my accident, and the hospital, I figured that she would politely get up from the table and say, "Thank you, it's been nice meeting you." But once again something strange happened. I found her to be greatly interested in what I had to say. She also showed genuine concern over the things that I had done with my life, and seemed pleased that I was alive.

After breakfast I walked her back to her office and gave her a friendly little hug. I asked her if I could have a business card, in case I wanted to return to Tucson. But this wasn't really why I wanted the number. This was just Phase One of my plan.

That afternoon, M. drove me to the airport. I thanked her for all that she had done, and I especially thanked her for introducing me to Karen.

"She's a wonderful lady, isn't she?" she said to me.

"She's a classy lady," I said, with a twinkle in my eye.

When I got to the airport I went immediately to the gift shop and bought an appropriate card that I would send to Karen from one of my next stops on the road. A few days later, I sent her another card from somewhere in the Midwest, and then reached into my wallet to get out her phone number at the hotel. "Hi, this is Jimmy Greenspoon of Three Dog Night," I said. "I just wanted to thank you again for your hospitality, and all that you did, and I will definitely be coming back to Tucson."

"Well, thank you very much for calling, Jimmy, and when you are coming back this way again, do not hesitate to get in touch with me," she said.

I thought to myself, *Don't worry, Karen Walden, I won't.* My scheme was now moving along quite smoothly, all in accordance with my carefully plotted plan.

While on tour in Canada, I began calling Karen every day. The longer we talked on the phone, the more intimate the conversation became. Finally, she invited me back to Tucson during a break in our tour. She set me up with a room at the downtown Sheraton and picked me up at the airport. When I stepped off of the plane and saw her, I realized that she was even more beautiful and classy than I had remembered from before. In a very short time, basically over the phone, we had become quite attracted to each other. Later that night, we consummated our relationship, and I knew then that this was something very special. I spent three wonderful days in Tucson with Karen, at which time I met her two teenaged daughters, Cheri and Kim, and instantly took a liking to them as well.

When I left to go back home to Los Angeles, I knew deep in my heart that I would be back very soon. I was only in L.A. for two days before Three Dog Night left for a week-long engagement at the Fairmont Hotel in San Francisco. I thought to myself, *Here I am paying $750 a month, for an apartment that I had hardly seen, and probably wouldn't even return to.* Every time I talked to Karen, I made subtle references to the possibility of my geographic relocation to someplace warm and wonderful — like Tucson.

I invited Karen to join me in San Francisco, and she immediately accepted. As far as I was concerned, I was head over heels in love with her, and although we had never said so to each other, I felt that she held the same feelings. I prepared for Karen's arrival by going downstairs to the Fairmont's drugstore/gift shop and purchasing over a dozen greeting cards with various "I Love You" messages inside of them. I then taped them to every mirror and drawer in my room.

She got there just before our showtime and was quite taken aback by my apparent affection and gestures of love toward her. In a move probably designed to discourage me from any serious relationship with her, she sat me down and told me there was something she had to explain. "I'm married," she told me.

"So?" I said, seeming to be only slightly put off by this minor setback. After inquiring further, I found out that she hadn't seen her husband in over two years, and that he was still in Cheyenne, Wyoming. The plan was for him to sell the house and to move down to Arizona to live with her and the kids. Unfortunately for him, and fortunately for me, the time that they were apart was so long that irreversible damage had already been done to their relationship. With this in mind, I asked her if she still loved him. Without giving her anytime to answer, I told her that I was madly in love with her. Everything was falling into place perfectly, and after relaying her similar feelings toward me, I was on "Cloud Nine." We were acting like a couple of teenagers in love for the first time — and it was wonderful.

When Karen left San Francisco, I told her that I would come down to Tucson and stay for a week or so. I temporarily moved my suitcase and a few articles of clothing into her small apartment. When I left to return to L.A. briefly, I made sure to leave behind a few things that would ensure my return.

I had my work cut out for me with Cheri and Kim. At first they resented me coming into their lives and disrupting what they thought was a perfect family. In time they realized that the situation had grown further away from their dad in Wyoming, and closer between Karen and myself. The barriers were soon broken down, and mutual admiration was apparent on both sides. The next order of business was that if Karen and I were as serious about each other as we said, she had to be legally divorced from her husband.

In a decision that I know was very difficult for her at the time, considering that she didn't know all that much about me and my life, she went ahead with the divorce. I went back on the road with Three Dog, and when I returned we made the mutual decision to live together in a larger place.

After about six months at our rented house, we stumbled upon a real estate deal that was too good to pass up. In a short time, I was once again a homeowner, and for the first time in my life I had a real family. My daughter Heather began to come down to Tucson frequently to visit us. Seeing how she got along with Karen and the girls, I decided to implement the last phase of my game plan. In my other failed marriages and relationships, I had learned a lot about life. With my new sobriety and family, it seemed to me that the only logical place to take this relationship was marriage. Although at first quite hesitant to make that commitment once again, Karen reluctantly agreed.

We set the date numerous times but had to keep pushing it back because of the group's ever-changing touring schedule. Finally, on June 21, 1987, Karen and I, in the presence of our daughters and close friends, were married at our church in Tucson. Even as we walked down the aisle, I think that Karen thought we wouldn't really go through with it.

That night, as we lay in bed together, I reflected on the events in my life that led up to this, the second most important thing to ever happen to me besides my sobriety. I had so much for which to be thankful. Just the fact that I was alive after all of these years of self-inflicted pain was a miracle. I knew that for the first time ever, I was truly in love with someone. Not only had I been given a second chance, but I had finally gotten my life together.

# *Epilogue* / **Tucson 1990**

Based on the journal I kept while in the hospital, I began writing about the events of my life. At the encouragement of my wife Karen and several friends, I decided to turn the writings into a book. The sole purpose behind it was to try to make people aware — through my mistakes — of the problems associated with drug abuse.

As of this writing, Three Dog Night is once again preparing for an extensive tour. Danny, Cory, and I are the only remaining original members. After twenty-two years in the group, although I do occasionally get tired of playing the same old songs, when I see the looks on the people's faces, and the fact that the fans are now grown up and bringing their own children to see us, I'm extremely grateful. Unless I get completely burnt out on touring, which could happen, I will probably remain with Three Dog Night for as long as people keep coming to our shows.

Danny and Laurie are happily married with two more sons and still living in L.A. Cory and his wife Mary are planning to move to Seattle. Floyd moved back in with his first wife, Sandy, to their old home in Hidden Hills, California. He continues to do various sessions and movie work with his ex-brother-in-law, Tommy Chong (of the comedy duo Cheech and Chong). Michael is happily married with a large family and has moved back to Modesto, California. In early 1991 he rejoined Three Dog Night. Joe is currently working on an upcoming record project with Floyd and Chuck.

Chuck is making a conscious effort to get his life on track, and I wish him only the best.

My mother is currently residing at the Santa Monica Convalarium, where she will probably remain for the rest of her life. I visit her there every chance I get.

My daughter Heather is doing fine, and after a rather rebellious period and her own bout with drugs, she has relocated to San Jose, California, and continues to make incredible progress in her life.

A few years ago Karen and I started our own travel business, called Entertainment Travel, which caters exclusively to the needs of the entertainment industry. Eventually both Cheri and Kim have come to work in our office. As an outgrowth of that company I also head up my own company called Desert Artist Management. At the present time I manage the career of a Tucson-based hard rock band called Bad Habit and San Francisco-based group About Face. For both groups recent recording sessions, I enlisted the help of my old friends Richard Podolor and Bill Cooper. I'm quite content as their manager, and in them I can see a lot of the same enthusiasm I had when I first started playing rock and roll. In 1991 I began work on an album project with old friends Michael Lloyd and Danny Belsky.

I'm fortunate to have a family who really loves me and the opportunity to be doing something not only useful but enjoyable. I especially get great satisfaction when I go to various schools, churches, or organizations and speak to kids about the horrors of drugs. It has a very therapeutic effect on me and is part of my ongoing recovery that will continue until the day that I die — because an addict is never really cured.

I have no regrets about anything that I've done in my life, even though I'm constantly reminded of the wreckage of my past. I realize now that I could have avoided a lot of unnecessary destruction had I found serenity and peace earlier in my life. Although I know I caused a lot of people a lot of pain — especially myself — I've made my amends and can now get on with living my life the way it was meant to be.

So much has been written to glorify the image of "sex and drugs and rock and roll," but people fail to realize the fact that living life under the pressures of stardom can destroy you. The public can place you on the highest pedestal, and just as quickly tear you down. Surrounded by supportive friends and a loving family, I fully realize how great life is. It was only after achieving success and throwing it all away that I finally discovered: one *is* the loneliest number.

# Jimmy Greenspoon Discography

## *Albums with Three Dog Night:*

(1) *THREE DOG NIGHT* (1969) * +
(ABC-Dunhill/MCA Records)
Produced by Gabriel Mekler
"One"
(Harry Nilsson)
"Nobody"
(Dick Cooper, Ernie Shelby, Beth Beatty)
"Heaven Is In Your Mind"
(Stevie Winwood, James Capaldi)
"It's For You"
(John Lennon, Paul McCartney)
"Let Me Go"
(Danny Whitten)
"Chest Fever"
(J. R. Robinson)
"Find Someone To Love"
(Johnny "Guitar" Watson)
"Bet No One Ever Hurt This Bad"
(Randy Newman)
"Don't Make Promises"

(Tim Harden)
"The Loner"
(Neil Young)
"Try A Little Tenderness"
(Campbell, Woods, Connelly)

(2) SUITABLE FOR FRAMING (1969) * +
(ABC-Dunhill/MCA Records)
Produced by Gabriel Mekler
"Feelin' Alright?"
(Dave Mason)
"Lady Samantha"
(Elton John, Bernie Taupin)
"Dreaming Isn't Good For You"
(Danny Hutton)
"A Change Is Gonna Come"
(Sam Cooke)
"Eli's Coming"
(Layra Nyro)
"Easy To Be Hard"
(G. MacDermot, J. Rado, G. Ragni)
"Ain't That A Lotta Love"
(W. D. Parker, H. Banks)
"King Solomon's Mines"
(Floyd Sneed)
"Circle For A Landing"
(D. Preston)
"Celebrate"
(Bonner, Gordon)

(3) *THREE DOG NIGHT CAPTURED LIVE AT THE FORUM* (1969) * +
(ABC-Dunhill/MCA Records)
Produced by Richard Podolor
"Easy To Be Hard"
(G. MacDermot, J. Rado, G. Ragni)
"One"
(Harry Nilsson)
"Eli's Ccming"
(Laura Nyro)
"Try A Little Tenderness"
(Campbell, Woods, Connelly)
"Chest Fever"
(J. R. Robinson)
"Nobody"

(Dick Cooper, Ernie Shelby, Beth Beatty)
"It's For You"
(John Lennon, Paul McCartney)
"Feelin' Alright?"
(Dave Mason)
"Heaven Is In Your Mind"
(Stevie Winwood, James Capaldi)

(4) *IT AIN'T EASY* (1970) * +
(ABC-Dunhill/MCA Records)
Produced by Richard Podolor
"Woman"
(A. Frazer, P. Rodgers)
"Cowboy"
(Randy Newman)
"It Ain't Easy"
(R. Davies)
"Out In The Country"
(Paul Williams, Roger Nichols)
"Good Feeling (1957)"
(A. Brakett, J. Merrill)
"Rock and Roll Widow"
(Mike Allsup, Jimmy Greenspoon, Danny Hutton, Chuck Negron, Joe Schermie, Floyd Sneed, Cory Wells)
"Mama Told Me (Not To Come)"
(Randy Newman)
"Your Song"
(Elton John, Bernie Taupin)
"Good Time Living"
(Barry Mann, Cynthia Weil)

(5) *NATURALLY* (1970) * +
(ABC-Dunhill/MCA Records)
Produced by Richard Podolor
"I Can Hear You Calling"
(P. Glan, R. Kenner, H. Sullivan, D. Troiano)
"One Man Band"
(T. Kaye, J. Tyme, B. Fox)
"I'll Be Creeping"
(A. Frazer, P. Rodgers)
"Fire Eater"
(Mike Allsup, Jimmy Greenspoon, Joe Schermetzler, Floyd Sneed)
"I Can't Get Enough Of It"

(Miller, Steve Winwood)
"Sunlight"
(J. C. Young)
"Heavy Church"
(Alan O'Day)
"Liar"
(Russ Ballard)
"I've Got Enough Heartache"
(Kellie, Gary Wright)
"Joy To The World"
(Hoyt Axton)

(6) *GOLDEN BISQUITS* (1971) *
(ABC-Dunhill/MCA Records)
Produced by Gabriel Mekler, and Richard Podolor
"One"
(Harry Nilsson)
"Easy To Be Hard"
(G. MacDermot, J. Rado, G. Ragni)
"Mama Told Me (Not To Come)"
(Randy Newman)
"Eli's Coming"
(Laura Nyro)
"Your Song"
(Elton John, Bernie Taupin)
"Celebrate"
(Bonner, Gordon)
"One Man Band"
(T. Kaye, J. Tyme, B. Fox)
"Out In The Country"
(Paul Williams, Roger Nichols)
"Nobody"
(D. Cooper, E. Shelby, B. Beatty)
"Woman"
(A. Frazer, Paul Rodgers)
"Don't Make Promises"
(T. Hardin)
"Try A Little Tenderness"
(Campbell, Woods, Connelly)

(7) *HARMONY* (1971) * +
(ABC-Dunhill/MCA Records)
Produced by Richard Podolor
"Never Been To Spain"
(Hoyt Axton)
"My Impersonal Life"

(Terry Furlong)
"An Old Fashioned Love Song"
(Paul Williams)
"I Never Dreamed You'd Leave In Summer"
(Stevie Wonder, Syreeta Wright)
"Jam"
(Mike Allsup, Jimmy Greenspoon, Danny Hutton, Chuck Negron, Joe Schermetzler, Floyd Sneed, Cory Wells)
"You"
(J. Goga, J. Bowen, I. Hunter)
"Night In The City"
(Joni Mitchell)
"Murder In My Heart For The Judge"
(D. Stevenson, J. Miller)
"The Family Of Man"
(Paul Williams, Jack Conrad)
"Intro Poem: Mistakes And Illusions"
(Paula Negron)
"Peace Of Mind"
(N. Woods)

(8) *SEVEN SEPARATE FOOLS* (1972) * +
(ABC-Dunhill/MCA Records)
Produced by Richard Podolor
"Black And White"
(D. Arkin, E. Robinson)
"My Old Kentucky Home (Turpentine and Dandelion Wine)"
(Randy Newman)
"Prelude To Morning"
(Jimmy Greenspoon)
"Pieces Of April"
(Dave Loggins)
"Going In Circles"
(T. Myers, Jaiananda)
"Chained"
(Russ Ballard)
"Tulsa Turnaround"
(A. Harvey, L. Collins)
"In Bed"
(Lynn Henderson, Wes Henderson, T. Baird)
"Freedom For The Stallion"
(Allen Toussaint)

"The Writings On The Wall"
(Dominic Troiano)
"Midnight Runaway"
(Gary Itri)

(9) *AROUND THE WORLD WITH THREE DOG NIGHT* (1973) *
(ABC-Dunhill/MCA Records)
Produced by Richard Podolor
"One Man Band"
(T. Kaye, J. Tyme, B. Fox)
"Never Been To Spain"
(Hoyt Axton)
"Going In Circles"
(T. Myers, Jaiananda)
"The Family Of Man"
(Paul Williams, J. Conrad)
"Midnight Runaway"
(Gary ltri)
"Liar"
(Russ Ballard)
"Good Feelin' 1957"
(A. Brackett, J. Merrill)
"Organ Solo"
(Jimmy Greenspoon)
"Eli's Coming"
(Laura Nyro)
"Joy To The World"
(Hoyt Axton)
"Black And White"
(D. Arkin, E. Robinson)
"Pieces Of April"
(Dave Loggins)
"Out In The Country"
(Paul Williams, Roger Nichols)
"Mama Told Me (Not To Come)"
(Randy Newman)
"Drum Solo"
(Floyd Sneed)
"An Old Fashioned Love Song"
(Paul Williams)
"Jam"
(Mike Allsup, Jimmy Greenspoon, Danny Hutton, Chuck Negron, Joe Schermetzler, Floyd Sneed, Cory Wells)

(10) *CYAN* (1973) * +
(ABC-Dunhill/MCA Records)
Produced by Richard Podolor
"Happy Song"
(Mike Allsup)
"Play Children Play"
(G. Stovall, K. Sprague)
"Storybook Feeling"
(Mike Allsup)
"Ridin' Thumb"
(Jimmy Seals)
"Shambala"
(Daniel Moore)
"Singer Man"
(C. Bernard)
"Let Me Serenade You"
(John Finley)
"Lay Me Down Easy"
(Daniel Moore)
"Into My Life"
(Mike Allsup)

(11) *HARD LABOR* (1974) * +
(ABC-Dunhill/MCA Records)
Produced by Jimmy Ienner
"Prelude"
(Public Domain)
"Sure As I'm Sittin' Here"
(John Hiatt)
"Anytime Babe"
(L. Weiss)
"Put Out The Light"
(Daniel Moore)
"Sitting In Limbo"
(Jimmy Cliff, G. Bright)
"I'd Be So Happy"
(Skip Prokop)
"Play Something Sweet (Brickyard Blues)"
(Allen Toussaint)
"On The Way Back Home"
(Daniel Moore)
"The Show Must Go On"
(Leo Sayer, Dave Courtney)

(12) *JOY TO THE WORLD — THEIR GREATEST HITS* (1974) * +
(ABC-Dunhill/MCA Records)
Produced by Richard Podolor, Gabriel Mekler, and Jimmy Ienner
"Joy To The World"
(Hoyt Axton)
"One"
(Harry Nilsson)
"Sure As I'm Sitting Here"
(John Hiatt)
"Old Fashioned Love Song"
(Paul Williams)
"Let Me Serenade You"
(John Finley)
"Shambala"
(Daniel Moore)
"Black And White"
(D. Arkin, E. Robinson)
"Never Been To Spain"
(Hoyt Axton)
"One Man Band"
(T. Kaye, J. Tyme, B. Fox)
"Play Something Sweet (Brickyard Blues)"
(Allen Toussaint)
"I'd Be So Happy"
(Skip Prokop)
"Liar"
(Russ Ballard)
"Family Of Man"
(Paul Williams, J. Conrad)
"The Show Must Go On"
(Leo Sayer, Dave Courtney)

(13) *COMING DOWN YOUR WAY* (1975)
(ABC Records)
Produced by Jimmy Ienner
" 'Til The World Ends"
(David Loggins)
"You Can Leave Your Hat On"
(Randy Newman)
"Good Old Feeling"
(Kent Sprague, Gary Stovall)
"Mind Over Matter"

(Allen Toussaint)
"Midnight Flyer"
(Skip Konte)
"Kite Man"
(Jay Gruska, Bonnie Spirit)
"Coming Down Your Way"
(Jack Lynton)
"When It's Over"
(Jeff Barry)
"Lean Back, Hold Steady"
(Daniel Moore)
"Yo Te Quiero Hablar (Take You Down)"
(Gregory Grandillo)

(14) *AMERICAN PASTIME* (1976)
(ABC Records)
Produced by Bob Monaco
"Everybody's A Masterpiece"
(G. Clinton, R. Reicheg)
"Easy Evil"
(Alan O'Day)
"Billy The Kid"
(B.& M. Lawrie)
"Mellow Down"
(Andy Fairweather Lowe)
"Yellow Beach Umbrella"
(C. Doerge, J. Henske)
"Hang On"
(J. Gruska, J. Spirit)
"Southbound"
(Hoyt Axton, M. Dawson)
"Drive On, Ride On"
(D. Grey, T. Seals)
"Dance The Night Away"
(D. Holster, B. Carpenter)

(15) *THE BEST OF THREE DOG NIGHT* (1982) +
(MCA Records)
Produced by Richard Podolor, Gabriel Mekler, and Jimmy Ienner
"Joy To The World"
(Hoyt Axton)
"Easy To Be Hard"
(G. MacDermot, J. Rado, G. Ragni)
"Family Of Man"

(Paul Williams, J. Conrad)
"Sure As I'm Sittin' Here"
(John Haitt)
"An Old Fashioned Love Song"
(Paul Williams)
"Mama Told Me (Not To Come)"
(Randy Newman)
"Try A Little Tenderness"
(Campbell, Woods, Connelly)
"Shambala"
(Daniel Moore)
"Let Me Serenade You"
(John Finley)
"Never Been To Spain"
(Hoyt Axton)
"Black And White"
(D. Arkin, E. Robinson)
"Pieces Of April"
(Dave Loggins)
"Liar"
(Russ Ballard)
"Out In The Country"
(Paul Williams, Roger Nichols)
"The Show Must Go On"
(Leo Sayer, D. Courtney)
"Eli's Coming"
(Laura Nyro)
"One Man Band"
(T. Kaye, J. Tyme, B. Fox)
"One"
(Harry Nilsson)
"Play Something Sweet (Brickyard Blues)"
(Allen Toussaint)
"Celebrate"
(Bonner, Gordon)

(16) *IT'S A JUNGLE* (1983)
(Passport Records)
Produced by Richard Podolor
"It's A Jungle Out There"
(Bill Moloney, Paul Pilger, Denny Polen)
"Shot In The Dark"
(Barry Devorzon, Michael Towers)
"Livin' It Up"

(Bill Labounty, Cynthia Weil, Barry Mann)
"I Can't Help It"
(Mark Anthony)
"Somebody's Gonna Get Hurt"
(Charlie Black, Richard Feldman, Marcy Levy)

* Certified Gold for sales in excess of 500,000 copies
** Certified "Double Platinum" for sales in excess of 2 million copies
+ Available on compact disc

## *Singles With Three Dog Night:*

1. "NOBODY" (1969) (peak chart position #73, #10 in L.A.)
2. "TRY A LITTLE TENDERNESS" (1969) (#29)
3. "ONE" (1969) (#5) ***
4. "EASY TO BE HARD" (1969) (#4)
5. "ELI'S COMING" (1969) (#10)
6. "CELEBRATE" (1970) (#15)
7. "MAMA TOLD ME NOT TO COME" (1970) (#1) ***
8. "OUT IN THE COUNTRY" (1970) (#15)
9. "ONE MAN BAND" (1970) (#19)
10. "JOY TO THE WORLD" (1971) (#1 for six weeks) + +
11. "LIAR" (1971) (#7)
12. "AN OLD FASHIONED LOVE SONG" (1971) (#4) ***
13. "NEVER BEEN TO SPAIN" (1971) (#1)
14. "THE FAMILY OF MAN" (1972) (#12)
15. "BLACK AND WHITE" (1972) (#1) ***
16. "PIECES OF APRIL" (1972) (#19)
17. "SHAMBALA" (1973) (#1) ***
18. "LET ME SERENADE YOU" (1973) (#17)
19. "THE SHOW MUST GO ON" (1974) (#1) ***
20. "SURE AS I'M SITTIN' HERE" (1974) (#16)
21. "PLAY SOMETHING SWEET (BRICKYARD BLUES)" (1974) (#33)
22. "TIL THE WORLD ENDS" (1975) (#32)

*** Certified Gold for sales in excess of one million copies
+ + Certified Platinum for sales in excess of two million copies

*Note: The chart figures from the songs were taken from the weekly music charts of either* Billboard, Cash Box *and/or* Record World. *Occasionally, the three charts differ in a given week's chart positions because of their different tallying methods.*